OXFORD MONOGRAPHS IN INTERNATIONAL HUMANITARIAN AND CRIMINAL LAW

General Editors

PAOLA GAETA
SALVATORE ZAPPALÀ

Fairness in International Criminal Trials

OXFORD MONOGRAPHS IN INTERNATIONAL HUMANITARIAN AND CRIMINAL LAW

The aim of this series is to publish original and innovative books on fundamental, topical, or cutting-edge issues in international humanitarian law and international criminal justice. The primary purpose of the series is to publish books which, in addition to critically surveying existing law, also suggest new avenues for improving the law.

Special attention will be given to works by young scholars.

Fairness in International Criminal Trials

YVONNE McDERMOTT

OXFORD
UNIVERSITY PRESS

OXFORD
UNIVERSITY PRESS

Great Clarendon Street, Oxford, OX2 6DP,
United Kingdom

Oxford University Press is a department of the University of Oxford.
It furthers the University's objective of excellence in research, scholarship,
and education by publishing worldwide. Oxford is a registered trade mark of
Oxford University Press in the UK and in certain other countries

First Edition published in 2016

Published in the United States of America by Oxford University Press
198 Madison Avenue, New York, NY 10016, United States of America

British Library Cataloguing in Publication Data
Data available

Library of Congress Control Number: 2015951307

ISBN 978–0–19–873981–4

To my parents

Foreword

At the opening of the International Military Tribunal at Nuremberg, United States Chief Prosecutor Robert Jackson famously said: 'We must never forget that the record on which we judge these defendants today is the record on which history will judge us tomorrow.' Seventy years later, those words remain as true for international criminal trials as they were for that seminal moment in the history of international justice.

International criminal trials have been said to have many goals. These include giving victims a voice, bringing peace to affected regions, and spreading the rule of law. Regardless of whether these goals are truly achievable, it is beyond question that the foremost priority for international criminal trials must be to do justice in a manner that is fair and impartial, that respects the presumption of innocence, and that gives the defendant an equal opportunity to present his or her case. It is fitting, then, that Yvonne McDermott has chosen to dedicate this important and far-reaching study to the examination of fairness in international criminal trials.

We cannot allow a creeping complacency to convince us that is sufficient for international criminal trials to be broadly fair, or fair for the most part. As McDermott convincingly argues, international criminal tribunals must set no less than the highest standards of fairness in their proceedings. It is beyond dispute that international criminal tribunals operate in a challenging legal environment, but as I argued in my Minority Opinion to the *Katanga* judgment, that is no excuse for derogation from the full protection of rights of the accused.

McDermott's study is both pragmatic and principled in its approach to international criminal procedure, including its commendation of existing practices and suggestions for improvement. She argues for a broader role for fairness in international criminal trials, beyond the four walls of the individual tribunal. She shows that references to 'balancing' the rights of the accused, be that against the rights of victims, the prosecution, or the international community, are misplaced and potentially very dangerous.

This book is essential reading for students of international criminal law and those with a broader interest in fair trial rights, and I have no doubt that it will be an important reference work for practitioners and judges in international criminal tribunals for many years to come.

Judge Christine Van den Wyngaert

The Hague, August 2015

Series Editors' Preface

The idea of establishing this series, the *Oxford Monographs in International Humanitarian and Criminal Law*, was that of our late mentor and friend Antonio (Nino) Cassese. In 2010, a few months after receiving the 2009 Erasmus Prize of the Praemium Erasmianum Foundation,[1] he conceived of this series and submitted the idea to OUP.

As was often the case with Nino, he managed to transform recognition for his accomplishments (the Prize) into new challenges that would require him (and sometimes his friends and associates) to face more work (the Series). Eager to continue in his lifelong pursuit of current and innovative scholarship, Nino planned to use the funds that he received from his prize to support young scholars, particularly non-native English speakers, to carry out and submit for publication their research in international humanitarian and international criminal law. Nino imagined this series to be an incubator of original and innovative books on fundamental, topical, or cutting-edge issues in international humanitarian law and international criminal justice.

Nino's untimely passing in 2011 led to delays in implementation of the series. Luckily, there were already two books in the pipeline at the time, and these were able to publish as planned.

In picking up the baton as Series Editors, we desire to carry on this initiative not only as part of Nino's legacy, but above all because we strongly believe in the 'cultural' dimension behind this project. While Nino's vision has not yet materialized, we continue in his belief of publishing books which, besides surveying existing law, also suggest new avenues for improving the law. This is part of a much larger endeavour linked both to the *Journal of International Criminal Justice* on the one hand, and also the many publications on the subject of International Criminal Law that Nino has authored or edited for OUP (from a Commentary on the Rome Statute of the ICC to a casebook and a textbook on International Criminal Law, to *The Oxford Companion to International Criminal Justice*[2]). The series is a vehicle for scholarship

[1] http://www.erasmusprijs.org/index.cfm?lang=en&page=Prijswinnaars&mode=detail&itemID=D591476D-F809-92BC-EF5B74E4909EBDF8&dateYear=2009.

[2] Antonio Cassese, Paola Gaeta, and John R.W.D. Jones (eds), *The Rome Statute of the International Criminal Court: A Commentary* (Oxford: OUP, 2002); Cassese's *International Criminal Law* (3rd edn, Oxford: OUP, 2013); Antonio Cassese, Guido Acquaviva, Mary Fan, and Alex Whiting, *International Criminal Law: Cases and Commentaries* (Oxford: OUP, 2011); Antonio Cassese (ed.), *The Oxford Companion to International Criminal Justice* (Oxford: OUP, 2009).

embracing the forward-looking approach to international humanitarian and criminal law that characterized Nino's career, and which we will strive to keep alive together with the authors of the books published in the series.

Fairness in International Criminal Trials by Dr Yvonne McDermott perfectly captures this mindset. In this book, the author tackles the procedural aspects of international criminal law with thorough and forward-looking approach. The book, the title of which mirrors an inspiring classic in international law,[3] deals with a central problem of international criminal justice: its fairness. By examining the fair trial guarantees of all actors involved in the proceedings, the book explores the theoretical concept as well as its practical implications and construes it in the light of systematic views of what can be considered another area of international criminal law: international criminal procedure.

For a long time this area of law has been neglected. Similar to the scholarship focusing on domestic criminal law, international criminal justice mechanisms were originally studied more through the lens of substantive law (international law, humanitarian law, and criminal law) than procedural. The reason for this neglect was probably that procedural issues were seen as ancillary and less relevant. In reality, experience has shown that one of the main challenges for the credibility of the international criminal justice system—from Nuremberg to the Hague—has revolved around procedural issues: from fairness to efficiency, from victim participation to prosecutorial discretion.

Nuremberg and Tokyo were criticized for their victor's justice dimension and the lack of several due process guarantees; it has been said that those tribunals were saved from the judgment of history because they ultimately provided for fair trials.[4] It seems likely that the fact that they at least afforded an opportunity for defendants to be heard was a major breakthrough.

Nearly fifty years later, in the statutes of the ICTY and ICTR, the Security Council, mirroring the provisions of the ICCPR, codified the principle that fair trial rights must be protected. Subsequently, the ICC and the hybrid or internationalized courts and tribunals (from Sierra Leone Special Court to Special Tribunal for Lebanon) have all reflected due-process guarantees in their statutes and the judges have implemented these in their case law.

One of the challenges confronting the contemporary, permanent system of international criminal law established around the ICC, is to a large extent procedural: it must improve its efficiency. The length of the proceedings,

[3] Thomas M. Franck, *Fairness in International Law and Institutions* (New York: OUP, 1998).

[4] Robert Badinter, 'Réflections générales' in Antonio Cassese and Mireille Delmas-Marty (eds), *Crimes internationaux et juridictions internationales* (Paris: Puf, 2002) 50.

and, at least for some critics, their ineffectiveness, is an issue that bears relevant implications for the application and interpretation of procedural law by the Court. And yet this can only happen through a careful balancing of any measures aimed at expediting proceedings against fairness, which ultimately remains the cornerstone of justice. As Dr McDermott explains, this is particularly true at the international level, where courts are also bound to set the example for their domestic counterparts.

Dr McDermott is a bright scholar, who has already published several contributions in the area of international criminal procedure; this book represents a *summa* of her efforts, providing a solid comparative analysis of the current state of the law, while also offering original and constructive recommendations for the way forward.

This book begins a new stage in this series, as we hope soon to receive several proposals from scholars with original and thought-provoking views on international humanitarian law and criminal law.

Paola Gaeta and Salvatore Zappalà

Acknowledgements

This book started life as a doctoral thesis, defended at the Irish Centre for Human Rights at the National University of Ireland, Galway, in 2013. Words cannot express my gratitude to my wonderful supervisor, William A. Schabas, who not only provided invaluable guidance throughout the drafting process, but also continues to be a mentor, friend, and inspiration post-graduation. I look forward to many more years of collaboration with him. My examiners, Andrew Ashworth and Noelle Higgins, offered excellent feedback and suggestions for transforming the thesis into a monograph, for which I am very grateful. I would also like to record my gratitude to the School of Law in NUI, Galway, for financial support in the form of a Doctoral Fellowship.

I am honoured that Judge Christine Van den Wyngaert, whose academic and judicial writings I have admired for many years now, agreed to write the foreword for this book.

The Irish Centre for Human Rights provided an ideal environment in which to write a thesis, and my experiences in Galway shaped me as an academic and left me with friends for life. This work benefitted enormously from the annual doctoral seminars, in particular. I am indebted to Ray Murphy for being a constant source of good counsel. I would like to thank my many friends from the ICHR and from my current academic home, Bangor University, for their collegiality and support. This book has benefitted enormously from many discussions at the Honourable Society of the Inner Temple, where I am an Academic Fellow.

I am especially grateful to those friends who took time out of their busy schedules to offer feedback on drafts and to discuss ideas—Aoife Daly, Michelle Farrell, Niamh Hayes, John Jackson, David Keane, Helen McDermott, Eadaoin O'Brien, Joe Powderly, His Honour Judge Jeremy Roberts, Evelyne Schmid, and Tara Smith. Alys Williams and Sarah Wilkinson provided invaluable research assistance.

The team at Oxford University Press: Merel Alstein, Emma Endean, Anthony Hinton, Nicole Leyland, and John Louth, have been wonderfully patient and helpful in dealing with my many queries.

Special thanks are owed to the extended McDermott and Rees clans: Mum, Dad, Ronan, Conor, Jane, Declan, Siân, Iwan, Siwan, Richard, Cadi, and Gwen. The biggest thanks of all go to Osian, for his tireless enthusiasm, patience and love. *Diolch, cariad.*

Contents

Table of Cases

INTERNATIONAL MILITARY TRIBUNAL AT NUREMBERG

INTERNATIONAL CRIMINAL TRIBUNAL FOR THE FORMER YUGOSLAVIA

INTERNATIONAL CRIMINAL TRIBUNAL FOR RWANDA

SITUATION IN THE DEMOCRATIC REPUBLIC OF THE CONGO (ICC-01/04)

Prosecutor v. Katanga and Ngudjolo Chui **(ICC-01/04-01/07)**

SITUATION IN THE REPUBLIC OF KENYA (ICC-01/09)

SITUATION IN UGANDA (ICC-02/04)

Prosecutor v. Kony **(ICC-02/04-01/05)**

Prosecutor v. Ongwen **(ICC-02/04-01/15)**

SPECIAL TRIBUNAL FOR LEBANON

In the case against Akhbar Beirut S.A.L and Al Amin **(STL-14-06)**

Prosecutor v. Ayyash et al. **(STL-11-01)**

In the case against New TV SAL and Al Khayat **(STL-14-05)**

In the Matter of El Sayed

Miscellaneous

INTERNATIONAL COURT OF JUSTICE

EUROPEAN COMMISSION ON HUMAN RIGHTS

EUROPEAN COURT OF HUMAN RIGHTS

HUMAN RIGHTS COMMITTEE

AFRICAN COMMISSION ON HUMAN AND PEOPLES' RIGHTS

INTER-AMERICAN COURT OF HUMAN RIGHTS

ENGLAND AND WALES

UNITED STATES

Table of Instruments

RULES OF PROCEDURE AND EVIDENCE OF THE INTERNATIONAL CRIMINAL TRIBUNALS

Rules of Procedure and Evidence of the International Criminal Tribunal for the former Yugoslavia

OTHER INTERNATIONAL LEGAL INSTRUMENTS

REPORTS OF THE UNITED NATIONS SECRETARY-GENERAL

TRAVAUX PRÉPARATOIRES

DOMESTIC LEGAL INSTRUMENTS

Bosnia and Herzegovina

Cambodia

Germany

Kenya

Netherlands

Rwanda

United Kingdom

United States of America

List of Abbreviations

ACHPR	African Charter on Human and Peoples' Rights
ACHR	American Convention on Human Rights
ADAD	Association des Avocats de la Défense
ADC	Association of Defence Counsel
Afr J Int'l & Comp L	*African Journal of International Law and Comparative Law*
AJIL	*American Journal of International Law*
Am Crim LR	*American Criminal Law Review*
Am J Comp L	*American Journal of Comparative Law*
Boston Coll LR	*Boston College Law Review*
Brit J Criminol	*British Journal of Criminology*
Brooklyn JIL	*Brooklyn Journal of International Law*
Buff LR	*Buffalo Law Review*
California LR	*California Law Review*
California Western Int'l L J	*California Western International Law Journal*
CAR	Central African Republic
Case Western Res JIL	*Case Western Reserve Journal of International Law*
Chicago Kent LR	*Chicago Kent Law Review*
CLF	*Criminal Law Forum*
Columbia Hum Rts LR	*Columbia Human Rights Law Review*
Columbia J Transnat'l L	*Columbia Journal of Transnational Law*
Connecticut JIL	*Connecticut Journal of International Law*
Cornell LR	*Cornell Law Review*
Crim L Q	*Criminal Law Quarterly*
Crim LR	*Criminal Law Review*
CUP	Cambridge University Press
Drake LR	*Drake Law Review*
DRC	Democratic Republic of the Congo
Duke J Comp & Int'l L	*Duke Journal of Comparative and International Law*
Duke L J	*Duke Law Journal*

ECCC	Extraordinary Chambers in the Courts of Cambodia
ECHR	European Convention on Human Rights
ECtHR	European Court of Human Rights
ECJ	European Court of Justice
EHRR	European Human Rights Reports
EJIL	*European Journal of International Law*
Eur J Crime Crim L & Crim Just	*European Journal of Crime, Criminal Law and Criminal Justice*
FRG	Federal Republic of Germany
Florida JIL	*Florida Journal of International Law*
Fordham Int'l L J	*Fordham International Law Journal*
GC	Grand Chamber of the European Court of Human Rights
Georgetown JIL	*Georgetown Journal of International Law*
Georgia LR	*Georgia Law Review*
GYIL	*German Yearbook of International Law*
Harv Int'l L J	*Harvard International Law Journal*
Harv LR	*Harvard Law Review*
HRLR	*Human Rights Law Review*
IACtHR	Inter-American Court of Human Rights
ICC	International Criminal Court
ICCPR	International Covenant on Civil and Political Rights
ICLQ	*International and Comparative Law Quarterly*
ICLR	*International Criminal Law Review*
ICTR	International Criminal Tribunal for Rwanda
ICTY	International Criminal Tribunal for the former Yugoslavia
IJTJ	*International Journal of Transitional Justice*
IMT	International Military Tribunal
IMTFE	International Military Tribunal for the Far East
Ind L J	*Indiana Law Journal*
Intl J Hum Rts	*International Journal of Human Rights*
Int'l Rev Red Cross	*International Review of the Red Cross*
Int'l Studies Rev	*International Studies Review*
Isr LR	*Israel Law Review*

J C & S L	*Journal of Conflict and Security Law*
J Crim L & Criminol	*Journal of Criminal Law and Criminology*
J Genocide Res	*Journal of Genocide Research*
JICJ	*Journal of International Criminal Justice*
J. Marshall LR	*John Marshall Law Review*
Law & Phil	*Law and Philosophy*
LCP	*Law and Contemporary Problems*
LJIL	*Leiden Journal of International Law*
LPR	*Law, Probability and Risk*
Max Planck Ybk UN L	*Max Planck Yearbook of United Nations Law*
Melbourne JIL	*Melbourne Journal of International Law*
Michigan JIL	*Michigan Journal of International Law*
MICT	Mechanism for the International Criminal Tribunals
MLR	*Modern Law Review*
N C J Int'l L & Com Reg	*North Carolina Journal of International Law and Commercial Regulation*
Netherlands Int'l LR	*Netherlands International Law Review*
NGO	Non-Governmental Organization
Nordic JIL	*Nordic Journal of International Law*
Nw U J Int'l Hum Rts	*Northwestern University Journal of International Human Rights*
NYU LR	*New York University Law Review*
OED	*Oxford English Dictionary*
OJLS	*Oxford Journal of Legal Studies*
OPCD	Office of Public Counsel for the Defence
Oregon Rev Int'l L	*Oregon Review of International Law*
OSCE	Organization for Security and Co-operation in Europe
OUP	Oxford University Press
Penn State Int'l LR	*Pennsylvania State University International Law Review*
Penn St LR	*Pennsylvania State University Law Review*
RIDP	*Revue Internationale de Droit Pénal*
RPE	Rules of Procedure and Evidence

RSCSL	Residual Special Court for Sierra Leone
RUF	Revolutionary United Front
S Cal LR	*Southern California Law Review*
SCSL	Special Court for Sierra Leone
SFOR	Stabilisation Force in Bosnia and Herzegovina
Stanford JIL	*Stanford Journal of International Law*
Stanford LR	*Stanford Law Review*
STL	Special Tribunal for Lebanon
Texas Int'l L J	*Texas International Law Journal*
UCLA J Int'l L & Foreign Aff	*University of California, Los Angeles Journal of International Law and Foreign Affairs*
UDHR	Universal Declaration of Human Rights
UN	United Nations
UNGA	United Nations General Assembly
UNHCR	United Nations High Commissioner for Refugees
UNICRI	United Nations Interregional Crime and Justice Research Institute
UNSC	United Nations Security Council
UNTAET	United Nations Transitional Administration in East Timor
UNTS	United Nations Treaty Series
U Penn LR	*University of Pennsylvania Law Review*
Va JIL	*Virginia Journal of International Law*
Va LR	*Virginia Law Review*
Wash U J L & Pol'y	*Washington University Journal of Law and Policy*
WCRO	War Crimes Research Office
Yale JIL	*Yale Journal of International Law*
Yale L J	*Yale Law Journal*

1

Introduction

In his opening statement before the International Military Tribunal at Nuremberg in 1945, United States Chief Prosecutor Robert Jackson noted that:

> To pass these defendants a poisoned chalice is to put it to our own lips as well. We must summon such detachment and intellectual integrity to our task that this Trial will commend itself to posterity as fulfilling humanity's aspirations to do justice ... [We] have undertaken the burden of participating in a complicated effort to give them fair and dispassionate hearings. That is the best-known protection to any man with a defence worthy of being heard.[1]

Almost fifty years later, on the establishment of the International Criminal Tribunal for the former Yugoslavia (ICTY), it was clear that the international community was no less concerned with the need to do justice in a fair and impartial manner. The United Nations Secretary General noted that it was 'axiomatic' that the Tribunal would 'fully respect internationally recognised standards regarding the rights of the accused at all stages of its proceedings'.[2] Fairness has remained a foremost concern for more recently-established international criminal tribunals, namely the International Criminal Tribunal for Rwanda (ICTR), Special Court for Sierra Leone (SCSL), International Criminal Court (ICC), and Special Tribunal for Lebanon (STL).

International criminal procedure as a discipline has reached a remarkably advanced stage of development.[3] Arguments have moved beyond questions of whether international criminal procedure is, or should be, most closely aligned with the adversarial or the inquisitorial legal tradition, and almost every international criminal law scholar now agrees that international criminal procedure represents a *sui generis* system which incorporates elements of criminal procedure from a vast range of countries, and some elements which are truly unique.[4]

[1] *Nuremberg Trial Proceedings, Vol. 2*, p. 100, 21 November 1945, Opening Statement of Mr Justice Jackson, Chief Prosecutor for the United States of America.

[2] Report of the Secretary-General Pursuant to Paragraph 2 of the Security Council Resolution 808 (1993) UN Doc. S/25704, 3 May 1993, para 106.

[3] Paul Roberts, 'The Priority of Procedure and the Neglect of Evidence and Proof: Facing Facts in International Criminal Law' (2015) 13 *JICJ* 479.

[4] See, amongst many others, Kai Ambos, 'International Criminal Procedure: "Adversarial", "Inquisitorial" or Mixed?' (2003) 3 *ICLR* 1; Mireille Delmas-Marty, 'The Contribution of

Procedure is no longer a chapter in international criminal law textbooks, but the subject of individual monographs,[5] and many have attempted to enunciate the precise scope of this burgeoning body of law. For example, the 'International Expert Framework on International Criminal Procedure', comprised of a team of forty-three expert researchers, attempted to identify and enunciate 'general rules and principles' of international criminal procedure.[6] With the acceptance of international criminal procedure as a self-sustaining discipline, and as the tribunals established to try the most serious crimes in the former Yugoslavia, Sierra Leone, and Rwanda have completed or are beginning to wind up their activities,[7] the time is ripe for a critical evaluation of these tribunals and their legacy.[8]

Comparative Law to a Pluralist Conception of International Criminal Law' (2003) 1 *JICJ* 13; Megan A. Fairlie, 'The Marriage of Common and Continental Law at the ICTY and Its Progeny, Due Process Deficit' (2004) 4 *ICLR* 243; William A. Schabas, 'Synergy or Fragmentation? International Criminal Law and the European Convention on Human Rights' (2011) 9 *JICJ* 609; Gideon Boas, 'Creating Laws of Evidence for International Criminal Law: The ICTY and the Principle of Flexibility' (2001) 12 *CLF* 41, and John D. Jackson, 'Finding the Best Epistemic Fit for International Criminal Tribunals: Beyond the Adversarial-Inquisitorial Dichotomy' (2009) 7 *JICJ* 17.

[5] Key texts include Karim Khan, Caroline Buisman and Christopher Gosnell (eds), *Principles of Evidence in International Criminal Justice* (Oxford: OUP, 2010); Nancy Combs, *Fact Finding without Facts: The Uncertain Evidentiary Foundations of International Criminal Convictions* (Cambridge: CUP, 2010); Christoph J.M. Safferling, *Towards an International Criminal Procedure* (Oxford: OUP, 2001); Salvatore Zappalà, *Human Rights in International Criminal Proceedings* (Oxford: OUP, 2003); Christoph J.M. Safferling, *International Criminal Procedure* (Oxford: OUP, 2012); Christine Schuon, *International Criminal Procedure: A Clash of Legal Cultures* (The Hague: T.M.C. Asser Press, 2010); Goran Sluiter and Sergey Vasiliev (eds), *International Criminal Procedure: Towards a Coherent Body of Law* (New York: Cameron May Publishing, 2009); and Goran Sluiter, Håkan Friman, Suzannah Linton, Salvatore Zappalà, and Sergey Vasiliev (eds), *International Criminal Procedure: Principles and Rules* (Oxford: OUP, 2013); Linda Carter and Fausto Pocar (eds), *International Criminal Procedure: The Interface of Civil Law and Common Law Legal Systms* (Cheltenham: Edward Elgar, 2013).

[6] The fruits of this labour were published in Sluiter et al. (eds) (ibid.).

[7] The SCSL completed its mandate in 2013 and transitioned to a residual mechanism, the Residual Special Court for Sierra Leone (RSCSL), which was established pursuant to an agreement between the United Nations and Sierra Leone, signed into law on 1 February 2012. The Mechanism for the International Criminal Tribunals (MICT) was established by Security Council Resolution 1966 (2010), UN Doc. S/RES/1966 (2010), 22 December 2010 to carry out the residual functions of the ICTY and ICTR upon completion of their mandates. The appeal for the final case before the ICTR commenced in April 2015: *Prosecutor v. Nyiramasuhuko et al.*, Transcript, Case No. ICTR-98-42-A, 14 April 2015. At the time of writing, the ICTY was expected to conclude its final trial by 2017: *Address to the UN Security Council*, Judge Theodor Meron, President, International Criminal Tribunal for the former Yugoslavia and Mechanism for International Criminal Tribunals, 10 December 2014, 2. For further discussion of the completion strategies of the international criminal tribunals in general, see further, Fidelma Donlon, 'The Role of the Judges in the Definition and Implementation of the Completion Strategies of the International Criminal Tribunals' in Shane Darcy and Joseph Powderly (eds), *Judicial Creativity at the International Criminal Tribunals* (Oxford: OUP, 2010) 353; Daryl A. Mundis, 'The Judicial Effects of the "Completion Strategies" on the Ad Hoc International Criminal Tribunals' (2005) 99 *AJIL* 142; and Dominic Raab, 'Evaluating the ICTY and its Completion Strategy: Efforts to Achieve Accountability for War Crimes and their Tribunals' (2005) 3 *JICJ* 82.

[8] Elena A. Baylis, 'Rebuilding National Courts through Transnational Networks' (2009) 50 *Boston Coll LR* 1, 82–3.

This book examines the right to a fair trial in international criminal proceedings, and asks what lessons can be learned from the practices of the contemporary international criminal tribunals. To this end, it seeks to analyse some key conceptual questions on the right to a fair trial in international criminal law, including: should international criminal tribunals set the highest standards of fairness, or is it sufficient for their practice to be just 'fair enough'? To whom does the right to a fair trial attach, and can actors such as the prosecution and victims be accurately said to benefit from that right? Does fairness require the full realization of a number of guarantees owed to the accused under the statutory frameworks of international criminal tribunals, or should we instead be concerned with the fairness of the trial 'as a whole'? What is the interplay between domestic and international courts on questions of procedural fairness? What are the elements of fairness in international criminal proceedings? And what remedies are available for breaches of fair trial rights?

These questions are analysed with reference to the law and practice of the contemporary international criminal tribunals, namely the ICC, ICTY, ICTR, SCSL, and STL. Reference will be made to the practices of historical international criminal tribunals, such as the International Military Tribunals at Nuremberg and Tokyo, and 'internationalized' criminal tribunals, such as the Extraordinary Chambers in the Courts of Cambodia (ECCC), where appropriate.

1.1 Context

As is widely known, the ICTY was established by the United Nations Security Council (UNSC) in 1993,[9] with the ICTR established in the same manner just over a year later.[10] On 17 July 1998, almost fifty years after the United Nations General Assembly (UNGA) considered that 'in the course of development of the international community, there will be an increasing need of an international judicial organ for the trial of certain crimes under international law',[11] 120 states adopted the Rome Statute, establishing the ICC. Unlike its predecessors, the ICC's mandate is not limited in its temporal or geographic scope.[12] In 2000, the SCSL was established by agreement between the United Nations (UN) and the Government of Sierra Leone.[13]

[9] Security Council Resolution 827 (1993), UN Doc. S/RES/827, 25 May 1993.

[10] Security Council Resolution 955 (1994), UN Doc. S/Res/955, 8 November 1994.

[11] General Assembly Resolution 260 (III) B, Annex, UN Doc. A/810 (1948), 9 December 1948.

[12] Rome Statute of the International Criminal Court, 17 July 1998, 2187 UNTS 90, entered into force 1 July 2002.

[13] UNSC, Report of the Secretary General on the Establishment of a Special Court for Sierra Leone, UN Doc. S/2000/915, 4 October 2000.

Owing to its composition of both international judges appointed by the UN Secretary General and judges appointed by the Government of Sierra Leone,[14] and its jurisdiction over domestic as well as international crimes,[15] there has been some debate as to whether the SCSL is more appropriately classified as a 'hybrid' or 'internationalized' criminal tribunal.[16] However, as Schabas has persuasively argued, a key determinant of whether a tribunal is best classified as international or 'internationalized' is whether its founding instrument is part of a domestic law instrument, or an international treaty or Security Council Resolution.[17] Thus, while an agreement reached between the government of Cambodia and the UN on the prosecution of crimes committed during the period of Democratic Kampuchea paved the way for the commencement of the ECCC's first trials,[18] a domestic law first promulgated in 2001 established the Chambers themselves.[19] Domestic law also established the War Crimes Chamber in the Court of Bosnia and Herzegovina,[20] and a Regulation of the Transitional Administration in East Timor founded the Special Panels of the Dili District Court.[21] The STL's establishment by Security Council Resolution in 2007[22] (after the speaker of the Lebanese Parliament blocked the ratification of the Agreement between the United Nations and the Lebanese Republic on the establishment of a Special Tribunal for Lebanon that had been signed

[14] Agreement between the United Nations and the Government of Sierra Leone on the Establishment of a Special Court for Sierra Leone, Annex to Report of the Secretary General on the Establishment of a Special Court for Sierra Leone, ibid., Article 2.

[15] Statute of the Special Court for Sierra Leone, Enclosure to Report of the Secretary General on the Establishment of a Special Court for Sierra Leone, ibid., Articles 2–5.

[16] Compare, for example, William A. Schabas, *The UN International Criminal Tribunals: The Former Yugoslavia, Rwanda and Sierra Leone* (Cambridge: CUP, 2006); Cesare P. Romano, André Nollkaemper, and Jann K. Kleffner (eds), *Internationalized Criminal Courts: Sierra Leone, East Timor, Kosovo, and Cambodia* (Oxford: OUP, 2004).

[17] William A. Schabas, *Unimaginable Atrocities: Justice, Politics and Rights at the War Crimes Tribunals* (Oxford: OUP, 2012) 19.

[18] General Assembly Resolution 57/228 B, UN Doc. A/Res/57/228 B, 22 May 2003.

[19] Law on the Establishment of Extraordinary Chambers in the Courts of Cambodia for the Prosecution of Crimes Committed during the Period of Democratic Kampuchea, with inclusion of amendments as promulgated on 27 October 2004, NS/RKM/1004/006, available online at http://www.eccc.gov.kh/sites/default/files/legal-documents/KR_Law_as_amended_27_Oct_2004_Eng.pdf (last accessed 30 June 2015).

[20] Law on Court of Bosnia and Herzegovina, Official Gazette of Bosnia and Herzegovina 29/00, 12 November 2000.

[21] United Nations Transitional Administration in East Timor (UNTAET), Regulation No. 2000/15 on the Establishment of Panels with Exclusive Jurisdiction over Serious Criminal Offences, 6 June 2000. UNTAET was vested with sole legislative authority at the time, pursuant to UNTAET Regulation No. 1999/1 on the Authority of the Transitional Administration in East Timor, 27 November 1999.

[22] Security Council Resolution 1757 (2007), UN Doc. S/Res/1757, 30 May 2007.

in January of that year) clearly renders it a tribunal of an international character, even though it only has jurisdiction over domestic Lebanese criminal law.[23]

As noted above, the Secretary General of the United Nations at the establishment of the ICTY stated that it was 'axiomatic' that criminal courts established by the international community should espouse the highest standards of human rights protection in their procedures.[24] The academic community was quick to call the same tribunal into account when early pronouncements both permitted the use of anonymous witnesses,[25] and likened international criminal tribunals to military tribunals in their operation.[26] Notwithstanding the fact that military tribunals are expected to grant the same corpus of rights as regularly-constituted courts,[27] this association quickly fell by the wayside, as did the use of anonymous witnesses in the practice of the ICTY and its contemporaries.[28] Nevertheless, the idealism that fostered near-universal academic support for the end of impunity through international justice[29] became tempered as commentators began to notice the rising costs and unwieldiness of these new institutions.[30] A new wave of scholarship on international criminal procedure began to examine issues such as

[23] Statute of the Special Tribunal for Lebanon, annexed to Security Council Resolution 1757, ibid., Article 2.

[24] Report of the Secretary-General Pursuant to Paragraph 2 of the Security Council Resolution 808 (1993) UN Doc. S/25704, 3 May 1993, para 106.

[25] *Prosecutor v. Tadić*, Decision on the Prosecutor's Motion Requesting Protective Measures for Victims and Witnesses, Case No. IT-94-1-T, 10 August 1995, para 86.

[26] ibid., para 28. For a critique, see Natasha Affolder, '*Tadić*, the Anonymous Witness and the Sources of International Procedural Law' (1997–8) 19 *Michigan JIL* 445.

[27] Human Rights Committee, *General Comment No. 32, Article 14: Right to equality before courts and tribunals and to a fair trial*, UN Doc. CCPR/C/GC/32 (2007) para 22 ('The provisions of Article 14 apply to all courts and tribunals within the scope of that article whether ordinary or specialized, civilian or military.'). See further, Evelyne Schmid, 'A Few Comments on a Comment: The UN Human Rights Committee's General Comment No. 32 on Article 14 of the ICCPR and the Question of Civilians Tried by Military Courts' (2010) 14 *Intl J Hum Rts* 1058.

[28] Discussed further below, Chapter 3. It must be noted, however, that the Special Tribunal for Lebanon disappointingly reintroduces the use of anonymous witnesses as permissible, per Rule 93 of its Rules of Procedure and Evidence. This re-introduction was discussed by the Tribunal's late President, who referred to the special nature of crimes of terrorism in its justification. See 'RPE—Explanatory Memorandum by the Tribunal's President', Special Tribunal for Lebanon, 10 November 2009, para 35. However, Rule 159 states that such statements may be excluded if their probative value is substantially outweighed by the need to ensure a fair trial, and that a conviction may not be based solely or decisively on them.

[29] Stephanos Bibas and William W. Burke-White, 'International Idealism meets Domestic Criminal Procedure Realism' (2009–10) 59 *Duke L J* 637.

[30] Augustine Brannigan, 'Is the Sun Setting on Cosmopolitan Justice?' (2011) 48 *Global Society* 420. The ICC cost $1 billion between 2002 and 2013: Stuart Ford, 'How Much Money Does the ICC Need?' in Carsten Stahn (ed.), *The Law and Practice of the International Criminal Court* (Oxford: OUP, 2015) 84, 85.

evidence,[31] the participation of victims,[32] and the length of trials[33] in greater detail. However, some key conceptual questions on fairness in international criminal trials remain under-examined in the existing literature, and it is with these questions that the current work is concerned.

1.2 Outline of the Book

Any attempt to comprehensively discuss fairness in international criminal trials must begin by asking what we mean by the term 'fairness' in this particular context. Chapter 2 examines a number of leading theories of fairness from the literature on legitimacy, procedural justice, and rule of law, and discusses their applicability to international criminal procedure. From this discussion, a number of key principles of fairness can be derived; these include transparency, consistency, equality, and impartiality. I argue that fairness in the context of the right to a fair trial is a unique legal construct which is comprised of a number of procedural guarantees derived from human rights standards in conjunction with these principles of fairness. This chapter discusses how the tribunals have defined and applied the concept of fairness in their procedures, and have answered questions such as whether the right to a fair trial requires the full realization of a number of minimum guarantees, or whether it is sufficient that the trial, taken as a whole, is seen to be fair.

[31] For example, Khan et al. (eds) (n 5); Combs (n 5); Alexander Zahar, 'The Problem of False Testimony at the International Criminal Tribunal for Rwanda' in Andre Klip and Goran Sluiter (eds), *Annotated Leading Cases of International Criminal Tribunals, Vol. XXV: The International Criminal Tribunal for Rwanda, 2006–2007* (Antwerp: Intersentia, 2010) 509; Megan A. Fairlie, 'Due Process Erosion: The Diminution of Live Testimony at the ICTY' (2003) 34 *California Western Int'l L J* 47; John D. Jackson, 'Transnational Faces of Justice: Two Attempts to Build Common Standards Beyond National Boundaries' in John D. Jackson, Máximo Langer, and Peter Tillers (eds), *Crime, Procedure and Evidence in a Comparative and International Context: Essays in Honour of Professor Mirjan R. Damaška* (Oxford: Hart Publishing, 2008) 221; and John D. Jackson and Sarah J. Summers, *The Internationalisation of Criminal Evidence: Beyond the Common Law and Civil Law Traditions* (Cambridge: CUP, 2012) chapter 5.

[32] Mirjan R. Damaška, 'Problematic Features of International Criminal Procedure' in Antonio Cassese et al. (eds), *The Oxford Companion to International Criminal Justice* (Oxford: OUP, 2009) 175, 178; Mirjan R. Damaška, 'The International Criminal Court: Between Aspiration and Achievement' (2009) 14 *UCLA J Int'l L & Foreign Aff* 19, 28–32; Yvonne McDermott, 'Some are More Equal than Others: Victim Participation in the International Criminal Court' (2008) 5 *Eyes on the ICC* 23; Yvonne McDermott, 'Victims and International Law: Remedies in the Courtroom?' (2009) 4 *Hague Justice Journal* 199; and Salvatore Zappalà, 'The Rights of Victims v. the Rights of the Accused' (2010) 8 *JICJ* 137.

[33] Stephane Bourgon, 'Procedural Problems Hindering Expeditious and Fair Justice' (2004) 2 *JICJ* 526; Jean Galbraith, 'The Pace of International Criminal Justice' (2009) 31 *Michigan JIL* 79.

Chapter 3 examines the elements of the right to a fair trial, with reference to the practice of the five tribunals. These elements are derived from the statutory provisions on the rights of the accused in the tribunals' statutes, as well as other rights that are recognized elsewhere in their legal frameworks or have been recognized in practice, such as the right to an appeal and the right to privacy. It also discusses fundamental principles of fairness in criminal law, including *ne bis in idem* and *nullum crimen sine lege*. A key finding in this chapter is that there are many elements of international criminal procedure that represent positive precedents worthy of emulation, but other areas, such as the right to an effective remedy and the right to trial without undue delay, have not been fully realized by all of the tribunals to date. Another observation is that there is a lack of consistency in procedure, not just between tribunals, but sometimes between different chambers of the same tribunal. This makes it difficult to reach conclusions on whether there are certain elements of the right to a fair trial that are always fully respected by international criminal trials. Instead, a more nuanced picture emerges, which points to both advances and areas for improvement by international criminal tribunals.

Chapter 4 then goes on to examine whether those components of the right to a fair trial are owed only to the accused, or whether others such as the prosecution, victims, and witnesses, and the international community can also be said to be holders of the right to a fair trial. It criticizes the extension of procedural fair trial rights to the prosecution and other actors, and argues that the defendant should be the only holder of procedural rights at trial.

Chapter 5 argues that international criminal tribunals have a role in setting the highest standards of fairness, contrary to other authors' assertions that they need to be just 'fair enough'.[34] A number of arguments are advanced in support of this hypothesis. First, the tribunals already embrace the position that their procedures represent the highest standards of fairness. Second, when international criminal tribunals fail to adhere to the highest standards of fairness, this gives an excuse to states that wish to derogate from or dilute the rights of the accused. As international legal institutions, the international criminal tribunals need to practically embody international fair trial standards to show states how they ought to work in practice. Last, setting the highest standards of fairness both aligns with the goals of international criminal tribunals and encourages state cooperation, which in turn bolsters the effectiveness of the institutions.

[34] Mirjan Damaška, 'Reflections on Fairness in International Criminal Justice' (2012) 10 *JICJ* 611, 616.

Chapter 6 discusses the interplay between domestic and international criminal jurisdictions on fair trial issues. I argue that practices like referrals from international criminal tribunals to domestic states can have a positive impact on the domestic protection of due process rights, and that this is evidenced in the Rule 11*bis* referral practice from the ICTY and ICTR. While the so-called 'due process hypothesis' on the principle of complementarity—that is, whether the fact that the state is willing and able to put the accused on trial, but unwilling or unable to guarantee a fair trial can serve as a basis for the ICC's jurisdiction—has been refuted by many scholars and some jurisprudence, it is posited that there is still a role for fair trial considerations in decisions relating to complementarity. The ICC's decisions on admissibility in the *Situation in Libya* have left the door open for the Court to declare a case admissible before it where the state has egregiously breached, or is egregiously breaching, the rights of the accused. The same argument can be made in relation to *ne bis in idem* considerations where an accused has been convicted or acquitted after a grossly unfair trial. These practices not only show that international criminal tribunals can encourage full respect for the rights of the accused by playing a role in assessing the fairness of domestic trials. They also further illustrate the need for the tribunals themselves to set the highest standards of fairness, given that these standards form the benchmark against which domestic trials will be measured.

1.3 The Nature of International Criminal Procedure

1.3.1 Classifying international criminal procedure

It is difficult to classify international criminal procedure within the confines of any one domestic criminal justice model. International criminal procedure represents a *sui generis* system that incorporates elements of criminal procedure from a vast range of countries, and some elements that are truly unique.[35] Indeed, there are divergences between the procedures espoused by the various international courts and tribunals themselves. For example, the STL permits *in absentia* trials, while the other tribunals do not; the ICC and STL allow victim participation in contrast to their predecessors, and the SCSL, ICC, and STL have established autonomous or semi-autonomous defence offices to provide legal aid and/or legal and administrative support to defence counsel, while in the ICTY and ICTR, this falls within the remit of the Registry.

[35] See above (n 4).

While a number of authors have argued for the need to move beyond the adversarial/inquisitorial dichotomy in assessing criminal procedure,[36] alternative models of classification do not readily assist in classifying international criminal procedure within one framework or another. For example, Jung has emphasized the need to take into account the meta-principles that guide criminal justice systems, instead of broadly classifying them by their procedural roots.[37] However, it is difficult to identify the key principle or principles that drive international criminal law. Judgments refer to the goals of fairness, giving victims a voice, assisting national peace and reconciliation, ending impunity, deterring future offenders, creating an accurate historical record, and strengthening domestic criminal justice systems, without any apparent hierarchy between those norms.[38] Thus, it becomes difficult to draw parallels between international and domestic justice systems based on their purported goals.

Another alternative to the classification of criminal justice models, aside from the adversarial/inquisitorial divide, is Packer's system of 'crime control' and 'due process' models. These two models, with their focus on policing and state authority, do not readily fit with the structure of international criminal law, which relies on the cooperation of states for its full realization. While deterrence is often mentioned in judgments,[39] 'crime control' is not a paramount feature of international criminal law in the sense of Packer's model. Nor does international criminal procedure fit neatly within the confines of Packer's 'due process' model, as he envisioned a system that would construct an 'obstacle course' for police conduct. By contrast, the conduct of arresting authorities is broadly disregarded when it comes to the trial phase of international criminal proceedings, unless any breaches of the rights of the accused at the arrest stage were particularly egregious.[40] Packer's 'due process' model placed the rights of defendants before all other considerations. International criminal

[36] Mireille Delmas-Marty, *Towards a Truly Common Law: Europe as a Laboratory for Legal Pluralism* (trans Naomi Norberg, Cambridge: CUP, 2002); Christopher Gane, 'Classifying Scottish Criminal Procedure' in Peter Duff and Neil Hutton (eds), *Criminal Justice in Scotland* (Aldershot: Ashgate, 1999) 56.

[37] Heike Jung, 'Nothing but the Truth? Some Facts, Impressions and Confessions about Truth in Criminal Procedure' in Anthony Duff, Lindsay Farmer, Sandra Marshall, and Victor Tadros (eds), *The Trial on Trial I: Truth and Due Process* (Oxford: Hart Publishing, 2004) 147, 152–3.

[38] Mirjan R. Damaška, 'What is the Point of International Criminal Justice?' (2008) 83 *Chicago Kent LR* 329; Immi Tallgren, 'The Sensibility and Sense of International Criminal Law' (2002) 13 *EJIL* 561.

[39] e.g. *Prosecutor v. Mucić et al.*, Appeal Judgment, Case No. IT-96-21-A, 20 February 2001, paras 799–896; *Prosecutor v. Tadić*, Sentencing Judgment, Case No. IT-94-1-T*bis*-R117, 11 November 1999, paras 7–9.

[40] *Prosecutor v. Nikolić*, Decision on Defence Motion Challenging the Exercise of Jurisdiction by the Tribunal, Case No. IT-94-2-PT, 9 October 2002, paras 112–14.

procedure not only refers to the rights of victims, witnesses, the prosecutor, and the international community,[41] but also purports to pursue goals outside of the due process model's goal of ensuring that innocent people are not wrongly convicted.

Some authors have defined procedural models on the basis of 'families' of legal systems. Most prominently, David and Brierley classified the criminal justice systems of the world into four 'families': common law, Romano-Germanic, socialist, and those based on religious or philosophical principles.[42] Vogler classified systems of justice as 'adversarial', 'inquisitorial', and 'popular', the latter of which included traditional justice mechanisms such as the *Gacaca* trials in Rwanda.[43] It is difficult to classify international criminal procedure as fitting squarely into any of those models, unless it can be regarded as its own family. However, this is unlikely because the division of systems into families is based on two factors: whether lawyers trained in one tradition can transfer to another with relative ease, and the principles that underpin the system.[44] Given that lawyers are not trained in international criminal procedure, but rather pass to the international criminal bar with relative ease from their own domestic systems,[45] the 'international justice as a new family' theory does not fit perfectly, but may come closest to categorizing the international criminal tribunals amongst the dominant theories of criminal procedure.

Perhaps the difficulties raised in attempting to classify international criminal procedure within established models of legal systems best illustrate that one cannot limit scholarly analysis of international criminal procedure to domestic legal constructs.[46] Some comparative legal scholars do reference the practice of the international criminal tribunals, but it is fair to say that this reference is fleeting and does not go to the heart of their classification of criminal justice systems.[47] For example, Vogler dedicated eight pages of his *World View of Criminal Justice* to the analysis of international criminal justice, remarking that there was an increased shift towards inquisitorial procedures in the international criminal tribunals, at a time when (in his view) domestic legal systems seemed to be ever shifting towards incorporating traditionally

[41] Discussed in detail at Chapter 5 below.

[42] René David and John E. C. Brierley, *Major Legal Systems in the World Today: An Introduction to the Comparative Study of Law* (3rd edn, London: Stevens & Sons, 1985).

[43] Richard Vogler, *A World View of Criminal Justice* (Aldershot: Ashgate, 2005).

[44] Vogler, ibid., 4.

[45] Rosemary Byrne, 'The New Public International Lawyer and the Hidden Art of International Criminal Trial Practice' (2010) 25 *Connecticut JIL* 243; Elena A. Baylis, 'Tribunal Hopping with the Post-Conflict Justice Junkies' (2008) 10 *Oregon Rev Int'l L* 361.

[46] Paul Roberts, 'On Method: The Ascent of Comparative Criminal Justice' (2002) 22 *OJLS* 539, 560–1.

[47] e.g. Mirjan R. Damaška, *Evidence Law Adrift* (New Haven: Yale University Press, 1997) 1.

common law elements.[48] He suggested that these increasingly inquisitorial facets of international criminal procedure were devoid of the checks and balances present domestically, and stated that 'these should be viewed with caution', given that 'international justice … is consciously intended to provide a blueprint for procedural reform around the world'.[49]

1.3.2 Procedural law-making at the international criminal tribunals

Regardless of the strength of Vogler's assessment of the purported trends in criminal procedure both internationally and domestically, or whether one would see his criticism of 'bureaucratic, inquisitorial' systems as well founded, he was correct in noting the creation of a more mixed procedural model over the lifetime of international criminal justice. The procedure in modern international criminal tribunals commenced in the ICTY with a set of Rules of Procedure and Evidence broadly similar to the Federal Rules for Criminal Procedure used in the United States of America. This was not caused by any major debate on the most appropriate procedural rules, but rather by pragmatism as the American Bar Association had provided the fullest working draft when the judges first sat down to draft the first set of Rules of Procedure and Evidence.[50] As a result, Jackson has suggested that judges may have been more driven by the exigencies of agreeing upon a draft set of rules than they were by formulating a human rights-based approach to rules of procedure and evidence.[51] The international criminal tribunals later moved towards incorporating more traditionally inquisitorial elements into their procedure, such as the creation of Pre-Trial Chambers,[52] the participation of victims,[53] the relaxation of rules relating to non-oral evidence,[54] and

[48] Vogler (n 43) 278–85. [49] ibid., 284–5. [50] Jackson (n 31) 236–7.

[51] See further Jackson (n 31) 236–7. See further, Daryl A. Mundis, 'From "Common Law" to "Civil Law": The Evolution of the ICTY Rules of Procedure and Evidence' (2001) 14 *LJIL* 367; Máximo Langer and Joseph W. Doherty, 'Managerial Judging Goes International, but Its Promise Remains Unfulfilled: An Empirical Assessment of the ICTY Reforms' (2011) 36 *Yale JIL* 241, 245.

[52] See William Pizzi, 'Overcoming Logistical and Structural Barriers to Fair Trials at International Tribunals' (2006) 4 *Int'l Commentary on Evidence* Issue 1, Article 4, available online at http://www.bepress.com/ice/vol4/iss1/art4, arguing that even more inquisitorial elements should have been adopted by the ad hoc tribunals. On the use of Pre-Trial Chambers in the ICC, see Jerome de Hemptinne, 'The Creation of Investigating Chambers at the ICC' (2007) 5 *JICJ* 402.

[53] See further, Chapter 4 below.

[54] Megan A. Fairlie, 'Due Process Erosion: The Diminution of Live Testimony at the ICTY' (2003) 34 *California Western Int'l L J* 47; Richard May and Marieke Wierda, *International Criminal Evidence* (Ardsley, NY: Transnational Publishers, 2002) 210–18; Patricia M. Wald, 'To "Establish Incredible Events by Credible Evidence": The Use of Affidavit Testimony in Yugoslavia War Crimes Tribunal Proceedings' (2001) 42 *Harv Int'l L J* 535; Peter Murphy, 'No Free Lunch,

a more managerial style of judging.[55] In a decision relating to the practice of witness proofing at the ICC, a great deal of emphasis was placed on these elements in illustrating that the Court's procedure was markedly different to that of its predecessors.[56] The status of international criminal procedure as a *sui generis* or mixed model is not in itself very remarkable. What is stunning, however, is the sheer pace of development and the fact that the procedure continues to grow and change over time.

We might question what the drivers of these developments are. Some authors have referred to individual events, such as the death of Slobodan Milošević before judgment could be issued in his case, as factors that lead to a re-evaluation of the efficiency and suitability of international criminal procedures.[57] Others have pointed to the 'completion strategies' for the ad hoc international tribunals as putting pressure on judges to finish trials as quickly as possible, even if that means relaxing some of the procedural safeguards that are in place for the rights of the accused.[58] On the other hand, the completion strategies do not seem to have hurried judges in issuing judgments; one 2011 judgment of the ICTR was issued almost three years after the close of trial.[59]

A key driver in the speedy pace of the development of international criminal procedure was almost certainly judicial creativity in solving problems as they arose.[60] Owing to this problem-solving approach, and the large degree of flexibility afforded to judges in such matters, particularly before the ad hoc tribunals, a significant degree of fragmentation between international criminal tribunals' procedures can be observed. By consequence, it becomes difficult (albeit not impossible) to refer to 'international criminal procedure' as though

No Free Proof: The Indiscriminate Admission of Evidence is a Serious Flaw in International Criminal Trials' (2010) 8 *JICJ* 539; Eugene O'Sullivan and Deirdre Montgomery, 'The Erosion of the Right to Confrontation under the Cloak of Fairness at the ICTY' (2010) 8 *JICJ* 511; and Colleen M. Rohan, 'Rules Governing the Presentation of Testimonial Evidence' in Khan et al. (eds) (n 5) 499.

[55] Máximo Langer, 'The Rise of Managerial Judging in International Criminal Law' (2005) 53 *AJIL* 835.

[56] *Situation in the DRC: Prosecutor v. Lubanga*, Decision Regarding the Practices Used to Prepare and Familiarise Witnesses for Giving Testimony at Trial, Case No. ICC-01/04-01/06, Trial Chamber, 30 November 2007.

[57] Jackson (n 31) 18.

[58] *Prosecutor v. Nyiramasuhuko et al.*, Decision in the Matter of Proceedings under Rule 15*bis* (D), Case No. ICTR-98-42-A15*bis*, 24 September 2003, Dissenting Opinion of Judge David Hunt, para 17.

[59] *Prosecutor v. Bizimungu et al.*, Judgment and Sentence, Case No. ICTR-99-50-T, 30 September 2011. The case closed on 5 December 2008: see *Prosecutor v. Bizimungu et al.*, Minutes of Proceedings: Trial Day 404, Case No. ICTR-99-50-T, 5 December 2008.

[60] O-Gon Kwon, 'Procedural Challenges Faced by International Criminal Tribunals and the Value of Codification' in Sluiter et al. (n 5) 1415.

it were a single entity or system. Indeed, we sometimes witness fragmentation not just between tribunals, but also even between different chambers of the same tribunal. For example, the ICTY's Trial Chamber in the *Milošević*, *Krajišnik*, and *Šešelj* cases imposed counsel on uncooperative accused,[61] whereas the *Šešelj* Appeals Chamber overturned the imposition of counsel.[62] In the *Stanišić and Simatović* case before the ICTY, the Trial Chamber held that the right to be present at trial could be derogated from in cases of 'substantial trial disruptions on the part of an accused',[63] even where this was unintentional, owing to illness. It based this reasoning on the rights of the accused and his co-accused to be tried without undue delay.[64] The Appeals Chamber overturned this ruling on the basis that the delay would not be 'so substantial as to warrant derogation from the fundamental right of the accused to be present at trial'.[65] The Appeals Chamber of the STL held that the Tribunal had jurisdiction over legal as well as natural persons for contempt offences,[66] but the Contempt Judge expressly departed from this finding just one month later.[67]

Judges have taken their place as procedural law-makers in the international criminal tribunals in one of two ways. First, some tribunals explicitly bestow judges with the power to create and amend their Rules of Procedure and Evidence (RPE), and this has been done frequently. In the ICTY, the RPE were amended fifty times between 1994 and 2014. Some of these changes

[61] *Prosecutor v. Šešelj*, Order Concerning Appointment of Standby Counsel and Delayed Commencement of Trial, Case No. IT-03-67-R77.2, 25 October 2006; *Prosecutor v. Krajišnik*, Decision on Momcilo Krajišnik's request to self-represent, on Counsel's motions in relation to appointment of amicus curiae, and on the Prosecution motion of 16 February 2007, Case No. IT-00-39-A, 11 May 2007; *Prosecutor v. Milošević*, Decision on Interlocutory Appeal of the Trial Chamber's Decision on the Assignment of Defence Counsel, Case No. IT-02-54-AR73.7, 1 November 2004.

[62] *Prosecutor v. Šešelj*, Decision on Assignment of Counsel, Case No. IT-03-67-T, 21 August 2006; *Prosecutor v. Šešelj*, Decision on Appeal against the Trial Chamber's Decision on Assignment of Counsel, Case No. IT-03-67-A, 20 October 2006; *Prosecutor v. Šešelj*, Reasons for Decision (No. 2) on Assignment of Counsel, Case No. IT-03-67-T, 27 November 2006; *Prosecutor v. Šešelj*, Decision on Appeal against the Trial Chamber's Decision (No. 2) on Assignment of Counsel, Case No. IT-03-67-A, 8 December 2006. For an excellent analysis, see Alexander Zahar, 'Legal Aid, Self-Representation, and the Crisis at the Hague Tribunal' (2008) 19 *CLF* 241.

[63] *Prosecutor v. Stanišić et al.*, Decision on Defence Appeal of the Decision on Future Course of Proceedings, Case No. IT-03-69-AR73.2, 16 May 2008, para 15.

[64] ibid., para 17. [65] ibid., para 18.

[66] *In the case against New TV SAL and Al Khayat*, Decision on Interlocutory Appeal Concerning Personal Jurisdiction in Contempt Proceedings, Case No. STL-14-05, 2 October 2014.

[67] *In the case against Akhbar Beirut S.A.L. and Al Amin*, Decision on Motion Challenging Jurisdiction, Case No. STL-14-06, 5 November 2014. This decision was, it probably goes without saying, overturned by the Appeals Chamber: *In the case against Akhbar Beirut S.A.L. and Al Amin*, Decision on Interlocutory Appeal Concerning Personal Jurisdiction in Contempt Proceedings, Case No. STL-14-06, 23 January 2015.

have been quite substantial, covering matters such as the removal of the preference for oral witness testimony,[68] provisions on continuing with a replacement judge or in the absence of a judge of a Chamber when they are unavailable,[69] and provisions on guilty pleas.[70] The ICTR's Rules were amended more than twenty times between 1995 and 2014, while the SCSL's Rules were amended twelve times in the Court's lifetime. Despite its status as a relatively new court, the STL's RPE underwent seven amendments in its first four years. The ICC's judge-made Regulations of the Court, designed to be those regulations 'necessary for its routine functioning',[71] have also been used creatively and have borne more importance than was probably intended for them, as particularly illustrated by the *Katanga* Regulation 55 debacle,[72] discussed further in Chapter 3 below.

Judges have also exercised their power to amend and adopt procedures by reference to 'the inherent competence of a judicial body, whether civil or criminal, to regulate its own procedure in the event of silence in the written rules, so as to assure the exercise of such jurisdiction as it has, and to fulfill itself, properly and effectively, as a court of law'.[73] This inherent powers doctrine was the basis for granting a stay of proceedings in the *Lubanga* case before the ICC, an interpretation later criticized by Judge Eboe-Osuji in the *Banda and Jerbo* case as being the very antithesis to the 'incidental jurisdiction' of the Court.[74] If the ICC's primary role was to end impunity, he argued, how could the granting of a stay of proceedings for abuse of process be incidental to that function?

The use of the inherent powers doctrine by the ICC is notable because the drafters of the Statute expressly removed the power to make and amend the RPE from the judges' hands. Nevertheless, the doctrine has been used

[68] Rule 90, Rules of Procedure and Evidence of the International Criminal Tribunal for the former Yugoslavia, UN Doc. IT/32/Rev.19, 1 and 13 December 2000 (deleting the former Rule 90(A)); see further Yvonne McDermott, 'The Admissibility and Weight of Written Witness Testimony in International Criminal Law: A Socio-Legal Analysis' (2013) 26 *LJIL* 971, 971–3.

[69] Rule 15*bis*, introduced by Rules of Procedure and Evidence of the International Criminal Tribunal for the former Yugoslavia, UN Doc. IT/32/Rev.26, 12 December 2002.

[70] Rule 62*bis*, introduced by Rules of Procedure and Evidence of the International Criminal Tribunal for the former Yugoslavia, UN Doc. IT/32/Rev.13, 10 July 1998.

[71] Article 52, ICC Statute.

[72] *Situation in the DRC: Prosecutor v. Katanga and Chui*, Decision on the Implementation of Regulation 55 of the Regulations of the Court and Severing the Charges against the Accused Persons, Case No. ICC-01/04-01/07, 21 November 2012.

[73] *Kanyabashi v. Prosecutor*, Dissenting Opinion of Judge Shahabuddeen, Case No. ICTR-96-15-A, 3 June 1999.

[74] *Situation in Darfur, Sudan: Prosecutor v. Banda and Jerbo*, Decision on the Defence Request for a Temporary Stay of Proceedings, Case No. ICC-02/05-03/09, 26 October 2012, Concurring Separate Opinion of Judge Eboe-Osuji, para 99.

to determine that the ICC does have the power to subpoena witnesses as an inherent component of its judicial function.[75] For the past sixteen years, commentators almost universally agreed that the ICC was not in a position to compel witness testimony, but rather to seek cooperation from state parties in these matters.[76] Nonetheless, the *Ruto and Sang* Trial Chamber concluded that the state parties did not intend to create an ICC that is 'in terms of substance, in truth a phantom'.[77]

Therefore, we can see that international criminal procedure remains a dynamic and evolving area of law. Judges of the international criminal tribunals have a key role, whether expressly granted to them or not, in shaping the procedures that govern their day-to-day activities. We will assess how that fluidity impacts on the legitimacy of their procedures in Chapter 2 below.

1.4 Finding the Best Lens for the Assessment of Fairness in International Criminal Trials

Many authors have grappled with the question of whether it would be appropriate to assess international criminal procedure through the lens of comparative criminal procedure, or by reference to a certain system or systems. Safferling, for example, looked at both United Kingdom and German procedural standards as well as those of the ICTY in developing his theory on an emerging international criminal procedure.[78] When assessing the fairness of

[75] *Situation in the Republic of Kenya: Prosecutor v. Ruto and Sang*, Decision on Prosecutor's Application for Witness Summonses and Resulting Request for State Party Cooperation, Case No. ICC-01/09-01/11, 17 April 2014. The Appeals Chamber declined to rule on the correctness of Trial Chambers' reliance on the implied powers doctrine or the concept of customary international criminal procedure, instead finding that the Statute and RPE clearly supported the Trial Chamber's findings: *Situation in the Republic of Kenya: Prosecutor v. Ruto and Sang*, Judgment on the Appeals of William Samoei Ruto and Mr Joshua Arap Sang against the decision of Trial Chamber V (A) of 17 April 2014 entitled 'Decision on Prosecutor's Application for Witness Summonses and resulting Request for State Party Cooperation', Case No. ICC-01/09-01/11, 9 October 2014, para 105.

[76] Robert Cryer, Håkan Friman, Darryl Robinson and Elizabeth Wilmshurst, *An Introduction to International Criminal Law and Procedure* (3rd edn, Cambridge: CUP, 2014) 520–2; William A. Schabas, *The International Criminal Court: A Commentary on the Rome Statute* (Oxford: OUP, 2010) 842; Bruce Broomhall and Claus Kress, 'Implementing Cooperation Duties under the Rome Statute' in Claus Kress, Bruce Broomhall, Flavia Lattanzi, and Valeria Santori (eds), *The Rome Statute and Domestic Legal Orders: Volume II* (Baden-Baden: Nomos, 2005) 515, 529.

[77] *Prosecutor v. Ruto and Sang*, Decision on Prosecutor's Application for Witness Summonses and Resulting Request for State Party Cooperation (n 75) para 124 (citing *The Betsy* (1797) 4 *International Adjudications* 179, 187.

[78] Safferling, *Towards an International Criminal Procedure* (n 5) 2: 'the aim must be a truly international criminal procedure which should not be used as a test for the credibility of domestic penal systems, but stand solidly on the various traditions of criminal procedure'.

procedures with reference to a certain domestic system or systems, however, one must be conscious of one's own legal background and the bias towards certain practices which may result.[79] Furthermore, as Roberts observed, comparative analyses may point out the benefits and disadvantages of a given procedure, but will fail to elaborate the values that ought to underpin criminal procedure.[80]

Human rights-based approaches to international criminal procedure, as perhaps most famously adopted by Zappalà,[81] have also been criticized. Mégret argued that human rights analyses are 'under-determinative', due to the following factors: (a) human rights treaties are not binding and have no formal status before international criminal tribunals; (b) the broad aims of human rights rarely prescribe a certain procedure; (c) human rights standards need to be contextualized within the broader goals of international criminal procedure; (d) human rights treaties are subject to a 'margin of appreciation' doctrine, which gives certain states leeway as to how to effectuate the standards therein; (e) there are internal inconsistencies in human rights treaties; (f) human rights case law depends on the actor claiming that their rights have been violated, and as a result, human rights courts do not have to deal with conflicting claims to rights as international criminal courts do when deciding between the rights of the accused and other actors at trial; (g) human rights law pushes for the end of impunity at any cost, and, as such, international criminal tribunals should not be limited by human rights standards in that shared quest for the end of impunity; and (h) human rights treaties allow for derogations in states of exception.[82] Mégret ended his analysis by noting that the debate between various legal traditions often finds itself looking to human rights law for guidance, only to find human rights law, in turn, seeking guidance from domestic law.[83]

A number of observations may be made on the under-determinacy of human rights law as a framework for analysing the fairness of procedures in

[79] Frederic Mégret, 'Beyond Fairness: Understanding the Determinants of International Criminal Procedure' (2009) 14 *UCLA J Int'l L & Foreign Aff* 37, 44 ('Judges associated with particular traditions have been known to, consciously or unconsciously, promote certain features of criminal procedure that they are familiar with.'). See also, Sarah J. Summers, *Fair Trials: The European Criminal Procedural Tradition and the European Court of Human Rights* (Oxford: Hart Publishing, 2007) 11, referring to 'legal nationalism' and the jealous guarding that some practitioners and commentators tend to have over their own legal traditions.

[80] Paul Roberts, 'Comparative Criminal Justice Goes Global' (2008) 28 *OJLS* 369, 375 ('Elaborating a principled set of values for criminal procedure is indeed an urgent—and relatively neglected—task for criminal justice scholarship.'); see also, Paul Roberts, 'Comparative Law for International Criminal Justice' in Esin Örücü and David Nelken (eds), *Comparative Law: A Handbook* (Oxford: Hart Publishing, 2007) 339, elaborating on 'seven concentric circles' of international criminal justice.

[81] Zappalá (n 5).

[82] Mégret (n 79) 49–58.

[83] ibid., 58.

international criminal law. First, the 'problem' of symbiosis between domestic and human rights systems is a non-issue; the relationship between the two is by its very nature a two-way street. Indeed, one would think that if human rights standards acted in a vacuum, it would be a better reason to disregard them as irrelevant to assessments of international criminal procedure.

Second, Mégret's reference to the principle that human rights law supports the end of impunity at any cost[84] may be something of a stretch. It is true that in *X v FRG*, the European Commission referred to the exceptional circumstances of post-World War II trials in stating that some of the fair trial principles were rendered inapplicable to those trials:

> The exceptional character of criminal proceedings involving war crimes committed during World War II renders, in the Commission's opinion, inapplicable the principles developed in case-law of the Commission and the Court of Human Rights in connection with cases involving other criminal offences.[85]

However, since that case, the European Court of Human Rights (ECtHR) has rejected the notion that society's interest in prosecution could override certain individual rights of the accused. In *Saunders v. UK*, for example, where the CEO of the Guinness Company was accused of white collar crime, it was argued that derogations from the right to silence were needed more in white collar criminal cases; this argument was rejected.[86] This decision could be said to comport with Dworkin's conceptualization of 'rights as trumps', where individual rights should 'trump' collective goals.[87] As Ashworth has pointed out, when a right is declared by a court to be 'fundamental', that same court cannot take it away again by showing that maybe it would be better if it did not exist in a certain limited situation.[88]

Last, while human rights treaties are not themselves binding before international criminal tribunals, the same fair trial standards are enshrined in the statutes of the international criminal tribunals, so it is unreasonable to regard the standards originally laid down in human rights legal instruments as irrelevant to international criminal procedure. Article 21 of the ICTY Statute, Article 20 of the ICTR Statute, Article 17 of the SCSL Statute, Article 16 of the STL Statute, and Article 67 of the ICC Statute are closely modelled

[84] ibid., 57.

[85] *X v. Federal Republic of Germany* (1976) 6 *Decisions and Reports* 114, 115–16.

[86] *Saunders v. UK*, Application No. 43/1994/490/572, Judgment, 17 December 1996.

[87] Ronald Dworkin, 'Rights as Trumps' in Jeremy Waldron (ed.) *Theories of Rights* (Oxford: OUP, 1984) 153. On the limits of this theory, see Aileen McHarg, 'Reconciling Human Rights and the Public Interest: Conceptual Problems and Doctrinal Uncertainty in the Jurisprudence of the European Court of Human Rights' (1999) 62 *MLR* 671.

[88] Andrew Ashworth, *Human Rights, Serious Crime and Criminal Procedure* (London: Sweet & Maxwell, 2002) 70–5.

on Article 14 of the International Covenant on Civil and Political Rights (ICCPR). All of these provisions embody the rights to equality before the law, the presumption of innocence, and a number of other minimum guarantees that must be observed in practice. Like the ICCPR, the statutes of the SCSL, ICTY, and ICTR lay out a total of seven minimum guarantees. The ICC's Statute adds to these the right to make an unsworn statement, the right to the disclosure of exculpatory materials, and the right not to have the burden of proof or onus of rebuttal imposed on the accused. It also requires the Court to interpret its law 'in accordance with international human rights standards'.[89] The STL's Statute qualifies the minimum guarantee of the accused to be tried in his/her presence, and adds a right to examine all of the evidence against him or her, whereas the other statutes refer only to the right to examine the witnesses against him or her. This close relationship between the standards set out in the ICCPR and regional human rights treaties and the standards set down in the international criminal tribunals' statutes means that we do not need to consider the extent to which human rights law sets standards that need to be followed by the tribunals—those standards are repeated verbatim in the tribunals' own law. Thus, the case law of the human rights tribunals can inform our understanding of the meaning of those standards.

The ICTY in *Tadić* determined that it could garner persuasive precedent from the jurisprudence of the ECtHR, along with domestic courts, but 'that these standards must be interpreted within the context of the unique object and purpose of the International Tribunal, particularly recognizing its mandate to protect victims and witnesses'.[90] It is quite remarkable that the Appeals Chamber in that case relied extensively on an ECtHR case (*Kostovski v. Netherlands*[91]) in reaching its decision that witness anonymity could be permitted, while the original ECtHR decision stated explicitly that the accused must be given the opportunity to challenge the witnesses against him or her.[92] In the words of former President of the Tribunal, the late Antonio Cassese:

> The Majority Opinion of the Trial Chamber was, of necessity, selective in its reliance on the *Kostovski* case. Indeed, it must be borne in mind that the finding of the majority ... was that fair trial guarantees were not violated with anonymous witnesses, whereas the finding of the European Court in *Kostovski* was that such guarantees were violated.[93]

[89] Article 21(3), ICC Statute.

[90] *Tadić* Decision on the Prosecutor's Motion Requesting Protective Measures for Victims and Witnesses (n 25) para 70.

[91] (1990) 12 EHRR 434, 20 November 1989.

[92] ibid., para 41.

[93] Antonio Cassese, 'The International Criminal Tribunal for the Former Yugoslavia and Human Rights' [1997] *European Human Rights Law Review* 329.

We might ask, given that ECtHR standards are not binding on the international criminal tribunals, why the Appeals Chamber (albeit selectively) relied so heavily on this adverse judgment in reaching its ruling. One can only assume that human rights case law has a legitimizing effect on some procedural decisions of the international criminal tribunals, and where there is a lacuna in the established law and procedure, the parties and the judges will look to such case law for guidance.

From the above, it is clear that human rights standards cannot be ignored in assessments of fairness in international criminal trials, for two key reasons. The first is that the fair trial provisions of the ICCPR and other international human rights instruments inspire the tribunals' own standards. The second is that the international criminal tribunals draw on international human rights jurisprudence in their interpretation of those standards, although occasionally their reliance on this case law is selective or seeks to distinguish international criminal trials from those in domestic contexts.

In spite of the clear importance of human rights standards, they fall short of providing the only standards of assessment, given that the jurisprudence only provides illustration on breaches of these rights, and by consequence, best practice is not enunciated. Moreover, assessments of whether the right to a fair trial has been breached take an approach based on the 'overall fairness' of the trial; therefore, these decisions do not enunciate the precise parameters of each individual component of the right to a fair trial, save in those rare cases where only one of the component guarantees is at issue. Last, by simply ruling on whether the right to a fair trial has been breached or not, human rights tribunals do not provide a great deal of guidance on the optimal conduct of criminal proceedings; indeed, a large margin of appreciation is given to states as regards their domestic criminal procedures.[94] Thus, international

[94] e.g. *Ruiz Torija v. Spain*, Application No. 18390/91, Judgment, 9 December 1994 (on the margin of appreciation doctrine as it relates to the right to a reasoned judgment); *Colozza v. Italy*, Application No. 9024/80, Judgment, 12 February 1985, para 30 ('The Contracting States enjoy a wide discretion as regards the choice of the means calculated to ensure that their legal systems are in compliance with the requirements of Article 6 para 1 ... The Court's task is not to indicate those means to the States, but to determine whether the result called for by the Convention has been achieved.'); *De Cubber v. Belgium* (1985) 7 EHRR 236, 26 October 1984, para 35 ('The Court's task is to determine whether the Contracting States have achieved the result called for by the Convention, not to indicate the particular means to be utilised.') See further, Yutaka Arai-Takahashi, *The Margin of Appreciation Doctrine and the Principle of Proportionality in the Jurisprudence of the ECHR* (Antwerp: Intersentia, 2002) 33–58. Compare Human Rights Committee, General Comment 32, para 4 ('Article 14 contains guarantees that States Parties must respect, regardless of their legal traditions and their domestic law. While they should report on how these guarantees are interpreted in relation to their respective legal systems, the Committee notes that it cannot be left to the sole discretion of domestic law to determine the essential content of Covenant guarantees.').

criminal procedure should be recognized as *sui generis* and its fairness should be examined through black-letter legal approaches as its own discipline. It is apposite, then, to turn to an analysis of the tribunals' own interpretations of what 'fairness' means, and how those interpretations might fit with established theories of fairness.

2

Interpreting Fairness in International Criminal Trials

This chapter examines a number of theories of fairness and how they might inform our understanding of what fairness means in the context of international criminal trials. The right to a fair trial is closely related to theories of legitimacy, procedural justice, and rule of law, and principles derived from those theories can inform our interpretation of fairness in international criminal trials. Such principles include that justice should be delivered openly and transparently—this relates to the right to a public trial; that the accused should be given a voice in the process—this relates to the right to challenge witnesses and evidence, and to self-representation or representation through counsel; and the principle of neutrality—this relates to the presumption of innocence and the right to trial by an independent and impartial tribunal.

In this context, we can see that the theoretical concept of fairness has a particular meaning when it pertains to the right to a fair trial. Human rights treaties, which are emulated by the statutes of the international criminal tribunals, outline a number of guarantees that must be met in order to ensure fairness in criminal trials. Concepts of fairness such as 'neutrality' can be translated to more concrete requirements on judicial impartiality. Thus, the second part of this chapter argues that the right to a fair trial represents a unique construct of fairness, comprised of several minimum guarantees and an overarching requirement that the accused should be given a fair opportunity to present his or her case in open, transparent, and impartial procedures, in accordance with clear law and procedures articulated in advance of trial. The final part of this chapter examines the interpretation of fairness by international criminal tribunals, including such questions as whether fairness should be assessed with reference to each constituent minimum guarantee, or whether it is sufficient for proceedings to be fair 'as a whole'. The international criminal tribunals have not developed a fully consistent definition of what fairness means in the context of their proceedings, although certain components have been recognized by their law and practice, as discussed further in Chapter 3.

2.1 Theories of Fairness and Their Interplay with International Criminal Proceedings

The concept of fairness is undeniably nebulous and the perceived fairness of a process is frequently based on the subjective view of the participants. In addition, 'fairness' in a general sense is a theoretical concept that scholars have referred to in order to answer questions of natural justice, equality, non-discrimination, and equitable distribution of wealth.[1] The remarks of the UN Secretary General at the time of the establishment of the ICTY, where he referred to the Tribunal's conformance to 'internationally recognized standards regarding the rights of the accused at all stages of its proceedings',[2] appear to support the interpretation taken in this work that 'fairness' in the sense of the rights of the accused bears a particular meaning, as it refers to the right to a fair trial as established by international human rights law and related practice. Nevertheless, some of the key theories of fairness and justice in a more general sense reveal the importance of principles such as consistency and legal certainty, and these principles can inform our assessment of the fairness of international criminal trials.

2.1.1 Fairness as legitimacy

Legitimacy in international law has been stated to affect the compliance of states, individuals and international organizations with the law.[3] Theories of legitimacy tend to fall into one of two types: constitutive legitimacy and process legitimacy.[4] The former examines the legitimacy of the process through which the rule in question was made, including the input into the rule's

[1] The leading works in this field include Amartya Sen, *The Idea of Justice* (London/New York: Allen Lane, 2009); John Rawls, *A Theory of Justice* (Cambridge, MA: Harvard University Press, 1971); John Rawls, *Justice as Fairness: A Restatement* (Cambridge, MA: Belknap Press, 2001) and Ronald Dworkin, *Taking Rights Seriously* (Cambridge, MA: Harvard University Press, 1977).

[2] Report of the Secretary-General Pursuant to Paragraph 2 of the Security Council Resolution 808 (1993) UN Doc. S/25704, 3 May 1993, para 106.

[3] Thomas M. Franck, *The Power of Legitimacy Among Nations* (Oxford: OUP, 1990) 16.

[4] As well as source and process legitimacy, a third facet is sometimes added: legitimacy of outcome. See e.g. Rüdiger Wolfrum, 'Legitimacy in International Law from a Legal Perspective: Some Introductory Remarks' in Rüdiger Wolfrum and Volker Röben (eds), *Legitimacy in International Law* (Berlin: Springer, 2008) 6.

formation by those who would be affected.[5] Weber's theory of sociological legitimacy can be seen as an early form of constitutive legitimacy.[6]

In *Tadić*, the accused challenged the legality of the establishment of the ICTY on the basis that it was not a 'tribunal established by law', as provided for in the fair trial provisions of human rights treaties.[7] The ICTY discussed elements of constitutive legitimacy in its examination of the phrase, 'tribunal established by law'. It determined that the phrase might refer to a separation of powers between branches of government in a domestic context, which had no relevance to an international law setting, given the absence of the traditional branches of power at international level.[8] It also found that the right to trial by a tribunal established by law necessitated the 'establishment … by a body which … has a limited power to take binding decisions', and that the Security Council was one such body.[9] Some theories of constitutive legitimacy also examine the effectiveness of a court or tribunal in achieving their stated goals.[10] In this respect, we observe the circular nature of legitimacy, in that effectiveness can be both a source of legitimacy and a result thereto.[11]

It would seem that the notion of 'process legitimacy' bears greater relevance when discussing international criminal procedure. The idea that outcomes are more likely to be accepted if the process followed is perceived to be fair was a key facet of Luhmann's theory of 'legitimation through procedure'.[12] A number of subsequent studies found that defendants' perceptions of court experiences were as much, if not more, based on the procedure followed than

[5] Samantha Besson, 'Institutionalising Global "Demoi"-cracy', in Lukas H. Meyer (ed.), *Legitimacy, Justice and Public International Law* (Cambridge: CUP, 2009) 58.

[6] Max Weber, *Economy and Society: An Outline of Interpretative Sociology* vol 1 (Guenther Roth and Claus Wittich (eds), originally published in 1922, Berkeley: University of California Press, 1978) 56. Shany has noted that the 'acceptance' of international courts may be measured by the acceptance of their jurisdiction, compliance with their judgments, or support of them as institutions: Yuval Shany, *Assessing the Effectiveness of International Courts* (Oxford: OUP, 2014) 139.

[7] Article 14(1), ICCPR.

[8] *Prosecutor v. Tadić*, Decision on the Defence Motion for Interlocutory Appeal on Jurisdiction, Case No. IT-94-1-T, 2 October 1995, para 43.

[9] ibid., para 44.

[10] Yuval Shany, 'Assessing the Effectiveness of International Courts: A Goal-Based Approach' (2012) 106 *AJIL* 225, 233; Cord Schmelzle, 'Evaluating Governance: Effectiveness and Legitimacy in Areas of Limited Statehood', SFB-Governance Working Paper Series 26, November 2011, 6; Michael J. Struett, *The Politics of Constructing the International Criminal Court: NGOs, Discourse, and Agency* (London: Palgrave Macmillan, 2008) 153.

[11] See also Yvonne McDermott and Wedad Elmaalul, 'Legitimacy and the Administration of International Justice' in William A. Schabas and Shannonbrooke Murphy (eds), *Research Handbook on International Courts and Tribunals* (Cheltenham: Edward Elgar, 2016) (forthcoming); Shany (n 6) 137–8, stating that internal legitimacy is a 'prerequisite for conferring external legitimization on other norms … and for facilitating the attainment of the court's ultimate ends'.

[12] Niklas Luhmann, *Legitimation durch Verhafen* (Darmstadt: Luchterhand, 1969). Luhmann's study examined legislative and administrative procedures as well as court processes.

on the ultimate outcome.[13] Lind and Tyler found that where the procedure as a whole is perceived as being fair, individual wrong decisions will be accepted, whereas unjust processes are seen to reflect badly on broader society.[14] In the context of international criminal trials, the defendant's perception that the process is fair and unbiased is crucial to their cooperation with the tribunal, and acceptance of its judgments.[15]

Process was key to the work of Thomas Franck, who noted that, '[i]t is only by reference to a community's evolving standards of what constitutes right process that it is possible to assert meaningfully that a … court's judgment … is legitimate.'[16] Franck's theory of fairness in international law incorporated his earlier theory of legitimacy, which comprised four elements—determinacy, symbolic validation, coherence, and adherence—in conjunction with an element of distributive justice.[17] The concept of determinacy requires that the message of a rule should be clear,[18] and in the context of international criminal procedure, would necessitate reasoned decisions on the meaning of rules of procedure and evidence where they are vague or parties require their further interpretation. Symbolic validation refers to ceremony ('ritual') and tradition ('pedigree') in establishing the rule-making authority of a body, and the use of the historic origin of that rule-making body or of the rule itself, to achieve compliance with a rule.[19] The fact that judges wear robes, the invocation of the scales of justice in tribunals' logos, and the manner in which court proceedings follow an established order may be seen as symbols of validation in the present context. Coherence, as may be obvious, relates to the degree to which a rule is applied consistently.[20] Adherence requires a consistency between primary and secondary rules of obligation,[21] so it would

[13] Tom R. Tyler, 'The Role of Perceived Injustice in Defendants' Evaluations of their Courtroom Experience' (1984) *Law and Society Review* 51–74; E. Allan Lind and Tom R. Tyler, *The Social Psychology of Procedural Justice* (New York: Plenum, 1988); Klaus F. Röhl, 'Procedural Justice: Introduction and Overview' in Klaus F. Röhl and Stefan Machura (eds), *Procedural Justice* (Dartmouth: Ashgate, 1997) 1.

[14] Lind and Tyler, ibid.; Tom R. Tyler, *Why People Obey the Law* (Princeton: Princeton University Press, 2006); Tom R. Tyler, *Why People Cooperate* (Princeton: Princeton University Press, 2010).

[15] Discussed further below, Section 5.2.4.

[16] Thomas M. Franck, *Fairness in International Law and Institutions* (New York: OUP, 1995) 29.

[17] ibid., 23. As distributive justice is concerned with the equitable distribution of monetary resources, this element of fairness falls outside the scope of the present work.

[18] Franck (n 3) 50.

[19] ibid., 92–4.

[20] ibid., 148. In his later work on fairness (see Franck (n 16) 77), however, Franck refined this position in asserting that the application of apparently straightforward rules resulting in patently unfair or absurd outcomes would require a balance to be struck between the legitimacy in doing so and the substantive justice at stake. For a discussion of this position, see Iain Scobbie, 'Tom Franck's Fairness' (2002) 13 *EJIL* 909, 914–16.

[21] Franck (n 3) 184.

require rules of procedure and evidence of the international criminal tribunals to adequately embody the standards set down in the tribunals' statutes.

In a similar vein to the adherence, coherence, and determinacy requirements, Fuller advocated eight attributes of the law, and these included the principles of consistency, articulateness, and concreteness.[22] The idea of legitimacy as an imperative requirement for establishing international criminal law as a mature system of law, rather than an incoherent set of laws and rules which do not bind together as a consistent whole, can be further seen in the work of May, who stated that '[i]nternational criminal law will not come to maturity as a system of law unless protections of fundamental fairness ... are put in place',[23] and Damaška's warnings on the dangers of picking and choosing divergent rules of procedure from domestic legal systems without having regard to the corresponding rules and principles that accompany them in their natural habitat.[24] Thus, it is clear that coherence, adherence, and determinacy, while they might not frequently be explicitly articulated by the international criminal tribunals in their jurisprudence on fairness, are key principles in ensuring the fairness of proceedings.

By embracing the highest standards of due process[25] and applying the law consistently and in full equality, the international criminal tribunals can bolster their legitimacy in the eyes of those affected.[26] As Judge Van den Wyngaert noted in her minority opinion to the *Katanga* judgment:

> In order for a court of law to have the legal and moral authority to pass legal and moral judgment on someone, especially when it relates to such serious allegations as international crimes, it is essential ... to scrupulously observe the fairness of the proceedings.[27]

[22] Lon L. Fuller, *The Morality of Law* (revised edn, New Haven and London: Yale University Press, 1969) 33–9. In this regard, the author argued, 'the word "procedural" should be assigned a special and expanded sense' (ibid., 96).

[23] Larry May, *Global Justice and Due Process* (New York/Cambridge: CUP, 2011) 67.

[24] Mirjan R. Damaška, 'Epistemology and Legal Regulation of Proof' (2003) 2 *LPR* 117, 121 ('In their natural habitat, each set of practices is part of a larger procedural whole, with its own internal coherence .... Creating a successful mixture is not like shopping in a boutique of detachable procedural forms, in which one is free to purchase some and reject others.').

[25] Discussed further at Chapter 5 below.

[26] David Luban, 'Fairness to Rightness: Jurisdiction, Legality, and the Legitimacy of International Criminal Law' in Samantha Besson and John Tasioulis (eds), *The Philosophy of International Law* (Oxford: OUP, 2010) 569; Hassan B. Jallow, 'Fair Trial in International Criminal Justice', *United Nations Audiovisual Library of International Law*, published online February 2015. Compare Anthony Duff, 'Authority and Responsibility in International Criminal Law' in Samantha Besson and John Tasioulis (eds), *The Philosophy of International Law* (Oxford: OUP, 2010) 589, who argues that the fairness of trials cannot bolster the authority of international criminal tribunals to try individuals where constitutive legitimacy is lacking.

[27] *Prosecutor v. Katanga*, Judgment, Case No. ICC-01/04-01/07, 7 March 2014, Minority Opinion of Judge Van den Wyngaert, para 311.

2.1.2 Fairness as procedural justice

'Justice' as a concept has been said to cover notions of retribution (or punishing those guilty of wrongdoing), deterrence (or discouraging others from committing those wrongs in future), and restoration (or reconciling the wrongdoers with their victims).[28] The procedures followed in achieving these end goals can be called 'methods of justice',[29] and, as such, might be seen as subsidiary to the substantive outcomes achieved. However, it is argued that procedure followed in international criminal trials is as important as their outcomes for two key reasons.

First, procedure is 'normatively prior'[30] to substantive law, in that the implementation of rights and duties depends on the proper administration of justice. The Genocide Convention, with its provision that genocide shall be prosecuted before 'such international penal tribunal as may have jurisdiction'[31] was some fifty years old by the time of the first conviction for genocide before an international criminal tribunal,[32] and that first ICTR judgment was significant in that it confirmed that rape and sexual violence could constitute acts of genocide.[33] Through the practice of the ICTR and its contemporaries, a deeper understanding of the elements of the crime of genocide, the evidential conditions that may give rise to a finding that the accused possessed genocidal intent, and the parameters of the ancillary crimes of genocide have developed. This is equally true for all of the international crimes, not least the category of war crimes committed in times of non-international armed conflicts, which has developed exponentially through the practice of international criminal tribunals. Thus, procedure clearly does matter, because it is only through following established processes that the law can be interpreted, understood, and scrutinized, and its integrity can be maintained.[34]

[28] Phil Clark, *The Gacaca Courts, Post-Genocide Justice and Reconciliation in Rwanda* (Cambridge: CUP, 2010) 38–40.

[29] ibid., 39.

[30] Paul Roberts, 'The Priority of Procedure and the Neglect of Evidence and Proof: Facing Facts in International Criminal Law' (2015) 13 *JICJ* 479.

[31] Convention on the Prevention and Punishment of the Crime of Genocide, 78 UNTS 227, 9 December 1948, entered into force 12 January 1951, Article VI.

[32] *Prosecutor v. Akayesu*, Judgment, Case No. ICTR-96-4-T, 2 September 1998. There were some convictions for genocide in the trials conducted under Control Council Law No. 10 after World War II: see further, William A. Schabas, *Genocide in International Law: The Crime of Crimes* (Cambridge: CUP, 2000) 47–50.

[33] ibid., para 731.

[34] Fuller (n 22) 81. Hart, by contrast, saw procedures as falling outside of the core of law: see further, H.L.A. Hart, 'Positivism and the Separation of Law and Morals' (1958) 71 *Harv LR* 593, and the discussion of this divergence of opinions in Larry May, 'International Criminal Law and the Inner Morality of Law', paper presented at a conference on the Hart/Fuller debates at the Law School of Australian National University, 18 December 2008.

Second, the courtroom is both the place where substantive rights can be taken away and the avenue through which an individual can prevent these rights from being taken away. In the context of their trials, through which such substantive rights as liberty, employment, privacy, and family life are at stake, international criminal tribunals are tasked with both adjudicating human rights violations alleged to have been committed by the suspect or accused, and upholding and exemplifying human rights standards. Death penalty scholars have argued that the way in which we treat violent murderers (seen to be the 'worst' members of society) reflects on society itself.[35] By the same token, the way in which the international community treats those accused of the gravest crimes known to mankind could be said to reflect the humanism of an international legal order. By granting accused individuals the procedural guarantees expected in the criminal justice system of any civilized nation, the international community shows that the international criminal law exercise is not one of mere retributivism.[36] As argued further in Chapter 5, if international criminal tribunals were to enunciate the highest standards of procedural fairness, they would exercise a dual instrumentalist function in advancing the rule of law: first, they would show that no one is above the law by putting those formerly holding positions of great power on trial; second, they would show that everybody is entitled to the strongest of judicial guarantees and the right to a fair trial, regardless of the charges against them or their resources.

Some have argued that procedural rights are not rights in themselves, but capable of assertion only to the extent that a substantive right—such as the denial of liberty—can be relied upon.[37] However, due process rights are embodied in human rights treaties on the same footing as substantive rights. Indeed, the matter of the right to a fair trial makes up a large chunk of adjudication before the international human rights tribunals; over half of the ECtHR's findings of violations between 1959 and 2009 concerned Article 6 of the ECHR.[38] This right is a fundamental element of the rule of law, and the procedure employed to realize that right acts as a bar to arbitrariness in the operation of the law.[39]

[35] Hans G. Franck, *The Barbaric Punishment: Abolishing the Death Penalty* (revised and edited by William A. Schabas, The Hague: Martinus Nijoff, 2003) 72.

[36] Compare Immi Tallgren, 'The Sense and Sensibility of International Criminal Law' (2002) 13 *EJIL* 561, arguing that ICL is essentially a retributivist exercise and that it merely upholds the myth of having other goals, such as deterrence.

[37] Larry Alexander, 'Are Procedural Rights Derivative Substantive Rights?' (1998) 17 *Law & Phil* 19.

[38] Ryan Goss, *Criminal Fair Trial Rights* (Oxford: Hart, 2014) 1.

[39] May (n 23) 53–4, citing Colleen Murphy, 'Lon Fuller and the Moral Value of the Rule of Law' (2005) 24 *Law & Phil* 239.

Thus, while high-profile acquittals (such as Schacht at Nuremberg) might indicate that the process was not completely skewed against the accused, we need to go beyond the fairness of the outcome and interrogate the process employed for a true evaluation of the fairness of the trial.[40] As Summers has recognized, certain rights that can rarely, when taken alone, have any effect on the outcome of the trial (such as the right to be physically present at trial), do have an inherent value.[41] Before examining the 'process values' seen as indispensible by procedural justice theorists, it is worthy of note that there is a clear interplay between the 'process legitimacy' theories discussed in the previous section, and theories of procedural justice. The difference between the two types of theory is that the process legitimacy theories treat equitable procedures as a means to the end of compliance with the rule, while procedural justice scholars treat fair procedures as an end in themselves, although they recognize that those procedures may have broader positive implications. For example, Rawls's theory of 'justice as fairness' is an example of a theory of process legitimacy, in that it centres around the two core components of liberty and the difference principle, but also recognizes the need for a procedure which, if properly followed, will result in a correct and fair outcome.[42] Procedural justice theorists, on the other hand, are principally concerned with the procedures themselves. Criminal trials follow what Rawls dubbed 'imperfect procedural justice',[43] as it is impossible to guarantee that the correct outcome will always be achieved through the procedure followed, but the outcome is likely to be considered just if certain independent procedural criteria for fairness are followed.[44]

Having established that the fairness of a process is itself as important as the outcome reached, we might ask what the components of procedural justice are. According to Schmidt, the following components are indispensible to a fair process. First, all relevant considerations should be taken into account.[45] In the context of an international criminal trial, this would mean that the defendant should be given the opportunity to put forward his or her

[40] Robert S. Summers, 'Evaluating and Improving Legal Process—A Plea for "Process Values" ' (1974) 60 *Cornell LR* 1.

[41] ibid. Compare D.J. Galligan, *Due Process and Fair Procedures: A Study of Administrative Procedures* (Oxford: Clarendon Press, 1996). Allan provides a very useful critique of Galligan's over-reliance on outcome in his defence of fair procedures: T.R.S. Allan, 'Procedural Fairness and the Duty of Respect' (1998) 18 *OJLS* 497, 499 *et seq.*

[42] John Rawls, *A Theory of Justice* (revised edn, Cambridge, MA: Harvard University Press, 1999) 74–5; 220; May (n 23) 59.

[43] John Rawls, *A Theory of Justice* (Harvard: Harvard University Press, 1971) 85.

[44] Samuel Freeman, *Rawls* (Abingdon: Routledge, 2007) 480.

[45] Volker H. Schmidt, 'Procedural Aspects of Distributive Justice' in Klaus F. Röhl and Stefan Machura (eds), *Procedural Justice* (Dartmouth: Ashgate, 1997) 161, 174–6.

side of the case. This is jeopardized where the accused is tried *in absentia*.[46] The requirement in some international criminal tribunals for the prosecution to investigate both exonerating and incriminating evidence goes some way to meeting this element.[47] Second, in a similar vein, all relevant information should be considered.[48] The tribunals' rules on admissibility of evidence focus on relevance,[49] although it is impossible to guarantee that all relevant information will be considered. Third, all those affected should be given a voice;[50] the enhanced role of victims in the ICC and STL attempts to give all those affected the opportunity to have their say, although this regime of victims' participation is not without its difficulties, as discussed in detail in Chapter 4. Fourth, the process should be public and transparent, insofar as it is possible.[51] Fifth, decisions should be reasoned;[52] by and large, the international criminal tribunals meet this criterion by providing exceptionally lengthy judgments. Last, there should be a possibility of reversal on appeal.[53] There has been some controversy in the international criminal tribunals where the prosecution is permitted appeal on an acquittal, and conviction on appeal is not subject to any further appeal. This is discussed further in Chapter 3. Others have developed principles of procedural justice that must be observed by the judiciary, such as treating the case with 'dignity, neutrality and importance',[54] or consistency and impartiality.[55] These principles have a clear bearing on international criminal trials.

2.1.3 Fairness as rule of law

That the right to a fair trial is an inherent component of the rule of law is probably an uncontroversial claim.[56] The definition of the concept of rule of law remains much less straightforward. Two of the Magna Carta's best-known chapters, 39 and 40, are frequently invoked as early evidence

46 See further below, Section 3.7.

47 Article 54(1)(a), ICC Statute.

48 Schmidt (n 45) 174–6.

49 Rule 149(C), STL RPE; Rule 89(C), ICTY RPE; Rule 89(C), ICTR RPE; Rule 89(C), SCSL RPE.

50 Schmidt (n 45) 174–6.

51 ibid.; the right to a public trial is discussed further in Chapter 3 below.

52 ibid.

53 ibid.

54 Neil Vidmar, 'Procedural Justice and Alternative Dispute Resolution' in Klaus F. Röhl and Stefan Machura (eds), *Procedural Justice* (Dartmouth: Ashgate, 1997) 121, 128.

55 John Kekes, 'Morality and Impartiality' (1981) 18 *American Philosophical Quarterly* 295.

56 Sergey Vasiliev, 'Fairness and Its Metric in International Criminal Procedure' in *International Criminal Trials: A Normative Theory* (Oxford: OUP, 2016) (forthcoming) available online at http://ssrn.com/abstract=2253177, 7, stating that the tribunals tasked themselves with compliance with international rule of law 'which in turn was interpreted principally as the duty to fully respect some objective and external … international standards of fair trial'.

of the core of rule of law. The former states that there can be no deprivation of a person's liberty 'except by the lawful judgment of his equals or by the law of the land', while the latter declares: 'To no-one shall we sell, to no-one deny or delay right of justice.' Dicey infamously declared that, 'no man is punishable ... except for a distinct breach of law established in the ordinary legal manner before the ordinary courts of the land', and that no person is above the law.[57] A popular contemporary definition comes from Lord Bingham: 'that all persons and authorities within the state, whether public or private, should be bound by and entitled to the benefit of laws publicly made, taking effect (generally) in the future and publicly administered in the courts'.[58] Tamanaha determined that the concept had three 'clusters' of meaning: first, that the government is limited by the law; second, that laws were subject to 'formal legality', that is, they are public, prospective, and 'with the qualities of generality, equality of application, and certainty'; and third, 'the rule of law, not man' must prevail.[59]

How can theories on the rule of law inform our understanding of the fairness of international criminal proceedings? A key component of all of the above theories is the principle of equality before the law, a principle enshrined in the statutes of the international criminal tribunals.[60] We can add the minimum components of the right to a fair trial, including the right to trial by an impartial and independent adjudicator, the right to a public trial, and the right to trial without undue delay.[61] That the law must be prospective is also reflected in the principle of *nullum crimen sine lege* found in the tribunals' statutes.[62] The need to treat 'like cases alike' is important in the context of the fragmentation of the international legal order,[63] as attempts are made to find coherence and commonalities in the procedures of international criminal tribunals.[64] Rule of law clearly also demands a measure of certainty or stability over time[65] if the international criminal tribunals are to show

[57] A.V. Dicey, *An Introduction to the Study of the Law of the Constitution* (1885; 9th edn, Macmillan, 1945) 193.

[58] Tom Bingham, *The Rule of Law* (London: Allen Lane, 2010) 8.

[59] Brian Z. Tamanaha, *On the Rule of Law* (Cambridge: CUP, 2004) 114–26.

[60] Article 67(1), ICC Statute; Article 21(1), ICTY Statute; Article 20(1), ICTR Statute; Article 17(1), SCSL Statute; Article 16(1), STL Statute.

[61] See below, Section 2.2, and Chapter 3.

[62] Joseph Raz, 'The Rule of Law and Its Virtue' in *The Authority of Law: Essays on Law and Morality* (Oxford: Clarendon Press, 1979) 210, 211–14.

[63] Jonathan I. Charney, 'Is International Law Threatened by Multiple International Tribunals?' (1998) 271 *Recuil des Cours* 101, 361.

[64] Goran Sluiter and Sergey Vasiliev (eds), *International Criminal Procedure: Towards a Coherent Body of Law* (New York: Cameron May Publishing, 2009) and Goran Sluiter, Håkan Friman, Suzannah Linton, Salvatore Zappalà, and Sergey Vasiliev (eds), *International Criminal Procedure: Principles and Rules* (Oxford: OUP, 2013).

[65] Fuller (n 22) preferred this formulation of relative stability over an outright principle of stability, which would of course render the law quite stagnant and ultimately unworkable. What he

that they respect the rule of law and do not simply act as 'rogue court[s] with rigged rules'.[66]

2.1.4 Theories of fairness: common elements

It would seem that the key common features that can be derived from the various theories on procedural justice, process legitimacy, and rule of law are as follows: adjudicators should be neutral and impartial; the law must be applied equally and consistently; the accused should have an effective defence, meaning that they should have the opportunity to put their side of the case forward; the process should be as open and transparent as possible; and the law and procedure should be clear and fully articulated in advance of the trial. In the context of international criminal trials, these principles are made more concrete through the articulation of specific rights. For example, related to the principle of an effective defence, certain sub-rights—such as the right to counsel, the right to examine evidence and witnesses, and the right to translation of documents and interpretation of court proceedings—are set down in the tribunals' statutes.

2.2 The Fair Trial as a Unique Construct of Fairness

While the above discussion illustrated that general theories of fairness give rise to principles such as equality, impartiality, and consistency, the concept of the 'fair trial' stands quite apart from the nebulous concept of 'fairness', in that it can be defined as the sum of a number of crucial parts. As Shany has noted:

> Legal standards offer us a particularly convenient yardstick for the evaluation of fairness in adjudication, as deviation from legally prescribed judicial procedures may suggest that some parties have been treated differently to other, similarly situated, parties. Deviation from legal prescriptions governing the judicial process may also suggest, to the extent that legal standards reflect our expectations for the regular and proper conduct of judicial institutions, that such expectations have been frustrated.[67]

sought to avoid with his principle of constancy was the enactment of 'such frequent changes in the rules that the subject cannot orient his action by them'. ibid., 39.

[66] Letter, 'The Anomalies of the International Criminal Tribunal are Legion', *The Times* (London: 17 June 1999). See further, Erik Voeten, 'Public Opinion and the Legitimacy of International Courts' (2013) 14 *Theoretical Inquiries in Law* 411, 435: 'in the minds of the general public, international courts may not be substitutes for poorly performing domestic courts, but rather extensions of a functioning rule of law system that they already trust'.

[67] Shany (n 6) 142–3.

Scholars seem to be largely in agreement about the legal standards necessary for a trial to be considered fair. Hildebrandt, for example, reduced the right to a fair trial down to six core guarantees: the right to a public trial; the right to test the evidence against one (the right of confrontation); the related right that judgments will not be based on evidence not heard in court; the right to equality of arms; the right to the presumption of innocence; and the right to an independent and impartial judiciary.[68] Trechsel listed the following 'universally recognized elements of fair trial or due process': the right to an independent and impartial tribunal; the right to a public trial; the right to an expeditious trial; the right to the presumption of innocence and freedom from self-incrimination; the right to challenge the evidence of the prosecution and to present evidence in one's defence; the right to be informed of the case against you; the right to appeal; and the right to 'be able effectively to present one's arguments'.[69] These principles are solidified by explicit fair trial guarantees laid out in the statutes of the international criminal tribunals.

The constituent elements of the right to a fair trial, as laid down in the statutes of the international criminal tribunals, include the accused's right: to a public trial;[70] to equality before the law;[71] to counsel (and to legal aid, where applicable);[72] to examine, or have examined, witnesses against him;[73] to obtain the attendance and examination of witnesses on his behalf under the same conditions as adverse witnesses;[74] to adequate facilities for the preparation of his or her defence;[75] to the presumption of innocence;[76] to

[68] Mireille Hildebrandt, 'Trial and "Fair Trial": From Peer to Subject to Citizen' in Anthony Duff et al. (eds), *The Trial on Trial, Volume II: Judgment and Calling to Account* (Oxford, Hart Publishing, 2006) 15, cited in Anthony Duff et al., *The Trial on Trial, Volume III: Towards a Normative Theory of the Criminal Trial* (Oxford, Hart Publishing, 2007) 51. Duff et al. added that these types of rights are found in both constitutional and human rights provisions which can be enforced by the individual against the state.

[69] Stefan Trechsel, 'Why Must Trials Be Fair?' (1997) 31 *Isr LR* 94, 95.

[70] Articles 19(4) and 20(2) ICTR Statute; Article 17(2) SCSL Statute; Articles 20(4) and 21(2) ICTY Statute; Article 67(1) ICC Statute.

[71] Article 16(4) STL Statute; Article 20(4) ICTR Statute; Article 17(4) SCSL Statute; Article 21(4) ICTY Statute; Article 67(1) ICC Statute.

[72] Article 16(4) STL Statute; Article 20(4) ICTR Statute; Article 17(4) SCSL Statute; Article 21(4) ICTY Statute; Article 67(1) ICC Statute.

[73] Article 16(4) STL Statute; Article 20(4) ICTR Statute; Article 17(4) SCSL Statute; Article 21(4) ICTY Statute; Article 67(1) ICC Statute.

[74] Article 16(4) STL Statute; Article 20(4) ICTR Statute; Article 17(4) SCSL Statute; Article 21(4) ICTY Statute; Article 67(1) ICC Statute.

[75] Article 16(4) STL Statute; Article 20(4) ICTR Statute; Article 17(4) SCSL Statute; Article 21(4) ICTY Statute; Article 67(1) ICC Statute.

[76] Article 16(3) STL Statute; Article 20(3) ICTR Statute; Article 17(3) SCSL Statute; Article 21(3) ICTY Statute; Articles 66 and 67(1) ICC Statute.

trial without undue delay;[77] to be informed of the charges against him;[78] to silence;[79] to be free from double jeopardy;[80] to interpretation into a language he understands;[81] and to be tried in his presence.[82]

Thus, we can see 'fairness' in the context of the right to a fair trial as a unique legal construct which is comprised of a number of procedural guarantees, in conjunction with principles of fairness such as consistency, publicity, non-retroactivity, equality before the law, and legal certainty.[83] In addition, the rights of accused persons before the tribunals extend to other human rights such as privacy and liberty, as illustrated by rules on privileged communications and provisional release.

The statutes of the tribunals set out a number of minimum guarantees owed to the accused,[84] but the overarching requirement of 'fairness' goes beyond these minimum guarantees to also cover such issues as disclosure of evidence and the independence of the judiciary. As stated in the *Milošević* trial:

> The Trial Chamber reads Article 21(4) of the Statute as setting out a bundle of rights, which are embraced within the principle that the accused must have a fair trial, which is itself set out in Article 21(2) of the Statute. The concept of fairness not only includes these specific rights but also has a much wider ambit, requiring that in all aspects the conduct of the trial must be fair to the accused. Hence, the specific rights are described as 'minimum guarantees'. Fairness is thus the overarching requirement of criminal proceedings.[85]

Therefore, outside of deeper questions on the meaning of the nebulous concept of fairness, an understanding of which is deeply founded in theories of legitimacy, rule of law, and procedural justice, this book recognizes that the

[77] Article 16(4) STL Statute; Article 20(4) ICTR Statute; Article 17(4) SCSL Statute; Article 21(4) ICTY Statute; Article 67(1) ICC Statute.

[78] Article 16(4) STL Statute; Article 20(3) ICTR Statute; Article 17(3) SCSL Statute; Article 21(3) ICTY Statute; Article 67(1) ICC Statute.

[79] Article 20(3) ICTR Statute; Article 17(3) SCSL Statute; Article 21(3) ICTY Statute; Article 67(1) ICC Statute.

[80] Article 9 ICTR Statute; Article 9 SCSL Statute; Article 10 ICTY Statute; Article 20 ICC Statute.

[81] Article 20(4) ICTR Statute; Article 17(4) SCSL Statute; Article 21(4) ICTY Statute; Article 67(1) ICC Statute.

[82] Article 21(4) ICTY Statute; Article 20(4) ICTR Statute; Article 17(4) SCSL Statute; Article 63 ICC Statute.

[83] In a similar vein, Bayles painted procedural justice as comprising of a number of elements, namely, impartiality, the ability to have one's side heard, and the 'formal justice' elements of consistency and adherence to precedent. Michael D. Bayles, *Procedural Justice* (Dordrecht: Kluwer, 1990).

[84] Article 67(1) ICC Statute; Article 16(4) STL Statute; Article 20(4) ICTR Statute; Article 17(4) SCSL Statute; Article 21(4) ICTY Statute.

[85] *Prosecutor v. Milošević*, Reasons for Decision on Assignment of Defence Counsel, Case No. IT-02-54-T, 22 September 2004, para 29.

notion of 'fairness' as part of the concept of the 'fair trial' may have a more concrete definition. It is a combination of a number of minimum guarantees found in human rights law instruments and a number of principles like equality before the law, access to procedures, coherence in the application of rules, and determinacy of the applicable standards. It relates only to the accused—an argument developed further in Chapter 4—and its component parts may be derogated from with the consent of the accused.[86] This understanding of fairness in the context of standard-setting by international criminal tribunals runs throughout this work.

The term, 'the highest standards of fairness', is set to be used throughout the present work. This is a nomenclature which comes from the courts' own jurisprudence and external statements of court representatives and the United Nations.[87] The term can be taken to mean full respect for the rights of the accused as established by international human rights standards and repeated in the statutes of the tribunals in a manner that is consistent with principles of fairness, such as neutrality, equality, and consistency. Whilst a trial might fail to respect a certain element of the right to a fair trial and still not be in breach of human rights standards, because the trial as a whole can be taken to be fair,[88] the highest standards of fairness necessarily require a greater respect for the rights of the accused, and this is the standard that is expected of international criminal tribunals.

2.3 The Interpretation of Fairness by International Criminal Tribunals

The international criminal tribunals have invoked facets of legitimacy, procedural justice, and the rule of law, as discussed above, in their decisions on fairness. In *Šešelj*, for example, the ICTY determined that the right to a fair trial was not just a fundamental right of the accused, 'but also a

[86] This argument is developed further below, at Section 3.8.

[87] See further below, Section 5.2.1.

[88] See especially the case law on breaches of Article 8 and their impact on the fairness of proceedings, e.g. *Bykov v. Russia*, Application No. 4378/02, Judgment, 10 March 2009 (Grand Chamber); *Khan v. UK* (2001) 31 EHRR 45, 12 May 2000; *P.G. and J.H. v. UK*, Application No. 44787/98, Judgment, 25 September 2001 (see especially the Partly Dissenting Opinion of Judge Tulkens on this matter). Outside the improperly-obtained evidence paradigm, examples include: *Sievert v. Germany*, Application No. 29881/07, Judgment, 19 July 2012 (where a violation on the right to examine witnesses against one was not sufficient to render the trial as a whole unfair); *Imbrioscia v. Switzerland* (1994) 17 EHRR 441, 24 November 1993 (on the right to legal assistance) and *S.N. v. Sweden* (2004) 29 EHRR 13, 2 July 2002 (on the right to cross-examination of witnesses).

fundamental interest of the Tribunal related to its own legitimacy.'[89] The ICC has held that the fair trial 'is the only means to do justice. If no fair trial can be held, the object of the judicial process is frustrated, and the process must be stopped.'[90] In relation to the rule of law, the ICTY has held that its main duty was 'to provide a fair and expeditious trial and to guarantee the rights of the accused. This adjudicatory process strengthens the rule of law, a fundamental principle shared by all members of the international community.'[91] Similarly, the SCSL noted that the states that had contributed to the funding of the Court had done so in the expectation that it would promote due process and the rule of law.[92] In *Prlić*, Judge Trechsel stated his view that 'the "justice" element ... in the administration of justice lies primarily in procedural justice.'[93]

There has been some debate as to the customary international law status of the right to a fair trial.[94] By asserting that the right is a requirement of customary international law, judges insulate it from being diluted on the basis of the unique context of the tribunals' legal framework.[95] Despite

[89] *Prosecutor v. Šešelj*, Decision on Prosecution Motion for Order Appointing Counsel to Assist Vojislav Šešelj with his Defence, Case No. IT-03-67-PT, 9 May 2003, para 21. See also, Jacob Katz Cogan, 'International Criminal Courts and Fair Trials: Difficulties and Prospects' (2002) 27 *Yale JIL* 111, quoting the first Chief Prosecutor of the ad hoc tribunals, Richard Goldstone, at 114: 'Whether there are convictions or whether there are acquittals will not be the yardstick of the [ICTY]. The measure is going to be the fairness of the proceedings ... '

[90] *Prosecutor v. Lubanga*, Judgment in the Appeal of Mr Thomas Lubanga Dyilo against a Decision on the Defence Challenge to the Jurisdiction of the Court Pursuant to Article 19(2)(a) of the Statute of 3 October 2006, Case No. ICC-01/04-01/06-722, 14 December 2006, para 37.

[91] *Prosecutor v. Blaškić*, Decision on the Objection of the Republic of Croatia to the Issuance of *Subpoena Duces Tecum*, Case No. IT-95-14, 18 July 1997, para 154. See also, *Prosecutor v. Tadić*, Decision on the Defence Motion for Interlocutory Appeal on Jurisdiction, Case No. IT-94-1-A, 2 October 1995, para 42.

[92] *Prosecutor v. Norman*, Decision on Preliminary Motion on Lack of Jurisdiction (Judicial Independence), Case No. SCSL-04-14-AR72, 13 March 2004, para 41. The emphasis on the rule of law principles of consistency and predictability has been clear in the STL decisions on the liability of corporations for contempt offences, particularly *In the Case against Akhbar Beirut SAL and Al Amin*, Decision on Interlocutory Appeal Concerning Personal Jurisdiction in Contempt Proceedings, Case No. STL-14-06/PT/AP/AR126.1, 23 January 2015, para 74 and Separate and Partially Dissenting Opinion of Judge Nosworthy, paras 27 and 38.

[93] *Prosecutor v. Prlić et al.*, Transcript, Case No. IT-04-74, 29 March 2007, 16626.

[94] Compare *Prosecutor v. Aleksovski*, Judgment, Case No. IT-95-14/1-A, 24 March 2000, para 104 (stating that the right to a fair trial was 'of course, a requirement of customary international law') and *Prosecutor v. Gbao*, Decision on Prosecution Motion for Immediate Protective Measures for Witnesses and Victims and for Non-Public Disclosure, Case No. SCSL-2003-09-PT, 10 October 2003, para 41 (taking the 'considered view that it has not been established that the right of the Accused to a fair trial has become part of customary international law').

[95] *Prosecutor v. Furundžija*, Appeals Judgment, Case No. IT-95-17/1-A, 21 July 2000, Separate Opinion of Judge Patrick Robinson, para 11 ('However, contextual interpretation highlighting this difference should not be taken too far, at any rate, not so far as to nullify fundamental rights which an accused has under customary international law.').

divergent state practice on criminal procedure, it would seem to be beyond question that there is significant state practice and *opinio juris* on the point that the right to a fair trial must be respected.[96] According to the ICTY's former President, Patrick Robinson, fairness was used 'as the plane to smooth the edges in the alignment of the legal systems',[97] illustrating that respect for the right to a fair trial was accepted by those from different legal systems, although there were elements of procedure that were fundamentally different.

The international criminal tribunals have taken different views as to whether they should be concerned with individual components of the right to a fair trial as minimum guarantees that must be respected and should be exceeded when appropriate, or whether their actions should be motivated by ensuring the overall fairness of trials, even if some aspects fall short of perfection. In *Nikolić*, for example, the 'Chamber observe[d] that these norms only provide for the absolute minimum standards applicable' which the Court could go beyond in ensuring due process,[98] and Judge Van den Wyngaert in her minority opinion in *Katanga* stated that, 'It is not good enough that most of the trial has been fair. All of it must be fair.'[99] On the contrary, Judge Shahabuddeen, in a dissenting opinion in *Milošević*, stated that 'the fairness of the trial need not require perfection in every detail. The essential question is whether an accused has had a fair chance of dealing with the allegations against him.'[100] The 'fairness as a whole' approach, which is taken by international human rights tribunals in their *ex post facto* assessments of the fairness of proceedings,[101] is unsuited to international criminal tribunals, which have to effectuate the right to a fair trial in their everyday practice. Moreover, to assert that some aspects of the right are somewhat dispensible is unhelpful, without a full exposition of which of those standards may be derogated from. Judge Shahabuddeen himself, in his extra-judicial writings, noted that a trial might be expeditious but not fair, but a trial lacking in

[96] Compare *Gbao* Decision on Prosecution Motion for Immediate Protective Measures for Witnesses and Victims and for Non-Public Disclosure (n 94), para 39.

[97] Patrick Robinson, 'Rough Edges in the Alignment of Legal Systems in the Proceedings at the ICTY' (2005) 3 *JICJ* 1037, 1058.

[98] *Prosecutor v. Nikolić*, Decision on Defence Motion Challenging the Exercise of Jurisdiction, Case No. IT-94-2-PT, 9 October 2002, paras 110–11.

[99] *Prosecutor v. Katanga*, Judgment, Minority Opinion of Judge Van den Wyngaert (n 27), para 311.

[100] *Prosecutor v. Milošević*, Separate Opinion of Judge Shahabuddeen, Decision on Admissibility of Evidence-in-Chief in the form of Written Statements, Case No. IT-02-54-AR 73.4, 30 September 2003, para 16.

[101] e.g. *Murray v. United Kingdom*, Application No. 18731/91, Grand Chamber Judgment, 8 February 1996, para 63. This approach has been criticized by Stefan Trechsel, *Human Rights in Criminal Proceedings* (Oxford: OUP, 2005) 87.

expeditiousness could not be fair,[102] suggesting that the right to trial without undue delay was one detail that did indeed require 'perfection'.

A more appropriate means of solving the 'minimum standards vs. overall fairness' debate would be to recognize that in the pursuit of the fairness of proceedings,[103] the tribunals may exceed the minimum guarantees set down in their statutes, but these standards must be complied with.[104] For example, the ICC in *Ngudjolo* recognized the right to privacy of the accused, even though this was not explicitly included in the Statute.[105] Various international criminal tribunals have recognized such fundamental principles of fairness to the accused as equality of arms,[106] *in dubio pro reo*,[107] and best evidence[108] in their jurisprudence.

[102] Mohamed Shahabuddeen, *International Criminal Justice at the Yugoslav Tribunal: A Judge's Recollection* (Oxford: OUP, 2012) 161.

[103] This general guarantee is included in the *chapeau* of Article 67(1), ICC Statute, and in Article 16(2), STL Statute; Article 21(2) ICTY Statute; Article 20(2), ICTR Statute, and Article 17(2), SCSL Statute. In addition, the ICC has to interpret its law in accordance with internationally recognized human rights, pursuant to Article 21(3) of its Statute. See further, *Situation in the DRC: Prosecutor v. Lubanga*, Judgment on the Appeal of Mr Thomas Lubanga Dyilo against the Decision on the Defence Challenge to the Jurisdiction of the Court pursuant to Article 19(2)(a) of the Statute of 3 October 2006, para 36.

[104] *Situation in the DRC: Prosecutor v. Lubanga*, Decision Establishing General Principles Governing Applications to Restrict Disclosure pursuant to Rule 81(2) and (4) of the Rules of Procedure and Evidence, Case No. ICC-01/04-01/06, 19 May 2006, para 37. See also, IACtHR, *Exceptions to the Exhaustion of Domestic Remedies (Arts. 46.1, 46.2.a and 46.2.b, American Convention on Human Rights)*, Advisory Opinion OC-11/90, 10 August 1990, para 24 ('By labelling these guarantees as minimum guarantees, the Convention assumes that other, additional guarantees may be necessary in specific circumstances to ensure a fair hearing.')

[105] *Situation in the DRC: Prosecutor v. Katanga and Ngudjolo Chui*, Decision on Request 1200 of the Prosecutor for Prohibition and Restrictive Measures against Mathieu Ngudjolo with Respect to Contacts Both Outside and Inside the Detention Centre, Case No. ICC-01/04-01/07, 24 June 2009, para 45; *Situation in the DRC: Prosecutor v. Katanga and Ngudjolo Chui*, Judgment on the Appeal of the Prosecutor against the 'Decision on Request 1200 of the Prosecutor for Prohibition and Restrictive Measures against Mathieu Ngudjolo with Respect to Contacts Both Outside and Inside the Detention Centre', Case No. ICC-01/04-01/07, 9 December 2009, para 52; *Situation in the DRC: Prosecutor v. Katanga and Ngudjolo Chui*, Decision further to the Appeals Chamber judgment of 9 December 2009 and Responding to Request 1959-Conf-Exp of the Office of the Prosecutor, Case No. ICC-01/04-01/07, 10 June 2010, para 38.

[106] Recognized in, amongst many others, *Prosecutor v. Tadić*, Judgment, Case No. IT-94-1-A, 15 July 1999, para 44; *Prosecutor v. Ayyash et al.*, Decision Authorising the Ayyash Defence and the Sabra Defence to File a Request for Reconsideration, Case No. STL-11-01/PT/TC, 22 May 2012, para 4; *Prosecutor v. Brima et al.*, Decision on Prosecution Request for Leave to Amend the Indictment, Case No. SCSL-04-16-PT, 6 May 2004, paras 27–8; *Kalimanzira v. Prosecutor*, Judgment, Case No. ICTR-05-88-A, 20 October 2010, paras 26–37; *Situation in Kenya: Prosecutor v. Ruto and Sang*, Decision on Prosecution's Application for Leave to Appeal the 'Decision on Mr Ruto's Request for Excusal from Continuous Presence at Trial', Case No. ICC-01/09-01-11, 18 July 2013, para 15.

[107] Translated as '[When] in doubt, favour the accused'. Seen, for example, in *Situation in Darfur, Sudan: Prosecutor v. Abu Garda*, Decision on the Confirmation of Charges, Case No. ICC-02/05-02/09, 8 February 2010, paras 42–3; *In the Matter of Contempt Proceedings Arising from the Case of The Prosecutor v. Charles Ghankay Taylor*, Judgment in Contempt Proceedings, Case No. SCSL-12-01-T, 19 October 2012.

[108] *Prosecutor v. Kupreškić et al.*, Decision on Appeal by Dragan Papić against Ruling to Proceed by Deposition, Case No. IT-95-16-AR73.3, 15 July 1999, para 20.

The only restrictions that can be imposed on the minimum guarantees enumerated in the statutes are those established in the text of the statutes themselves. For example, the right to translated materials under the ICC Statute extends only to those translations that 'are necessary to meet the requirements of fairness', and only applies when the proceedings or documents 'are not in a language which the accused fully understands and speaks'.[109] Outside of those inherent restrictions, it is incorrect to assume that individual derogations from these standards are permissible, provided that the overall fairness of proceedings is preserved.

Thus, the ICC's adoption of the principle of proportionality and the ECtHR's finding that any restrictions on the rights of the accused 'must be sufficiently counterbalanced by procedures followed by the judicial authorities'[110] is problematic, because it is founded on the assumption that the rights of the accused are necessarily in conflict with the rights or interests of other parties,[111] and allows the fundamental rights of the accused to be diluted. As Judges Sajó and Karakaş highlighted in their partly dissenting opinion to the ECtHR Grand Chamber's decision in *Al-Khawaja and Tahery*:

> When the Convention singled out paragraph 3 rights this meant that these basic rights of the defence were necessary to counterbalance the dominant power of the prosecution, in the interests of fairness. To balance these rights a second time against the interests of the administration of justice ... is to give the prosecution and the interests of administering justice (namely, to punish) a clear advantage.[112]

Al-Khawaja provides clear evidence of the dangers of taking 'counterbalancing factors' into account, where the presence of additional evidence supporting the untested witness statement that was the sole or decisive basis of a conviction was found to be sufficient to conclude that there had been no breach of Article 6.[113] As Hoyano has pointed out, this is not a question of 'counterbalancing' in the sense of remedying the prejudice suffered by the accused with some favourable procedural safeguard; the Grand Chamber

[109] Article 67(1)(f), ICC Statute. This is discussed further in Section 3.6 below.

[110] *Lubanga* Decision Establishing General Principles Governing Applications to Restrict Disclosure pursuant to Rule 81(2) and (4) of the Rules of Procedure and Evidence (n 104) paras 13, 32.

[111] This assumption has been roundly challenged; see, inter alia, Laura Hoyano, 'What Is Balanced on the Scales of Justice? In Search of the Essence of the Right to a Fair Trial' [2014] *Crim LR* 4; Andrew Ashworth and Mike Redmayne, *The Criminal Process* (3rd edn, Oxford: OUP, 2010), 41–2.

[112] *Al-Khawaja and Tahery v. United Kingdom*, Application Nos 26766/05 and 22228/06, Grand Chamber Judgment, 15 December 2011, Joint Partly Dissenting and Partly Concurring Opinion of Judges Sajó and Karakaş.

[113] *Al-Khawaja and Tahery v. United Kingdom*, Grand Chamber Judgment, ibid., paras 153–8.

found 'balance' in 'other evidence further loading the prosecution's pan on the scales of justice'.[114] This illustrates the dangers in allowing a culture of 'balance' to permeate the international criminal tribunals' practice on the right to a fair trial, which, as will be argued further in Chapter 4, should be seen as being principally owed to the accused.

Conclusion

At the outset of this chapter, we examined several key theories of fairness related to legitimacy, procedural justice, and rule of law, and found that common principles such as consistency, equality, and impartiality could be derived from those theories. Section 2.3 illustrated how the international criminal tribunals refer—albeit intermittently—to these principles in some of their decisions on fairness.

However, it was argued that the right to a fair trial represents a unique construct of fairness, which has been reinforced by human rights law and practice, and principles of customary international law on the right to a fair trial. This interpretation is more fully supported by the practice of the international criminal tribunals, which see fairness as the sum of a number of constituent rights, outlined in their statutes, which can be exceeded in the interest of their overall need to respect the fundamental rights of accused persons. An approach of full respect for each of the rights of the accused is preferable to some of the limited jurisprudence that seeks to refer to the fairness 'as a whole' of proceedings or that leans towards the perilous rhetoric of 'balancing' such rights against the public interest and/or the rights or interests of other parties. The next chapter will analyse the jurisprudence on these constituent rights in detail.

[114] Hoyano (n 111) 14.

3

The Right to a Fair Trial in Practice in International Criminal Trials

The practice of the contemporary international criminal tribunals in enforcing the rights of the accused is important not just for their legitimacy, as discussed in the previous chapter, but also for their legacy. The ICTY published a *Manual on Developed Practices* in 2009, which noted Judge Pocar's emphasis on the legacy of the Tribunal during his Presidency,[1] while the SCSL's annual reports contained a distinct section on 'legacy' in the Court's final years.[2] It is clear that this legacy can inform not just other international criminal trials, but also sets precedents for the conduct of complex criminal proceedings for international crimes domestically.[3] In recent years, a number of guidelines and model codes on the rights of the accused have been informed by the practice of international criminal tribunals.[4]

This chapter examines each of the component parts of the right to a fair trial in detail, and points to synergies and divergences between the practices of the tribunals. Where practice falls short of the highest standards of fairness (a concept addressed in detail in Chapter 5), recommendations are made for future practice. This is timely, given that the ICTY and ICTR were, at the time of writing, nearing the end of their mandates, and the SCSL had already finished its operations. It is hoped that lessons can be learned from

[1] ICTY/UNICRI, *ICTY Manual on Developed Practices* (Turin, 2009).

[2] e.g. *Eighth Annual Report of the President of the Special Court for Sierra Leone*, May 2011, 47.

[3] See, for example, Gideon Boas, *The Milošević Trial: Lessons for the Conduct of Complex International Criminal Proceedings* (Cambridge: CUP, 2007); William W. Burke-White and Anne-Marie Slaughter, 'The Future of International Law Is Domestic (or, the European Way of Law)' (2006) 47 *Harv Int'l L J* 327; and Jenia Iontecheva Turner, 'Nationalizing International Criminal Law' (2005) 41 *Stanford JIL* 1 for arguments that international criminal prosecutions will increasingly be conducted by domestic courts in the future. This is discussed further in Chapter 6.

[4] e.g. Amnesty International, *Fair Trial Manual* (2nd edn, London, 2014); Hague Institute for Global Justice, *Model Code for the Investigation and Prosecution of International Crimes* (in process, 2015).

their procedures for the continuing proceedings before the ICC and STL, and future proceedings before domestic and international tribunals.

3.1 Presumption of Innocence

The general principle of law that every person accused of a crime has the right to be presumed innocent until proven guilty has been described as the 'golden thread' in the web of criminal trials.[5] The subjective presumption of the accused's innocence is of course difficult to prove, but it can be condensed into a number of objectively measurable components. Pending trial, the presumption means that statements and press releases by court organs should clearly indicate that the individual is a suspect, and has not been found responsible for any of the crimes alleged.[6] Before an arrest warrant or indictment is issued, prosecuting authorities have a duty to prevent the suspect from being exposed to negative publicity, and this may entail keeping their identity confidential until the individual is formally indicted.[7]

Once an accused is brought into the custody of a tribunal, he or she has the right to be detained separately from those who have been convicted,[8] and to provisional release pending trial.[9] The practice on provisional release has been

[5] *Woolmington v. DPP* [1935] AC 462: 'Throughout the web of the English Criminal Law one golden thread is always to be seen, that it is the duty of the prosecution to prove the prisoner's guilt … '

[6] *Situation in Libya*, Decision on the OPCD 'Requête relative aux propos publics de Monsieur le Procureur et au respect de la presomption d'innocence', Case No. ICC-01/11, 8 September 2011; *Situation in the DRC: Prosecutor v. Mbarushimana*, Decision on the Defence Request for an Order to Preserve the Impartiality of Proceedings, Case No. ICC-01/04-01/10, 31 January 2011; *Prosecutor v. Popović*, Transcript, Case No. IT-05-88-T, 26 March 2007; *Prosecutor v. Lubanga*, Transcript, Case No. ICC-01/04-01/06, 9 November 2006. This clearly also applies during trial: *Prosecutor v. Lubanga*, Decision on the Press Interview with Ms Le Fraper du Hellen, Case No. ICC-01/04-01/06, 12 May 2010.

[7] *Situation in Kenya*, Decision on the 'Application for Leave to Participate in the Proceedings before the Pre-Trial Chamber relating to the Prosecutor's Application under Article 58(7)', Case No. ICC-01/09, 11 February 2011, para 22.

[8] President of the International Tribunal, Order to the Registrar to Separate Convicted and Non-Convicted Detainees Held in the Detention Unit, Case No. IT-06-89-Misc.1, 15 June 2006.

[9] There is some debate as to whether provisional release is a function of the presumption of innocence at all: Judge Robinson in *Prosecutor v. Krajisnik et al.*, Decision on Momcilo Krajisnik's Notice of Motion for Provisional Release, Case No. IT-00-39&40-PT, 8 October 2001, Dissenting Opinion of Judge Patrick Robinson explicitly linked provisional release to the presumption of innocence. The Appeals Chamber of the SCSL, on the other hand, found that the presumption had nothing to do with provisional release, 'since innocent defendants may nevertheless try to avoid a lengthy trial or to threaten those who have made statements against them': *Prosecutor v. Norman et al.*, Fofana—Appeal Against Decision Refusing Bail, Case No. SCSL-04-14-AR65, 11 March 2005, para 37.

enhanced significantly over time; the earliest drafts of the RPE for the SCSL, ICTR, and ICTY only permitted provisional release in 'exceptional circumstances', but by today, provisional release may be granted if the accused can prove that they will appear for trial if released and that they will not pose a danger to victims or witnesses while on release.[10] The ICC Statute and STL RPE go further, by imposing a positive obligation on the Pre-Trial Chamber to release the accused, unless continued detention is necessary to ensure the accused's appearance at trial, to ensure that the accused does not obstruct the investigation or later trial, or to prevent the continuing commission of the crime with which the accused is charged.[11] Early practice on provisional release before the ICC was impeded by a lack of state cooperation,[12] but this was eventually overcome by the Court determining that if the suspect was the national of a state, or the holder of a valid visa for a state, no negotiations were required with that state before releasing him or her to the state.[13] Before the ICTY, release has been aided significantly by the fact that various Balkan states were willing to host defendants for the duration of the bail period, and to guarantee their return to the seat of the Tribunal.[14] No accused person was ever provisionally released by either the ICTR or SCSL.[15] At the time

[10] Rules 65(B) ICTY, ICTR, and SCSL RPE.

[11] Article 60(2), ICC Statute; Rule 102, STL RPE. See also, *Situation in the CAR: Prosecutor v. Bemba*, Decision on the Interim Release of Jean-Pierre Bemba Gombo and Convening Hearings with the Kingdom of Belgium, the Republic of Portugal, the Republic of France, the Federal Republic of Germany, the Italian Republic, and the Republic of South Africa, Case No. ICC-01/05-01/08, 14 August 2009, para 77 (stating that the decision on release is 'not of a discretionary nature' when all of the conditions are met).

[12] Following the decision in *Prosecutor v. Bemba*, Decision on the Interim Release of Jean-Pierre Bemba Gombo and Convening Hearings with the Kingdom of Belgium, the Republic of Portugal, the Republic of France, the Federal Republic of Germany, the Italian Republic, and the Republic of South Africa (n 11), the identified countries appeared unwilling to allow Mr Bemba to spend his provisional release on their territory.

[13] *Situation in the CAR: Prosecutor v. Bemba et al.*, Decision ordering the release of Aimé Kilolo Musamba, Jean-Jacques Mangenda Kabongo, Fidèle Babala Wandu and Narcisse Arido, Case No. ICC-01/05-01/13, 21 October 2014, 5–6.

[14] A recent example is *Prosecutor v. Šešelj*, Order on the Provisional Release of the Accused *Propio Motu*, Case No. IT-03-67-T, 6 November 2014. Upon release to Serbia, the accused made public statements to the effect that those who co-operated with the Tribunal were traitors, and stated publicly that he would never return to The Hague. The ICTY refused to revoke his provisional release, finding that the former 'unfortunate' statements did not constitute threats or attempts to interfere with witnesses, while the latter constituted 'mere declarations of intent' and thus, the conditions of provisional release had not been violated: *Prosecutor v. Šešelj*, Decision on Prosecution Motion to Revoke Provisional Release, Case No. IT-03-67-T, 13 January 2015, paras 12–13.

[15] See further, Karel de Meester et al., 'Investigation, Coercive Measures, Arrest, and Surrender' in Goran Sluiter et al. (eds), *International Criminal Procedure: Principles and Rules* (Oxford: OUP, 2013) 171, 328–9. The term 'bail' is used instead of 'provisional release' in Rule 65, SCSL RPE.

of writing, the STL had no accused persons in custody, so the question of provisional release had obviously not arisen.

At trial, the clearest manifestation of the presumption of innocence is that the burden rests with the prosecution to prove the guilt of the accused beyond reasonable doubt.[16] If the prosecution fails to do so, the accused must be acquitted.[17] The *in dubio pro reo* principle demands that any doubt should be interpreted in favour of the accused, and this applies to factual findings as well as ultimate findings on culpability.[18] No reverse burden may be placed on the accused,[19] although the tribunals have determined that in certain circumstances—for example, where the accused wishes to invoke a defence of insanity,[20] or where mitigating circumstances are raised for the purposes of sentencing[21]—it will be for the defence to prove these elements on the balance of probabilities. In *Bemba*, the ICC Appeals Chamber found that the Trial Chamber had unjustifiably reversed the onus when it admitted the totality of prosecution witness statements into evidence, leaving it to the defence to disprove their admissibility.[22]

One controversial area of practice has been the taking of 'judicial notice' of certain facts. All of the tribunals allow for judicial notice to be taken of facts of common knowledge or those facts that cannot reasonably be disputed,[23] and this is the standard applied in a number of domestic criminal justice systems.[24] In addition, the RPE of all tribunals apart from the ICC

[16] Article 16(3), STL Statute; Article 66, ICC Statute; Article 21(3), ICTY Statute; Article 20(3), ICTR Statute; Article 17(3), SCSL Statute. See also, opening statement of Robert Jackson at Nuremberg, Second Day, 21 November 1945: 'Despite the fact that public opinion already condemns their acts, we agree that here they must be given a presumption of innocence, and we accept the burden of proving criminal acts and the responsibility of these defendants for their commission.'

[17] Report of the International Law Commission on the work of its forty-fifth session (3 May–23 July 1993), UN Doc. A/48/10, 119; *Prosecutor v. Delalić et al.*, Judgment, Case No., IT-96-21-T, 16 November 1998, para 600.

[18] *Prosecutor v. Limaj et al.*, Judgment, Case No. IT-03-66-A, 27 September 2007, para 21.

[19] Article 67(1)(i), ICC Statute.

[20] *Prosecutor v. Delalić et al.*, Judgment, Case No. IT-96-21-A, 20 February 2001, para 582. By contrast, there is no onus on the accused to prove an alibi, if one is raised; the Prosecutor must show that, despite the alibi evidence introduced, the accused is still guilty beyond reasonable doubt: *Prosecutor v. Kunarac*, Judgment, Case No. IT-96-23-T, 22 February 2001, para 625.

[21] *Prosecutor v. Sikirika et al.*, Sentencing Judgment, Case No. IT-95-8-S, 13 November 2001, para 188.

[22] *Prosecutor v. Bemba*, Judgment on the appeals of Mr Jean-Pierre Bemba Gombo and the Prosecutor against the decision of Trial Chamber III entitled 'Decision on the admission into evidence of materials contained in the prosecution's list of evidence', ICC-01/05-01/08-1386, 3 May 2011, para 73.

[23] Article 69, ICC Statute; Rules 94, ICTY, ICTR, and SCSL RPE; Rule 160, STL RPE.

[24] For example, United States: Federal Rules of Evidence, Rule 201(b); Kenya: Evidence Act 1963, s. 60; England and Wales: *Commonwealth Shipping Representative v. P & O Branch Services* [1923] AC 191, 212; Germany: Code of Criminal Procedure in the version published on 7 April

allow judicial notice to be taken of 'adjudicated facts' from proceedings of the tribunal itself or from other international or domestic criminal proceedings, that relate to matters at issue in the ongoing proceedings.[25] Some Chambers have taken quite an expansive approach to judicial notice—in *Karadžić*, for example, the Trial Chamber took judicial notice of over 2,000 adjudicated facts,[26] including that Serb forces removed non-Serbs from certain areas, were involved in the mistreatment, severe beating, and execution of detainees, and conducted attacks on Muslim areas.[27] The ICTR has taken judicial notice of the genocide in Rwanda.[28] The taking of judicial notice means that an adjudicated fact does not need to be proven in later proceedings, but, before most tribunals, the accuracy of a fact may be challenged at trial.[29] This could be seen as reversing the burden of proof, in placing an onus on the defence to rebut judicially noticed facts. Judge Shahabuddeen, in a separate opinion in the *Milošević* case, disagreed with this position, stating that there was a distinction to be drawn between 'facilitating proof' and 'dispensing with proof', and that judicial notice was an example of the former.[30] However, the doctrine was developed to save court energies on adjudicating matters that cannot be subject to reasonable dispute,[31] and it would seem appropriate to

1987 (Federal Law Gazette [*Bundesgesetzblatt*] Part I p. 1074, 1319), as most recently amended by Article 3 of the Act of 23 April 2014 (Federal Law Gazette Part I p. 410), s. 244(3).

[25] Rule 160 of the STL RPE adds that these adjudicated facts cannot relate to the acts and conduct of the accused; this was one of the criteria for taking judicial notice of a given fact developed in the case law of the ICTY (e.g. *Prosecutor v. Stanković*, Decision on Prosecution Motion for Judicial Notice Pursuant to Rule 94(B), Case No. IT-96-23/2-PT, 16 May 2003, para 10). Compare, however *Prosecutor v. Karemera et al.*, Decision on Prosecutor's Interlocutory Appeal of Decision on Judicial Notice, Case No. ICTR-98-44-AR73(C), 16 June 2006, para 48, finding that only those facts that have some bearing on the culpability of the accused would be relevant and thus eligible for judicial notice.

[26] *Prosecutor v. Karadžić*, Decision on First Prosecution Motion for Judicial Notice of Adjudicated Facts, Case No. IT-95-5/18-PT, 5 June 2009; *Prosecutor v. Karadžić*, Decision on Second Prosecution Motion for Judicial Notice of Adjudicated Facts, Case No. IT-95-5/18-PT, 9 October 2009; *Prosecutor v. Karadžić*, Decision on Third Prosecution Motion for Judicial Notice of Adjudicated Facts, Case No. IT-95-5/18-PT, 9 July 2009; *Prosecutor v. Karadžić*, Decision on Fourth Prosecution Motion for Judicial Notice of Adjudicated Facts, Case No. IT-95-5/18-T, 14 June 2010.

[27] *Karadžić* Decision on Fourth Prosecution Motion for Judicial Notice of Adjudicated Facts, ibid., Appendix A.

[28] *Karemera* Decision on Prosecutor's Interlocutory Appeal of Decision on Judicial Notice (n 25). This has been criticized in, inter alia, Kirk G. Shannon, 'Passing the Poisoned Chalice: Judicial Notice of Genocide by the ICTR' (2006) 19(2) *Revue Québécoise de Droit International* 95.

[29] *Prosecutor v. Milošević*, Decision on the Prosecution's Interlocutory Appeal against the Trial Chamber's 10 April 2003 Decision on Prosecution Motion for Judicial Notice of Adjudicated Facts, Case No. IT-02-54-AR73, 28 October 2003, para 14; ibid., Separate Opinion of Judge Shahabuddeen, paras 14 and 23.

[30] ibid., para 24.

[31] The early literature on judicial notice assumes that it will be limited to facts of common knowledge: see, for example, James B. Thayer, 'Judicial Notice and the Law of Evidence' (1890) 3(7)

limit judicial notice to such facts.[32] This position further comports with the SCSL's decision that, once judicially noticed, facts cannot be challenged;[33] to allow this would defeat the purpose of the doctrine.[34]

Another manifestation of the presumption of innocence through the prosecutorial burden of proof is the existence of so-called 'no case to answer' determinations at the ICTY, SCSL, ICTR, and STL.[35] Under this procedure, following the close of the prosecution case, the Trial Chamber can determine that, even if taken at its highest, the evidence on a particular count charged in the indictment is insufficient to sustain a conviction, and may enter a judgment of acquittal on any such counts.[36] There is no equivalent procedure before the ICC, presumably because the Prosecutor already has to prove that there is sufficient evidence 'to establish substantial grounds to believe that the person committed each of the crimes charged'[37] at the confirmation of the charges hearing before the trial can commence. However, it remains open to the Trial Chamber to adopt such a procedure, pursuant to its general powers under Article 64(3)(a) of the Statute, should it be deemed necessary to facilitate the fair and expeditious conduct of proceedings.[38]

3.2 Right to Silence and Freedom from Self-Incrimination

Closely related to the presumption of innocence is the accused's right to remain silent and not to be compelled to testify against himself or herself; this right is enshrined in all of the tribunals' statutes as a minimum guarantee.[39] The ICC and STL Statutes add that the exercise of the right to silence cannot be considered in the determination of the guilt or innocence

Harvard Law Review 285, and Arthur John Keefe, William B. Landis, Jr and Robert B. Shaad, 'Sense and Nonsense about Judicial Notice' (1950) 2(4) *Stanford Law Review* 664.

[32] See further, *Milošević* Decision on the Prosecution's Interlocutory Appeal against the Trial Chamber's 10 April 2003 Decision on Prosecution Motion for Judicial Notice of Adjudicated Facts (n 29), Dissenting Opinion of Judge Hunt.

[33] *Prosecutor v. Norman et al.*, Decision on Appeal Against 'Decision on Prosecution's Motion for Judicial Notice of Adjudicated Facts, Case No. SCSL-04-14-AR73, 16 May 2005, para 32.

[34] ibid., Separate Opinion of Judge Robertson, para 9.

[35] Rules 98*bis*, ICTR and ICTY RPE; Rule 98, SCSL RPE; Rule 167, STL RPE.

[36] One such acquittal was ordered in *Prosecutor v. Jelisić*, Transcript, Case No. IT-95-10-T, 19 October 1999.

[37] Article 61(5), ICC Statute.

[38] Håkan Friman et al., 'Charges', in Goran Sluiter et al. (eds), *International Criminal Procedure: Principles and Rules* (Oxford: OUP, 2013) 381, 430.

[39] Article 21(4)(g), ICTY Statute; Article 20(4)(g), ICTR Statute; Article 16(4)(h), STL Statute; Article 17(4)(g), SCSL Statute; Article 67(1)(g), ICC Statute.

of the accused.[40] Under the ICC's legal framework, the accused may not be compelled to testify at all,[41] whereas the other tribunals' statutes refer only to the right not to be compelled to testify against oneself or to confess guilt.[42] The freedom from compulsion extends beyond testimonial evidence and also incorporates a right to refuse to give physical evidence, such as handwriting samples.[43] In this respect, the international criminal jurisprudence goes beyond the ECtHR's approach, which has developed a number of qualifications to the general right to silence in recent years.[44]

During investigations, the Prosecutor has a duty to inform the accused that he or she has the right to silence, and to caution that any statements made may be used in evidence.[45] Where an accused has not been adequately informed of his or her rights, the statement in question will be excluded from the evidence.[46] The onus is on the Prosecutor to show that a statement was given voluntarily and in the absence of coercion.[47] In *Sesay*, reference to off-tape conversations and the accused's apparent misapprehension that he was a suspect, rather than an accused, raised doubts as to the compliance of the statements with the applicable rules and procedures.[48] Later, the Appeals Chamber found that the accused was 'labouring under a misapprehension'[49] that his cooperation with prosecution investigators might enable him to avoid prosecution and excluded the confessional statements given during those interviews from evidence.[50] A key factor in that decision was the fact

[40] Article 67(1)(g), ICC Statute; Article 15(b), STL Statute. The ICTR in *Prosecutor v. Niyitegeka*, Judgment and Sentence, Case No. ICTR-96-14-T, 16 May 2003, para 46 confirmed that no adverse inference would be drawn from the accused's choice not to testify.

[41] Article 67(1)(g), ICC Statute.

[42] Article 21(4)(g), ICTY Statute; Article 20(4)(g), ICTR Statute; Article 16(4)(h), STL Statute; Article 17(4)(g), SCSL Statute.

[43] *Prosecutor v. Delalić*, Decision on the Prosecution's Oral Requests for the Admission of Exhibit 155 into Evidence and for an Order to Compel the Accused, Zdravko Mucić, to Provide a Handwriting Sample, Case No. IT-96-21-T, 19 January 1998.

[44] John Jackson, 'Re-conceptualizing the Right of Silence as an Effective Fair Trial Standard' (2009) 58 *ICLQ* 835.

[45] Rules 42(A)(iii) and 63(B), ICTR, SCSL, and ICTY RPE; Rules 65(A) and 85, STL RPE; Article 55(2)(b), ICC Statute.

[46] *Prosecutor v. Delalić et al.*, Decision on Zdravko Mucić's Motion for the Exclusion of Evidence, Case No. IT-96-21-T, 2 September 1997, para 41.

[47] ibid., para 42; *Prosecutor v. Prlić*, Decision on the Admission into Evidence of Slobodan Praljak's Evidence in the case of Naletelić and Martinović, Case No. IT-04-74-T, 5 September 2007, para 19; *Prosecutor v. Sesay et al.*, Ruling on *Voir Dire*—Written Reasons, Case No. SCSL-04-15-T, 2 November 2007, para 15.

[48] *Sesay*, Ruling on *Voir Dire*—Written Reasons, ibid., para 18.

[49] *Prosecutor v. Sesay et al.*, Written Reasons—Decision on the Admissibility of Certain Prior Statements of the Accused Given to the Prosecution, Case No. SCSL-04-15-T, 30 June 2008, para 50.

[50] ibid., para 68.

that discussions during breaks in recording were not recapitulated when recording recommenced.[51] By contrast, in *Halilović*, no evidence supported the defence position that the accused was offered a withdrawal of the indictment in return for cooperation with the prosecution,[52] and it was found that the offer to support the accused's application for provisional release did not constitute an inducement.[53]

A corollary to the right to freedom from self-incrimination is the accused's right to make an unsworn statement. This was first included in an amendment to the ICTY RPE in 1999,[54] and has since been listed as a minimum guarantee owed to the accused under Article 67(1)(h) of the ICC Statute—a development described by Schabas as a 'genuine innovation' in the Statute.[55] Where the accused opts to make such a statement, the Prosecutor does not have the right to cross-examine him or her on that statement, as to do so would contravene the presumption of innocence.[56] Such statements may attract evidentiary weight,[57] but this is at the discretion of the Chamber.[58]

3.3 Right to Trial by an Independent and Impartial Tribunal

Unlike their counterparts in the ICCPR and other human rights legal instruments,[59] the statutes of the ICTY, ICTR, STL, and SCSL do not contain an explicit right to be tried by an impartial and independent tribunal, although their statutes do demand that judges must be persons of 'high moral character,

[51] ibid., para 49.

[52] *Prosecutor v. Halilović*, Decision on Admission into Evidence of Interview of the Accused, Case No. IT-01-48-T, 20 June 2005, paras 15–17.

[53] ibid., para 14. [54] Rule 84*bis*, ICTY RPE.

[55] William A. Schabas, 'Article 67' in Otto Triffterer (ed.), *Commentary on the Rome Statute: Observers' Notes, Article-by-Article* (2nd edn, Munich: Beck, 2008) 1247, 1257.

[56] *Situation in the CAR: Prosecutor v. Bemba*, Decision on unsworn statement by the accused pursuant to Article 67(l)(h) of the Rome Statute, Case No. ICC-01/05-01/08, 1 November 2013, para 8.

[57] *Situation in the DRC: Prosecutor v. Ngudjolo*, Decision on the Prosecutor's request to establish parameters for Mr Ngudjolo's personal address at the appeal hearing, Case No. ICC-01/04-02/12-217, 17 October 2014, para 9.

[58] Schabas (n 55), 1278. See also, *Situation in Darfur, Sudan: Prosecutor v. Abu Garda*, Decision on the Confirmation of the Charges, Case No. ICC-02/05-02/09, 8 February 2010, para 55 (declining to treat the accused's unsworn statement as evidence).

[59] e.g. Article 6, ECHR; Article 7(1)(d), ACHPR (mentioning only impartiality, not independence). Article 8(1) of the ACHR and Article 14(1) of the ICCPR add 'competence' to their requirements of independence and impartiality.

impartiality and integrity'.[60] The ICC's legal framework not only incorporates the right to a fair hearing conducted impartially,[61] it also develops a detailed set of provisions on the competence of judges,[62] procedures for their election,[63] and their recusal if there are issues surrounding their independence or impartiality.[64] The ICC Statute also determines that the Registrar, Deputy Registrar, Prosecutor, and Deputy Prosecutor must be impartial in the exercise of their functions.[65]

The issue of judicial impartiality has been subject to quite extensive jurisprudence before the international criminal tribunals. The international criminal judiciary has established that it is imperative to the fairness of proceedings that judges must not only be free from bias, they must also be free from any reasonable apprehension of bias.[66] The Appeals Chamber of the ICC stated that it was 'the absence of bias, real or apparent ... [that] legitimizes a judicial body to administer justice'.[67]

There is an assumption that judges will be impartial, and it is for the moving party to prove any alleged lack of impartiality or independence.[68] Allegations of bias may arise from any one of a number of circumstances. Some obvious examples are where a judge has a personal or professional relationship with one of the parties,[69] or where he or she has expressed an opinion that might cause a

[60] Article 13, ICTY Statute; Article 12, ICTR Statute; Rule 15 (A) of the ICTY and ICTR Rules of Procedure and Evidence (RPE); Article 41 of the Rome Statute and Rule 34 of the ICC Rules of Procedure and Evidence; Article 9, STL Statute; SCSL Statute.

[61] Article 67(1), ICC Statute. [62] Article 36, ICC Statute. [63] ibid.

[64] Article 41, ICC Statute. [65] Articles 42 and 43, ICC Statute.

[66] *Prosecutor v. Furundžija*, Judgment, Case No. IT-95-17/1-A, 21 July 2000, para 182; *Prosecutor v. Rutaganda*, Judgment, Case No. ICTR-96-3-A, 26 May 2003, para 39 *et seq.*; *Prosecutor v. Sesay*, Decision on Defence Motion Seeking the Disqualification of Justice Robertson from the Appeals Chamber, Case No. SCSL-2004-15-AR15, 13 March 2004, para 15; *Prosecutor v. Norman*, Decision on the Motion to Recuse Judge Winter from the Deliberation in the Preliminary Motion on the Recruitment of Child Soldiers, Case No. SCSL-2004-14-PT, 28 May 2004.

[67] *Situation in the DRC: Prosecutor v. Katanga and Ngudjolo*, Judgment in the Appeal by Mathieu Ngudjolo Chui of 27 March 2008 against the Decision of Pre-Trial Chamber I on the Application of the Appellant for Interim Release, Case No. ICC-01/04-01/07, 9 June 2008, para 10.

[68] *Prosecutor v. Blagojević*, Decision on Motion for Disqualification, Case No. IT-02-60-R, 2 July 2008; *Prosecutor v. Šešelj*, Decision on Motion for Disqualification, Case No. IT-03-67-PT, 16 February 2007, para 5; *Furundžija* Judgment (n 66), para 196; *In the matter of El Sayed*, Decision on Mr El Sayed's Motion for the Disqualification of Judge Chamseddine from the Appeals Chamber Pursuant to Rule 25, Case No. CH/PRES/2010/09, 5 November 2010, para 17; *Prosecutor v. Mladić*, Decision Concerning Defence Motion to Exceed Word Count and Defence Motion Pursuant to Rule 15(B) Seeking Disqualification of Presiding Judge Alphons Orie, Case No. IT-09-92-T, 22 January 2014, 3; *Prosecutor v. Mladić*, Decision Concerning Defence Motion to Exceed Word Count and Defence Motion Pursuant to Rule 15(B) Seeking Disqualification of Presiding Judge Christoph Flügge, Case No. IT-09-92-T, 22 January 2014, 2–3.

[69] Rule 34(1)(a), ICC RPE; *Prosecutor v. Karemera et al.*, Reasons for Decision on Interlocutory Appeals Regarding the Continuation of Proceedings with a Substitute Judge and on Nzirorera's Motion for Leave to Consider New Material, Case No. ICTR-98-44-AR15*bis*.2, 22 October 2004, para 69.

reasonable observer to question his or her impartiality.[70] The SCSL found that comments expressed by Judge Robertson in his book *Crimes Against Humanity* referred to the RUF, which the accused was a member of, and this constituted sufficient grounds for his recusal.[71] In *Šešelj*, a leaked email message written by Judge Harhoff, wherein he decried recent acquittals by the ICTY and referred to 'more or less set practice at the court' to convict military commanders, formed the basis of his disqualification from the case.[72] By contrast, before the ICC, when Judge Song referred to the *Lubanga* judgment as setting 'a crucial precedent in the fight against impunity' and a 'landmark judgment', it was held that a fair-minded observer would not see these comments as referring to the merits of the case, and the Plenary of Judges declined to recuse him from the appeal.[73]

Many international criminal judges have had some involvement in extra-judicial causes relevant to international criminal law, either before their appointment as a judge or during their time in office. This will, generally speaking, not be sufficient grounds for recusal, and indeed, may serve as proof of the judge's competence in the field.[74] Equally, earlier judicial involvement with cases arising from the same set of facts will generally not suffice to find an unacceptable of bias, 'unless they display a deep-seated favoritism or antagonism that would make fair judgment impossible'.[75] In *Karadžić*, the accused alleged that Judge Picard could not judge his case impartially,

[70] Rule 34(1)(d), ICC RPE.

[71] *Sesay* Decision on Defence Motion Seeking the Disqualification of Justice Robertson from the Appeals Chamber (n 66).

[72] *Prosecutor v. Šešelj*, Order on the Prosecution Motion for the Disqualification of Judge Frederik Harhoff, Case No. IT-03-67-T, 14 January 2008.

[73] *Situation in the DRC: Prosecutor v. Lubanga*, Decision of the Plenary of Judges on the Defence Application of 20 February 2013 for the Disqualification of Judge Sang-Hyun Song from the case of *The Prosecutor v. Thomas Lubanga Dyilo*, Case No. ICC-01/04-01/06, 11 June 2013, paras 13–19.

[74] ibid., paras 21–32; *Norman* Decision on the Motion to Recuse Judge Winter from the Deliberation in the Preliminary Motion on the Recruitment of Child Soldiers (n 66) 30; *Furundžija* Judgment (n 66), paras 195–215.

[75] *Prosecutor v. Karemera et al.*, Decision on Motion by Karemera for Disqualification of Trial Judges, Case No. ICTR-98-44-T, 17 May 2004, para 12. See also, *In the Case Against Akbar Beirut S.A.L and Al Amin*, Decision on the Motion for Disqualification of Judge Lettieri, Case No. STL-14-06/PT/OTH/R25, 5 September 2014, para 21; *Prosecutor v. Galić*, Judgment, Case No. IT-98-29-A, 30 November 2006, para 42; *Prosecutor v. Krajišnik*, Decision on the Defence Application for Withdrawal of a Judge from the Trial, Case No. IT-00-39-PT, 22 January 2003; *Prosecutor v. Kordić and Čerkez*, Order on Accused's Application Requesting Disqualification of Judges Jorda and Riad, Case No. IT-95-14/2-PT, 4 May 1998; *Nahimana et al. v. Prosecutor*, Judgment, Case No. ICTR-99-52-A, 28 November 2007, para 78; *Situation in the DRC: Prosecutor v. Katanga*, Decision of the Plenary of Judges on the Application of the Legal Representative for Victims for the disqualification of Judge Christine Van den Wyngaert from the case of *The Prosecutor v. Germain Katanga*, Case No. ICC-01/04-01/07, 22 July 2014; *In the matter of El Sayed*, Decision on Mr El Sayed's Motion for the Disqualification of Judge Riachy from the Appeals Chamber Pursuant to Rule 25, Case No. CH/PRES/2010/08, 5 November 2010, para 32.

given her former role as President of the Human Rights Chamber of Bosnia and Herzegovina, which made findings on the genocide in Srebrenica.[76] This motion was denied, on the basis that a fair-minded informed observer would recognize that the determination of the accused's individual criminal responsibility was 'materially and fundamentally different from the necessary findings and determinations of state responsibility for human rights violations by the Human Rights Chamber'.[77] Along the same vein, a judge's involvement with a decision granting protective measures to witnesses before the STL did not demonstrate that the judge would be lacking in impartiality in contempt cases involving the disclosure of those witnesses' identities.[78] In *Taylor*, the SCSL Appeals Chamber dubbed the assertion that Judge Sebutinde's judicial independence was marred by her appointment to the ICJ 'unsupported, disingenuous and ridiculous'.[79]

There is some divergence in practice on whether earlier judicial involvement in the case itself will give rise to grounds for recusal. At the ICC, where a judge has participated in the pre-trial phase of a case, he or she may not sit on the Trial Chamber for that case.[80] Two Appeals Chamber judges recused themselves from hearing an appeal because of their earlier membership of the Pre-Trial Chamber in the case.[81] By contrast, the legal frameworks of the ICTY, ICTR, and SCSL explicitly state that a judge who confirmed the indictment against the accused shall not be precluded from sitting on the Trial Chamber for that case.[82] The STL's legal framework is silent on this issue. Jurisprudence of the European Court of Human Rights is not entirely consistent on this point,[83] but it would seem appropriate that judges who are involved in the issuance of an arrest warrant or an indictment should recuse

[76] *Prosecutor v. Karadžić*, Decision on Motion to Disqualify Judge Picard and Report to the Vice-President Pursuant to Rule 15(B)(ii), Case No. IT-95-05/18-PT, 22 July 2009.

[77] ibid., para 19.

[78] *In the Case Against Akbar Beirut S.A.L and Al Amin*, Decision on the Motion for Disqualification of Judge Fransen, Case No. STL-14-06/PT/OTH/R25.2, 12 August 2014.

[79] *Prosecutor v. Taylor*, Judgment, Case No. SCSL-03-01-A, 26 September 2013, para 635.

[80] Article 39(4), ICC Statute.

[81] *Situation in the DRC: Prosecutor v. Katanga and Ngudjolo*, Decision on the Request to be Excused from Sitting on the Appeal against the Decision on Admissibility in the case of *The Prosecutor v. Germain Katanga and Mathieu Ngudjolo Chui* pursuant to Article 41 of the Rome Statute, Case No. ICC-01/04-01/07-1266-AnxII, 3 July 2009.

[82] Rules 15(C), ICTY and ICTR RPE; Rule 15(D), SCSL RPE. The SCSL and ICTY RPE add that such a judge will not be disqualified from sitting on the Appeals Chamber for the case on the basis of their earlier involvement.

[83] *Ben Yaacoub v. Belgium* (1991) 13 EHRR 418, 27 November 1987; *De Cubber v. Belgium* (1985) 7 EHRR 236, 26 October 1984; *Kyprianou v. Cyprus*, Application No. 73797/01, Judgment, 15 December 2005; *Hauschildt v. Denmark* (1990) 12 EHRR 266, 24 May 1989; *Fey v. Austria* (1993) 16 EHRR 387, 24 February 1993; compare *Saraivo de Carvalho v. Portugal* (1994) 18 EHRR 534, 22 April 1994.

themselves on the basis that it may give rise to an appearance of bias, even though the judges themselves may not actually be tainted by bias.[84]

3.4 Right to Trial without Undue Delay

The right to be tried without undue delay is a minimum guarantee provided for in each of the tribunals' statutes.[85] International criminal tribunals have broadly employed the standards laid down in human rights law[86] as regards the factors that should be assessed in analysing whether a delay can be said to be 'undue'. These are: the complexity of the case,[87] the conduct of the authorities,[88] the

[84] See also, Yvonne McDermott, 'The Judicial Duty to Ensure Fairness of Proceedings' in Sluiter et al. (eds) (n 38); *In the Case against Florence Hartmann*, Report of Decision on Defence Motion for Disqualification of Two Members of the Trial Chamber and of Senior Legal Officer, Case No. IT-02-54-R77.5, 27 March 2009, Separate Opinion of Judge Flügge Concurring in Result, para 2. Compare *Prosecutor v. Blagojević et al.*, Decision on Joint Defence Motion for Reconsideration of Trial Chamber's Decision to Review All Discovery Materials Provided to the Accused by the Prosecution, Case No. IT-02-60-PT, 21 January 2003, 6; and *Prosecutor v. Galić*, Decision on the Defence Motion for Withdrawal of Judge Orie, Case No. IT-98-29-T, 3 February 2003, para 8 ('The Judges of this Tribunal are professional Judges with solid experience in handling information in the criminal legal context and notably distinguishing between facts established at trial and facts derived from elsewhere'); *Hartmann* Report of Decision on Defence Motion for Disqualification of Two Members of the Trial Chamber and of Senior Legal Officer, ibid., para 44.

[85] Article 20(4)(c) ICTR Statute; Article 17(4)(c) SCSL Statute; Article 21(4)(c) ICTY Statute; Article 67(1)(c) ICC Statute; Article 16(4)(c) STL Statute.

[86] African Commission on Human and Peoples' Rights, *Principles and Guidelines on the Right to a Fair Trial and Legal Assistance in Africa*, Principle N(3)(1)(c) ('Factors relevant to what constitutes undue delay include the complexity of the case, the conduct of the parties, the conduct of other relevant authorities, whether an accused is detained pending proceedings, and the interest of the person at stake in the proceedings'); *Union Alimentaria Sanders, S.A. v. Spain* (1989), 12 EHRR 24, 7 July 1989; *Martins Moreira v. Portugal* (1991) 13 EHRR 517, 26 October 1988; *Guincho v. Portugal* (1982) 29 *Decisions and Reports* 129, 28 June 1984; *X v. France* (1992) Series A No. 234-C, 31 March 1992; *Suárez Rosero Case*, IACtHR, 12 November 1997.

[87] e.g. *Prosecutor v. Bizimungu et al.*, Decision on Prosper Mugiraneza's Interlocutory Appeal from Trial Chamber II Decision of 2 October 2003 Denying the Motion to Dismiss the Indictment, Case No. ICTR-99-50-AR73, 27 February 2004, 3; *Prosecutor v. Perišić*, Decision on Motion for Sanctions for Failure to Bring the Accused to Trial without Undue Delay, Case No. IT-04-81-PT, 23 November 2007, para 12; *Prosecutor v. Bizimungu et al.*, Decision on Prosper Mugiraneza's application for a hearing or other relief on his motion for dismissal for violation of his right to a trial without undue delay, Case No. ICTR-99-50-T, 3 November 2004, para 26; *Prosecutor v. Bizimungu et al.*, Decision on Justin Mugenzi's Motion for Stay of Proceedings or in the Alternative Provisional Release (Rule 65) and in Addition Severance (Rule 82(B)), Case No. ICTR-99-50-I, 8 November 2002, para 36; *Situation in the CAR: Prosecutor v. Bemba Gombo*, Decision on application for interim release, Case No. ICC-01/05-01/08, 16 December 2008, paras 46–7.

[88] e.g. *Prosecutor v. Bizimungu et al.*, Decision on Prosper Mugiraneza's application for a hearing or other relief on his motion for dismissal for violation of his right to a trial without undue delay (n 87) paras 31–2; *Prosecutor v. Bizimungu et al.*, Decision on Prosper Mugiraneza's Second Motion

conduct of the accused,[89] and the prejudice suffered by the accused.[90] The burden of proof lies with the accused to show that delay was undue.[91]

'Complexity' can be assessed by the examination of a number of factors, including the number of charges, the volume of evidence, the number of witnesses, and the complexity of the applicable factual backdrop and legal provisions.[92] Bearing this in mind, it is undeniable that trials before international criminal tribunals are exceptionally complex. At the investigative stage, they involve the unpicking of intricate command structures, political factors, and historical backdrops to identify individual roles in atrocities committed on an enormous scale, often in an environment where states and witnesses are unwilling to co-operate with the institution.[93] At trial, the tribunals have to deal with counsel who may not yet be entirely familiar with the structures and rules of the international tribunal, having often practised in a drastically different domestic criminal procedural system,[94] evidence records

to Dismiss for Deprivation of his Right to Trial without Undue Delay, Case No. ICTR-99-50-T, 29 May 2007, paras 32–36.

[89] e.g. *Prosecutor v. Norman et al.*, Decision on Prosecution Motion for a Ruling on the Admissibility of Evidence, Case No. SCSL-04-14-PT, 24 May 2005, Dissenting Opinion of Justice Pierre Boutet, para 30; *Prosecutor v. Bizimungu et al.*, Decision on Prosper Mugiraneza's application for a hearing or other relief on his motion for dismissal for violation of his right to a trial without undue delay (n 87) para 32; *Prosecutor v. Bagosora et al.*, Decision on the Prosecutor's motion for joinder, Case Nos. ICTR-96-7, ICTR-96-12, ICTR-97-34 and ICTR-97-30, 29 June 2000, para 147; *Prosecutor v. Blagojević et al.*, Decision on independent counsel for Vidoje Blagojević's motion to instruct the Registrar to appoint new lead and co-counsel, Case No. IT-02-60-T, 3 July 2003, para 113.

[90] e.g. *Prosecutor v. Barayagwiza*, Appeal against the Trial Chamber II's 'Decision on the extremely urgent motion by the defence for orders to review and/or nullify the arrest and provisional detention of the suspect' of 17 November 1998, Case No. ICTR-97-19-AR72, 3 November 1999, paras 75–7; *Prosecutor v. Bizimungu et al.*, Decision on Jérôme-Clément Bicamumpaka's Motion Seeking Permanent Stay of Proceedings, Case No. ICTR-99-50-AR73, 27 February 2009, para 18.

[91] *Prosecutor v. Bizimungu et al.*, Decision on Prosper Mugiraneza's application for a hearing or other relief on his motion for dismissal for violation of his right to a trial without undue delay (n 87) para 33.

[92] *Prosecutor v. Norman et al.*, Decision on Prosecution Motion for a Ruling on the Admissibility of Evidence, Case No. SCSL-04-14-PT, 24 May 2005, Dissenting Opinion of Justice Pierre Boutet, para 30; *Prosecutor v. Bizimungu et al.*, Decision on Prosper Mugiraneza's application for a hearing or other relief on his motion for dismissal for violation of his right to a trial without undue delay (n 87) para 26.

[93] *Situation in the DRC: Prosecutor v. Lubanga*, Decision on the Application for the interim release of Thomas Lubanga Dyilo, Case No. ICC-04/01-01/06, 18 October 2006, 7 (considering the volume of evidence and the fact that a large amount of evidence had to be garnered from abroad as evidence of the complexity of the case).

[94] Rosemary Byrne, 'The New Public International Lawyer and the Hidden Art of International Criminal Trial Practice' (2010) 25 *Connecticut JIL* 243, 252. Lawyers often do not stay in one institution long enough to create an 'institutional memory' that can be passed on to newer members of staff—see Elena A. Baylis, 'Tribunal Hopping with the Post-Conflict Justice Junkies' (2008) 10 *Oregon Rev Int'l L* 361.

that run to tens of thousands of pages,[95] and extended forms of liability that are unique to international criminal law.[96] It might be argued, therefore, that it is unreasonable to impose standards devised with the 'ordinary' criminal trial in mind to international criminal proceedings.[97]

In *Kovačević*, for example, Judge Shahabuddeen warned that 'peculiarities and difficulties of unearthing and assembling material for war crimes prosecutions' called for 'judicial flexibility'.[98] Indeed, in a European Commission of Human Rights case concerning war crimes prosecutions in Germany, it was held that the unique features of such prosecutions permitted some derogation from the principles governing expedience in criminal trials.[99] The Commission stated that: 'The exceptional character of criminal proceedings involving war crimes committed during World War II renders, in the Commission's opinion, inapplicable the principles developed in case-law of the Commission and the Court of Human Rights in connection with cases involving other criminal offences.'[100] However, as pointed out by van Dijk and van Hoof, the complexity of the case is just one of the factors that is to be taken into account when assessing whether a delay has been a breach of the applicant's human rights; therefore, the Commission was incorrect in declaring the overall principles of the right to a fair trial inapplicable in this case.[101] Moreover, the provisions of Article 1 clearly state that the protections laid out in the Convention apply to 'everyone', so the distinction

[95] To give an example, the *Đorđević* Trial Chamber received some 2,518 pieces of documentary evidence 'from the bar table' and the trial record encompasses 14,534 pages of transcript. See also, *Situation in the Republic of Kenya, Prosecutor v. Ruto, Kosgey and Sang*, Urgent Defence Application for Postponement of the Confirmation Hearing and Extension of Time to Disclose and List Evidence, Case No. ICC-01/09-01/11, 11 August 2011, para 3, where the pre-trial proceedings alone involved over 900 pages of disclosed information to the defence. On the practice of 'flooding' the defence, see Colleen Rohan, 'Protecting the Rights of The Accused in International Criminal Proceedings: Lip Service Or Affirmative Action?' in William A. Schabas, Yvonne McDermott, and Niamh Hayes (eds), *The Ashgate Research Companion to International Criminal Law: Critical Perspectives* (Aldershot: Ashgate, 2013) 289.

[96] Darryl Robinson, 'The Identity Crisis of International Criminal Law' (2008) 21 *LJIL* 925, 927.

[97] Mirjan R. Damaška, 'Reflections on Fairness in International Criminal Justice' (2012) 10 *JICJ* 611, 612, referring to the 'challenging international environment' in which international criminal tribunals operate.

[98] *Prosecutor v. Kovačević*, Decision stating reasons for Appeals Chamber's order of 29 May 1998, Case No. IT-97-24-AR73, 2 July 1998, Separate Opinion of Judge Shahabuddeen, 4–5 (cited in *Prosecutor v. Delalić et al.*, Decision on the Prosecution's Alternative Request to Reopen the Prosecution's Case, Case No. IT-96-21-T, 19 August 1998, para 9).

[99] *X v. Federal Republic of Germany*, Commission, Application No. 6946/75, Decision of 6 July 1976 on the admissibility of the application, 6 *Decisions and Reports* 114.

[100] ibid., 115–16.

[101] Paul van Dijk and G.J.H. van Hoof, *Theory and Practice of the European Convention on Human Rights* (3rd edn, The Hague [etc.]: Kluwer Law International, 1998) 450.

drawn in *X v Federal Republic of Germany* (FRG) was illogical.[102] Given that the Commission applied Article 6 as normal to a later war crimes suspect in *Menten*,[103] and more recent ECtHR jurisprudence has considered the fair trial rights of those accused of war crimes,[104] it would seem that we can treat *X v FRG* as a curiosity rather than established precedent. This means that the complexity of the case should be seen as a consideration to be taken into account when assessing whether a delay was undue rather than a factor excluding the defendant from the full scope of protection afforded by international human rights standards.

The complexity of international criminal trials alone should not itself serve as sufficient justification for judicial derogations from the right to a speedy trial. Domestic criminal proceedings often deal with complex situations, such as political corruption, Ponzi schemes, criminal gangs, and stock market fraud, which also involve reams of evidence records, unclear chains of command, and uncooperative witnesses. Even though the trial of Thomas Lubanga Dyilo on a sole charge relating to child soldiers could be said to be far less complex on the facts than some domestic cases, both the Pre-Trial and Appeals Chambers relied on the complexity of the case as justification for declaring the defendant's pre-trial detention period to have been of reasonable length.[105] Lubanga's trial lasted over eight years, from the date of his transfer to the custody of the ICC in March 2006, to the issuance of the Appeals Chamber judgment in the case on 1 December 2014. The furore that led to two stays of proceedings in the case as a result of the prosecution's non-disclosure of exculpatory materials in the first instance and the identity of an intermediary in the second is well-documented and need not be restated here.[106] Suffice to say that those two stays of proceedings added

[102] ibid.

[103] *Menten v. The Netherlands*, Application No. 9433/81, D & R 27 (1982) 233, cited in van Dijk and van Hoof (n 101), 450.

[104] *Van Anraat v. The Netherlands*, Application No. 65389/09, 6 July 2010; *Kononov v. Latvia*, Application No. 36376/04, 24 July 2008.

[105] *Situation in the DRC: Prosecutor v. Lubanga*, Decision on the Application for the Interim Release of Thomas Lubanga Dyilo, Case No. ICC-01/04-01/06, 18 October 2006; *Situation in the DRC: Prosecutor v. Lubanga*, Judgment on the Appeal of Thomas Lubanga Dyilo against the Decision of Pre-Trial Chamber I entitled 'Décision sur la demande de mise en liberté provisoire de Thomas Lubanga Dyilo', Case No. ICC-01/04-01/06, 13 February 2007, paras 118–24.

[106] *Situation in the DRC: Prosecutor v. Lubanga*, Decision on the consequences of the non-disclosure of exculpatory materials covered by Article 54(3)(e) agreements and the application to stay the proceedings of the accused, together with certain other issues raised at the Status Conference on 10 June 2008, Case No. ICC-01/04/01/06, 13 June 2008; *Situation in the DRC: Prosecutor v. Lubanga*, Judgment on the Appeal of the Prosecutor against the Decision of Trial Chamber I entitled 'Decision on the Release of Thomas Lubanga Dyilo', Case No. ICC-01/04-01/06, 21 October 2008; *Situation in the DRC: Prosecutor v. Lubanga*, Decision on the Prosecution's Urgent Request for Variation of the Time-Limit to Disclose the Identity of

an extra eight months to the duration of the trial; the first stay of proceedings lasted from 13 June 2008 to 18 November 2008, while the second lasted from 8 July 2010 to 8 October 2010.

Given that the conduct of the authorities is one of the factors to be assessed in judging whether a delay was undue, one might have expected that Thomas Lubanga's defence team were in a strong position when they alleged in their submissions before the sentencing hearing that the Trial Chamber should 'take into consideration the breach of the fundamental rights of Mr Lubanga as it comes to its determination'.[107] An earlier abuse of process motion, asking for a permanent stay of proceedings on the grounds that the accused's rights had been breached by these two stays and other instances where the Prosecutor had failed to disclose evidence, had been denied in March 2011, on the grounds that the alleged violations did not render it 'odious' or 'repugnant' to continue with the trial.[108] In its judgment, the Trial Chamber insisted that it had taken adequate steps to vindicate the rights of the accused throughout the trial, and 'had addressed any potential prejudice to the accused arising from incomplete or late disclosure'.[109] The allegations raised in the sentencing hearing on the alleged breaches of the accused's rights to adequate facilities for the preparation of his defence and to trial without undue delay were given similarly summary analysis. The Chamber held that these factors did not call for his sentence to be reduced, as the length of time spent in detention would be deducted from his sentence.[110] For what it was worth, the Chamber did go on to note Mr Lubanga's cooperation with the court throughout the trial, despite the 'particularly onerous circumstances' he faced,[111] which was unlikely to have provided a great deal of consolation to the accused. The Appeals Chamber later refused to entertain Lubanga's arguments on trial without undue delay, finding instead that the accused ought to have sought remedial action from the Trial Chamber.[112]

Intermediary 143 or Alliteratively to Stay Proceedings Pending Further Consultations with the VWU, Case No. ICC-01/04-01/06, 8 July 2010; *Situation in the DRC: Prosecutor v. Lubanga*, Judgment on the Appeal of Prosecutor against the Oral Decision of Trial Chamber I of 15 July 2010 to Release Thomas Lubanga Dyilo, Case No. ICC-01/04-01/06, 8 October 2010.

[107] *Situation in the DRC: Prosecutor v. Lubanga*, Transcript, Case No. ICC-01/04-01/06, 13 June 2012.

[108] *Situation in the DRC: Prosecutor v. Lubanga*, Redacted Decision on the 'Defence Application Seeking a Permanent Stay of the Proceedings', Case No. ICC-01/04-01/06, 2 March 2011.

[109] *Situation in the DRC: Prosecutor v. Lubanga*, Judgment Pursuant to Article 74 of the Statute, Case No. ICC-01/04-01/06, 14 March 2012, paras 120–1.

[110] *Situation in the DRC: Prosecutor v. Lubanga*, Decision on Sentence pursuant to Article 76 of the Statute, Case No. ICC-01/04-01/06, 10 July 2012, para 90.

[111] ibid., para 91.

[112] *Situation in the DRC: Prosecutor v. Lubanga*, Judgment on the Appeal of Mr Thomas Lubanga Dyilo against his Conviction, Case No. ICC-01/04-01/06, 1 December 2014, para 159.

As well as disclosure violations, some have pointed to the amount of time between close of trial and the issuance of judgment taken by some Trial Chambers as an unacceptable practice.[113] In *Prlić et al.*, for example, judgment was issued in May 2013, almost nine years since the transfer of the accused individuals to the Tribunal,[114] and over two years since proceedings were brought to a close.[115] In *Bizimungu et al.*, before the ICTR, almost three years passed from the close of trial to the issuance of judgment, and by this time, the four accused, two of whom were acquitted in the trial judgment, had been in detention for over twelve years.[116] By the time of their acquittal on appeal in 2013, the remaining two accused in this case, Mugenzi and Mugarineza, had spent almost fourteen years on trial. In its judgment, the Trial Chamber dealt with a motion on trial without undue delay filed by the accused Mugenzi, who had asserted that there had been a breach of his right to trial without undue delay owing to the Tribunal's failure to prioritize the case, by assigning judges to different cases.[117] While the Trial Chamber acknowledged that 'the increased workload of the presiding judges ... contributed to this delay',[118] the motion was denied, based on the complexity of the case, and encompassing factors such as the number of co-accused and the number of witnesses heard.[119]

However, these factors do not adequately explain why it should take almost three years to issue a judgment.[120] The defendant's motion was dismissed as being in disregard of 'the common challenges of trial administration of a multi-accused case with a complicated procedural history'.[121] Regardless of those challenges, the task of issuing a judgment after the trial has been completed is not quite an administrative function in the managerial or organizational sense. Instead, it is the imperative and overarching purpose of the trial, and it should be treated as the Chamber's utmost priority, particularly

[113] e.g. Yvonne McDermott, 'The Legacy of the International Criminal Tribunal for Rwanda in Promoting Respect for International Due Process Standards' [2013] *African Yearbook of International Humanitarian Law* 45.

[114] The six accused made their initial appearances before the Tribunal on 6 April 2004: see ICTY Press Release, 'Prlić, Stojić, Praljak, Petković, Corić and Pušić Initial Appearance', ICTY Ref. JM/P.I.S./836e, The Hague, 6 April 2004.

[115] *Prosecutor v. Prlić*, Transcript, Case No. IT-04-74-T, 2 March 2011, 52976.

[116] *Prosecutor v. Bizimungu et al.*, Judgment and Sentence, Case No. ICTR-99-50-T, 30 September 2011.

[117] ibid., paras 66–79. [118] ibid., para 74. [119] ibid., paras 66–79.

[120] See also, Yvonne McDermott, 'Rights in Reverse: A Critical Analysis of Fair Trial Rights under International Criminal Law' in William A. Schabas, Yvonne McDermott, and Niamh Hayes (eds), *The Ashgate Research Companion to International Criminal Law: Critical Perspectives* (Aldershot: Ashgate, 2013) 165.

[121] *Bizimungu et al.*, Judgment and Sentence (n 116) para 79.

when defendants are deprived of their liberty in waiting for a judgment. The Chamber must have made its decision to acquit two of the co-accused some time in advance of the 2011 judgment; they should have moved swiftly to release those men by issuing a summary judgment as soon as it became apparent that these two defendants were going to be acquitted.[122] The issuance of summary judgments before the final judgment is released has expedited matters in some cases,[123] but in others, it still took the Trial Chamber over a year to issue the judgment in summary form.[124]

The extent to which a delay is attributable to the parties' conduct is also relevant when considering the length taken to deliver decisions on the confirmation of the charges before the ICC. Pursuant to Regulation 53, such decisions shall be delivered within sixty days from the end of the confirmation hearing, but in practice, only the *Lubanga* and *Katanga* confirmation decisions have been issued within this timeframe, with other confirmation decisions taking significantly longer.[125] In *Gbagbo*, the accused was transferred to the Court on 30 November 2011, but the confirmation of the charges decision was not issued until 12 June 2014.[126] This delay was due, in part, to the fact that the prosecution case (in light of the excessive reliance on anonymous hearsay found in NGO reports and press articles) was deemed not to meet the evidentiary threshold for the confirmation of the charges in June 2013 and on that basis, the Pre-Trial Chamber adjourned the confirmation hearing and requested further evidence from the prosecution, pursuant to Article 61(7)(c) of the Statute.[127]

Trial Chambers will take steps to ensure that undue delay is not caused by the Prosecutor's actions, such as by refusing to amend an indictment to

[122] McDermott (n 113) 57.

[123] e.g., *Prosecutor v. Karemera et al.*, Judgment and Sentence, Case No. 98-44-T, 2 February 2012.

[124] *Prosecutor v. Bagosora et al.*, Judgment and Sentence, Case No. ICTR-98-41-T, 18 December 2008; *Prosecutor v. Taylor*, Judgment, Case No. SCSL-03-01-T, 18 May 2012.

[125] Yvonne McDermott, 'Some Thoughts on the Ntaganda and Gbagbo Confirmation of the Charges Decisions at the ICC', *PhD Studies in Human Rights*, 14 June 2014, available online at http://humanrightsdoctorate.blogspot.ie/2014/06/some-thoughts-on-ntaganda-and-gbagbo.html (last accessed 22 June 2015). Cassese criticized the delay in issuing the *Lubanga* confirmation decision (*Situation in the DRC: Prosecutor v. Lubanga*, Decision on the Confirmation of Charges, Case No. ICC-01/04-01/06, 29 January 2007), ten months after the accused's first appearance in March 2006, even though the confirmation hearing was held between 9 and 28 November 2006: Antonio Cassese, 'The International Criminal Court Five Years On: *Andante* or *Moderato*?' in Carsten Stahn and Goran Sluiter (eds), *The Emerging Practice of the International Criminal Court* (Leiden: Martinus Nijhoff, 2009) 21, 29.

[126] *Situation in Côte d'Ivoire: Prosecutor v. Laurent Gbagbo*, Decision on the Confirmation of Charges against Laurent Gbagbo, Case No. ICC-02/11-01/11, 12 June 2014.

[127] *Situation in Côte d'Ivoire: Prosecutor v. Laurent Gbagbo*, Decision Adjourning the Hearing on the Confirmation of Charges pursuant to Article 61(7)(c)(i) of the Rome Statute, Case No. ICC-02/11-01/11, 3 June 2013.

include additional counts,[128] denying a joinder of cases,[129] or severing an individual's case from a joint trial where their ill-health may jeopardize the rights of their co-accused.[130] The ICTR in *Barayagwiza* found that, in exceptional circumstances, unjustifiable delay owing to the Prosecutor's lack of due diligence might lead to the charges being dropped with prejudice to the prosecution.[131] In *Kenyatta*, following a refusal to grant the Prosecutor's request for an 'indefinite adjournment', the ICC ordered that she either declare that she was ready to proceed to trial or drop the charges against the accused.[132] The charges were subsequently withdrawn.[133]

The final element that will be examined is whether the accused has suffered prejudice as a result of the undue delay. This differs somewhat from the human rights jurisprudence on trial without undue delay, which examines the interest of the person at stake in the proceedings as opposed to prejudice suffered. 'Prejudice' in the context of international criminal tribunals' assessements can be defined as any impairment on the defendant's ability to present an effective defence, or any 'threat to … an accused's significant stakes, psychological, physical and financial'.[134] It could be said that any delay will always cause prejudice to the accused in a criminal trial in terms of their physical and psychological wellbeing, insofar as their continued liberty remains unclear until all proceedings have been completed, but this argument has been unsuccessful in practice. In *Bizimungu*, one of the accused argued that the fact of his continued incarceration and the resulting infringements on his right to private and family life should have been sufficient to establish a *prima facie* case for prejudice.[135] This position would appear to

[128] *Prosecutor v. Kovačević*, Decision on Prosecutor's Request to File an Amended Indictment, Case No. IT-97-24-T, 5 March 1998; this decision was later overturned in *Prosecutor v. Kovačević*, Decision Stating Reasons for Appeals Chamber's Order of 29 May 1998, Case No. IT-97-24-AR73, 2 July 1998.

[129] *Prosecutor v. Kvočka et al. & Prosecutor v. Kolundžija*, Decision on Prosecutor's Motion for Joinder, Case Nos. IT-98-30/1-T & IT-95-8-T, 19 October 1999, para 13; *Prosecutor v. Bagosora et al.*, Dismissal of Indictment, Case No. ICTR 98-37-I, 31 March 1998, 10–11.

[130] *Prosecutor v. Brđanin & Talić*, Decision on the Prosecutor's Oral Request for the Separation of Trials, Case No. IT-99-36-T, 20 September 2002, para 10.

[131] *Prosecutor v. Barayagwiza*, Decision, Case No. ICTR-97-19-AR72, 3 November 1999. The decision to release the accused was later overturned in *Prosecutor v. Barayagwiza*, Decision (Prosecutor's Request for Review or Reconsideration), Case No. ICTR-97-19-AR72, 31 March 2000.

[132] *Situation in Kenya: Prosecutor v. Kenyatta*, Decision on Prosecution's application for a further adjournment, Case No. ICC-01/09-02/11, 3 December 2014.

[133] *Situation in Kenya: Prosecutor v. Kenyatta*, Notice of withdrawal of the charges against Uhuru Muigai Kenyatta, Case No. ICC-01/09-02/11, 5 December 2014.

[134] *Black's Law Dictionary* (5th edn, St. Paul, MN, USA: West Publishing Co., 1979) 1062.

[135] *Prosecutor v. Bizimungu et al.*, Decision on Prosper Mugiraneza's application for a hearing or other relief on his motion for dismissal for violation of his right to a trial without undue delay (n 87) para 7.

have particular resonance with the unique context of international trials, where individuals can spend up to a decade or more in custody many thousands of miles away from their families, with their prospects of provisional release hampered by uncooperative states.[136] However, this argument was rejected, with the Trial Chamber saying:

> As far as prejudice to the Accused is concerned, the Chamber notes that the Defence has failed to show how the delay of four years, six months and 28 days has prejudiced [the] Accused such as to prevent a fair trial ... The burden for proving prejudice does indeed lie with the Defence.[137]

The international criminal tribunals are in a difficult position from the outset, insofar as their trials relate to incidents that happened years, and often decades, before. With each passing month, witnesses' memories are likely to fade, and individual witnesses will die or move away from their last known residence. In addition, accused persons are often detained for many years in a country far from their families while the trial is ongoing. These factors place an additional imperative on international criminal tribunals to ensure that trials are conducted in as expedient a fashion as possible. Thus, once an undue delay has been proven, the need to show resultant prejudice should not be an insurmountable barrier to cross.

It could be surmised that this unwillingness to recognize a breach in the right to trial without undue delay may arise from a fear that if the Chamber holds that the rights of the accused have been violated in this manner, he or she should be released without charge. Indeed, this is the remedy often sought by defendants.[138] It is suggested that this perception is ill-founded, because human rights jurisprudence clearly establishes that a reduction in sentence and/or compensation where a defendant is convicted is an adequate remedy, while those acquitted should be entitled to compensation upon acquittal.[139] In the words of van Hoof and van Dijk:

[136] See above, Section 3.2.

[137] *Prosecutor v. Bizimungu et al.,* Decision on Prosper Mugiraneza's application for a hearing or other relief on his motion for dismissal for violation of his right to a trial without undue delay (n 87) para 7.

[138] Dismissal of the indictment was the relief sought in the motions at issue in the many decisions listed above (n 87).

[139] *Neubeck v. Germany* (1985) 41 *Decisions and Reports* 13; *Eckle v. Germany* (1983) 5 EHRR 1, 15 July 1972; *Beck v. Norway*, Application No. 26390/95, 26 June 2001. See also *Prosecutor v. Bizimungu et al.*, Decision on Prosper Mugiraneza's Fourth Motion to Dismiss Indictment for Violation of Right to Trial without Undue Delay, Case No. ICTR-99-50-AR73, 23 June 2010, Partially Dissenting Opinion of Judge Emile Francis Short and *Bizimungu et al.*, Judgment and Sentence (n 116), Dissenting Opinion of Judge Emile Francis Short.

[T]he public interest in the prosecution and conviction of the criminal may be so great that the prosecution should not be stopped for the sole reason that the reasonable time has been transgressed; another, more proportionate compensation should be awarded to the victim of that transgression.[140]

The same public interest can undoubtedly be said to apply to international criminal proceedings. International criminal courts should be secure in the knowledge that the validity of their convictions will not be called into question by an unreasonable delay in proceedings;[141] in that regard, where the length of proceedings was in violation of the accused's rights under the Statute, compensation should be offered in the event of an acquittal, and a reduced sentence should be offered in the event of a conviction.[142]

It is difficult to point to any of the issues—or parties—discussed above as the sole cause of the extremely lengthy nature of trials before international criminal tribunals. More likely, it is a combination of these and other factors, including requests from both parties for additional time to prepare their cases at the pre-trial stage, the number of witnesses and the volume of evidence involved, and the unavailability of witnesses that lead to the unprecedented length of international criminal trials, where it is not uncommon for defendants to be in custody for the best part of a decade. However, as shall be seen below,[143] by setting such a low precedent for the length of trials, the courts send a message to states that such elongated proceedings are acceptable. On the other hand, the withdrawal of the charges in the *Kenyatta* case, while criticized by some as exemplifying the 'failures' of the ICC,[144] sends a powerful message to Prosecutors that investigations will not be permitted to drag on indefinitely until they are happy to proceed to trial on the evidence gathered.

I have noted elsewhere some concerns on the 'reverse application' of the right to trial without undue delay in international criminal trials,[145] which do not need to be restated at length here but are worthy of a brief mention. This occurs when an accused's right to trial without undue delay is used against him or her when they have requested a particular course of action, often to

140 van Dijk and van Hoof (n 101) 450.

141 *Eckle v. Germany* (n 139) para 20.

142 See further, Section 3.16 below.

143 Section 5.2.3.

144 See e.g. 'First Kenya, now Sudan: The International Criminal Court takes another bad knock', *The Economist* (20 December 2014), available online at http://www.economist.com/news/middle-east-and-africa/21636780-international-criminal-court-takes-another-bad-knock-first-kenya-now-sudan (last accessed 4 June 2015); 'Kenyatta failure deals blow to ICC', *Al Jazeera* (11 December 2014), available online at http://america.aljazeera.com/opinions/2014/12/uhuru-kenyatta-crimesagainsthumanityinternationalcriminalcourt.html (last accessed 4 June 2015).

145 McDermott (n 120).

protect other components of the right to a fair trial. A key example comes from the ICTR case of *Nyiramasuhuko et al.*, where one of three trial judges was not re-elected to the Tribunal.[146] Under an earlier version of Rule 15*bis*, continuation of proceedings in the long-term absence of a judge after the trial had started could 'only be ordered with the consent of the accused'.[147] However, this Rule was amended in May 2003 to qualify that consent.[148] Under the new Rule 15*bis*(D), if the accused withheld his consent, the two remaining judges could decide to proceed with a substitute judge anyway 'if, taking all the circumstances into account, they determine[d] unanimously that doing so would serve the interests of justice'. In this case, only the accused Nsabimana had agreed to proceeding with a substitute judge.[149] The five co-accused objected to this course of action, which was understandable, given that twenty-two of the twenty-three witnesses who had been heard by the Chamber by that time were subject to protective measures and therefore their evidence had not been recorded; this meant that the substitute judge would not have been able to assess their demeanour by looking at the trial record.[150] Nonetheless, Judges Sekule and Ramaroson noted that the substitute judge would have had to confirm that they had familiarized themselves with the trial record, and on that basis, held that it would be in the interests of justice to continue with a substitute judge rather than to start again with three new judges, which would have the effect of making proceedings 'drag on endlessly'.[151] As regards the rights of the accused, the two judges held that a recommencement of the trial with a new judge, in the manner requested by the accused, would 'prejudice the rights of the accused more than it … [would] advance them'.[152] In a situation like this, where the accused is clearly aware that an alternative course of action will lengthen his or her trial but nonetheless requests it rather than continue in a manner that he or she sees as prejudicial, judges should take account of that 'forfeit'. As 'the conduct of

[146] *Prosecutor v. Nyiramasuhuko et al.*, Decision in the matter of proceedings under Rule 15*bis*(D), Case No. ICTR 98-42-T, 15 July 2003.

[147] This was contained in the original Rule 15(E) ICTR RPE (UN Doc. ITR/3/Rev.1, International Criminal Tribunal for Rwanda, 29 June 1995) and repeated as Rule 15*bis*(C) in the 11th amendment to the RPE (UN Doc. ITR/3/Rev.11, International Criminal Tribunal for Rwanda, 31 May 2001).

[148] Rules of Procedure and Evidence, UN Doc. ITR/3/Rev.13, International Criminal Tribunal for Rwanda, 27 May 2003.

[149] *Nyiramasuhuko et al.*, Decision in the matter of proceedings under Rule 15*bis*(D) (n 146) 3.

[150] *Prosecutor v. Nyiramasuhuko et al.*, Decision in the Matter of Proceedings under Rule 15*bis*(D), Case No. ICTR-98-42-A15*bis*, 24 September 2003, Dissenting Opinion of Judge David Hunt, para 27.

[151] *Nyiramasuhuko et al.*, Decision in the matter of proceedings under Rule 15*bis*(D) (n 146) paras 33–4.

[152] ibid., para 34.

the parties' is a deciding factor in assessing whether the right to trial without undue delay has been breached, the courts will not fall afoul of this recognition.

In a similar vein, the imposition of the right to trial without undue delay as a bar to a course of action requested by the accused can be observed in *Blagojević et al.*, where the accused Blagojević had requested a replacement of his defence counsel.[153] The Trial Chamber denied this request on the grounds that 'the ensuing delay in proceedings … [would constitute] a violation of their [the accuseds'] right to an expeditious trial.'[154] This wording suggests that the Chamber was concerned not only with the rights of Blagojević's co-accused, whose case it could ultimately have severed if it were concerned about the added duration of proceedings, but also of Blagojević himself. Of course, this is not to suggest that the request of the accused should have been granted; the point is, rather, that it is quite remarkable that a person's rights should be used against them in this manner.

3.5 Right to be Informed of the Charges

All of the tribunals' statutes set out the right of the accused person to be informed promptly and in detail of the nature and cause of the charge against him or her.[155] The ICC Statute uses the phrase 'nature, cause and content of the charge', but in reality, 'there may be no meaningful distinction between "cause" and "content", except perhaps a message of exhaustivity'.[156] The Prosecutor has an obligation to set out the material facts of the case with enough detail to enable the defendant to prepare his or her defence.[157] Where interviews have been conducted without fully informing the accused of the case against him or her, it would be contrary to the dictates of fairness to permit such interviews to be admitted as evidence.[158] The RPE of the

[153] *Prosecutor v. Blagojević et al.*, Decision on independent counsel for Vidoje Blagojević's motion to instruct the Registrar to appoint new lead and co-counsel, Case No. IT-02-60-T, 3 July 2003.

[154] ibid., para 113.

[155] Article 21(4)(a), ICTY Statute; Article 20(4)(a), ICTR Statute; Article 17(4)(a), SCSL Statute; Article 16(4)(a), STL Statute; Article 67(1)(a), ICC Statute.

[156] William A. Schabas, *The International Criminal Court: A Commentary on the Rome Statute* (Oxford: OUP, 2010) 803.

[157] *Prosecutor v. Kupreškić et al.*, Judgment, Case No. IT-95-16-A, 23 October 2001, para 88; *Prosecutor v. Taylor*, Decision on Urgent Defence Motion Regarding a Fatal Defect in the Prosecution's Second Amended Indictment Relating to the Pleading of JCE, Case No. SCSL-03-1-T-752, 27 February 2009, para 57.

[158] *Prosecutor v. Simić*, Reasons for Decision on Prosecutor's Motion to Use Telephone Interviews, Case No. IT-95-9-T, 11 March 2003.

non-permanent tribunals and the ICC Regulations provide further detail as to what exactly is required to ensure that the accused is fully aware of the scope and content of the charges against him or her.[159] In *Kupreškić*, the Appeals Chamber of the ICTY found that 'the thrust of' an allegation against two of the accused changed so greatly over the course of the prosecution case that it was not a reflection of what was pleaded in the indictment,[160] thereby rendering the trial unfair.[161]

A major area of controversy for the ICC has been the operation of Regulation 55 of its Regulations of the Court, which permits a Trial Chamber to amend the legal characterization of the facts underlying the charges. The exercise of the Chamber's discretion in this regard must be 'without exceeding the facts and circumstances described in the charges and any amendments to the charges',[162] a limitation that is reflected in Article 74(2) of the Statute, which states that the Trial Chamber's judgment must not exceed the facts and circumstances set out in the charges.

In *Lubanga*, the Trial Chamber considered that it could potentially re-characterize the facts to encompass charges relating to sexual violence.[163] In overcoming the difficulty posed by the proviso that such re-characterization may not exceed the charges, the Chamber considered that Regulation 55 envisioned two separate regimes: under Regulation 55(1), the facts could be re-characterized in the judgment itself, but this re-characterization must fall within the ambit of the charges, as confirmed, while under Regulation 55(2), re-characterization can happen at any stage of the trial, and this re-characterization was not limited to the charges.[164] The Appeals Chamber overturned this ruling, finding that Article 74(2) 'confines the scope of Regulation 55 to the facts and circumstances described in the charges and any amendment thereto',[165] regardless of what stage of the trial the modification of the legal characterization of those facts and circumstances occurs.

[159] Rule 121, ICC RPE; Regulation 52, ICC Regulations; Rules 47, ICTY, ICTR, and SCSL RPE; Rule 68, STL RPE.

[160] *Kupreškić* Appeal Judgment (n 157), para 93.

[161] ibid., para 122.

[162] Regulation 55(1), ICC Regulations.

[163] *Situation in the DRC: Prosecutor v. Lubanga*, Decision Giving Notice to the Parties and Participants that the Legal Characterisation of the Facts may be Subject to Change in Accordance with Regulation 55(2) of the Regulations of the Court, Case No. ICC-01/04-01/06, 14 July 2009.

[164] ibid., paras 27–8.

[165] *Situation in the DRC: Prosecutor v. Lubanga*, Judgment on the Appeals of Mr Lubanga Dyilo and the Prosecutor against the Decision of Trial Chamber I of 14 July 2009 entitled 'Decision Giving Notice to the Parties and Participants that the Legal Characterization of the Facts may be Subject to Change in Accordance with Regulation 55(2) of the Regulations of the Court', Case No. ICC-01/04-01/06, 8 December 2009, para 93.

In *Katanga and Ngudjolo*, the defendants were originally charged with committing crimes within the jurisdiction of the Court through 'indirect co-perpetration', under Article 25(3)(a) of the Statute.[166] The Trial Chamber, after the close of trial and just before its judgment was expected, re-characterized Katanga's mode of liability to common purpose liability under Article 25(3)(d)(ii).[167] Ngudjolo was acquitted shortly thereafter.[168] Katanga argued that the decision breached his right to be promptly informed of the charges, affected his ability to prepare adequately for trial, and that his defence strategy, including his decision to testify, might have been different, had he known that the form of participation charged could have changed at the late stage in proceedings that it did.[169] The Appeals Chamber rejected this argument, finding that 'there is no reason of principle as to why, without more, the timing of the notice of re-characterization would result in a violation of Mr Katanga's right to be informed promptly of the charges',[170] and that it would be for the Trial Chamber to counteract any potential unfairness.[171] However, as Rigney has pointed out, it is impossible to take measures to ensure the 'effective preparation of the defence' pursuant to Regulation 55(3) when the trial has already ended.[172] Moreover, the decision on the re-characterization of the facts provided insufficient detail on the new charge—it was unclear who the other members of the group acting with a common purpose were, for example[173]—so even if the changing of the mode of liability after the close of trial could hypothetically conform with fair trial requirements by taking extra measures to assist the preparation of the defence, in this instance, the decision was in breach of Article 67(1)(a)'s 'nature, cause and content of the charge' requirements. It is acknowledged that one of the

[166] *Situation in the DRC: Prosecutor v. Katanga and Ngudjolo*, Decision on the Confirmation of Charges, Case No. ICC-01/04-01/07, 30 September 2008, paras 575–7.

[167] *Situation in the DRC: Prosecutor v. Katanga and Ngudjolo*, Decision on the Implementation of Regulation 55 of the Regulations of the Court and Severing the Charges against the Accused Persons, Case No. ICC-01/04-01/07, 21 November 2012.

[168] *Situation in the DRC: Prosecutor v. Ngudjolo*, Judgment Pursuant to Article 74 of the Statute, Case No. ICC-01/04-02/12, 18 December 2012.

[169] *Situation in the DRC: Prosecutor v. Katanga*, Judgment on the Appeal of Mr Germain Katanga against the Decision of Trial Chamber II of 21 November 2012 entitled 'Decision on the Implementation of Regulation 55 of the Regulations of the Court and Severing the Charges against the Accused Persons', Case No. ICC-01/04-01/07, 27 March 2013, paras 66–8.

[170] ibid., para 94.

[171] ibid., para 91.

[172] Sophie Rigney, '"The Words Don't Fit You": Recharacterisation of the Charges, Trial Fairness, and *Katanga*' (2014) 15(2) *Melbourne JIL* 515, 527.

[173] *Katanga*, Judgment on the Appeal of Mr Germain Katanga against the Decision of Trial Chamber II of 21 November 2012 entitled 'Decision on the Implementation of Regulation 55 of the Regulations of the Court and Severing the Charges against the Accused Persons' (n 169), para 102; ibid., Dissenting Opinion of Judge Cuno Tarfusser, paras 22–7.

key purposes of adopting Regulation 55 was to promote efficiency by discouraging cumulative or alternative charging in the indictment.[174] Inefficient as such charging practices might be, at least the defendant is on notice of the alternate modes of liability charged and can prepare his or her defence accordingly, whereas the uncertain possibility of Regulation 55 being applied leaves defence counsel to contend with a limitless and vague set of possible modes of liability not delineated from the outset of the trial. Thus, the more recent practice of charging alternative modes of liability is preferable,[175] and Regulation 55 should be used cautiously.

The international criminal tribunals' statutes add that the accused should be informed of the charges in a language that he or she understands;[176] the ICC Statute mandates that he or she should 'fully' understand and speak the language in question.[177] This is discussed in greater detail in the next section.

3.6 Right to an Interpreter

As well as having the right to be informed of the charges against them in a language that they understand, accused persons before international criminal tribunals have the right to free assistance of an interpreter, if they cannot understand or speak the language used by the tribunal.[178] The ICC's provision expands on this right, by stating that the accused is entitled to an interpreter if he or she does not 'fully' understand or speak the language of proceedings.[179] In its early jurisprudence, the Court had to determine the extent of the right to translation in this context. An early decision in

[174] Jennifer Easterday, 'A Closer Look at Regulation 55 at the ICC', *International Justice Monitor*, 28 May 2013, available online at http://www.ijmonitor.org/2013/05/a-closer-look-at-regulation-55-at-the-icc/ (last accessed 4 June 2015).

[175] *Situation in Côte d'Ivoire, Prosecutor v. Blé Goudé*, Decision on the 'Defence Request to Amend the Document Containing the Charges for Lack of Specificity', Case No. ICC-02/11-02/11, 1 September 2014, paras 7–8.

[176] Article 21(4)(a), ICTY Statute; Article 20(4)(a), ICTR Statute; Article 17(4)(a), SCSL Statute; Article 16(4)(a), STL Statute; Article 67(1)(a), ICC Statute.

[177] Article 67(1)(a), ICC Statute.

[178] Article 16(4)(g), STL Statute; Article 20(4)(f), ICTR Statute; Article 21(4)(f), ICTY Statute; Article 17(4)(f), SCSL Statute; Article 67(1)(f), ICC Statute. Suspects also have the right to be assisted by an interpreter during investigations, pursuant to Article 15, STL Statute; Article 17(3), ICTR Statute; Article 18(3), ICTY Statute; Article 55(1)(c), ICC Statute.

[179] Article 67(1)(f), ICC Statute. See further, *Situation in the DRC: Prosecutor v. Katanga*, Judgment on the appeal of Mr Germain Katanga against the decision of the Pre-Trial Chamber I entitled 'Decision on the defence request concerning languages', Case No. ICC 01/04-01/07, 27 May 2008, para 49 ('There must be a difference between an entitlement to a language one understands or speaks (or simply understands) and a language one fully understands and speaks.')

Katanga noted the Registry's observation that the accused could understand and communicate in French, and denied him an interpreter in the language of his choice, Lingala.[180] The Appeals Chamber found this to be an erroneous interpretation of the higher standard set down in the Court's Statute, and that 'an accused's request for interpretation into a language other than the Court's language must be granted as long as he or she is not abusing his or her rights under Article 67 of the Statute'.[181] It found that an accused will be considered to 'fully' understand and speak a language when he or she is completely fluent in the language in ordinary, non-technical conversation; if there is any doubt as to their competence, their request should be accommodated.[182]

The right to an interpreter also extends to the translation of such documents 'as are necessary to meet the requirements of fairness'.[183] The ECtHR has held that 'all those documents or statements in the proceedings instituted against [the accused] which it is necessary for him to understand in order to have the benefit of a fair trial' must be translated.[184] The ICC has held that the right to translation extends to all those documents necessary for the accused's understanding of the charges or preparation of their defence.[185] Where the accused and his or her team of defence counsel is fluent in one of the working languages of the Court, but proceedings are being conducted in the other working language, as was the case in *Lubanga*, translations of certain key documents and an interpreter will be made freely available to the accused and the defence team.[186] Where the accused is not assisted by counsel, but is conducting his or her defence in person, a more extensive range of evidentiary documents will need to be translated to meet the requirements of fairness.[187]

[180] *Situation in the DRC: Prosecutor v. Katanga*, Decision on the Defence Request Concerning Languages, Case No. ICC-01/04-01/07, 21 December 2007.

[181] *Situation in the DRC: Prosecutor v. Katanga*, Judgment on the appeal of Mr Germain Katanga against the decision of the Pre-Trial Chamber I entitled 'Decision on the defence request concerning languages', Case No. ICC 01/04-01/07, 27 May 2008, para 62.

[182] ibid., para 61.

[183] Article 67(1)(f), ICC Statute.

[184] *Leudicke and ors v. Germany*, Judgment, Series A No. 29, 28 November 1978, para 48.

[185] *Situation in the CAR: Prosecutor v. Bemba et al.*, Decision on the Defence request for an order requiring the translation of evidence, Case No. ICC-01/05-01/13-177, 11 February 2014, para 6. See also, *Situation in Côte d'Ivoire, Prosecutor v. Gbagbo*, Decision on Mr Gbagbo's request for translation and an extension of time for the filing of a response to the document in support of the appeal, ICC-02/11-01/11-489, 22 August 2013, para 12.

[186] *Situation in the DRC: Prosecutor v. Lubanga*, Decision on the Requests of the Defence of 3 and 4 July 2006, Case No. ICC-01/04-01/06, 4 August 2006.

[187] *Situation in Uganda: Prosecutor v. Ongwen*, Decision Setting the Regime for Evidence Disclosure and Other Related Matters, Case No. ICC-02/04-01/15, 27 February 2015, para 33.

3.7 Right to Trial in the Presence of the Accused

Although the right to be present at trial is not specifically laid down in the majority of international criminal law statutes (with the exception of Article 67(1)(d) of the ICC Statute and Article 16(4)(d) of the STL Statute, both of which include exceptions to the right), the international criminal tribunals have developed quite an extensive case law on the right to trial in the presence of the accused.[188] There are, broadly speaking, three types of absence from trial. The first is where the accused has persisted in disruptive behaviour and has been given a warning that continued disruption will result in removal from the courtroom.[189] In *Gbao*, the Chamber held that:

> [I]t is a clear indication that it is not the policy of the criminal law to allow the absence of an accused person or his disruptive conduct to impede the administration of justice or frustrate the ends of justice. To allow such an eventuality to prevail is tantamount to judicial abdication of the principle of legality and a capitulation to a frustration of the ends of justice without justification.[190]

Removal from the courtroom for disciplinary reasons is permissible under human rights law, according to Trechsel, provided that the exclusion for the courtroom only persists for as long as is strictly necessary to maintain courtroom decorum.[191] If the accused promises to cease the disruption, he or she should not continue to be excluded as a form of punishment.[192] In the interest of protecting the accused's right to be present in proceedings, some tribunals have made provision for the removed defendant to follow proceedings via video-link in this situation,[193] which seems to be a sensible compromise. Where the disruption is unintentional, for example, where it is caused by

[188] See e.g. *Prosecutor v. Zigiranyirazo*, Decision on Interlocutory Appeal, Case No. ICTR-2001-73-AR73, 30 October 2006 ('*Zigiranyirazo* Interlocutory Appeal Decision'), paras 11–12; see also, *Prosecutor v. Karemera et al.*, Decision on Nzirorera's Interlocutory Appeal Concerning his Right to be Present at Trial, Case No. ICTR-98-44-AR73.10, 5 October 2007 ('*Niziroera* Interlocutory Appeal') paras 11–15. The right to be present at trial is included in Article 14(3)(d) of the ICCPR. It has also been recognized by the European Court of Human Rights in *Colozza v. Italy* (1985) 7 EHRR 516, 12 February 1985, para 27 and *Stanford v. UK* (1994) Series A No. 282-A, 23 February 1994, para 26.

[189] Rules 80(B), ICTY, ICTR, and SCSL RPE; Article 63(2), ICC Statute and Rule 170, ICC RPE.

[190] *Prosecutor v. Gbao*, Ruling on the Issue of the Refusal of the Third Accused, Augustine Gbao, to Attend Hearing of the Special Court for Sierra Leone on 7 July 2004 and Succeeding Days, Case No. SCSL-2004-15-T, 12 July 2004, para 8.

[191] Stefan Trechsel, *Human Rights in Criminal Proceedings* (Oxford: OUP, 2006) 253.

[192] ibid.

[193] Rule 80(B), SCSL RPE.

illness, it would be disproportionate to continue with proceedings in the absence of the accused.[194]

The second type of absence from trial is where the accused has explicitly waived his or her right to be present. It is generally accepted that proceedings may continue in the absence of the accused where he or she has asked to be excused for a short period of time and has consented to the trial's continuation in his or her absence.[195] The Appeals Chamber of the ICC has set down the following conditions for voluntary absence from trial:

> (i) the absence of the accused can only take place in exceptional circumstances and must not become the rule; (ii) the possibility of alternative measures must have been considered, including, but not limited to, changes to the trial schedule or a short adjournment of the trial; (iii) any absence must be limited to that which is strictly necessary; (iv) the accused must have explicitly waived his or her right to be present at trial; (v) the rights of the accused must be fully ensured in his or her absence, in particular through representation by counsel; and (vi) the decision as to whether the accused may be excused from attending part of his or her trial must be taken on a case-by-case basis, with due regard to the subject matter of the specific hearings that the accused would not attend.[196]

In 2013, the ICC RPE were amended to reflect this jurisprudence. Under the new Rules 134 *bis, ter* and *quater*, an accused person can make a request to be present via video-link technology only or to be absent during part of the trial, provided that he or she is represented by counsel. In making its determination on such requests, the Trial Chamber will be guided by the rights of the accused, the interests of justice, and whether alternative measures are possible.

194 *Prosecutor v. Karemera et al.*, Decision on Joseph Nzirorera's Motion for Stay of Proceedings while Unfit to Attend Trial or Certification to Appeal, Case No. ICTR-98-44-T, 11 July 2007; *Prosecutor v. Stanišić et al.*, Decision on Defence Appeal of the Decision on Future Course of Proceedings, Case No. IT-03-69-AR73.2, 16 May 2008.

195 *Situation in the DRC: Prosecutor v. Lubanga*, Transcript, Case No. ICC-01/04-01/06-T-172-Red3-ENG, 12 May 2009, 1–2; *Situation in the CAR: Prosecutor v. Bemba*, Transcript, Case No. ICC-01/05-01/08-T-183-Red-ENG, 7 November 2011, 1–2; *Situation in the CAR: Prosecutor v. Bemba*, Transcript, Case No. ICC-01/05- 01/08-T-306-Red-ENG, 12 April 2013, 62; *Situation in the CAR: Prosecutor v. Bemba*, Transcript, Case No. ICC-01/05-01/08-T-324-ENG, 17 June 2013, 16–17; *Situation in the CAR: Prosecutor v. Bemba*, Transcript, Case No. ICC-01/05-01/08-T-331-CONF-ENG, 27 June 2013, 2–3; *Situation in Kenya: Prosecutor v. Ruto and Sang*, Judgment on the appeal of the Prosecutor against the decision of Trial Chamber V(a) of 18 June 2013 entitled 'Decision on Mr Ruto's Request for Excusal from Continuous Presence at Trial', Case No. ICC-01/09-01/11, 25 October 2013.

196 *Ruto and Sang*, Judgment on the appeal of the Prosecutor against the decision of Trial Chamber V(a) of 18 June 2013 entitled 'Decision on Mr Ruto's Request for Excusal from Continuous Presence at Trial', ibid., para 2.

The third, and most controversial, type of absence from trial is when the accused can be said to have implicitly waived his or her right to be present by absconding from the trial or by evading arrest. Article 12 of the IMT Charter allowed the Tribunal to try any defendant in their absence, if they had not been found or if the Tribunal deemed it necessary in the interests of justice. The ICTY, ICTR, and SCSL did not envision allowing *in absentia* trials in this context; upon establishment of the ICTY, the UN Secretary General expressed the view that this would not be consistent with Article 14 of the International Covenant on Civil and Political Rights (ICCPR).[197] The ICC Trial Chamber suggested that a trial *in absentia* might feasibly be possible where the accused had absconded, on the basis that it would 'hold the Court hostage to impunity by negating the power of the Chamber to proceed with the trial of an accused who deliberately absconded from his own trial in circumstances that are precisely calculated to frustrate the trial and the course of justice'.[198] This suggestion was strongly refuted by the Appeals Chamber, which found that the purpose behind Article 63(1) of the Statute was to preclude any interpretation of Article 67(1)(d) allowing trials *in absentia* when the accused absconded or failed to appear for trial.[199]

The STL expressly permits trials *in absentia*, where the accused has either expressly waived his or her right to be present, has not been transferred to the Tribunal by a state, has absconded or cannot be found and all reasonable steps have been taken to secure his or her appearance and inform him or her of the charges.[200] In the case of hearings being conducted in the accused's absence, the STL must ensure that the following conditions are met:

(a) The accused has been notified, or served with the indictment, or notice has otherwise been given of the indictment through publication in the media or communication to the State of residence or nationality;
(b) The accused has designated a defence counsel of his or her own choosing, to be remunerated either by the accused or, if the accused is proved to be indigent, by the Tribunal;
(c) Whenever the accused refuses or fails to appoint a defence counsel, such counsel has been assigned by the Defence Office of the Tribunal with a view to ensuring full representation of the interests and rights of the accused.[201]

[197] UN Doc. S/25704, para 101.

[198] *Situation in Kenya: Prosecutor v. Ruto and Sang*, Decision on Mr Ruto's Request for Excusal from Continuous Presence at Trial, Case No. ICC-01/09-01/11, 18 June 2013, para 44.

[199] *Ruto and Sang*, Judgment on the appeal of the Prosecutor against the decision of Trial Chamber V(a) of 18 June 2013 entitled 'Decision on Mr Ruto's Request for Excusal from Continuous Presence at Trial' (n 195), para 54.

[200] Article 22(1), STL Statute.

[201] Article 22(2), STL Statute.

Where the accused is convicted *in absentia*, the accused has the right to be retried by the STL, unless he or she designated counsel for the original trial or has accepted the judgment.[202] Much ink has been spilled on the conformity or otherwise of this provision with international human rights standards.[203] While it would seem that some limited support can be found in the jurisprudence of the Human Rights Committee and ECtHR for *in absentia* trials in certain circumstances,[204] the STL's provisions fall short in a number of respects. First, they appear to allow an *in absentia* trial to be held where the Tribunal assumes that the accused knows of the indictment, through its publication in the media or its communication to the state of residence or nationality; the HRC in *Maleki* held that an assumption of knowledge was insufficient—it must be shown that the accused has actually been informed of the proceedings.[205] Second, as Jordash and Parker have noted, the right to retrial has the potential to be ineffective, given that the STL has a limited mandate and may have closed its doors by the time any individual who has been convicted *in absentia* is apprehended.[206]

There is perhaps a broader point to be made on the practical utility of holding total *in absentia* trials. In the early days of the ICTY, some commentators predicted that such high-profile accused persons as Karadžić, Mladić, and Kordić would evade justice, thereby justifying their trials *in absentia*.[207] Yet, as we know, all of these high-profile accused were ultimately transferred to the Tribunal and stood trial. What value would an *in absentia* trial have offered? As the ICTY itself noted in *Blaškić*, 'it would not be appropriate to

[202] Article 22(3), STL Statute.

[203] Paola Gaeta, 'To Be (Present) or Not To Be (Present): Trials *In Absentia* before the Special Tribunal for Lebanon' (2007) 5 *JICJ* 1165; Wayne Jordash and Tim Parker, 'Trials *in Absentia* at the Special Tribunal for Lebanon: Incompatibility with International Human Rights Law' (2010) 8 *JICJ* 487; Charles C. Jalloh, 'Self-representation and the Use of Assigned, Standby and Amicus Counsel', in Linda Carter and Fausto Pocar (eds), *International Criminal Procedure: The Interface of Civil Law and Common Law Legal System* (Cheltenham: Edward Elgar, 2013), 155; Cecile Aptel, 'Some Innovations in the Statute of the Special Tribunal for Lebanon' (2007) 5 *JICJ* 1123; Ralph Riachy, 'Trial in Absentia in the Lebanese Judicial System and at the Special Tribunal for Lebanon: Challenge or Evolution?' (2010) 8 *JICJ* 1305; Mohammad H. Zakerhossein and Anne-Marie De Brouwer, 'Diverse Approaches to Total and Partial *In Absentia* Trials by International Criminal Tribunals' (2015) 26 CLF 181.

[204] *Mbenge v. Zaire*, Communication No. 16/1977, UN Doc. CCPR/C/18/D/16/1977; *Maleki v. Italy*, Communication No. 699/1996, UN Doc. CCPR/C/66/D/699/1996; *Colozza v. Italy*, Application No. 9024/80, Judgment, 12 February 1985; *Somogyi v. Italy*, Application No. 67972/01, Judgment, 18 May 2004.

[205] *Maleki v. Italy*, ibid., paras 9.3–9.4; *Somogyi v. Italy*, ibid., para 72 ('Article 6 of the Convention imposes on every national court an obligation to check whether the defendant has had the opportunity to apprise himself of the proceedings against him.').

[206] Jordash and Parker (n 203) 498.

[207] Herman Schwartz, 'Trials in Absentia' (1996) 4(1) *Human Rights Brief* 12.

hold *in absentia* proceedings against persons falling under the primary jurisdiction of the International Tribunal … it would prove extremely difficult or even impossible for an international criminal court to determine the innocence or guilt of that accused.'[208] Arguably, trial without the presence of the accused and full participation in their own defence would have encouraged the ICTY's retractors who seek to portray it as a biased and unfair institution, and would have discouraged state cooperation with the Tribunal in later years. Moreover, trials *in absentia* appear to run contrary to the goals of international criminal justice; they cannot achieve retribution because a convicted person who is not present at the seat of the tribunal is unlikely to ever serve their sentence, and their didactic or truth-establishing function is lessened by the absence of the defendant—a central character in any criminal trial (this, according to Jordash and Parker, is akin to staging '*Hamlet* without the Prince'[209]). The STL itself recognized that trial in an accused's presence was in the best interests of the Tribunal 'with its purpose of achieving a fair and efficient trial to establish truth and promote reconciliation within Lebanon';[210] nevertheless, the legal framework of the Tribunal gives a Chamber little choice but to proceed *in absentia* where the conditions of Article 22 are met,[211] and the first *in absentia* trial commenced in January 2014.[212]

3.8 Right to Self-Representation or Representation through Counsel

Although the accused person has the right to counsel of his or her choosing,[213] this right is fettered somewhat by provisions on counsel competence, experience, and qualifications set down in the tribunals' RPE.[214] Where the accused is indigent, the international criminal tribunal will pay for his or her defence; the administration of legal aid is part of the Registry's functions.[215] In May 2014,

[208] *Prosecutor v. Blaškić*, Judgment on the Request of the Republic of Croatia for Review of the Decision of Trial Chamber II of 18 July 1997, Case No. IT-95-14-T, 29 October 1997, para 59.

[209] Jordash and Parker (n 203) 501.

[210] *Prosecutor v. Ayyash et al.*, Decision to Hold Trial *In Absentia*, Case No. STL-11/01/I/TC, 1 February 2012, para 20.

[211] ibid., para 41 (stating that to await the arrest of the accused would be to defeat the purpose of the Tribunal's Statute and Rules).

[212] *Prosecutor v. Ayyash et al.*, Transcript, Case No. STL-11-01, 16 January 2014.

[213] Article 21(4)(d) ICTY Statute; Article 20(4)(d) ICTR Statute; Article 17(4)(d) SCSL Statute; Article 67(1)(d) ICC Statute; Article 16(4)(d) STL Statute.

[214] Rules 44–5, ICTY, ICTR, and SCSL RPE; Rules 58–9, STL RPE; Rule 22, ICC RPE; Regulations 67–73, ICC Regulations.

[215] Rule 21, ICC RPE; Rule 45, ICTY and ICTR RPE. This comes under the remit of the Defence Offices before the STL and SCSL: Rule 57, STL RPE; Rule 45, SCSL RPE.

the Registry of the ICTY ordered one accused, Praljak, to repay almost three million euro to cover the costs of Tribunal-paid defence counsel provided during trial, when it discovered that the accused had sufficient resources to fund his own defence.[216] Shortly thereafter, Praljak, who had opted to self-represent on appeal when paid counsel was withdrawn from him, requested a stay of proceedings until translations were received by him, given that he did not speak either English or French.[217] The Appeals Chamber ordered the Registry to assign counsel to Praljak, to be reimbursed by him, despite the fact that he had not yet reimbursed the Registry for earlier legal services provided, finding that to halt proceedings until past costs were recovered would run contrary to the interests of justice.[218] This shows the difficult balance that Chambers have to strike; while the tribunals' legal frameworks provide that counsel should be paid for by the tribunal only where the accused 'does not have sufficient means' to pay for their own counsel, they also have a duty to ensure adequate legal representation and that proceedings are not unduly delayed for co-accused individuals.

The question of whether an accused person before an international tribunal should be afforded the right to represent themselves has been one of the thorniest issues before the SCSL, ICTR, and ICTY. While it had not, at the time of writing, afforded much scope for debate before the STL or the ICC, it will doubtless become an issue at some point in future proceedings. The conundrum raised by self-representation is that it is a right recognized by almost all of the leading international and regional human rights tribunals,[219] as well as the statutes of the tribunals,[220] but there is the danger that accused persons will use the right as a vehicle for political diatribes or propaganda.[221]

[216] *Prosecutor v. Prlić et al.*, Order on the Registrar's Application Pursuant to Rule 45(E) of the Rules, Case No. IT-04-74-A, 13 May 2014.

[217] *Prosecutor v. Prlić et al.*, Decision on Praljak's Request for Stay of Proceedings, Case No. IT-04-74-A, 27 June 2014, para 9.

[218] ibid., para 17.

[219] Article 14(3)(d), ICCPR; Article 6(3)(c), ECHR; Article 8(2)(d), ACHR. Article 7(1)(c) of the Banjul Charter does not explicitly reference the right of the accused to defend himself or herself in person.

[220] Article 21(4)(d), ICTY Statute; Article 20(4)(d), ICTR Statute; Article 17(4)(d), SCSL Statute; Article 67(1)(d), ICC Statute; Article 16(4)(d), STL Statute.

[221] Nina H. B. Jorgensen, 'The Problem of Self-Representation at International Criminal Tribunals' (2006) 4 *JICJ* 64, 76. There is a wide body of literature on this element of international criminal procedure, including: Gillian Higgins, 'The Development of the Right to Self-Representation before the International Criminal Tribunals' in Shane Darcy and Joseph Powderly (eds), *Judicial Creativity at the International Criminal Tribunals* (Oxford: OUP, 2010) 252; Jarinde Temminck Tuinstra, 'The ICTY's Continuing Struggle with the Right to Self-Representation' in Bert Swart, Alexander Zahar, and Göran Sluiter (eds), *The Legacy of the International Criminal Tribunal for the Former Yugoslavia* (Oxford: OUP, 2011) 345; Rachel K. Jones, 'Untangling the Right to Self-Representation in the International Criminal Tribunal for the Former Yugoslavia' (2009) 43 *Georgia LR* 1285; Eugene Cerruti, 'Self-Representation in the International Arena: Removing a

Tribunal practice is far from consistent on how best to resolve the issues that self-representation raises, but some approaches have been both principled and pragmatic, and ought to be welcomed. In *Milošević*, for example, the Tribunal recognized that it was appropriate to follow the Human Rights Committee's guidance on the matter, and declined to impose counsel on an unwilling accused.[222] It did note, however, the provisions in its Rules under which obstreperous defendants could be removed from the courtroom, and stated that if the accused did decide to obstruct proceedings whilst representing himself, he could be said to have relinquished his right to self-represent, and counsel would have to be imposed for such a time as he was absent from proceedings.[223] This approach had the advantage of both respecting the rights of the accused and ensuring that self-representation could not be used to hijack the trial. By contrast, some Chambers have taken a rather paternalistic approach to the issue of self-representation by imposing counsel apparently in the interests of ensuring the best legal representation for the accused.[224]

Even though counsel may be able offer a more effective defence to self-representing defendants, the accused can be seen as having been willing to take that risk, and so long as he or she does not disrupt proceedings or use his or her self-representation as a vehicle for spreading propaganda, he or she should be allowed to proceed in that manner.[225] As Fletcher has argued, where an individual has capacity to consent and consents to something that would, without consent, be a clear breach of his rights—such as having medical treatment or testifying against themselves—that conduct can no longer be said to be a violation of the person's rights, owing to the consent.[226] Counsel should only be imposed with the agreement of the accused, or where he or she has failed to co-operate with the tribunal by refusing to appear for trial, or has deliberately obstructed proceedings. Where an accused has

False Right of Spectacle' (2009) 40 *Georgetown JIL* 919; Nina H. B. Jorgensen, 'The Right of the Accused to Self-Representation Before International Criminal Tribunals' (2004) 98 *AJIL* 711; Michael P. Scharf, 'Self-Representation Versus Assignment of Defence Counsel before International Criminal Tribunals' (2006) 4 *JICJ* 31, and Joanne Williams, 'Slobodan Milošević and the Guarantee of Self-Representation' (2006–2007) 32 *Brooklyn JIL* 553.

222 *Prosecutor v. Milošević*, Reasons for Decision on the Prosecution Motion concerning Assignment of Counsel, Case No. IT-02-54-T, 4 April 2003, paras 36–7.

223 ibid., paras 40–1.

224 See e.g. *Prosecutor v. Norman*, Decision on the Application of Samuel Hinga Norman for Self Representation under Article 17(4)(d) of the Statute of the Special Court, Case No. SCSL-2004-14-T, 8 June 2004.

225 This risk taken by the accused was recognized in *Prosecutor v. Krajišnik*, Decision on Krajišnik Request and on Prosecution Motion, Case No. IT-00-39-A, 11 September 2007, para 41.

226 George P. Fletcher, *Basic Concepts of Legal Thought* (Oxford: OUP, 1996) 109.

decided to self-represent, they can be said to have willingly accepted that they may not be as adequately represented as if their case were presented by qualified legal counsel.

A balance between the right to self-representation and the adequacy of representation was struck in *Krajišnik*, where the accused opted to self-represent on appeal. The accused had requested in the middle of the trial that he proceed to represent himself, having previously been represented by allegedly incompetent defence counsel. This request was denied.[227] It was recognized that the accused was inadequately represented at trial and the accused was permitted to represent himself for the appeal stage of proceedings. However, conscious that he may not have been able to argue the intricacies of joint criminal enterprise mode of responsibility, Krajišnik requested the appearance of an American lawyer, Alan Dershowitz, on his behalf for this limited purpose. On 28 February 2008, the Chamber granted this request, holding that, '[t]here is no fundamental reason why a defendant may not make different choices—self-representing or engaging legal counsel—with regard to different issues.'[228] This approach appears to have been a sensible resolution to seeing that self-representing accused individuals who are forbidden from giving instruction to standby counsel or *amici curiae*[229] are adequately represented. This outcome is far more preferable than those decisions which have placed self-representation and assistance by counsel in binary opposition, holding that an accused must opt for one form of representation or the other.[230]

Counsel has been imposed on self-representing defendants on occasions when their behaviour has been seen to be disruptive to proceedings.[231] Judge

[227] *Prosecutor v. Krajišnik*, Reasons for Oral Decision denying Mr Krajišnik's Request to Proceed Unrepresented by Counsel, Case No. IT-00-39-T, 18 August 2005.

[228] *Prosecutor v. Krajišnik*, Decision on Momčilo Krajišnik's motion to reschedule status conference and permit Alan Dershowitz appear, Case No. IT-00-39-A, 28 February 2008, para 8; see further, Yvonne McDermott, 'Case commentary: *Prosecutor v. Krajišnik*, Decision on Momčilo Krajišnik's motion to reschedule status conference and permit Alan Dershowitz appear' in André Klip and Göran Sluiter (eds), *Annotated Leading Cases of International Criminal Tribunals: Vol XXXV: The International Criminal Tribunal for the Former Yugoslavia 2007–2008* (Antwerp: Intersentia, 2012) 181.

[229] See *Prosecutor v. Krajišnik*, Decision on Motion Requesting Permission for *Amicus Curiae* to File Submission on Matters Arising out of Appellant's Appeal Brief, Prosecution Response and Appellant's Reply, Case No. IT-00-39-A, 23 November 2007, and *Prosecutor v. Krajišnik*, Decision on *Amicus Curiae* Motion for Guidance, Case No. IT-00-39-A, 11 June 2008, stating that '*amicus curiae* remain[ed] under an obligation to work independently from Mr Krajišnik'.

[230] *Prosecutor v. Krajišnik*, Decision on Krajišnik Request and on Prosecution Motion, Case No. IT-00-39-A, 11 September 2007, paras 40-41. *Prosecutor v. Milošević*, Decision on Interlocutory Appeal of the Trial Chamber's Decision on the Assignment of Defence Counsel, Case No. IT-02-54-AR73.7, 1 November 2004, para 11.

[231] *Prosecutor v. Šešelj*, Order Concerning Appointment of Standby Counsel and Delayed Commencement of Trial, Case No. IT-03-67-R77.2, 25 October 2006; *Prosecutor v. Krajišnik*,

Schomburg advised that this should only be used sparingly and only in the circumstance of continued violations, noting that '[d]omestic law rarely regards obstructive behaviour as a reason to impose counsel, although this is certainly possible. Rather, such conduct is usually addressed by sanctioning an accused without touching upon issues of representation.'[232] The jurisprudence of the ECtHR recognizes that it may sometimes be necessary to impose counsel in order to preserve the decorum of proceedings, and that the right to represent oneself is not unlimited.[233] In the case of *Šešelj*, however, the Appeals Chamber could be said to have gone too far on the rights of the accused by twice overruling Trial Chamber decisions on the imposition of counsel on a disruptive defendant.[234] The overly-protective approach to the right to represent oneself espoused by the Appeals Chamber in *Šešelj* is inconsistent with the practice of most states.[235]

It could be argued that this approach, by going beyond the limitations on the right set down in the jurisprudence of the European Court of Human Rights, actually embraces the highest standards of fairness. But the highest standards of fairness do not translate as ensuring that the accused is granted their every request. The abuse of one's right to self-represent to defame fellow participants in the trial,[236] prevent the tribunal from carrying out its day-to-day activities,[237] or to abuse and intimidate witnesses,[238] as Šešelj has, clearly implies that the accused has forfeited his rights, in

Decision on Momcilo Krajišnik's request to self-represent, on Counsel's motions in relation to appointment of *amicus curiae*, and on the Prosecution motion of 16 February 2007, Case No. IT-00-39-A, 11 May 2007.

[232] *Prosecutor v. Krajišnik*, Decision on Momcilo Krajisnik's request to self-represent, on Counsel's motions in relation to appointment of amicus curiae, and on the Prosecution motion of 16 February 2007, Case No. IT-00-39-A, 11 May 2007, Fundamentally Dissenting Opinion of Judge Schomburg, para 4.

[233] *Croissant v. Germany* (1993) 16 EHRR 135, 25 September 1992, para 29; *Mayzit v. Russia* (2006) 43 EHRR 38, 20 January 2005.

[234] *Prosecutor v. Šešelj*, Decision on Assignment of Counsel, Case No. IT-03-67-T, 21 August 2006; *Prosecutor v. Šešelj*, Decision on Appeal against the Trial Chamber's Decision on Assignment of Counsel, Case No. IT-03-67-A, 20 October 2006; *Prosecutor v. Šešelj*, Reasons for Decision (No. 2) on Assignment of Counsel, Case No. IT-03-67-T, 27 November 2006; *Prosecutor v. Šešelj*, Decision on Appeal against the Trial Chamber's Decision (No. 2) on Assignment of Counsel, Case No. IT-03-67-A, 8 December 2006. For an excellent analysis, see Alexander Zahar, 'Legal Aid, Self-Representation, and the Crisis at the Hague Tribunal' (2008) 19 *CLF* 241.

[235] *Prosecutor v. Milošević*, Decision on Interlocutory Appeal of the Trial Chamber's Decision on the Assignment of Defence Counsel, Case No. IT-02-54-AR73.7, 1 November 2004, para 12, referring to state practice from around the world.

[236] See the various defamatory and abusive submissions of the accused cited in *Prosecutor v. Šešelj*, Decision on Assignment of Counsel (n 234) paras 34–65.

[237] *Prosecutor v. Norman*, Decision on the Application of Samuel Hinga Norman for Self-Representation under Article 17(4)(d) of the Statute of the Special Court, (n 224) para 26.

[238] *Prosecutor v. Šešelj*, Decision on Assignment of Counsel (n 234) paras 63–5.

the same way that a defendant who deliberately causes delay to the trial reneges on his right to trial without undue delay for those periods of delay caused by him.[239] This argument was recognized by the Trial Chamber in *Milošević* that reasoned that since the right to be present at trial could be waived in situations of continued disruption, so too could the right to represent oneself.[240]

3.9 Right to a Public Trial

The late Judge Cassese once remarked that it was 'not enough … simply to administer international criminal justice impartially and with due regard for the rights of the accused. It must also carry out this activity under the scrutiny of the international community.'[241] Thus, the accused has the right to a public hearing, and the transparency of proceedings itself adds to the fairness of trials by allowing members of the public to observe the conduct of trials and assess first-hand whether proceedings are carried out fairly.[242] However, the right to a public trial is explicitly subject to conditions in the tribunals' statutes.[243] It is clear that proceedings can be held in closed session to protect confidential or sensitive information,[244] or to protect witnesses,[245] state agents,[246] or the accused.[247] In addition, a range of measures for witnesses, including using video technology, voice distortion, and/or shielding the witness from the view of the public gallery, may be implemented to protect witnesses and prevent traumatization, particularly for child witnesses and victims of sexual violence.[248]

[239] See above, Section 3.4, 62–63.

[240] *Prosecutor v. Milošević*, Decision on Interlocutory Appeal of the Trial Chamber's Decision on the Assignment of Defence Counsel, Case No. IT-02-54-AR73.7, 1 November 2004, para 13.

[241] 'Foreword by Judge Antonio Cassese, former President of the International Criminal Tribunal for the former Yugoslavia', (1997) *International Review of the Red Cross*, No. 321, 602.

[242] For example, Byrne's work on the ICTR is based on an empirical trial observation study: Rosemary Byrne, 'The New Public International Lawyer and the Hidden Art of International Criminal Trial Practice' (2010) 25 *Connecticut JIL* 243. Rule 79(C) of the SCSL RPE explicitly permits the Chamber to allow representatives of monitoring agencies to remain where the public has been excluded. It also states that such representatives may be granted access to the transcript of closed sessions, where appropriate.

[243] Article 21(2), ICTY Statute; Article 20(2), ICTR Statute; Article 17(2), SCSL Statute; Article 16(2), STL Statute; Articles 64(7) and 67(1), ICC Statute.

[244] Article 64(7), ICC Statute; Rule 137, STL RPE; Rules 79, ICTY, ICTR, and SCSL RPE.

[245] Article 68(2), ICC Statute; Rule 137, STL RPE; Rules 79, ICTY, ICTR, and SCSL RPE.

[246] Article 68(6), ICC Statute.

[247] Article 68(2), ICC Statute.

[248] Article 68(1), ICC Statute; Rules 75, SCSL, ICTY, and ICTR RPE; Rule 85(D), SCSL RPE; Rule 133, STL RPE.

Where a closed session is entered into, the Chamber must make public the reasons for this.[249] The explicit list of reasons for excluding the press and public from the proceedings varies between tribunals, but they can be generally classified as reasons pertaining to national security;[250] to protecting the privacy, security or identity of a victim or witness,[251] public order or morality,[252] or other reasons in the interests of justice.[253] The SCSL is unique in that it permits representatives of monitoring agencies to remain in the courtroom when the court is in closed session, where appropriate.[254] Where the reasons for redaction of transcripts no longer exist, a Chamber may decide to reclassify all or part of the transcript as public.[255]

Article 64(7) of the ICC Statute sets out two explicit exceptions to the principle of publicity of proceedings: the first is for the purposes of protecting victims, witnesses, or the accused under Article 68, and the second is 'to protect confidential or sensitive information'. Article 68(2) permits the conduct of proceedings *in camera* or the presentation of evidence by electronic or other means.[256] It states that such measures shall be ordered in the case of child victims or witnesses or victims of sexual violence, unless the Court decides otherwise, taking the views of the victim or witness into account. It may seem curious that the protection of the accused is included within the ambit of this provision, given that the accused has the right to a public trial pursuant to Article 67. Perhaps it might be deemed appropriate to enter into an *in camera* session to protect the physical security of the

[249] Regulation 20(1), ICC Regulations; Rules 79, ICTR, ICTY, and SCSL RPE; Rule 137, STL RPE.

[250] Rule 79, SCSL RPE; Rule 137, STL RPE. The STL RPE has separate subsections for 'security' and 'a state's national security interests'; it can be assumed that the first refers to the security of the Tribunal and those present at trial.

[251] Article 68(2), ICC Statute; Rules 79, ICTR, ICTY, and SCSL RPE; Rule 137, STL RPE.

[252] Rules 79, ICTR and ICTY RPE; Rule 137, STL RPE.

[253] Rules 79, ICTY, ICTR, and SCSL RPE; Rule 137, STL RPE.

[254] Rule 79(C), SCSL RPE.

[255] Regulation 20(3), ICC Regulations; *Situation in the DRC: Prosecutor v. Katanga and Ngudjolo*, Ordonnance portant instructions en vue de favoriser la publicité de la procédure, ICC-01/04-01/07, 31 January 2012, para 2.

[256] Rule 87, ICC RPE. The use of voice and image distortion, together with the use of pseudonyms, is quite commonplace, as evidenced by, inter alia, *Situation in the DRC: Prosecutor v. Lubanga*, Transcript, Case No. ICC-01/04-01/06, 16 January 1999; *Situation in the DRC: Prosecutor v. Katanga and Ngudjolo*, Order on Protective Measures for Certain Witnesses called by the Prosecutor and the Chamber (Rules 87 and 88 of the Rules of Procedure and Evidence), Case No. ICC-01/04-01/07, 9 December 2009, para 12. Where pseudonyms are used, the identities of the victims or witnesses are disclosed to the accused; see further, Schabas, *The International Criminal Court: A Commentary on the Rome Statute* (n 156) 825.

accused,[257] but the security of high-profile accused persons has been assured through less intrusive means by the tribunals, and this would not justify limitations on broadcasting hearings under Regulation 21. Donat-Cattin argues that in exceptional cases where the identity of an accused should be shielded from the public, technology could be used to hide his or her voice and face, and measures could be taken to prevent the location of the accused being made known, but to exclude the public from the entirety of the trial would appear extreme.[258] According to Bedont, the reason behind the inclusion of the accused in Article 68(2) is attributable to the fact that '[o]n certain issues, the delegates felt compelled to extract symbolic concessions in order to allay their egos, even if the compromise language did not further their objectives'.[259] In this instance, one delegation had proposed excluding the public from cases involving sexual violence, on the basis that this information might impact upon public morality; when other delegations resisted, one 'compromise' offered was that the accused would be included under the ambit of Article 68, and while this did not address the state's concern in any way, it was accepted.[260]

On the second exception to a public trial, the ICC Statute allows states to make an application to protect 'confidential or sensitive information'.[261] Article 72 sets out a detailed framework for such applications. Pursuant to Article 72(4), where it discovers that information or documents pertaining to the state have been or are likely to be disclosed in the course of proceedings and it believes that this disclosure would prejudice national security interests, a state has the right to intervene to request a resolution of the issue. This right is not limited to state parties to the Statute. Attempts will be made to resolve the issue,[262] but if the state continues to maintain that the information in question cannot be disclosed, it will notify the Prosecutor or the Court of the specific reasons for this ('unless a specific description of the reasons would itself necessarily result in such prejudice to the State's national security interests').[263] The Court will then determine whether the information is 'relevant and necessary' for the purposes of establishing the guilt or innocence of the accused.[264] If so, where the information in question was subject to a request for cooperation under Part 9, or where an individual has

[257] David Donat-Cattin, 'Article 68' in Otto Triffterer (ed.), *Commentary on the Rome Statute of the International Criminal Court: Observers' Notes, Article by Article* (3rd edn, Baden-Baden: Beck, 2015) 1677.

[258] ibid., 1689.

[259] Barbara Bedont, *Internal Report on the Diplomatic Conference* of *the International Center for Human Rights and Democratic Development* (unpublished), cited in Donat-Cattin, ibid.

[260] ibid. [261] Article 68(6), ICC Statute. [262] Article 68(5), ICC Statute.

[263] Article 72(6), ICC Statute. [264] Article 72(7), ICC Statute.

been requested to give this information or evidence, the Court may either request further consultations, refer the state to the Assembly of State Parties or the Security Council for its non-cooperation, or draw inferences on the existence or non-existence of a fact.[265] Article 72(7)(b) refers to 'all other circumstances', and this can be assumed to apply when the state or individual has not been directly asked to provide the information in question, but is concerned about that information being disclosed in Court. As such, the state's objection poses a threat to the publicity of the trial. In such circumstances, the Court can either order disclosure or not order disclosure.[266] Where it decides against ordering disclosure, the Court can 'make such inference ... as to the existence or non-existence of a fact, as may be appropriate in the circumstances'.[267]

Article 72 has been criticized for its ambiguity,[268] and rightly so. The drafting of this provision was very much overshadowed by events in the *Blaškić* case, where the ICTY Appeals Chamber determined that the Tribunal was not barred from examining documents raising national security concerns.[269] States were clearly concerned that they might be forced to hand over sensitive information, and that the Court would be the final arbiter of whether national security would be affected by such disclosure.[270] Article 72 was unsuccessfully raised in the *Kenya* situation before the ICC, where it was held that a reference to 'State House' in the document containing the charges was insufficient to substantiate the government's claims that national security interests were at risk, and the government's objections appeared to be based on a particular reading of the document containing the charges.[271]

3.10 Right to Present and Examine Evidence and Witnesses

Closely related to the right to a public trial is the right of the accused to examine the witnesses against him or her and obtain witnesses on his or

[265] Article 72(7)(a), ICC Statute. [266] Article 72(7)(b), ICC Statute. [267] ibid.

[268] Donald K. Piragoff, 'Protection of National Security Information' in Roy S. Lee (ed.), *The International Criminal Court: The Making of the Rome Statute* (The Hague: Kluwer Law International, 1999) 270.

[269] *Blaškić*, Judgment on the Request of the Republic of Croatia for Review of the Decision of Trial Chamber II of 18 July 1997 (n 208) paras 61–6.

[270] Schabas, *The International Criminal Court: A Commentary on the Rome Statute* (n 156) 865.

[271] *Situation in Kenya: Prosecutor v. Muthaura et al.*, Decision on the 'Request by the Government of Kenya in Respect of the Confirmation of Charges Proceeding', Case No. ICC-01/09-02/11, 20 September 2011, para 11.

her behalf under the same conditions as those against him or her. Some of the same concerns relating to national security and protection of victims and witnesses that apply to the publicity of proceedings, as discussed in the previous section, may also impact upon this right. The right is also an obvious component of the principle of equality of arms, which 'is intended ... to ensure that the Defence has the means to prepare and present its case equal to those available to the Prosecution'.[272] The accused has the right to present any evidence in his or her defence and to examine, or have examined, witnesses on his or her behalf under the same conditions as the evidence or witnesses against him or her,[273] and the ICTR has held that divergences in the means in which prosecution and defence evidence is presented may constitute a breach of equality of arms.[274] This section will analyse three aspects of the right to examine evidence and witnesses: disclosure, the powers of the tribunals in securing evidence, and the right to cross-examination of witnesses.

3.10.1 Disclosure

Disclosure of both inculpatory and exculpatory materials is easily one of the most litigated fair trial rights before international criminal tribunals, and that trend shows no signs of abating.[275] The disclosure regime, and the types of material that must be disclosed, varies slightly between the ICC and the other international criminal tribunals. Before the ICTR, SCSL, STL, and ICTY, the prosecution must disclose, within thirty days of the accused's initial appearance, evidence in support of the indictment and any prior statements of the accused in its possession.[276] Within a time limit prescribed by the Trial Chamber, the prosecution must also provide the witness statements of any witnesses that it intends to call at trial, along with copies of any documentary evidence to be tendered.[277] The statements of any additional prosecution witnesses must also be provided in advance of their testimony, when a decision has been made to call those witnesses.[278]

[272] *Prosecutor v. Tadić*, Decision on Prosecution Motion for Production of Defence Witness Statements, Case No. IT-94-1-T, 27 November 1996, Separate Opinion of Judge Vohrah, para 4.

[273] Articles 16(4)(e) and (f), STL Statute; Article 17(4)(e), SCSL Statute; Article 20(4)(e), ICTR Statute; Article 21(4)(e), ICTY Statute; Article 67(1)(e), ICC Statute.

[274] *Prosecutor v. Munyakazi,* Decision on the Prosecutor's Request for Referral of Case to the Republic of Rwanda, Case No. ICTR-97-36- R11*bis*, 28 May 2008, para 65.

[275] Alex Whiting, 'Disclosure Challenges at the ICC' in Carsten Stahn (ed.), *The Law and Practice of the International Criminal Court* (Oxford: OUP, 2015) 1007..

[276] Rule 66(A)(i) ICTR, SCSL, and ICTY RPE; Rule 110(A)(i) STL RPE.

[277] Rule 66(A)(ii) ICTR, SCSL, and ICTY RPE; Rule 110(A)(ii) STL RPE.

[278] Rule 66(A)(ii), ICTR, SCSL, and ICTY RPE; Rule 110(A)(ii) STL RPE. The prosecution need only provide the names, and not the statements, of any rebuttal witnesses that it intends to call, *per* Rules 67(B)(ii), ICTR, SCSL, and ICTY RPE and Rule 112(B)(ii) STL RPE.

The second prong of the disclosure obligation requires the prosecution to disclose any material in its possession which may exculpate the accused or call the credibility of prosecution evidence into question,[279] and which is not in the public domain.[280] There is a distinction to be drawn between material of 'public character' and that which is in the 'public domain', however; in *Blaškić*, the Appeals Chamber emphasized 'that unless exculpatory material is reasonably accessible to the accused, namely, available to the Defence with the exercise of due diligence, the Prosecution has a duty to disclose the material itself'.[281] The responsibility over deciding whether material is exculpatory lies with the prosecution.[282] In order to be successful, defence motions seeking the disclosure of material are required to be specific as to exactly what material is in the prosecution's possession and how it might be exculpatory; 'fishing expeditions' are expressly prohibited.[283]

Due to the added stage of the confirmation hearing, the ICC's disclosure regime differs slightly. The disclosure of inculpatory material is designed to take place across two stages: the material upon which the Prosecutor intends to rely at the confirmation hearing should be disclosed 'within a reasonable time before the hearing',[284] whilst any prior statements made by witnesses whom the prosecution intends to call must be disclosed 'sufficiently in advance' of trial.[285] Under Article 67(2) of the Statute, any exculpatory material[286] must be disclosed 'as soon as practicable'. A tension between this obligation and Article 54(3)(e), which permits the Prosecutor to enter into an agreement with information providers agreeing not to disclose any information gathered on the condition of confidentiality and solely for the purpose of generating new evidence, was apparent in the *Lubanga* case. Trial Chamber I

[279] Rules 68, ICTR, SCSL, and ICTY RPE; Rule 113, STL RPE.

[280] *Prosecutor v. Blaškić*, Decision on the Appellant's Motions for the Production of Material, Suspension or Extending of the Briefing Schedule, and Additional Filings, Case No. IT-95-14-A, 26 September 2000, para 38.

[281] *Prosecutor v. Blaškić*, Judgment, Case No. IT-95-14-A, 29 July 2004, para 296.

[282] See e.g. *Prosecutor v. Blaškić*, Decision on the Production of Discovery Materials, Case No. IT-95-14-PT, 27 January 1997, para 47.

[283] *Prosecutor v. Bizimungu et al.*, Decision on Jerome-Clement Bicamumpaka's Submissions for Stay of Proceedings and Motion for Disclosure Concerning Witness GKB, Case No. ICTR-99-50-T, 19 May 2009, para 6.

[284] Article 61(3)(b) ICC Statute.

[285] Article 64(3)(c), ICC Statute; Rule 76, ICC RPE.

[286] The statutory provision actually refers to prosecution 'evidence' of an exculpatory character, but the Pre-Trial Chamber in *Lubanga* held that Article 67(2) applies to all exculpatory material: *Situation in the DRC: Prosecutor v. Lubanga*, Decision on the Final System of Disclosure and the Establishment of a Timetable, Case No. ICC-01/04-01/06, 15 May 2006, 8. Rule 77 imposes a broad duty to disclose any evidence in the possession of the prosecution that is 'material to the preparation of the defence'.

held that a stay of proceedings must be imposed, because the Prosecutor's inability to disclose this exculpatory material to the accused rendered a fair trial impossible.[287]

The prosecutorial disclosure obligation cannot be slotted in neatly along the adversarial/inquisitorial spectrum, and has been described as 'an inquisitorial modification of a pure adversary system'.[288] It is clear, however, that it can be best regarded as a human rights obligation as much as it is a procedural rule. Human rights courts and international criminal tribunals alike have linked the disclosure obligation to the right to have adequate time and facilities for the preparation of one's defence,[289] and to the principle of equality of arms.[290] A failure to disclose relevant materials might also lead to a breach of the right to trial without undue delay, having regard to all of the other circumstances of the case.[291]

Of course, there may be valid reasons for non-disclosure or delayed disclosure on the part of the prosecution, and these are foreseen in the tribunals' legal frameworks. If disclosure of the information could endanger the security of a state, victim or witness, or jeopardize ongoing investigations, the Prosecutor can be relieved of those disclosure obligations, following a Trial

[287] *Situation in the DRC: Prosecutor v. Lubanga*, Decision on the Consequences of Non-Disclosure of Exculpatory Materials covered by Article 54(3)(e) Agreements and the Application to Stay the Prosecution of the Accused, together with Certain Other Issues raised at the Status Conference on 10 June 2008, Case No. ICC-01/04-01/06, 13 June 2008, para 93. A solution was ultimately reached in *Situation in the DRC: Prosecutor v. Lubanga*, Reasons for Oral Decision Lifting the Stay of Proceedings, Case No. ICC-01/04-01/06, 23 January 2009.

[288] Kent Roach, 'Wrongful Convictions: Adversarial and Inquisitorial Themes' (2010) 35 *NC J Int'l L & Com Reg* 387, 395; see also, Rudolf B. Schlesinger, 'Comparative Criminal Procedure: A Plea for Utilizing Foreign Experience' (1977) 26 *Buff LR* 361, 372, and Sergey Vasiliev, 'The Role and Legal Status of the Prosecutor in International Criminal Trials', 25 November 2010, available online at http://papers.ssrn.com/sol3/papers.cfm?abstract_id=1715465 (last accessed 2 May 2015) 8–10.

[289] e.g. *Blaškić* Decision on the Appellant's Motions for the Production of Material, Suspension or Extending of the Briefing Schedule, and Additional Filings (n 280), para 52; *Situation in the DRC: Prosecutor v. Mbarushimana*, Decision on 'Defence Request to Deny the Use of Certain Incriminating Evidence at the Confirmation Hearing' and Postponement of Confirmation Hearing, Case No. ICC-01/04-01/10, 16 August 2011, para 14; *Jespers v. Belgium* (1981) 5 EHRR 305.

[290] *Situation in the CAR: Prosecutor v. Bemba*, Judgment on the Appeal of Mr Jean-Pierre Bemba Gombo against the decision of Pre-Trial Chamber III entitled 'Decision on Application for Interim Release', Case No. ICC-01/05-01/08, 16 December 2008, para 32. *Edwards v. UK* (1993) 15 EHRR 417, para 36, held that disclosure pertains more generally 'to the requirement of [overall] fairness under paragraph 1 of Article 6'. The same approach was taken in *Situation in the DRC: Prosecutor v. Katanga*, Judgment on the Appeal of Mr Germain Katanga against the decision of Pre-Trial Chamber I entitled 'First Decision on the Prosecution Request for Authorisation to Redact Witness Statements', Case No. ICC-01/04-01/07, 13 May 2008, para 63.

[291] *Beggs v. UK*, Application No. 25133/06, Judgment, 6 November 2012, para 265; see further above, Section 3.4.

Chamber determination of the matter.[292] In *Katanga*, Trial Chamber II held that 'early disclosure dictated solely by a concern to better protect the rights of the Defence would … contravene the spirit and the purpose of the Statute if this resulted in witnesses called to give evidence facing real risks', and that the right of the accused to the disclosure of materials must be balanced with the rights of witnesses.[293] So long as, in accordance with Article 68(5), any evidence used at trial or in the confirmation hearing is disclosed to the accused sufficiently in advance to allow him or her to prepare for trial, this does not in principle violate the rights of the accused.[294]

In practice, however, the precise parameters of the prosecution's disclosure obligation, hearings on applications for non-disclosure and decisions on allegations of non-compliance with disclosure obligations have elongated proceedings. To give an example, in the *Karadžić* case, no less than 100 motions relating to disclosure issues had been filed by July 2015,[295] and the Trial Chamber has acknowledged a number of disclosure violations committed by the prosecution in the case.[296] In one of the longest trials before the ICTR, which ultimately resulted in the acquittal of the four accused, the Appeals Chamber recognized that the prosecution had violated its disclosure obligations at numerous junctures over the course of the trial,[297] but the Appeals Chamber saw it sufficient to 'firmly remind … the Prosecution of the fundamental importance of its positive and continuous obligation to disclose exculpatory material under Rule 68 of the Rules',[298] and declined to grant financial compensation to the acquitted men. In the *Kenya* situation before the ICC, the key witness relied upon by the prosecution for the confirmation hearing against Muthaura and Kenyatta recanted some of his statement, and had admitted taking bribes,[299] and ultimately the charges against both

[292] Rules 66(C) and 67, ICTY, ICTR, and SCSL RPE; Rule 116, STL RPE; Rules 81-84, ICC RPE.

[293] *Situation in the DRC: Prosecutor v. Katanga and Ngudjolo*, Public redacted version of the Decision on the protection of prosecution witnesses 267 and 353 of 20 May 2009, Case No. ICC-01/04-01/07, 28 May 2009, para 31.

[294] See further, Nicholas A. J. Croquet, 'The International Criminal Court and the Treatment of Defence Rights: A Mirror of the European Court of Human Rights' Jurisprudence?' (2011) 11 *HRLR* 91, 118.

[295] *Prosecutor v. Karadžić*, Decision on Accused's One Hundreth Disclosure Violation Motion, Case No. IT-95-5/18-T, 13 July 2015.

[296] e.g. ibid.; *Prosecutor v. Karadžić*, Decision on Accused's Motion for New Trial for Disclosure Obligations, Case No. IT-95-5/18-T, 3 September 2012, para 14.

[297] *Prosecutor v. Mugenzi and Mugiraneza*, Appeals Judgment, Case No. ICTR-99-50-A, 4 February 2013, para 63.

[298] ibid.

[299] *Situation in Kenya: Prosecutor v. Muthaura and Kenyatta*, Prosecution notification of withdrawal of the charges against Francis Kirimi Muthaura, Case No. ICC-01/09-02/11, 11 March 2013, para 11; *Situation in Kenya: Prosecutor v. Muthaura*, Decision on the Withdrawal of Charges

accused were dropped.[300] Even though this information was available to the prosecution in advance of the confirmation hearing, it was not disclosed to the defence in advance, and the prosecution later acknowledged its clear failing to comply with its disclosure obligations.[301]

The lack of consequences for disclosure breaches in *Lubanga*, discussed above,[302] raises the question of whether the consequences of failing to disclose materials are sufficiently punitive to deter prosecutorial carelessness when it comes to these obligations. Sanctions are rarely imposed;[303] statements like this one from *Bagosora*, where the Trial Chamber held that the prosecution had failed to fulfil its disclosure obligations, and 'exhort[ed] … the Prosecution to be more cooperative with the Defence Counsel in general, and with respect to disclosure in particular'[304] are much more common. There are some exceptions: in *Karemera*, for example, the Chamber formally drew the attention of the Prosecutor, who has a disciplinary role over the prosecution team, to the misconduct of prosecution counsel.[305] In *Haradinaj*, however, individual censure of the lead counsel for the prosecution on the grounds of its failure to comply with disclosure obligations was later overturned on the grounds that the Office of the Prosecutor acts as a whole, and individual lawyers could not be penalized in this manner under Rule 68.[306]

It could be argued that the Trial Chamber's finding in *Lubanga* that the delays caused solely by the misconduct of the prosecution would be deducted

against Mr Muthaura, Case No. ICC-01/09-02/11, 18 March 2013, para 11. See further, Karim A. A. Khan and Caroline Buisman, 'Sitting on Evidence? Systematic Failings in the ICC Disclosure Regime—Time for Reform' in *The Law and Practice of the International Criminal Court: A Critical Account of Challenges and Achievements* (Oxford: OUP, 2014) 1029.

[300] *Situation in Kenya: Prosecutor v. Muthaura*, Decision on the Withdrawal of Charges against Mr Muthaura, ibid.; *Situation in Kenya: Prosecutor v. Kenyatta*, Decision on the Withdrawal of Charges against Mr Kenyatta, Case No. ICC-01/09-02/11, 13 March 2015.

[301] *Situation in Kenya: Prosecutor v. Muthaura and Kenyatta*, Public redacted version of the 25 February 2013 Consolidated Prosecution response to the Defence applications under Article 64 of the Statue to refer the confirmation decision back to the Pre-Trial Chamber, Case No. ICC-01/09-02/11, 25 February 2013, para 37.

[302] See above, text to n 112.

[303] Kate Gibson and Cainnech Lussiaa-Berdou, 'Disclosure of Evidence' in Karim Khan, Caroline Buisman, and Christopher Gosnell (eds), *Principles of Evidence in International Criminal Justice* (Oxford: OUP, 2010) 306, 327; Rohan (n 95) 293–4; Michele Caianiello, 'Law of Evidence at the International Criminal Court: Blending Accusatorial and Inquisitorial Models' (2011) 36 *N C J Int'l L & Com Reg* 287, 311–12.

[304] *Prosecutor v. Bagosora*, Decision on the Motion by the Defence Counsel for Disclosure, Case No. ICTR-96-7-T, 27 November 1997.

[305] *Prosectuor v. Karemera et al.*, Decision on Motion for Disclosure of RPF Material and for Sanctions against Prosecution, Case No. ICTR-98-44-T, 19 October 2006, para 17.

[306] *Prosecutor v. Haradinaj et al.*, Decision on Prosecutor's Motion for Reconsideration of Relief Ordered Pursuant to Rule 68*bis*, Case No. IT-04-84*bis*-T, 27 March 2012.

from the defendant's sentence sends a message that permits complacency, because prosecutorial teams will not worry too much about prolonging the accused's time in detention; it will just be taken away from their sentence in the end. A number of alternative sanctions, such as disciplinary measures[307] or reporting individuals to the professional body that regulates the conduct of counsel in their country of qualification, may serve a greater deterrent function.[308]

Alternatively, if a piece of evidence has not been disclosed in sufficient time to allow the accused sufficient opportunity to prepare his case, that evidence (or the related witness where it is a witness statement that has not been disclosed) should not be allowed as evidence in the trial record. This would follow from the non-permanent tribunals' RPE (under which evidence can be excluded where its probative value is outweighed by the right to a fair trial)[309] and Article 69(4) of the ICC Statute, which states that the probative value and the possible prejudice to the accused will be taken into account in decisions on the relevance or admissibility of evidence.

Perhaps the most reasonable solution, especially in the light of the duty incumbent on the ICC Prosecutor to investigate exonerating circumstances equally,[310] would be to allow open access to all evidentiary materials, including the prosecution's CaseMap file,[311] in the form of a dossier. This would also relieve some of the criticisms that are often laid against prosecution teams in relation to the practice of 'flooding' the defence, whereby thousands of pages of documents are disclosed to the defence just in advance of trial, without indicating precisely which parts are exculpatory, which means that defence teams have to analyse vast quantities of evidence within a short time-frame.[312] Furthermore, this would solve the problem whereby the defence regards a piece of evidence as exculpatory, the prosecution believes it to be inculpatory, and the Chamber has a third view insofar as it sees the evidence as potentially exculpatory but not for the reasons proposed by the defence, as was the case in *Karadžić*.[313]

The defence, of course, also has disclosure obligations, but a failure to notify the prosecution of its intention to raise a defence or alibi[314] will not

307 Article 47, ICC Statute and Rule 25, ICC RPE.

308 Caianiello (n 303).

309 Rule 89, ICTY, ICTR, and SCSL RPE; Rule 118(I), STL RPE.

310 Article 54(1)(a) ICC Statute.

311 Geoffrey Nice and Philippe Vallières-Roland, 'Procedural Innovations in War Crimes Trials', in Hirad Abtahi and Gideon Boas (eds), *The Dynamics of International Criminal Justice: Essays in Honour of Sir Richard May* (Leiden: Nihoff, 2006) 141, 165.

312 Rohan (n 95), 294–7.

313 *Prosecutor v. Karadžić*, Decision on Accused's Eighty-Ninth and Ninetieth Disclosure Violation Motions, Case No. IT-95-5/18-T, 16 April 2014, para 17. See further, Whiting (n 275), 1022.

314 Rules 67, ICTR, ICTY, and SCSL RPE; Rule 112, STL RPE; Rule 79, ICC RPE.

relieve the prosecution of its own disclosure obligations. However, a failure to inform the prosecution of a key line of defence may lead to delayed disclosure of exculpatory materials, as the Prosecutor, obviously, may not recognize the exculpatory value of a piece of evidence until he or she is aware of the defence, and therefore delayed disclosure might be a consequence of late defence disclosure.[315]

3.10.2 Collection of evidence

Equality of arms necessitates that the defence and the prosecution should be given equal opportunity in presenting their cases, and this may require intervention by the tribunal to encourage state cooperation with investigations. The difficulties posed by certain states' unwillingness to co-operate with the defence was illustrated in *Tadić*, where the defence cited its inability to access evidence and witnesses (in contrast to the significant amount of state cooperation granted to the prosecution) in arguing that substantial inequalities resulted.[316] The Appeals Chamber stressed that the Trial Chamber must 'provide every practicable facility it is capable of granting under the Rules and Statute when faced with a request by a party for assistance in presenting its case'.[317] While the Appeals Chamber reiterated that equality of arms meant that the prosecution and defence must be equal before the tribunal, it also found that a 'more liberal' approach to the principle was necessitated by the context of international criminal tribunals.[318] In fact, the 'more liberal' approach was a misnomer, in that it effectively allowed a more restrictive, and therefore less liberal, interpretation of the notion of 'equality'—the Appeals Chamber held that inequality caused by no fault of the Trial Chamber would not be a breach of the right to equality of arms.[319] However, inequality between the parties, however caused, is still inequality, and to determine that certain inequalities are permissible simply because they cannot be directly attributed to the Trial Chamber renders the concept of 'equality' meaningless.

Later cases have illustrated that the tribunals' powers in ordering state cooperation are quite limited. In *Nahimana*, the defence requested a stay of proceedings on the basis that its investigative efforts had been hampered

[315] *Situation in the DRC: Prosecutor v. Lubanga*, Judgment on the Appeal of Mr Lubanga Dyilo against the Oral Decision of Trial Chamber I of 18 January 2008, Case No. ICC-01/04-01/06, 11 July 2008, para 36.

[316] *Prosecutor v. Tadić*, Judgment, Case No. IT-94-1-A, 15 July 1999, para 32.

[317] ibid., para 52. [318] ibid. [319] ibid., paras 53–4.

by Rwanda's unwillingness to co-operate.[320] The Trial Chamber recalled its efforts in helping the defence to gain access to evidence, and that the defence 'had in fact received some measure of co-operation from the Rwandan authorities',[321] yet declined to comment on the sufficiency of that 'measure of co-operation' in relation to the defendant's right to obtain the attendance and examination of witnesses on his behalf under the same conditions as the witnesses against him. While the tribunals have the power to issue such orders as may be necessary for investigations or trials,[322] their ability to enforce these orders is limited. As discussed above, where a state has failed to comply with a request to cooperate with the ICC, it can refer the matter to the Assembly of States Parties, or in the case of a Security Council referral, to the Security Council.[323] The ad hoc tribunals can also refer the matter of non-cooperation to the Security Council,[324] but in practice the Security Council has not been especially active in imposing punitive measures upon states for non-compliance.[325]

Unlike the IMT and IMTFE, which had the power to summon witnesses to testify,[326] some of the contemporary international criminal tribunals' power to subpoena witnesses was not explicit at the outset, and has been described as 'essentially judge made'.[327] In *Blaškić*, the ICTY determined that

[320] *Prosecutor v. Nahimana et al.*, Decision on the Motion to Stay the Proceedings in the Trial of Ferdinand Nahimana, Case No. ICTR-99-52-T, 5 June 2003.

[321] ibid., para 15.

[322] Article 19(2), ICTY Statute; Article 18(2), ICTR Statute; Rule 8, SCSL RPE; Article 18(2), STL Statute; Articles 57(3) and 64(6), ICC Statute; Rule 54, ICTY, ICTR and SCSL RPE; Rule 77, STL RPE; Rule 54*bis*, ICTY RPE.

[323] Articles 72(7) and 87(7), ICC Statute.

[324] Rule 7*bis*, ICTY and ICTR RPE. The SCSL and STL have a slightly different cooperation regime. Non-compliance by Lebanon with the STL can be referred to the Security Council under Rule 20 of the STL RPE. In the case of third states, Rule 21 states that the matter will be dealt with in accordance with any agreement of cooperation with the Tribunal it has entered into, or, if no such agreement is in force, by means of consultation with that state's authorities. Rule 8 of the SCSL RPE leaves it to the President of the Court to take 'appropriate action' in the face of non-compliance with orders by states.

[325] Most notably, perhaps, in relation to the Sudan situation before the ICC, following such decisions as *Situation in Darfur, Sudan: Prosecutor v. Harun and Ali*, Decision informing the United Nations Security Council about the lack of cooperation by the Republic of the Sudan, Case No. ICC-02/05-01/07, 15 September 2010 and *Situation in Darfur, Sudan: Prosecutor v. Al Bashir*, Decision on the Prosecutor's Request for a Finding of Non-Compliance Against the Republic of the Sudan, Case No. ICC-02/05-01/09, 9 March 2015. See further, Rod Rastan, 'Testing Co-operation: The International Criminal Court and National Authorities' (2008) 21(2) *LJIL* 431, 438.

[326] Article 17(a), IMT Charter; Article 11(a), IMTFE Charter. See further, Nancy Combs, 'Fact-Finding Powers', in Goran Sluiter et al. (eds), *International Criminal Procedure: Principles and Rules* (Oxford: OUP, 2013) 689, 706.

[327] Mark Klamberg, *Evidence in International Criminal Trials: Confronting Legal Gaps and the Reconstruction of Disputed Events* (Leiden: Nijhoff, 2013) 243.

the power to summon witnesses was in line with 'the spirit and purpose of the Statute', along with ancillary statutory provisions on the powers of the Prosecutor and Trial Chamber under Articles 18 and 19 of the Statute.[328] The ICC Statute refers to the 'voluntary appearance of persons as witnesses',[329] and for many years, observers believed that the Court had no power to compel witnesses to appear.[330] In 2014, however, Trial Chamber V held that the ICC has the power to summon witnesses to appear, and to oblige state parties to serve such summonses and compel the attendance of witnesses.[331]

3.10.3 Cross-examination

The early RPE of the ICTY embraced a preference for oral testimony,[332] but over time, this was abolished by both the ICTY and SCSL.[333] By today, all of the international criminal tribunals allow for written statements or prior recorded testimony to be introduced in lieu of oral testimony where that testimony does not go to the acts and conduct of the accused,[334] and most tribunals allow such evidence to be admitted, even when it does go to the acts and conduct of the accused, where the witness is dead or genuinely unavailable,[335] or where the Trial Chamber is satisfied that the witness has been subject to intimidation.[336] In addition, the ICTY, SCSL, and STL allow written statements and transcripts to be admitted in lieu of examination-in-chief where the witness is present in court, has attested that the statement reflects what he or she would have said if examined, and the parties and judges have had the opportunity to cross-examine him or her.[337] The ICC had a similar provision under its original Rule 68, which determined that prior recorded testimony could be admitted before the Court only where both prosecution

[328] *Blaškić*, Judgment on the Request of the Republic of Croatia for Review of the Decision of Trial Chamber II of 18 July 1997 (n 208), paras 47–8.

[329] Article 93, ICC Statute.

[330] Goran Sluiter, '"I Beg You, Please Come Testify"—The Problematic Absence of Subpoena Powers at the ICC' (2009) *New Criminal Law Review* 590, 592.

[331] *Situation in Kenya: Prosecutor v. Ruto and Sang*, Decision on Prosecutor's Application for Witness Summonses and Resulting Request for State Party Cooperation, Case No. ICC-01/09-01/11, 17 April 2014, para 193.

[332] Rule 90(A), ICTY RPE.

[333] Rules 90(A), ICTY and SCSL RPE were amended to remove the preference for oral testimony in Rules of Procedure and Evidence, UN Doc. IT/32/Rev.17, International Criminal Tribunal for the former Yugoslavia, 17 November 1999 and Rules of Procedure and Evidence of the Special Court for Sierra Leone, 30 October 2003.

[334] Rules 92*bis*, ICTY, ICTR, and SCSL RPE; Rule 68(2)(b), ICC RPE; Rule 155, STL RPE.

[335] Rules 92*quater*, ICTY and SCSL RPE; Rule 158, STL RPE; Rule 68(2)(c), ICC RPE.

[336] Rule 92*quinquies*, ICTY RPE; Rule 68(2)(d), ICC RPE.

[337] Rules 92*ter*, SCSL and ICTY RPE; Rule 156, STL RPE.

and defence had the opportunity to examine the witness when the testimony was recorded,[338] or where the witness was present before the Court, did not object to the admission of the statement, and the parties and Chamber had the opportunity to examine the witness.[339]

In November 2013, however, the Assembly of State Parties to the ICC amended Rule 68,[340] effectively rendering its legal framework on this issue similar to that of the ICTY, which has been criticized for its liberal approach towards written statements without cross-examination.[341] Under the new Rule 68, prior recorded testimony can be admitted in lieu of oral testimony where: the parties had the opportunity to cross-examine the witness at the time the statement was made;[342] the statement does not go to the acts and conduct of the accused;[343] the witness is dead or unavailable;[344] or the witness has been subject to interference.[345] It is unclear why these extensive amendments were introduced in 2013. One suggestion was that they were designed to improve the efficiency of proceedings,[346] but this does not stand up to scrutiny. As mentioned above,[347] the *Lubanga* trial lasted over eight years from arrest to final Appeals judgment, but a total of only sixty-seven witnesses were heard over the course of the trial.[348] It is clear that the delays in the trial were not caused by the number of witnesses heard live in court, but

[338] Rule 68(a), ICC RPE, as originally adopted.

[339] Rule 68(b), ICC RPE, as originally adopted.

[340] Assembly of States Parties, Resolution ICC-ASP/12/Res.7, adopted at the 12th plenary meeting on 27 November 2013, by consensus, para 2.

[341] Amongst others, see Patricia M. Wald, 'To "Establish Incredible Events by Credible Evidence": The Use of Affidavit Testimony in Yugoslavia War Crimes Tribunal Proceedings' (2001) 42 *Harv. Int'l L J* 535; Megan A. Fairlie, 'Due Process Erosion: The Diminution of Live Testimony at the ICTY' (2003) 34 *California Western Int'l L J* 47; John D. Jackson, 'Finding the Best Epistemic Fit for International Criminal Tribunals: Beyond the Adversarial-Inquisitorial Dichotomy' (2009) 7 *JICJ* 17; Peter Murphy, 'No Free Lunch, No Free Proof: The Indiscriminate Admission of Evidence is a Serious Flaw in International Criminal Trials' (2010) 8 *JICJ* 539; Christian DeFrancia, 'Due Process in International Criminal Courts: Why Procedure Matters' (2001) 87 *Va LR* 1381, 1397–9; 1424–30, Eugene O'Sullivan and Deirdre Montgomery, 'The Erosion of the Right to Confrontation under the Cloak of Fairness at the ICTY' (2010) 8 *JICJ* 511; Colleen M. Rohan 'Rules Governing the Presentation of Testimonial Evidence' in Karim Khan et al. (eds), *Principles of Evidence in International Criminal Justice* (Oxford: OUP, 2010) 499; Yvonne McDermott, 'The Admissibility and Weight of Written Witness Testimony in International Criminal Law: A Socio-Legal Analysis' (2013) 27 *LJIL* 971; Steven Kay, 'The Move from Oral Evidence to Written Evidence: "The Law is always Too Short and Too Tight for Growing Humankind"' (2004) 2 *JICJ* 495.

[342] Rule 68(2)(a), ICC RPE. This was the case under the old Rule 68(a).

[343] Rule 68(2)(b), ICC RPE.

[344] Rule 68(2)(c), ICC RPE.

[345] Rule 68(2)(d), ICC RPE.

[346] [Draft] Report of the Study Group on Governance, 20 September 2013, para 18, as cited in International Bar Association, ICC Programme Legal Opinion, *Rule 68 Amendment Proposal*, 12 November 2013, 1.

[347] See above, Section 3.4.

[348] *Lubanga* judgment (n 109), para 11.

by the stays of proceedings that had to be imposed. Further, Rules 68(2)(c) and (d) on dead, unavailable, and intimidated witnesses do not enhance efficiency, but rather may cause proceedings to drag on when the Chamber considers whether there is good reason to allow admission of this testimony, whether the testimony bears sufficient indicia of reliability, and whether the interests of justice are best served by admitting the evidence in question.[349] Moreover, it will be difficult for a Chamber to satisfy itself that a lack of cooperation from a witness is attributable to intimidation, as illustrated by proceedings in the *Ruto and Sang* case. There, the Prosecutor alleged that prior recorded testimony of a prosecution witness who later recanted their testimony should be admitted because that witness had been intimidated.[350] The defence countered that the witness merely decided to tell the truth when they were under oath in the witness stand, and the prosecution had not taken the opportunity to cross-examine their 'hostile witness' to determine whether they had indeed been subject to intimidation.[351]

The amendments to allow the admission of prior recorded testimony that does not go to the acts and conduct of the accused may seem sanguine, and indeed the International Bar Association deemed it 'less controversial' than the new Rules on dead, unavailable, or intimidated witnesses.[352] However, this overlooks the fact that this so-called 'crime base' evidence might be crucial to an ultimate finding of guilt, as it makes it difficult for the accused to challenge, for example, that there was no widespread or systematic attack for the purposes of crimes against humanity. For example, a key issue in the ongoing *Gbagbo* trial is whether there was a state or organizational policy in place for the commission of crimes against humanity;[353] evidence that does not go to the alleged acts and conduct of the accused himself might be admitted under the new Rule 68(2)(b), and this might be deemed sufficient to prove that a policy was in existence.

The admission of unavailable or intimidated witnesses is also problematic from the perspective of the accused's right to examine the witnesses against him or her, given that such evidence can go towards proving the acts and conduct of the accused. This goes against the principle, set out in Article 69(2) of the ICC Statute, that 'the testimony of a witness at trial shall be given in person', and that any measures taken to derogate from this principle 'shall not be prejudicial to or inconsistent with the rights of the accused'.[354] As regards allegedly intimidated witnesses, there is a danger that the Court

[349] Rules 68(2)(c) and (d), ICC RPE.

[350] *Situation in Kenya: Prosecutor v. Ruto and Sang*, Transcript, Case No. ICC-01/09-01/11, 25 June 2015.

[351] ibid. [352] International Bar Association (n 346), 2.

[353] *Situation in Côte d'Ivoire: Prosecutor v. Gbagbo*, Decision on the Confirmation of the Charges against Laurent Gbagbo, Case No. ICC-02/11-01/11, 12 June 2014, paras 213–21; 268–77.

[354] Article 69, ICC Statute.

might rely on Rule 68(2)(c) and admit the prior recorded testimony of such witnesses without cross-examination, where the rights of both the accused and the witness could have been better protected through witness protection measures.[355]

3.11 Right to Time and Facilities for the Preparation of One's Defence and to Free Communication with Counsel

In accordance with the principle of equality of arms, the accused has the right to adequate time to prepare his or her defence.[356] What constitutes adequate time will be assessed on a case-by-case basis, bearing in mind the complexity of the case and the rights of co-accused persons, amongst other considerations.[357] The imposition by the ICC of a strict time limit to prepare for the confirmation of charges hearing in *Ruto, Kosgey and Sang* has been criticized.[358] In April 2011, the prosecution was ordered to disclose the document containing the charges and the list of evidence by 1 August 2011 and a strict deadline of 16 August 2011 was set for defence disclosure, in advance of the 1 September 2011 confirmation hearing.[359] Given that the prosecution disclosure amounted to almost 9,000 pages of evidence, and there were various operational issues facing the defence teams, including the fact that the defence teams had not been given office space by the Registry, the defence requested an extension of these deadlines.[360] The defence argued that a postponement of the date for the confirmation hearing was necessary to allow for adequate time to prepare, and to avoid possible self-incrimination that might arise from disclosing defence material without having a full opportunity to consider the almost 9,000 pages of prosecution material.[361] The Single Judge dismissed these concerns as being attributable to a 'lack of proper organisation on the part of the

[355] International Bar Association (n 346), 5.

[356] Article 67(1)(b), ICC Statute; Article 20(4)(b), ICTY Statute; Article 19(4)(b), ICTR Statute; Article 17(4)(b), SCSL Statute; Article 16(4)(b), STL Statute.

[357] *Prosecutor v. Delalić et al.*, Decision on Applications for Adjournment of Trial Date, Case No. IT-96-21-T, 3 February 1997, para 19.

[358] Khan and Buisman (n 299), 1035.

[359] *Situation in Kenya: Prosecutor v. Ruto, Kosgey and Sang*, Decision on the Prosecution's application requesting disclosure after a final resolution of the Government of Kenya's admissibility challenge and Establishing a Calendar for Disclosure Between the Parties, Case No. ICC-01/09-01/11, 20 April 2011.

[360] *Situation in Kenya: Prosecutor v. Ruto, Kosgey and Sang*, Decision on the Urgent Defence Application for Postponement of the Confirmation Hearing and Extension of Time to Disclose and List of Evidence, Case No. ICC-01/09-01/11, 12 August 2011, para 6.

[361] ibid., para 16.

defence',[362] and she went so far as to suggest that the request was an abuse of the rights of the accused under Article 67.[363] Whilst it is important that trials are as expedient as possible, it is equally important for judges to embrace some degree of flexibility when unexpected hurdles arise, in order to fully respect the rights of the accused. Moreover, defence teams should not be discouraged from seeking the full support needed in order to defend their client's rights, and to suggest that a request for an extra couple of weeks to prepare for the confirmation hearing is an abuse of those rights seems excessive.

The question of adequate facilities for the preparation of the defence has been one of the most vexed over the course of the tribunals' lifetimes. Clearly, this is a multi-faceted obligation, covering the financial resources to pay a defence team,[364] as well as other logistical and technical resources[365] and access to documents and records necessary for the preparation of the defence.[366] The allocation of resources is normally a decision to be made by the Registry, but the Chamber will interfere with the Registry's decisions in this area where there are compelling reasons to do so, in order to ensure fairness to the accused.

Some tribunals include a defence office as part of the Registry[367] or as an independent organ of the Court.[368] These offices can assist defence teams

[362] ibid., para 11. [363] ibid., para 16.

[364] Amongst many others, examples include *Prosecutor v. Milutinović et al.*, Decision on Interlocutory Appeal on Motion for Additional Funds, Case No. IT-99-37-AR73.2, 13 November 2003; *Situation in the DRC: Prosecutor v. Lubanga*, Decision Reviewing the Registry's Decision on Legal Assistance for Mr Thomas Lubanga Dyilo pursuant to Regulation 135 of the Regulations of the Registry, Case No. ICC-01/04-01/06, 20 August 2011; *Situation in the DRC: Prosecutor v. Ngudjolo*, Decision on Mr Ngudjolo's Request for Review of the Registrar's Decision Regarding the Level of Remuneration during the Appeal Phase and Reimbursement of Fees, Case No. ICC-01/04-02/12, 11 February 2014; *Niyitegeka v. Prosecutor*, Decision on Niyitegeka's Urgent Request for Legal Assistance, Case No. ICTR-96-14-R, 20 June 2005.

[365] e.g. *Prosecutor v. Prlić et al.*, Decision on the Oral Request of the Accused Jadranko Prlić for Authorisation to Use a Laptop Computer at Hearings or to be Seated Next to his Counsel, Case No. IT-04-74-T, 29 June 2006; *Prosecutor v. Taylor*, Joint Decision on Defence Motions on Adequate Facilities and Adequate Time for the Preparation of Mr Taylor's Defence, Case No. SCSL-03-1-PT, 23 January 2007, para 13. See further, Charles C. Jalloh and Amy di Bella, 'Equality of Arms in International Criminal Law: Continuing Challenges' in William A. Schabas, Yvonne McDermott, and Niamh Hayes (eds), *The Ashgate Research Companion to International Criminal Law: Critical Perspectives* (Aldershot: Ashgate, 2013) 251.

[366] See above, Section 3.10.1.

[367] Rule 45, SCSL RPE, and Regulation 77, ICC Regulations. The ICTY created a Defence Counsel Unit (later renamed as the Office for Legal Aid and Detention matters) in 2000: ICTY, Seventh Annual Report of the International Tribunal for the Prosecution of Persons Responsible for Serious Violations of International Humanitarian Law Committed on the Territory of the Former Yugoslavia since 1991, UN Doc. A/55/273-S/2000/777, 26 July 2000, para 229. The ICTR's Defence Counsel and Detention Management Section was established in 1997. In addition, the ICTY and ICTR have incorporated the nearest equivalents to bar associations at an international level—the Association of Defence Counsel (ADC) and the Association des Advocats de la Défence (ADAD)—into their activities, such that membership of the ADC is now a prerequisite to practicing before the ICTY, per Rule 44(A), ICTY RPE.

[368] Articles 7 and 13, STL Statute.

through providing legal research assistance, support in gathering evidence, and training. The creation of the first independent defence office at the STL was welcomed,[369] given that the work of the SCSL Defence Office was initially hampered by its subordination to—and dependence on—the Registry to provide resources.[370]

There have been issues on the provision of resources to defence teams since the inception of the contemporary international criminal tribunals. For example, defence counsel in the Charles Taylor trial reported having to use cafés to work in,[371] and having inadequate access to a photocopier.[372] In a letter sent to the Court, Taylor noted that he had just one lawyer to appear in court on his behalf, compared to nine prosecution lawyers,[373] and ultimately requested that his counsel cease to represent him on that basis.[374] It emerged that the Registrar had deemed it unnecessary for the accused to meet with the Principal Defender, and had refused to fund the Principal Defender's travel from Freetown to The Hague for these purposes.[375] This decision was overturned by the Trial Chamber,[376] which also ordered the Principal Defender to assemble a defence team for the accused, comprising of one lead counsel, two co-counsels, and one senior investigator.[377]

While judicial interventions to overturn Registry decisions and ensure adequate legal representation are to be welcomed, the conceptualization of the principle of equality of arms remains problematic. The ICTY, ICTR, and SCSL have consistently held that 'equality' does not require the same, or even similar,[378] financial and/or personal resources, but rather whether the accused has been placed at a disadvantage when presenting their case.[379] It has been stated that a lack of strict equality is justified, because the prosecution bears

[369] John R.W.D. Jones and Misa Zgonec-Rožej, 'Rights of Suspects and Accused', in Amal Alamuddin, Nidal Nabil Jurdi, and David Tolbert (eds), *The Special Tribunal for Lebanon: Law and Practice* (Oxford: OUP, 2014) 177, 191–2.

[370] Antonio Cassese, *Report on the Special Court for Sierra Leone submitted by the Independent Expert, Antonio Cassese*, 12 December 2006, available online at http://www.rscsl.org/Documents/Cassese%20Report.pdf (last accessed 2 June 2015), para 136.

[371] *Prosecutor v. Taylor*, Transcript, Case No. SCSL-2003-01-T, 4 June 2007, 256.

[372] *Prosecutor v. Taylor*, Transcript, Case No. SCSL-2003-01-T, 25 June 2007, 366. See also, Cassese Report (n 370), para 145.

[373] *Prosecutor v. Taylor*, Transcript, Case No. SCSL-2003-01-T, 4 June 2007, 249.

[374] ibid., 260–7. [375] ibid., 338. [376] ibid., 340.

[377] *Prosecutor v. Taylor*, Transcript, Case No. SCSL-2003-01-T, 25 June 2007, 44.

[378] *Prosecutor v. Perisić*, Decision on Motion to Appoint *Amicus Curiae* to Investigate Equality of Arms, Case No. IT-04-81-PT, 18 June 2007, para 9.

[379] *Prosecutor v. Kayishema and Ruzindana*, Judgment (Reasons), Case No. ICTR-95-1-A, 1 June 2000, para 69; *Prosecutor v. Stakić*, Judgment, Case No.: IT-97-24-A, 22 March 2006, para 149; *Prosecutor v. Norman et al.*, Decision on the Impermissibility of Eliciting Evidence Involving the Second Accused through Cross-Examination of Witnesses Called by the Third Accused, Case No. SCSL-04-14-T, 10 November 2006, para 20.

the burden of presenting a coherent narrative, whereas the defence's role is limited to picking holes in that narrative.[380] This observation is not universally true—defence strategies more commonly involve challenging several aspects of the prosecution case, including the elements of the crimes and the mode(s) of liability charged. This exercise requires an overall assessment of the prosecution case at the outset, and then a rigorous analysis of each of the constituent elements of the case to determine where those weak points in the case can be found, and then finding the relevant evidence to support the counter-argument. There is nothing to suggest that the preparation of a defence case is any less onerous than a prosecution case in this respect. Moreover, as Jalloh and DiBella have noted, if, in light of this depiction of the Prosecutor's role, he or she is granted more resources and more time to meet the prosecutorial burden, 'then claims of parity between the parties become meaningless'.[381]

By contrast, in a leading decision on equality of arms, Trial Chamber I in *Lubanga* did not adopt the language of 'whether the accused would be placed at a substantial disadvantage' or determine that the notion of 'equality' did not strictly mean equality in this context.[382] The issue at hand was whether defence counsel could be kept in service between the close of trial and the issuance of judgment. The Registrar believed this to be unnecessary, but the defence argued that to not pay counsel during this period would mean that members of the legal team would have to find other work, and would not therefore be available to respond when the judgment was issued. The Chamber found that it would be disruptive for the accused to have to hire a new legal team to handle his appeal in the event of conviction,[383] and additionally, this would create an unequal position between the parties, insofar as prosecution counsel remain in service following the concluding submissions,[384] and therefore ordered the Registry to retain a defence team of lead counsel, co-counsel and two legal assistants until the judgment was issued.[385] This interpretation of equality as simply meaning equality, and not the absence of substantial disadvantage, is to be welcomed.

The right to free communication with counsel is frequently associated with the right to time and facilities for the preparation of one's defence.[386]

[380] *Prosecutor v. Orić*, Interlocutory Decision on Length of Defence Case, Case No. IT-03-68-AR73.2, 20 July 2005, para 7.

[381] Jalloh and Di Bella (n 365), 276.

[382] *Situation in the DRC: Prosecutor v. Lubanga*, Decision Reviewing the Registry's Decision on Legal Assistance for Mr Thomas Lubanga Dyilo pursuant to Regulation 135 of the Regulations of the Registry, Case No. ICC-01/04-01/06, 30 August 2011.

[383] ibid., paras 56–7. [384] ibid., para 57.

[385] ibid., para 63.

[386] Article 16(4)(b), STL Statute; Article 17(4)(b), SCSL Statute; Article 20(4)(b), ICTR Statute; Article 21(4)(b), ICTY Statute; Article 67(1)(b), ICC Statute.

The STL has declared that the right to free and private communication with counsel has customary international law status 'as one of the fundamental human rights relating to due process',[387] and lawyer-client privilege is explicitly recognized by the tribunals' rules.[388] Contrary to previous ICTY case law that suggested that communication with counsel may be restricted when the accused is testifying in his or her own defence, in *Prlić*, the Appeals Chamber found that the right was 'one of the most important basic rights of an accused' and that there was a presumption in favour of the right to consult with counsel, even when the accused was acting as a witness.[389] The privilege might also be waived where there are allegations of criminal activity between the accused and his or her lawyer, such as engaging in fee-splitting[390] or interfering with witnesses.[391]

3.12 Right to an Appeal

One of the more controversial aspects of the Nuremberg and Tokyo tribunals was the fact that their judgments were final and not subject to appeal.[392] By contrast, the contemporary international criminal tribunals all recognize the right to appeal,[393] which the UN Secretary General described at the time of the ICTY'S establishment as 'a fundamental element of individual civil and political rights'.[394] Both the convicted individual and the prosecution can lodge appeals of final judgments,[395]

[387] President of the Special Tribunal for Lebanon, Order on Conditions of Detention, Case No. CH/PRES/2009/01/rev, 21 April 2009, para 16.

[388] Rule 97 ICTY, ICTR, and SCSL RPE; Rule 73 ICC RPE; Rule 163 STL RPE. See further, Yvonne McDermott, 'General Duty to Ensure the Integrity of the Proceedings' in Goran Sluiter et al. (eds), *International Criminal Procedure: Principles and Rules* (Oxford: OUP, 2013) 743.

[389] *Prosecutor v. Prlić*, Decision on Prosecution's Appeal against Trial Chamber's Order on Contact Between the Accused and Counsel During an Accused's Testimony Pursuant to Rule 85(C), Case No. IT-04-74-AR73.10, 5 September 2008, paras 16–19.

[390] Rule 97(B), ICTR RPE.

[391] *Situation in Central African Republic*, Decision on the Prosecutor's 'Request for judicial order to obtain evidence for investigation under Article 70', Case No. ICC-01/05, 3 February 2014.

[392] Article 26, IMT Statute; Article 17, IMTFE Statute.

[393] Articles 81–4, ICC Statute; Article 20, SCSL Statute; Article 26, STL Statute; Article 24, ICTR Statute; Article 25, ICTY Statute.

[394] Report of the SG on establishment of ICTY, para 116.

[395] Article 81, ICC Statute; Article 20, SCSL Statute; Article 26, STL Statute; Article 24, ICTR Statute; Article 25, ICTY Statute. The STL has extended the right to appeal certain interlocutory decisions to victims: *Prosecutor v. Ayyash et al.*, Decision on Appeal by Legal Representative of Victims against Pre-Trial Judge's Decision on Protective Measures, Case No. STL-11-01/PT/AC/AR136.3, 10 April 2013.

although the ICC Statute allows broader grounds of appeal for convicted persons, incorporating also any ground that affects the fairness or reliability of the proceedings or decision.[396] There has been some criticism of the prosecutorial right to appeal, insofar as an individual who has been acquitted at trial could be convicted on appeal, and he or she would have no effective right to appeal this conviction.[397] The ICC Statute does include a provision that a higher sentence cannot be imposed on appeal, but this only applies where the convicted person has lodged an appeal, and the prosecution has not.[398]

Generally speaking, appeals can be classified as pertaining either to alleged errors of fact or errors of law.[399] The standard of appeal is higher for errors of fact—it must be demonstrated that the Trial Chamber 'committed a clear error, namely, misappreciated the facts, took into account irrelevant facts, or failed to take into account relevant facts',[400] and, additionally for the non-permanent international criminal tribunals, that this error occasioned a miscarriage of justice.[401] Even where the Appeals Chamber might have reached a different conclusion, it will not replace the Trial Chamber's evaluation of the evidence unless it can be shown to be 'wholly erroneous' or a conclusion that no reasonable trier of fact could have reached.[402] Given this high threshold, it is perhaps unsurprising that alleged errors of fact tend not to attract a great deal of success on appeal. By contrast, for errors of law, 'The Appeals Chamber does not review the Trial Chamber's findings ... merely to determine whether they are reasonable, but rather to determine whether they are correct.'[403]

396 Article 81(1)(b), ICC Statute.

397 *Prosecutor v. Mrkšić and Šljivančanin*, Review Judgement, Case No. IT-95-13/1-R.1, 8 December 2010, Partially Dissenting Opinion of Judge Pocar, paras 1–13.

398 Article 83(2) ICC Statute.

399 Article 20, SCSL Statute; Article 26, STL Statute; Article 24, ICTR Statute; Article 25, ICTY Statute. Article 81 ICC Statute adds 'any procedural error' as a ground for appeal.

400 *Situation in the DRC: Prosecutor v. Lubanga*, Judgment on the appeals of the Prosecutor and Mr Thomas Lubanga Dyilo against the 'Decision on Sentence pursuant to Article 76 of the Statute', Case No. ICC-01/04-01/06, 1 December 2014, para 21.

401 Article 20(1)(b), SCSL Statute; Article 26(1)(b), STL Statute; Article 24(1)(b), ICTR Statute; Article 25(1)(b), ICTY Statute. Before the ICC, the error must have 'materially affected the determination': see Article 83(2), ICC Statute and *Situation in Uganda: Prosecutor v. Kony et al.,* Judgment on the appeal of the Defence against the 'Decision on the admissibility of the case under Article 19 (1) of the Statute' of 10 March 2009, Case No. ICC-02/04-01/05, 16 September 2009, para 80.

402 *Kupreškić* Appeal Judgment (n 157), para 41.

403 *Prosecutor v. Krnojelac*, Appeal Judgment, Case No. IT-97-25-A, 17 September 2003, para 10. The SCSL, STL, ICTY, and ICTR Statutes state that the error of law must be one that 'invalidates the decision'; the ICC will assess whether the error materially affected the decision.

3.13 *Nullum Crimen, Nulla Poena Sine Lege*

The principle of legality, or that there can be no crime or punishment without law, is a well-established principle of fairness. The judicial development and expansion of definitions of crimes, modes of liability, and other aspects of international criminal law is widely documented,[404] and it is obvious that this expansionist approach may clash with the principle of legality. Van Schaack has argued that the tribunals overcame this tension and found that the principle had not been breached 'through a series of interpretive devices, analytical claims, and methodological choices'.[405] More recently, the STL has faced allegations that its definition of terrorism as an international crime and use of extended modes of liability violated the legality principle.[406]

The drafters of the ICC Statute, apparently conscious of this tide of judicial law-making at the ad hoc tribunals, introduced the first explicit reference to the twin principles of *nullum crimen sine lege* and *nulla poena sine lege* in an international criminal statute, under Articles 22 and 23. The ICC has determined that where a crime is defined with 'sufficient particularity' in the Rome Statute, this effectively solves any questions of *nullum crimen*.[407] Less clear is whether this would suffice where the situation concerns a non-state party, in the case of Security Council referrals or ad hoc acceptance of jurisdiction under Article 12(3).[408] In such a scenario, Broomhall argues that 'the only legitimate basis for establishing the criminal responsibility of individuals would presumably—in the absence of relevant national criminal prohibitions at the time of the alleged conduct—be that of customary law'.[409]

[404] See e.g. Mohamed Shahabuddeen, 'Judicial Creativity and Joint Criminal Enterprise' in Shane Darcy and Joseph Powderly (eds), *Judicial Creativity at the International Criminal Tribunals* (Oxford: OUP, 2010) 188; Shane Darcy, *Judges, Law, and War: The Judicial Development of International Humanitarian Law* (Cambridge: CUP, 2014).

[405] Beth Van Schaack, 'Legality and International Criminal Law' (2009) *ASIL Proceedings* 101, 102.

[406] STL Appeals Chamber, Interlocutory decision on Applicable Law: Terrorism, Conspiracy, Homicide, Perpetration, Cumulative Charging, Case No. STL-11-01/I, 16 February 2011. See further, Philippa Webb, 'Individual Criminal Responsibility', in Amal Alamuddin, Nidal Nabil Jurdi, and David Tolbert (eds), *The Special Tribunal for Lebanon: Law and Practice* (Oxford: OUP, 2014) 88.

[407] *Situation in the DRC: Prosecutor v. Lubanga*, Decision on the Confirmation of Charges, Case No. ICC-01/04-01/06, 29 January 2007, paras 302–3.

[408] Bruce Broomhall, 'Article 22: *Nullum Crimen Sine Lege*' in Otto Triffterer (ed.), *Commentary on the Rome Statute of the International Criminal Court—Observers' Notes, Article by Article* (2nd edn, Munich: Beck, 2008) 713, 720.

[409] ibid.

3.14 *Ne Bis in Idem*

The statutes of the international criminal tribunals prevent a person from being tried by another court for a crime for which they have already been convicted or acquitted by the international tribunal.[410] In addition, the *ne bis in idem* principle will act as a bar for the Court in proceeding against an individual who has already been tried for the same crimes before a national court, unless it can be shown that the proceedings were for the purposes of shielding that individual from the jurisdiction of the Court,[411] were not carried out independently or impartially, or the case was not diligently prosecuted.[412]

The ICTY in *Tadić* found that *ne bis in idem* will only apply where an individual has been finally acquitted or convicted.[413] The ICTY, ICTR, and SCSL Statutes make explicit that where an individual has been tried for an ordinary crime, the international criminal tribunal can try that conduct as an international crime.[414] Article 20(3) of the ICC Statute uses the term 'for conduct also proscribed under Article 6, 7, or 8', implying that where an individual has been tried for a domestic crime, the ICC cannot try the person again for the same conduct as an international crime.[415] The STL Statute obviously does not make this distinction, given that the Tribunal applies Lebanese criminal law.[416]

The ICC Statute adds that the Court itself may not try an individual for crimes based on conduct that has already formed the basis of a conviction or acquittal by the Court.[417] Thus, for example, if an individual was acquitted of genocide, the Prosecutor could not have a 'second bite of the cherry' by later charging the individual with crimes against humanity based on the same conduct. This seems unlikely, given that the more common practice would be to charge that individual with both genocide and crimes against humanity at the outset.

[410] Article 20(2), ICC Statute; Article 10(1), ICTY Statute; Article 9(1), ICTR Statute; Article 5(1), STL Statute; Article 9(1), SCSL Statute.

[411] Article 20(3)(a), ICC Statute; Article 10(2)(b), ICTY Statute; Article 9(2)(b), ICTR Statute; Article 9(2)(b), SCSL Statute; Article 5(2), STL Statute.

[412] Article 10(2)(b), ICTY Statute; Article 9(2)(b), ICTR Statute; Article 9(2)(b), SCSL Statute; Article 5(2), STL Statute. Article 20(3)(b) of the ICC Statute uses a slightly different formulation for the diligent prosecution requirement: the Court will instead examine whether the proceedings were conducted in such a way that they were 'inconsistent with bringing the person concerned to justice'.

[413] *Prosecutor v. Tadić*, Decision on the Defence Motion on the Principle of *Non-Bis-In-Idem*, Case No. IT-94-1-T, 14 November 1995, para 24.

[414] Article 10(2), ICTY Statute; Article 9(2), ICTR Statute; Article 9(2), SCSL Statute.

[415] Mohammed El Zeidy, *The Principle of Complementarity in International Criminal Law* (Leiden: Nijhoff, 2008) 283–98.

[416] Article 2, STL Statute.

[417] Article 20(1), ICC Statute.

3.15 Other Human Rights

The international criminal tribunals have considered the accused's human rights more generally on a number of occasions, particularly before the ICC, where the Court has an obligation to interpret and apply the law in accordance with internationally recognized human rights.[418] Pursuant to the right to family life, they have authorized visits from the family members of detainees, and the ICC found that the Court has a positive obligation to fund such visits 'in order to give effect to a right which would otherwise be ineffective in the particular circumstances of the detainee'.[419] The Registry has the authority to decide whether it would be appropriate to authorize a family visit, in light of the circumstances of the case.[420] In 2014, Charles Taylor, who was serving a 50-year sentence in the United Kingdom, applied to the Residual SCSL (RSCSL) for transfer to Rwanda, given that it had proven impossible for his wife and children to visit him in prison, due to the denial of their visa applications by the United Kingdom authorities.[421] The RSCSL held that Mrs Taylor had failed to comply with United Kingdom visa requirements and had not availed of offers by the Registry to assist her in re-applying,[422] and thus there was no interference with Taylor's right to family life by either the United Kingdom authorities or the RSCSL.[423]

The ICC has also considered that the right to privacy applies to searches carried out in pursuit of an investigation.[424] It was noted that the indiscriminate nature of the search and seizure of hundreds of items carried out by Congolese authorities in the presence of an ICC investigator was in violation of the accused's right to privacy.[425] Nevertheless, it found that this violation was not so serious as to warrant exclusion of the evidence obtained in this manner.[426] The right to private life also extends to private telephone

[418] Article 21(3), ICC Statute.

[419] *Situation in the DRC: Prosecutor v. Katanga and Ngudjolo*, Decision on 'Mr Mathieu Ngudjolo's Complaint Under Regulation 221(1) of the Regulations of the Registry Against the Registrar's Decision of 18 November 2008', Case No. ICC-RoR-217-02/08, 10 March 2009, para 37.

[420] A detained witness was denied a family visit in 2012, and this was upheld by the Presidency in Decision on Application for Judicial Review Dated 5 November 2012, Case No. ICC-RoR-221-04/12, 22 February 2013.

[421] *In the Matter of Charles Ghankay Taylor*, Decision on Public with Public and Confidential Annexes Charles Ghankay Taylor's Motion for Termination of Enforcement of Sentence in the United Kingdom and for Transfer to Rwanda, Case No. SCSL-03-01-ES, 30 January 2015.

[422] ibid., paras 85–90. [423] ibid., para 121.

[424] *Situation in the DRC: Prosecutor v. Lubanga*, Decision on the Confirmation of the Charges, Case No. ICC-01/04-01/06, 29 January 2007, paras 62–91.

[425] ibid., para 78. [426] ibid., para 90.

conversations and written communications with family members, and any restrictions on these communications must be proportionate to the aim sought.[427]

3.16 Remedies and Compensation

Of the international criminal tribunals, only the ICC and the STL recognize a right to compensation following a miscarriage of justice or unlawful arrest or detention in their legal frameworks.[428] The President of the ICTY in 2002 denied the requests of two acquitted persons for compensation on the basis that the Tribunal had no power to rule on such requests.[429] By contrast, the ICTR has determined that the power to grant compensation is inherent to its judicial function.[430] It has also found that a reduction of sentence would be an appropriate remedy where an accused whose rights have been breached is ultimately convicted.[431]

To date, only one defendant has ever been given compensation for a breach of their rights at the hands of an international criminal tribunal—the ICTR granted Rwamakuba $2,000 in 2007 because he was denied access to a lawyer for 125 days following his arrest.[432] In the *Bizimungu et al.* judgment (the case discussed above in relation to trial without undue delay, where three years passed between the close of trial and issuance of judgment[433]), Judge Short opined that the two acquitted men should have been declared to be entitled to compensation

[427] *Situation in the DRC: Prosecutor v. Katanga and Ngudjolo Chui*, Decision on Request 1200 of the Prosecutor for Prohibition and Restrictive Measures against Mathieu Ngudjolo with Respect to Contacts Both Outside and Inside the Detention Centre, Case No. ICC-01/04-01/07, 24 June 2009, paras 35 and 45; *Situation in the DRC: Prosecutor v. Katanga and Ngudjolo Chui*, Judgment on the Appeal of the Prosecutor against the 'Decision on Request 1200 of the Prosecutor for Prohibition and Restrictive Measures against Mathieu Ngudjolo with Respect to Contacts Both Outside and Inside the Detention Centre', Case No. ICC-01/04-01/07, 9 December 2009, para 52; *Situation in the DRC: Prosecutor v. Katanga and Ngudjolo Chui*, Decision further to the Appeals Chamber judgment of 9 December 2009 and Responding to Request 1959-Conf-Exp of the Office of the Prosecutor, Case No. ICC-01/04-01/07, 10 June 2010, para 38.

[428] Article 85, ICC Statute; Rule 170, STL RPE.

[429] Ninth Annual Report of the International Criminal Tribunal for the former Yugoslavia, UN Doc. A/57/379-S/2002/985, 4 September 2002, para 28.

[430] *Prosecutor v. Rwamakuba*, Decision on Appropriate Remedy, Case No. ICTR-98-44C-T, 31 January 2007, para 31.

[431] *Prosecutor v. Barayagwiza*, Decision (Prosecutor's Request for Review or Reconsideration), Case No. ICTR-97-19-AR72, 31 March 2000; *Semanza v. Prosecutor,* Decision, Case No. ICTR-97-20-A, 31 May 2000.

[432] ibid.; *Prosecutor v. Rwamakuba*, Decision on Appeal against Decision on Appropriate Remedy, Case No. ICTR-98-44C-A, 13 September 2007.

[433] Section 3.4 above.

as a result of the failure to issue a judgment in good time, whilst the two convicted men should have been given a reduction in sentence in recognition of the violation of their rights,[434] but the majority did not concur. On appeal, where the two remaining defendants were acquitted, Judge Robinson stated that he would have given them compensation of $5,000 each for the breach of their rights.[435] He found that at least one year of the delay could be considered to have been 'undue', owing to the delay in issuing a judgment, and concluded that 'Mugenzi and Mugiraneza suffered psychological non-pecuniary damage which cannot be sufficiently compensated by the mere finding of a violation; cases show that in such circumstances financial compensation is warranted.'[436] Again, because only the dissenting judge favoured the granting of compensation, no such compensation was awarded.

The strict approach to compensation following a miscarriage of justice was again illustrated by the ICTR in *Zigiranyirazo*.[437] Although the Trial Chamber noted that Article 85(3) of the ICC Statute on compensation reflected customary international law,[438] and that the Appeals Chamber had explicitly held that a miscarriage of justice had occurred in Zigiranyirazo's case,[439] it noted that he had waited over two years after his acquittal before submitting his claim.[440] It denied his claim on that basis, and also on the basis that the errors that occurred were not of sufficient gravity to warrant compensation.[441] However, as Judge Park pointed out in his dissenting opinion, the violations were far more grave than those for which Rwamakuba was compensated.[442]

Conclusion

It will be recalled that Chapter 2 argued that the concept of fairness in the context of international criminal trials stands quite apart from general theories of fairness, insofar as the notion of a 'fair trial' is composed of a number of individual due process rights that must be respected, together with key principles of fairness. This chapter examined these components in detail,

[434] *Bizimungu et al.*, Judgment and Sentence (n 116) Partially Dissenting Opinion of Judge Emile Francis Short.

[435] *Prosecutor v. Mugenzi and Mugiraneza*, Appeals Judgment (n 297) Partially Dissenting Opinion of Judge Robinson, para 12.

[436] ibid., para 9.

[437] *Zigiranyirazo v. Prosecutor*, Decision on Protais Zigiranyirazo's Motion for Damages, Case No. ICTR-2001-01-073, 18 June 2012.

[438] ibid., para 19. [439] ibid., para 21. [440] ibid. [441] ibid., paras 21–42.

[442] ibid., Partially Dissenting Opinion of Judge Park, para 4.

going beyond the statutory provisions on the rights of the accused to also incorporate such rights as the right to appeal, the right to an effective remedy and the right to privacy, and fundamental principles of fairness in criminal law, including *ne bis in idem* and *nullum crimen sine lege*.

There are a number of areas of international criminal practice that are worthy of commendation for setting the highest standards of fairness. These include the granting of provisional release by some tribunals; the proceedings on 'no case to answer' in most tribunals, which illustrate the presumption of innocence in action, and the jurisprudence on judicial impartiality which finds that a judge must not only be free from subjective bias, he or she must also be free from any appearance of bias. In addition, the expansive translation rights at the ICC, while they may be costly for the Court, are to be welcomed insofar as they illustrate the highest standards of fairness.

Some other areas of trial practice in some of the tribunals leave some room for improvement. A number of suggestions were made in this chapter for the enhancement of the rights of the accused in the areas of disclosure, judicial notice, remedies for breaches of rights, the length of trials, and resources for the defence pursuant to the equality of arms principle in a number of the tribunals. In addition, some issues specific to individual tribunals, such as *in absentia* trials before the STL and the impact of Regulation 55 before the ICC on the right to be informed of the charges, were discussed.

Given the lack of coherence and consistency between the procedural practices of the various tribunals, and occasionally between chambers of the same tribunal, it is difficult to draw overall conclusions on whether international criminal trials are fair or unfair as a whole. Indeed, it would be unhelpful to attempt to do so, given that such an assessment might overlook some pressing issues in particular tribunals, or might fail to recognize some of the positive precedents set by the international criminal tribunals. Instead, this chapter highlighted some of the positive aspects of international criminal procedure and some areas where some work was needed in order to bring the tribunals in line with their self-declared 'highest standards of fairness'. This concept will be addressed in greater detail in Chapter 5, but the next chapter will first deal with a key conceptual issue on fairness—that is, to whom does the right to a fair trial attach?

4

Procedural Actors and the Right to a Fair Trial

This chapter examines the extension of fair trial rights to actors beyond the accused in the context of international criminal trials. It will be shown that the Prosecutor has, on occasion, been held to possess specific procedural entitlements that were designed and set out in human rights instruments and international criminal statutes with only the accused in mind. The extension of procedural guarantees such as the right to trial without undue delay to other parties with an interest in the outcome of proceedings, such as victims and the international community, shall also be discussed.

In addition, this chapter considers the need to protect the rights of witnesses, in particular where the witness's life or safety is at risk. A consideration of whether those rights are imperilled by the trial, it shall be seen, is justified where it involves a balancing of two individual's human rights—for example, the accused's right to a fair trial on one hand and the witness's right to life on the other. By contrast, the balancing exercise that international criminal tribunals have occasionally entered into, in pursuit of equilibrium between the 'prosecutor's rights' and the 'accused's rights' is fundamentally flawed, because the alleged procedural rights of the Prosecutor have no basis in law. The prosecution does possess certain interests laid down in the statutes, designed to ensure that its case is put before the court in a coherent and complete manner, but it shall be argued that these interests should not outweigh the rights of the accused, which ought to stand at the apex of any considerations by the court. The question instead should be whether the prosecution has been unduly hampered in its presentation of the case. As shall be seen in some of the examples discussed in this chapter, the impact of these extensions on the rights of the accused have been far from theoretical.

4.1 Theoretical Considerations: The Place of Other Procedural Actors in Achieving the Highest Standards of Fairness

Before entering into a full analysis of the extension of fair trial rights to the prosecution and other actors at trial, it is apposite to consider how this chapter fits in with one of this book's core hypotheses, discussed in Chapter 5 in greater detail—that international criminal tribunals are under a duty to set the highest standards of fairness in their procedure. Some might argue that by developing a body of procedural entitlements for victims, witnesses, the prosecution, and other interested parties, international criminal tribunals have gone beyond minimalist conceptions of the right to a fair trial as interpreted by domestic and human rights jurisdictions, and have thereby embraced higher standards of fairness than those embodied by human rights and domestic standards.[1] This viewpoint could be particularly championed by victims' groups, who for many years have bemoaned the victim's status as 'bystander' or 'uninvited guest' to criminal trials, both in certain legal systems[2] and internationally.[3] Indeed, some of the very notions that drove the establishment of international criminal tribunals in the first place, such as the idea of achieving 'justice for all' through these courts, might well be advanced as a very good reason why international criminal tribunals need to place other actors on a relatively equal footing vis-à-vis the rights of the accused.

However, as discussed in Chapter 2 above, there is a distinction to be drawn between fairness as a meta-juridical concept, which can embrace elements of restorative justice, distributive justice, and the right to an effective remedy, and the right to a fair trial as a standalone concept, which is defined most extensively in Article 14 of the ICCPR.[4] Article 14 has formed the basis of the right to a fair trial in the tribunals' statutes, and as such, these tribunals

[1] Mirjan R. Damaška, 'Reflections on Fairness in International Criminal Justice' (2012) 10 *JICJ* 611, 614–15.

[2] William F. McDonald, 'Towards a Bicentennial Revolution in Criminal Justice: The Return of the Victim' (1976) 13 *Am Crim LR* 649; Nils Christie, 'Conflicts as Property' (1977) 17 *Brit J Criminol* 1. A huge number of victims' rights instruments and legislation have been passed in recent decades: see Marc S. Groenhuijsen and Rianne M. Letschert (eds), *Compilation of International Victims' Rights Instruments* (Nijmegen: Wolf Legal Publishers, 2012).

[3] See e.g. the comments by the Colombian delegation to the ICC Preparatory Conference that 'the victim … was an uninvited guest, a spectator, which exacerbated the conflict'. *Proposal by Colombia: Comments on the report on the international seminar on victims' access to the International Criminal Court*, PNCICC/1999/WGRPE/DP.37, 10 August 1999.

[4] See further above, Section 2.2.

should seek to maximize the realization of the *lege lata* before expanding rights to other actors as a matter of the *lege ferenda*. Even if international tribunals were to expand these rights on the basis of a conceptual understanding of 'fairness' or 'justice', it is argued that the interpretation of rights and duties within the confines of the judicial system must necessarily be based on sound legal authority and a full discussion of the principles that drive this expansion. In practice, however, as shall be discussed below, the conceptual underpinnings of the meaning of fairness and justice have not been discussed when extending rights in this manner, and the rights of the prosecution and other actors have often been asserted without a great deal of legal reasoning.

Therefore, there is a case to be made that the conceptualizations of fairness and justice, which extend beyond the confines of the courtroom, should be of limited concern to the judicial system. To expect the international criminal judiciary to achieve, for example, justice for all victims affected by the atrocities of the past may be over-ambitious.[5] In any event, it is unlikely that such ends could be achieved by allowing victims the right to legal representation or permitting them to present evidence.[6]

There is a need to distinguish 'service rights' from 'procedural rights' in the context of the international criminal trial.[7] I have argued elsewhere that victims would be far better served by the provision of service rights than by the extension of procedural rights at trial.[8] Service rights include information about proceedings, reparations, and counselling, while procedural rights include participation in proceedings, the presentation of evidence, and influence over prosecutorial decision-making.[9] The current regime of procedural rights at the ICC and STL may produce a greater inequality in effect, because it grants broad swathes of procedural rights to a limited number of victims of mass atrocities, whereas their fellow victims are excluded. It can also lead to disappointment where victims' expectations surpass what the Court can actually offer. There is a clear need to carefully analyse the procedural

[5] Lorraine Smith, 'Victims' Participation at the International Criminal Court: Benefit or Burden?' in William A. Schabas, Yvonne McDermott, and Niamh Hayes (eds), *The Ashgate Research Companion to International Criminal Law: Critical Perspectives* (Aldershot: Ashgate, 2013) 181, 188.

[6] Yvonne McDermott, 'Some are More Equal than Others: Victim Participation in the International Criminal Court' (2008) 5 *Eyes on the ICC* 23.

[7] The term 'procedural rights' was coined by Andrew Ashworth in his article, 'Victim Impact Statements and Sentencing' (1993) *Crim LR* 498, 499, according to Helen Fenwick, 'Procedural "Rights" of Victims of Crime: Public or Private Ordering of the Criminal Justice Process?' (1997) 60 *MLR* 317, 318.

[8] Yvonne McDermott, 'Victims and International Law: Remedies in the Courtroom?' (2009) 4 *Hague Justice Journal* 199.

[9] ibid., 203.

safeguards in place for the rights of the accused when measures such as victim participation are introduced in the interests of restorative justice.[10]

When it comes to prosecutorial fair trial rights, the link to the goals of international criminal law is tenuous. Perhaps it could be argued that by allowing the prosecution to avail itself of fair trial rights, the goal of 'ending impunity' is pursued because it makes it easier for such rights to be asserted in pursuit of a conviction. The circumstances surrounding the *Haradinaj* retrial, discussed in detail below, serves as a prime example, where some might suggest that the prosecution's 'right' to a fair trial in this regard effectively gave it a second chance to argue its case.[11] But such incidents add fuel to the fire of these courts' detractors who wish to argue that the cards are stacked against the defendants in these trials.[12] Ultimately, then, the overall impact of such extensions may take away from the goal of pursuing justice in a transparent and unbiased manner, rather than aiding the realization of that goal.

In light of the limited and definite paradigm of the right to a fair trial as defined by international human rights legal instruments, the inescapable conclusion is that that such rights should only apply to the accused. This is also supported by the *travaux preparatoires* of the ICC Statute—Articles 63 and 67 of the Draft Statute of the ICC referred exclusively to the rights of suspects and accused persons.[13] In spite of the fact that Article 6 is one of the most litigated provisions before the European Court of Human Rights, the ECtHR has never dealt with cases where a breach of Article 6 has been alleged because the prosecution has been deprived of these rights. The rights of victims tend to fall under the aegis of the right to an effective remedy.[14]

Nevertheless, all of the international criminal tribunals have recognized that fairness is a duty owed principally but not solely to the accused.

[10] Andrew Ashworth, 'Responsibilities, Rights and Restorative Justice' (2002) 42 *Brit J Criminol* 578.

[11] Yvonne McDermott, 'Double Speak and Double Standards: Does the Jurisprudence on Retrial following Acquittal under International Criminal Law Spell the End of the Double Jeopardy Rule?' in David Keane and Yvonne McDermott (eds), *The Challenge of Human Rights: Past, Present and Future* (Cheltenham: Edward Elgar, 2012) 176.

[12] See also, Section 5.2.3 below.

[13] Report of the Preparatory Committee on the Establishment of an International Criminal Court, A/CONF.183/2/Add.1, 14 April 1998.

[14] See e.g. *Kaya v. Turkey* (1998) 28 EHRR 1, 19 February 1998. Compare *Gulec v. Turkey* (1999) 28 EHRR 121, 27 July 1998, holding that Article 2 of the ECHR gives rise to a state obligation to investigate and prosecute serious crimes. The Inter-American Court of Human Rights has extended the due process rights contained in Article 8 (the right to a fair trial) to victims: *Paniagua Morales et al.* Case, Judgment of March 8, 1998, Inter-Am. Ct. H.R. (Ser. C) No. 37 (1998) para 155, and to the relatives of victims: *Blake* Case, Judgment of January 24, 1998, Inter-Am. Ct. H.R. (Ser. C) No. 36 (1998) para 97.

A number of decisions have stated that other actors, such as the prosecutor, victims, or the international community may be regarded as holders of such rights.

The next section of this chapter shall examine the rights extended to the prosecution in the tribunals' jurisprudence. Section 4.3 shall discuss the extension of the rights of the accused to victims, witnesses, and the international community; the need to achieve a balance between the rights of the accused and the fundamental rights of witnesses; and the theory that witness protection issues are the only considerations that should be balanced against the rights of the accused.

4.2 The Prosecutor's Right to a Fair Trial

In the *Prlić* case, the ICTY Prosecutor argued that by reducing the time allocated to it in the interests of the accused's right to an expeditious trial,[15] the Trial Chamber of the ICTY had violated 'the fundamental right of the victims, the Prosecution, and the international community to a fair trial'.[16] The Appeals Chamber, in holding that the requirement of a fair trial was 'not uniquely predicated on the fairness accorded to any one party',[17] found that the Trial Chamber had failed to adequately take into account the effect that the reduction of time might have had on the prosecution's right to fairly present its case.[18] This was in spite of the fact that a key reason behind the impugned decision was that just 30 per cent of the sitting time of the Trial Chamber had been used by the prosecution in the six preceding months.[19] In light of this leisurely pace adopted by the prosecution and in the interests of hurrying it along, the Chamber had reduced the time allocated to the prosecution for presenting its case by one-third, and had offered suggestions as to how the prosecution could use its time more wisely.[20] As a result of the Appeals Chamber's reversal of this decision, the presentation of the prosecution case proceeded for some eight months longer than planned: the Trial Chamber had ordered the prosecution to complete the presentation of its case by July 2007, but the prosecution case did not in fact close until February 2008.

[15] *Prosecutor v. Prlić*, Decision on Adoption of New Measures to Bring the Trial to an End within Reasonable Time, Case No. IT-04-74-T, 13 November 2006, para 14.

[16] *Prosecutor v. Prlić*, Decision on Prosecution Appeal Concerning the Trial Chamber's Ruling Reducing Time for the Prosecution Case, Case No. IT-04-74-AR73.4, 6 February 2007, para 13.

[17] ibid., para 14. [18] ibid., para 16.

[19] *Prlić* Decision on Adoption of New Measures to Bring the Trial to an End within Reasonable Time (n 15) para 6.

[20] ibid., paras 20–1.

The Appeals Chamber judgment seems to go against the principle that it should be for the Trial Chamber to decide on the time limits that need to be set for the presentation of cases, in full accordance with the rights of the accused.[21]

The ICTY Appeals Chamber in *Martić* had to decide whether it would be in the interests of justice to allow the evidence of a prosecution witness who had died before the defence could conclude its cross-examination of him to remain on the trial record.[22] The Trial Chamber had held that the rights of the accused did not outweigh the probative value of the evidence.[23] By so doing, the Trial Chamber applied the correct standard of assessment laid out in the tribunal's Rules of Procedure and Evidence, which state that a piece of evidence can be admitted if its probative value is not 'substantially outweighed' by the need to ensure a fair trial.[24] While the outcome was itself correct and recognized the court's truth-seeking function, the Trial Chamber and Appeals Chamber decisions on the issue are remarkable because they based their decision on the Prosecutor's right to a fair trial. The accused sought to appeal on the grounds that the 'only type of unfairness envisaged by the Statute ... [was] unfairness to the accused'.[25] The Appeals Chamber, in dismissing this claim, noted that the Prosecutor acts on behalf of victims and the international community, and that it would be difficult to find that a trial had been fair where the prosecution had been disadvantaged owing to the Chamber's granting of rights to the accused 'beyond a strict compliance with those fundamental protections'.[26] This seems to suggest that the rights of the accused need to be realized in their most minimalist form, and that any higher realization, where it was 'at the expense of the Prosecution',[27] would be fallacious.

This interpretation fails to take into account the fact that Prosecutors before some international criminal tribunals are often in an institutionally privileged position because they serve as the 'public face' of the court,[28] which enhances the

[21] See Rules 73*bis*(C) and 73*ter*(F) ICTY RPE.

[22] *Prosecutor v. Martić*, Decision on Appeal against the Trial Chamber's Decision on the Evidence of Witness Milan Babić, Case No. IT-95-11-AR73.2, 14 September 2006.

[23] *Prosecutor v. Martić* Decision on Motion to Exclude the Testimony of Witness Milan Babić, Together with Associated Exhibits, from Evidence, Case No. IT-95-11-T, 9 June 2006.

[24] Rule 89(D) ICTY RPE.

[25] *Martić* Decision on Appeal against the Trial Chamber's Decision on the Evidence of Witness Milan Babić (n 22) para 10.

[26] ibid., para 13. See also *Prosecutor v. Aleksovski*, Decision on Prosecutor's Appeal on Admissibility of Evidence, Case No. IT-95-14/1-AR73, 16 February 1999, para 25.

[27] *Prosecutor v. Aleksovski*, Decision on Prosecutor's Appeal on Admissibility of Evidence, Case No. IT-95-14/1-AR73, 16 February 1999, para 25.

[28] Charles C. Jalloh and Amy DiBella, 'Equality of Arms in International Criminal Law: Continuing Challenges' in Schabas, McDermott, and Hayes (eds) (n 5) 251, 263–4,

cooperation between state and non-governmental organizations, and prosecution investigators and counsel, while defence teams' ability to carry out investigations,[29] secure witnesses,[30] and benefit from the cooperation of non-governmental organizations[31] is necessarily hampered by a wider unwillingness to assist the defence.[32] Defence counsel lawyers have, on occasion, even been arrested in the country of investigation as a result of their activities.[33] Of course, the prosecution needs to receive an equal opportunity to present its case,[34] but the position that any trial that is 'too fair' on the rights of the accused will result in an unfair trial when the prosecution is in any way disadvantaged, seems to be a bridge too far. This perception of the fair trial as a balancing exercise between the rights of the accused and the interests of the prosecution can only result in inequity in practice, considering the prosecution's already-privileged position.

The STL has also explicitly recognized the 'prosecutor's right to a fair trial', and has recognized an equally dangerous balancing exercise between the rights of the defence and the interests of the prosecution. In a decision pertaining to a prosecution request to amend its exhibit list, the Trial Chamber noted that it had 'carefully balanced the right of the Prosecution to present evidence supporting its case with the rights of counsel to adequately prepare for trial' and, in light of that balancing exercise, deemed it appropriate to permit the prosecution to amend its exhibit list.[35] As mentioned in Chapter 2 above, the rhetoric of 'balance' in the criminal law is especially dangerous, because it allows the rights of the accused to be outweighed by other factors.[36]

The ICTR's approach in *Zigiranyirazo* seems to strike a more appropriate balance.[37] It recalled the Chamber's role in ensuring full respect for the

pointing to the fact that Prosecutors often represent their international court or tribunal before the Security Council.

[29] See the analysis of evidence-gathering in the *Blaškić* case in Jacob Katz Cogan, 'International Criminal Courts and Fair Trials: Difficulties and Prospects' (2002) 27 *Yale JIL* 111, 122–4.

[30] Mark S. Ellis, 'Achieving Justice before the International War Crimes Tribunal: Challenges for the Defense Counsel' (1996–1997) 7 *Duke J Comp & Int'l L* 519, 534 (stating that, in *Tadić*, witnesses in the Prijedor region who were members of the police or armed forces were prohibited from speaking to defence teams).

[31] Jalloh and DiBella (n 28) 263. [32] ibid.

[33] Kate Gibson, 'The Arrest of ICTR Defense Counsel Peter Erlinder in Rwanda' (2010) 14 *ASIL Insights*; 'ICC Promises to Investigate Libya Staff if Released', *BBC News* (London, 23 June 2012).

[34] See also, *Prosecutor v. Milutinović et al.*, Decision on Prosecution's Request for Certification of Rule 73*bis* Issue for Appeal, Case No. IT-05-87-T, 30 August 2006, para 10.

[35] *Prosecutor v. Ayyash et al.*, Decision on Prosecution Motion to Amend its Exhibit List and Oneissi Defence Request to Stay the Proceedings, Case No. STL-11-01/T/TC, 13 April 2015, para 47.

[36] Section 2.3 above.

[37] *Prosecutor v. Zigiranyirazo*, Decision on the Prosecution Joint Motion for Re-Opening its Case and for Reconsideration of the 31 January 2006 Decision on the Hearing of Witness Michel Bagaragaza via Video-Link, Case No. ICTR-2001-73-T, 16 November 2006.

rights of the accused and held that the question to be asked was whether the prosecution had been 'unduly hampered in the presentation of its case'.[38] Similarly, the ICC Appeals Chamber in the *Ngudjolo* case found it unnecessary to enter into a discussion as to whether the Prosecutor was owed the right to a fair trial.[39] Instead, it framed the contestation that the Prosecutor's right to challenge witnesses had been breached as, 'a fundamental aspect of the trial, which touches upon the core functions of both the Prosecutor and the Trial Chamber, namely the objective of establishing the truth as well as the Prosecutor's ability to present evidence in order to prove the charges against the accused'.[40] However, the concept of the Prosecutor's 'right' to a fair trial was reintroduced in *Ruto and Sang*, where the prosecution requested that the statements and transcripts of recorded interviews of witnesses who later recanted their testimony be admitted to the trial record as proof of their contents.[41] In its oral submissions, the prosecution argued that to refuse admission of these documents would breach its right to a fair trial.[42]

A number of decisions have based the extension of fair trial rights to the prosecution on the fair trial principle of equality of arms.[43] Judge Vohrah, in an early pronouncement in the *Tadić* case, held that the equality guarantee was a right that attached to the accused alone, as it was designed to ensure that the defence was not disadvantaged vis-à-vis the prosecution.[44] He said:

> This proposition that the equality of arms principle was intended to elevate the Defence to the level of the Prosecution, as much as possible, in its ability to prepare and present its case is evident in the case law arising out of the European Convention for the Protection of Human Rights and Fundamental Freedoms 1950 ('the ECHR') and the International Covenant on Civil and Political Rights 1966

[38] ibid., para 18.

[39] *Situation in the DRC: Prosecutor v. Ngudjolo Chui*, Judgment, Case No. ICC-01/04-02/12, 27 February 2015, para 256.

[40] ibid.

[41] *Situation in Kenya: Prosecutor v. Ruto and Sang*, Public Redacted Version of 'Prosecution's Request for the Admission of Prior Recorded Testimony of [REDACTED] Witnesses', Case No. ICC-01/09-01/11, 29 April 2015.

[42] *Situation in Kenya: Prosecutor v. Ruto and Sang*, Transcript, Case No. ICC-01/09-01/11, 25 June 2015.

[43] e.g. *Aleksovski*, Decision on Prosecutor's Appeal on Admissibility of Evidence (n 26) para 25; *Situation in Uganda*, Decision on the Prosecution's Application for Leave to Appeal the Decision on Victims' Applications for Participation a/0010/06, a/0064/06 to a/0070/06, a/0081/06 to a/0104/06 and a/0111/06 to a/0127/06, Case No. ICC-02/04-01/05, 19 December 2007, para 27; *Situation in Uganda: Prosecutor v. Kony et al.*, Decision on the Prosecutor's Application for Leave to Appeal Dated the 15th day of May 2006, Case No. ICC-02/04-01/05, 10 July 2006, para 24.

[44] *Prosecutor v. Tadić*, Decision on Prosecution Motion for Production of Defence Witness Statement, Separate Opinion of Judge Vohrah, Case No. IT-96-1-T, 27 November 1996.

('the ICCPR') both of which incorporate the principle of equality of arms in the concept of a fair trial.[45]

This interpretation recognizes the fact that the prosecution will have more power and resources at its disposal than the defence, in both international and domestic criminal trials.[46] However, later interpretations have ruled that 'procedural equality means what it says, equality between Prosecution and Defence, and to suggest otherwise is tantamount to a procedural inequality in favour of the Defence and against the Prosecution'.[47]

This is an incorrect interpretation of the equality clause for a number of reasons. First, the provision from which the equality guarantee in international criminal law is derived states that 'all *persons* shall be equal before the International Tribunal',[48] not that all *parties* should be equal before the tribunal. Second, if we look at the context of the reference to equality, we observe that this reference is made under the chapeau of 'rights of the accused', indicating that this equality was intended as being between accused persons, as opposed to ensuring that the prosecutor should be treated 'as equally' as the defendants.[49] Finally, the statutory provisions on rights of the accused were designed to ensure that the rights of accused as laid down in international human rights treaties were fully transposed into the law of the international criminal tribunals. Because those human rights provisions interpret the equality of arms guarantee as a right of the accused only,[50] broader interpretations run contrary to the object and purpose of the statutory provision.

The extension of rights to the prosecution in the interests of fairness or the Prosecutor's alleged right to a fair trial can have a real effect on the rights of the accused, and this is probably best illustrated by the *Haradinaj* retrial fiasco, which I have discussed at length elsewhere,[51] but the facts are worthy of restatement here. The three accused (Ramush Haradinaj, Idriz Balaj, and Lahi Brahimaj) were transferred to the International Criminal Tribunal for the former Yugoslavia on 9 March 2005. In April 2008, Haradinaj and Balaj were acquitted on all counts in the indictment, and Brahimaj was acquitted

[45] ibid. [46] See also, *Jespers v. Belgium* (1981) 5 EHRR 305.

[47] *Aleksovski* Decision on Prosecutor's Appeal on Admissibility of Evidence (n 26) para 23.

[48] Article 18(1), SCSL Statute; Article 20(1), ICTR Statute; Article 21(1), ICTY Statute (author's emphasis).

[49] See further on this point, Sergey Vasiliev, 'The Role and Legal Status of the Prosecutor in International Criminal Trials', 25 November 2010, available online at http://papers.ssrn.com/sol3/papers.cfm?abstract_id=1715465 (last accessed 2 March 2015).

[50] See the authority cited in Judge Vohrah's dissenting opinion above (n 44).

[51] Yvonne McDermott, 'Rights in Reverse: A Critical Analysis of Fair Trial Rights under International Criminal Law' in Schabas, McDermott, and Hayes (eds) (n 5) 165; McDermott (n 11).

on all counts but two.[52] For reasons pertaining to the Prosecutor's right to a fair trial, the Appeals Chamber ordered a retrial in respect of several counts of the indictment in July 2010.[53] The three accused were acquitted of all counts in the retrial judgment, issued on 29 November 2012.[54] In effect, therefore, the three accused spent an extra four and a half years on trial, as a consequence of the alleged breach of the prosecution's right to a fair trial during the original trial.[55]

'The prosecution's right to a fair trial' was the term used in the 2010 Appeals Chamber judgment, but a corrigendum was issued a number of days later which changed the reference to 'the Trial Chamber's duty to safeguard the fairness of proceedings'.[56] This corrigendum may well have been issued in the knowledge that the original explicit reference to the prosecution's right to a fair trial, and the clear consequences for the accused in this instance, would be highly controversial. The nomenclature changed again slightly by the time of the retrial judgment. The newly-constituted Trial Chamber noted that the successful prosecutorial appeal alleged '*inter alia*, that the Trial Chamber breached *its right to a fair trial* by not allowing it additional time to secure the evidence of two critical witnesses'.[57] Therefore, this case can be taken as a clear example of the Prosecutor's right to a fair trial in action.

Throughout the duration of the *Haradinaj et al.* trial, the Chamber had to contend with allegations of intimidation of prosecution witnesses and difficulties in securing the testimony of such witnesses. Protective measures were issued for a number of witnesses in order to encourage them to testify.[58] Ultimately, the Chamber heard from over ninety witnesses, some of whom only appeared following the Trial Chamber's issuance of subpoenas for their appearance.[59] Of the eighteen witnesses for whom subpoenas were issued, seventeen testified during the trial.[60] It was arranged for the remaining subpoenaed witness, Naser Lika, to testify via video-link on 13 November 2007.[61] Two days after he failed to appear to testify on the scheduled date, he

[52] *Prosecutor v. Haradinaj et al.*, Judgment, Case No. IT-04-84-T, 3 April 2008.

[53] *Prosecutor v. Haradinaj et al.*, Judgment, Case No. IT-04-84-A, 21 July 2010.

[54] *Prosecutor v. Haradinaj et al.*, Retrial Judgment, Case No. IT-04-84*bis*-T, 29 November 2012.

[55] The Appeals Chamber held that the Trial Chamber had 'prioritised logistical considerations over the Prosecution's right to a fair trial': *Haradinaj* Appeal Judgment (n 53) para 46.

[56] *Prosecutor v. Haradinaj et al.*, Corrigendum to Judgment of 19 July 2010, Case No. IT-04-94-A, 23 July 2010, 1.

[57] *Haradinaj* Retrial Judgment (n 54) para 3 (author's emphasis).

[58] ibid., para 22.

[59] Subpoenas were issued to eighteen witnesses for the prosecution—see *Haradinaj* Trial Judgment (n 52) Annex A, 'Procedural History', para 20.

[60] Three of these witnesses required some coaxing—one testified via video-link and two only agreed to testify once contempt proceedings had been initiated against them (*Haradinaj* Trial Judgment (n 52) Annex A, 'Procedural History', paras 22–4).

[61] ibid., para 24.

was arrested by the Canadian authorities.[62] A new date was organized but the authorities were unable to bring the witness to the location in time.[63] A third date was then arranged to hear this witness's testimony, but the witness fell ill and was admitted to hospital before he could testify.[64] The prosecution informed the Chamber that it would be more than a week before it could even provide an estimate as to when the witness might be in a position to testify,[65] which the Trial Chamber obviously considered too long to wait because it declared the prosecution case closed some four days later. The prosecution took umbrage at this development, and Naser Lika was one of two key witnesses at issue in the prosecutor's appeal and request for a retrial.

The other witness, Shefqet Kabashi, appeared at the seat of the tribunal but refused to answer any questions put to him.[66] Arrangements were made for him to testify via video link from the United States, but he was unco-operative via this medium as well.[67] In response, the Chamber ordered the Prosecutor to make the indictment against that witness public, which was probably the only remaining power it had to encourage the witness to testify. Nonetheless, the Prosecutor alleged that the Chamber had not done enough to secure the testimony of Kabashi as well as Lika. The Appeals Chamber agreed and ordered a retrial.[68]

At the retrial, the evidence of some fifty-six witnesses, including the two key witnesses who were the subject of the successful appeal, was tendered for the prosecution.[69] When witness Kabashi (who had been sentenced to two months in prison for contempt[70]) appeared on the stand, he refused to co-operate or to answer questions, and he further alleged that his testimony given in the *Limaj* trial had been falsified.[71] The transcript of this testimony was entered onto the record under Rule 89(D), but the Chamber noted that it would need to be corroborated to form the basis of a conviction.[72] One might wonder why the prosecution did not move to introduce the *Limaj* transcript in this manner during the original trial. Regardless, as it happened, the relevant portions of Kabashi's testimony were not corroborated, even though the prosecution had been granted permission to introduce new witnesses.[73] Despite the prosecution having been given something of a second

[62] ibid. [63] ibid. [64] ibid. [65] ibid. [66] ibid. [67] ibid.

[68] *Haradinaj* Appeal Judgment (n 53) para 49.

[69] *Haradinaj* Retrial Judgment (n 54) para 4.

[70] *Prosecutor v. Kabashi*, Sentencing Judgment, Case No. IT-04-84-R77.1, 16 September 2011.

[71] *Prosecutor v. Haradinaj et al.*, Transcript, T.332-435, Case No. IT-04-84*bis*-T, 22-24 August 2011.

[72] *Prosecutor v. Haradinaj et al.*, Decision on Joint Defence Oral Motion pursuant to Rule 89(D), Case No. IT-04-84*bis*-T, 28 September 2011.

[73] *Prosecutor v. Haradinaj et al.*, Appeal Brief on Behalf of Ramush Haradinaj on Scope of Partial Retrial, Case No. IT-04-84*bis*-AR73.1, 10 February 2011, para 20; *Prosecutor v. Haradinaj*

chance in the form of the *Haradinaj et al.* retrial, the evidence was still insufficient to prove the guilt of the three accused beyond reasonable doubt on the charges, and they were acquitted on all counts.[74]

It would seem, therefore, that the prosecution had not been unduly hampered in the presentation of its original case at trial, since the testimony of the two 'crucial' witnesses proved insufficient at retrial to establish the alleged culpability of the accused. Of course, it is easy to make that assessment with the benefit of hindsight. Nevertheless, this example again illustrates that the most appropriate standard of assessment for issues pertaining to the prosecution's interests at trial is whether the prosecution was unduly hampered in the presentation of its case,[75] and not whether the prosecution's rights had been 'outweighed' by the rights of the accused. Had the proposed standard been adopted by the Appeals Chamber in 2010, it is unlikely that the accused in *Haradinaj et al.* would have been deprived of their liberty for an additional two years. The crude balancing act that pits the Prosecutor's 'rights' against the accused's right to a fair trial is neglectful of every court's fundamental role in protecting the rights of defendants deprived of their liberty and facing trial before it. In allowing those rights to be 'balanced' against the interests of the prosecution, which is already in a privileged position deriving from its role as an organ of the court, these decisions effectively create an imbalance to the detriment of the accused.

4.3 The Rights of Victims, Witnesses, and the International Community

As mentioned at the outset, broader conceptions of fairness have not just extended fair trial rights to the prosecution. Following emerging domestic and international practice recognizing the rights of victims, international criminal trials have had increasing regard for victims' rights. The ICC Statute explicitly recognizes that victims have a right to present their views and concerns at appropriate stages of proceedings.[76] Of course, it would be ridiculous to suggest that the accused's rights should trump the human rights of other affected actors at all times. Where, for example, there is a clear risk

et al., Decision on Haradinaj's Appeal on Scope of Partial Retrial, Case No. IT -04-84*bis*-AR 73.1, 31 May 2011, para 26.

[74] *Haradinaj* Retrial Judgment (n 54), paras 682–5.

[75] Following *Zigiranyirazo*, Decision on the Prosecution Joint Motion for Re-Opening its Case and for Reconsideration of the 31 January 2006 Decision on the Hearing of Witness Michel Bagaragaza via Video-Link (n 37).

[76] Article 68(3), ICC Statute.

to a witness's right to life by respecting the accused's right to a public trial, it is clear where the burden should fall. This conclusion is supported by the European Court of Human Rights decision in *Doorson*, which found that:

> Such interests of witnesses and victims [as the right to life] are in principle protected by other, substantive provisions of the Convention, which imply that Contracting States should organise their criminal proceedings in such a way that those interests are not unjustifiably imperilled.[77]

This formulation, which treats victims and witnesses' human rights as interests that must not be jeopardized by the trial, is reflected in, inter alia, Article 64(2) of the ICC Statute, which mandates that the Trial Chamber must ensure that the trial 'is conducted with full respect for the *rights* of the accused and due regard for the *protection* of victims and witnesses'.[78]

The need to ensure that witnesses do not come to any harm as a result of their cooperation with the international criminal tribunal, and to balance any protection measures imposed to achieve this end with the rights of the accused to a public trial and to the disclosure of both exculpatory and incriminating evidence, is unquestionably challenging. The tribunals lack the power to protect witnesses in the same way as domestic legal systems can, where the police can impose witness protection programmes. However, units have been established as part of the registries of the international criminal tribunals to protect witnesses and victims and to provide them with information and assistance through counselling and other services, and can provide witness protection through relocation in exceptional circumstances.[79]

Witness protection measures that seek to shield the witness's identity from the public or other parties to proceedings have a potential impact on the rights to a public trial, to adequate time and facilities for the preparation of one's defence and to confront one's accusers. In *Bagosora*, the Chamber considered equality of arms and the need to ensure a balance between the positions of the prosecution and defence as a factor in deciding whether to grant protective measures to defence witnesses.[80] It is for this reason that the international criminal tribunals have been extremely unwilling to permit witness anonymity. The *Tadić* Protective Measures Decision can be seen as an outlier in this respect, as it has not been followed in later decisions.[81]

[77] *Doorson v. The Netherlands* (1997) 23 EHRR 330, 26 March 1996, para 70.

[78] Author's emphasis. See also, Article 16(2), STL Statute.

[79] See Rule 34, ICTY, ICTR, and SCSL RPE; Rule 50, STL RPE; Article 43(6), ICC Statute.

[80] *Prosecutor v. Bagosora et al.*, Decision on Kabiligi Motion for Protection of Witnesses, Case No. ICTR-98-41-T, 1 September 2003, para 2.

[81] *Prosecutor v. Tadić*, Decision on the Prosecutor's Motion Requesting Protective Measures for Victims and Witnesses, Case No. IT-94-1-T, 10 August 1995. Compare: *Prosecutor v. Blaškić*,

Disappointingly, the STL introduces an elaborate procedure that permits the testimony of anonymous witnesses to be taken,[82] and to be admitted into the record provided that its probative value is not 'substantially outweighed' by the need to ensure a fair trial.[83]

On the other hand, if witnesses cannot be assured of their safety, they will be unwilling to testify.[84] As is the case in domestic proceedings, child witnesses and victims of sexual violence are especially vulnerable and their privacy and dignity need to be respected in the course of proceedings.[85] In such cases, testimony via video-conference link or other means may be appropriate, as may measures to shield their identity from the public or the media.[86] The ICC RPE sets out a number of principles of evidence for sexual violence cases: first, the general rule that a Chamber shall not impose a general rule that evidence needs to be corroborated applies in particular to sexual violence crimes;[87] second, consent must be genuine and cannot be inferred where there was a threat or use of force, an inability to consent on the part of the victim, or through silence,[88] and last, evidence on the prior sexual conduct of the victim is irrelevant[89] and therefore inadmissible.[90]

There is a lack of uniformity between the tribunals on when witness protection measures will be granted. The ICTY has arguably set down the most stringent pre-requisites for granting witness protection, and has required that witnesses show they have reasonable and genuine fears before protective measures will be granted.[91] The STL requires 'persuasive evidence'[92] showing that the protective measures are appropriate, and has dismissed

Decision on the Application of the Prosecutor Dated 17 October 1996 Requesting Protective Measures for Victims and Witnesses, Case No. IT-95-14-T, 5 November 1996.

[82] Examination of such witnesses is to be conducted by the Pre-Trial judge *ex parte*, per Rule 93 of the STL RPE, and only applies where there is a serious risk of harm to the witness, to a person close to him or her, or to imperative national security interests.

[83] Rules 93, 149(D) and 159, STL RPE.

[84] Guido Acquaviva and Mikaela Heikkilä, 'Protective and Special Measures for Witnesses' in Goran Sluiter, Håkan Friman, Suzannah Linton, Salvatore Zappalà, and Sergey Vasiliev (eds), *International Criminal Procedure: Principles and Rules* (Oxford: OUP, 2013) 818, 819.

[85] Anna-Marie L.M. de Brouwer, *Supranational Criminal Prosecution of Sexual Violence* (Antwerp: Intersentia, 2005) 231–78.

[86] Rule 133, STL RPE; Rule 75, ICTR, ICTY, and SCSL RPE; Article 68(2), ICC Statute.

[87] Rule 63(4), ICC RPE.

[88] Rule 70, ICC RPE. See also, Rule 96, SCSL, ICTR, and ICTY RPE.

[89] Rule 70(d), ICC RPE.

[90] Rule 71, ICC RPE.

[91] e.g. *Prosecutor v. Popović et al.*, Decision on Urgent Prosecution Motion for Additional Protective Measures for Witness KDZ084, Case No. IT-05-88-A, 10 May 2012, 3.

[92] *Prosecutor v. Ayyash et al.*, Reasons for Decision Denying Certification to Appeal the Decision on Protective Measures for Witness PRH-566, Case No. STL-11/01/T/TC, 19 February 2014, para 11.

applications for protective measures that are overly broad and insufficiently specific.[93] By contrast, the ICTR has been more lenient in finding generalized factors, such as the security situation in Rwanda, to be sufficient in this regard.[94] The SCSL granted witness protection to all witnesses resident in Sierra Leone who had not expressly waived their right to protective measures.[95] Nonetheless, and despite the relatively widespread nature of witness protection measures which has continued into the practice of the ICC,[96] the extent of such protective measures should not be overstated. The most common protective measure is the ordering of 'delayed disclosure'.[97] In order to allow adequate time[98] for the preparation of the defence case, the identity of the witness is disclosed at least twenty-one days before their appearance,[99] and often longer.[100] The most important point to note is that witness anonymity was granted in only one early case,[101] and has not been followed in later jurisprudence,[102] although the possibility remains open that

[93] *Prosecutor v. Ayyash et al.*, Consolidated Decision on the Prosecution Motions for Protective Measures Regarding Ten Witnesses, Case No. STL-11/01/T/TC, 2 July 2014, para 14.

[94] *Prosecutor v. Simba*, Decision on Defence Request for Protection of Witnesses, Case No. ICTR-01-76-I, 25 August 2004, para 6. See further, Goran Sluiter, 'The ICTR and the Protection of Witnesses' (2005) 3 *JICJ* 962, 968

[95] *Prosecutor v. Norman et al.*, Decision on Prosecution Motion for Modification of Protective Measures for Witnesses, Case No. SCSL-04-15-PT-180, 8 June 2004, para 41.

[96] All witnesses bar three in the *Lubanga* case before the ICC were granted protective measures according to William A. Schabas, *The International Criminal Court: A Commentary on the Rome Statute* (Oxford: OUP, 2010) 825.

[97] Acquaviva and Heikkilä (n 84) 836. See e.g. *Prosecutor v. Prlić et al.*, Decision Establishing Guidelines for Requests for Protective Measures for Defence Witnesses, Case No. IT-04-74-T, 22 February 2008, 2–3 (distinguishing between these two types of protective measure).

[98] Rule 69(C) ICTY, ICTR, and SCSL RPE.

[99] e.g. *Prosecutor v. Bizimungu*, Decision on the Prosecutor's Motion for Protective Measures for Witnesses, Case No. ICTR-99-50-T, 22 September 2000, paras 14–15 and *Prosecutor v. Brima et al.*, Decision on the Prosecution Motion for Immediate Protective Measures for Witnesses and Victims, Case No. SCSL-2003-13-PT, 24 November 2003, para 44.

[100] For example, disclosure was delayed until forty-five days before the witness was scheduled to testify in *Situation in the DRC: Prosecutor v. Katanga and Ngudjolo*, Public redacted version of the Decision on the Protection of Prosecution Witnesses 267 and 353 of 20 May 2009, Case No. ICC-01/04-01/07, 28 May 2009.

[101] *Tadić* Decision on the Prosecutor's Motion Requesting Protective Measures for Victims and Witnesses (n 81), paras 59–66. This decision was heavily criticized in, inter alia, Natasha Affolder, '*Tadić*, the Anonymous Witness and the Sources of International Procedural Law' (1997–98) 19 *Michigan JIL* 445; Monroe Leigh, 'The Yugoslav Tribunal: Use of Unnamed Witnesses against Accused' (1996) 90 *AJIL* 235, and Monroe Leigh, 'Witness Anonymity is Inconsistent with Due Process' (1997) 91 *AJIL* 80. Compare Christine Chinkin, 'Due Process and Witness Anonymity' (1997) 91 *AJIL* 75.

[102] In *Blaškić*, the Trial Chamber held that witness anonymity could only be granted where 'fundamental exceptional circumstances' existed. See *Prosecutor v. Blaškić*, Judgment, Case No. IT-95-14-T, 3 March 2000, para 50.

the STL and other international criminal tribunals might allow anonymous witnesses in future cases.

The need to protect the accused from anonymous accusers has been extended to the participation of victims before the ICC. In *Lubanga*, it was stated that 'the fundamental principle prohibiting anonymous accusations would be violated if ... [victims] were permitted to add any point of fact or evidence at all to the Prosecution's case-file' and that, therefore, victims should not be permitted to question witnesses.[103] Other Chambers have, however, embraced a more expansive approach to victim participation. In *Bemba*, for example, victims were permitted to question witnesses.[104]

Suffice to say that these measures can impact on the rights of the accused, but that this is one of the excusable situations foreseen by the statutes where the rights of the accused can be fettered by the rights of others.[105] A distinction can be drawn between victims' participatory rights as 'status rights' and the human rights that are at issue when we discuss the witness's right to life or to respect for their private lives, and the right of the accused to a fair trial. Universally-accepted human rights should prevail over status rights, and when it comes to a clash between two human rights, the courts will have to strike a very delicate balance.

More relevant to the present chapter, however, are instances where procedural rights of the accused are extended to other actors. The SCSL, for example, has held that the right to a speedy trial attaches not just to the accused, but to victims and the international community as well, stating:

> It appears in the ICCPR as a right guaranteed to a defendant, but for international human rights law it offers a vital and concomitant guarantee to victims of war crimes and crimes against humanity ... Victims and relatives of victims are entitled

[103] *Situation in the DRC: Prosecutor v. Lubanga*, Decision on the Arrangements for Participation of Victims a/0001/06, a/0002/06 and a/0003/06 at the Confirmation Hearing, Case No. ICC-01/04-01/06, 22 September 2006, 7. See further, Christine H. Chung, 'Victims' Participation at the International Criminal Court: Are Concessions of the Court Clouding the Promise?' (2007–2008) 6 *Nw U J Int'l Hum Rts* 459.

[104] *Situation in the CAR: Prosecutor v. Bemba*, Decision (i) Ruling on Legal Representatives' Applications to Question Witness 33 and (ii) Setting a Schedule for the Filing of Submissions in Relation to Future Applications to Question Witnesses, Case No. ICC-01/05-01/08, 9 September 2011.

[105] See e.g. Article 67(1) ICC Statute ('having regard to the provisions of this Statute') and Article 68(2); Article 17(2) SCSL Statute ('subject to measures ordered ... for the protection of victims and witnesses'.); ICTR Statute, Article 20(2) ('subject to Article 21 of the Statute'); ICTY Statute, Article 21(2). See further *Prosecutor v. Bagosora et al.*, Decision and scheduling order on the prosecution motion for harmonization and modification of protective measures for witnesses, Case No. ICTR-98-41-I, 5 December 2001, para 14.

to have those accused of hideous offences which have caused them so much grief to be tried expeditiously.[106]

This finding was made despite the fact that the SCSL Statute explicitly says that the accused is entitled to the right to trial without undue delay, and does not mention any other parties in this regard.[107] The accused's motion in this case argued that Rule 72 of the Rules of Procedure and Evidence, which sent certain matters straight to the Appeals Chamber for consideration, violated the right to appeal to a higher authority.[108] The majority denied this appeal based on a finding that the rule served to enhance 'the basic right to expeditious justice'.[109] A more logical basis for denying the appeal was found in the Separate Opinion of Judge King, who recalled that the right to final appeal applied only to final appeal of a conviction, as opposed to appeals on procedural matters.[110]

Similarly, the interest of the international community in seeing the completion of international trials was put forward by the prosecution in a submission arguing against temporary release in *Šainović et al.*[111] The rights of victims and the international community have also been considered in referral decisions pursuant to Rule 11*bis*. Although the Referral Bench in *Ademi and Norac* recognized that Rule 11*bis* only explicitly required that the accused could be guaranteed a fair trial, it considered that this requirement was 'complemented by a concern for fairness towards other interested parties, such as victims and the international community', and that fairness to those actors was a policy consideration that needed to be taken into account in making referral decisions.[112] In principle, there should be nothing wrong with extending the fair trial rights of the accused to other persons with an interest in the outcome or with a role in proceedings. Problems arise, however, when those rights start to impinge on the rights of the accused, which is a risk if the early practice of the ICC regarding victim participation is to be followed in later jurisprudence.

Victims before the ICC have the right to 'present their views and concerns ... in a manner which is not prejudicial to or inconsistent with the rights of

[106] *Prosecutor v. Norman et al.*, Decision on the Application for a Stay of Proceedings and Denial of Right to Appeal, Case No. SCSL-2003-09-PT, 4 November 2003, para 8.

[107] Article 17(4)(c) SCSL Statute.

[108] *Norman et al.*, Decision on the Application for a Stay of Proceedings and Denial of Right to Appeal (n 106), para 9.

[109] ibid., para 30.

[110] ibid., Separate Opinion of Judge King, para 10.

[111] *Prosecutor v. Šainović et al.*, Decision on Ojdanic Motion for Temporary Provisional Release, Case No. IT-05-87-T, 7 December 2007, para 5.

[112] *Prosecutor v. Ademi and Norac*, Decision for Referral to the Authorities of the Republic of Croatia Pursuant to Rule 11*bis*, Case No. IT-04-78-PT, 14 September 2005, para 53.

the accused and a fair and impartial trial'.[113] The Court's formative years were widely criticized for their broad interpretations of the rights of victims in this regard.[114] Some of the rights that have been recognized include the right to examine evidence, the right to be notified about developments in the proceedings, the right to reparations, and the right to make submissions.[115] Victims have also been granted the right to introduce evidence pertaining to the guilt or innocence of the accused, and to challenge the admissibility and relevance of evidence tendered by other parties.[116] It has been suggested that these provisions effectively mean that the accused faces more than one accuser, in violation of the equality of arms principle.[117] Furthermore, unlike the ICC Prosecutor, participating victims do not bear an obligation to disclose exculpatory material to the defence, notwithstanding the fact that they now have a related right to lead evidence pertaining to the guilt or innocence of the accused.[118] What this means, in theory, is that a participating victim can call a witness to testify as to the guilt of the accused, and if they have some information to suggest that this witness is actually grossly unreliable, there is no duty on the witness to disclose that fact.

In the case of a clash between the participatory rights of victims and the procedural rights of the accused, it is clear from the formulation of Article 68(3) of the ICC Statute and Article 17 of the STL Statute that the rights of the accused should prevail. It is for this reason that these extensions of victims' rights into areas such as the leading of evidence should be treated with

[113] Article 68(3) ICC Statute.

[114] See, amongst many others, Smith (n 5); McDermott (n 6); McDermott (n 8); Christine Van den Wyngaert, 'Victims before International Criminal Courts, Some Views and Concerns of an ICC Trial Judge', Lecture delivered to Case Western Reserve University, 21 November 2011; Mirjan R. Damaška, 'Problematic Features of International Criminal Procedure' in Antonio Cassese *et al.* (eds), *The Oxford Companion to International Criminal Justice* (Oxford: OUP, 2009) 175, 178; Elisabeth Baumgartner, 'Aspects of Victim Participation in the Proceedings of the International Criminal Court' (2008) 90(870) *Int'l Rev Red Cross* 411; War Crimes Research Office, *Victims Participation at the Case Stage of Proceedings* (February 2009); Mirjan R. Damaška, 'The International Criminal Court: Between Aspiration and Achievement' (2009) 14 *UCLA J Int'l L & Foreign Aff* 19, 28–32, and Salvatore Zappalà, 'The Rights of Victims v. the Rights of the Accused' (2010) 8 *JICJ* 137.

[115] *Situation in the DRC: Prosecutor v. Katanga and Chui*, Decision on the Set of Procedural Rights attached to Procedural Status of Victim at the Pre-Trial Stage of the Case, Case No. ICC-01/04-01/07, 13 May 2008.

[116] *Situation in the DRC: Prosecutor v. Lubanga*, Judgment on the Appeals of the Prosecutor and the Defence against Trial Chamber I's Decision on Victims' Participation of 18 January 2008, Case No. ICC-01/04-01-06, 26 February 2008.

[117] War Crimes Research Office (n 114), 8.

[118] *Situation in the DRC: Prosecutor v. Lubanga*, Judgment on the Appeals of the Prosecutor and the Defence against Trial Chamber I's Decision on Victims' Participation of 18 January 2008 (n 116); see also the dissenting opinion of Judge Pikis and Partly Dissenting Opinion of Judge Kirsch.

caution. A further issue that arose from the early practice of victims' participation was its impact on the right to trial without undue delay.[119] However, later decisions have enunciated a more cautious approach towards the modalities of victim participation.[120]

Conclusion

This chapter primarily focused on the burgeoning jurisprudence on the prosecution's right to a fair trial and the impact that it can have on the rights of the accused, as perhaps most sharply illustrated by the *Haradinaj* retrial decision of 2010. This jurisprudence runs contrary to all human rights interpretations of the right to a fair trial, which have not recognized the prosecution as a holder of the right to a fair trial. Furthermore, it is dangerous insofar as it allows the accused's right to a fair trial to be balanced against the alleged procedural rights of the prosecution.

Despite concerns raised about the applicability of rights to the prosecution as a whole, the fact remains that all tribunals have some jurisprudence on the extension of fair trial rights to the prosecution. In the light of this emerging principle of international criminal procedure, questions need to be asked about its precise parameters. It was suggested that the correct test to be used by tribunals in assessing the balance between the Prosecutor's interests and the rights of the accused is, 'Does this course of action *unduly hamper* the prosecution in the presentation of its case?' If not, then the accused's rights should prevail. This test would pave the way for the international criminal tribunals to lay down the highest standards of fairness. A move away from the 'strict compliance with fundamental protections' for the rights of the accused standard that was embraced by *Martić* and *Aleksovski* was recommended in this regard.

The extension of procedural rights of the accused to other actors, such as victims and the international community, also gives rise to concern. The rights of the already-nebulous concept of 'the international community' as regards the outcome and conduct of proceedings are far from clear, and seem to have been asserted in an ad hoc fashion. While this is far less widespread than the extension of rights to the prosecution, it was worthy of mention. Particular attention was paid to certain facets of victims' participation before the ICC. The extension of victims' rights to include, for example, the

[119] *Situation in Kenya: Prosecutor v. Muthaura and Kenyatta*, Decision on Victims' Participation and Representation, Case No. ICC-01/09-02/11, 3 October 2012, para 35.

[120] ibid.

introduction of evidence, without concomitant procedural safeguards, represents a worrying trend and caution should be exercised to ensure that the procedural rights extended to victims do not encroach upon the rights of the accused.

In contrast to some of the 'rights' of other actors recognized by the tribunals, which can be more accurately defined as 'interests' or 'status rights', witnesses are the only party at trial whose rights need to be balanced against the rights of the accused, because their rights are properly recognized as competing human rights to the human right to a fair trial. The standard applied by the ECtHR in ensuring the rights of witnesses and the rights of the accused are protected asks whether the former would be 'unjustifiably imperilled' by giving testimony in a particular manner, and this is the standard that the international criminal tribunals should adopt. To this end, witness protection measures will generally be able to ensure that the rights of witnesses are not jeopardized by the trial, whilst still protecting the rights of the accused.

5

Setting the Highest Standards of Fairness, or Just 'Fair Enough'?

In observing the ILC Draft Statute for the ICC in 1995, the Ad Hoc Committee of the General Assembly noted that 'in view of the considerable powers [the Court] would enjoy in relation to individuals, [it] should be bound to apply the highest standards of justice, integrity and due process'.[1] However, in recent years, some high-profile authors have attempted to argue that the notion of 'the highest standards of fairness' sets the bar too high for international criminal trials, and that it should be sufficient for their procedures to be just 'fair enough'.[2] This chapter aims to rebut that argument and make an argument that international criminal tribunals should set the highest standards of fairness in their proceedings.

The chapter commences with a general discussion on the goals of international criminal law, and opines that setting the highest standards of fairness corresponds with some of the main goals of international criminal law. The second section of this chapter expands upon the case for standard-setting in international criminal procedure. Some reasons in favour of international criminal tribunals espousing the highest fair trial standards include the risk of wrongful conviction and the fact that the legitimacy of their judgments rest, at least in part, upon an external evaluation of fairness in the procedure leading to that judgment. Moreover, given that the international criminal tribunals themselves declare their procedures to be an embodiment of the highest standards of fairness, to fall below a true reflection of the very highest standards is to provide an excuse for a dilution of the rights of the accused by states that can point to the practice of international criminal tribunals as justification for their own imperfect practices. In order to pre-empt some of the counter-arguments that may be raised, the third section expands upon

[1] General Assembly, Report of the Ad Hoc Committee on the Establishment of an International Criminal Court, UN Doc. A/50/22, 1995, para 129.

[2] Mirjan R. Damaška, 'Reflections on Fairness in International Criminal Justice' (2012) 10 *JICJ* 611, 616.

some of the challenges that may be set forth against this hypothesis and analyses them in detail.

5.1 Goals of International Criminal Procedure

There are many declared and implied goals of international criminal law; indeed, some authors have argued that there is an 'overabundance' of goals,[3] and that the absence of a clear hierarchy of goals has led to inconsistencies in their application.[4] This point is perhaps illustrated in the previous chapter on the actors imbued with fair trial rights. Therein, it becomes clear that there is a tension between all the boxes that international criminal procedure seek to tick: they want to do justice for the victims, and to do so in an expedient manner, whilst ensuring the safety of the witnesses and respect for the interests of the international community in the outcomes of their trials. Occasionally, and not always persuasively, a trading-off exercise is entered into; Chapter 4 of this work argued that this is often at the expense of the accused. Arguably, the problem of competing goals is not unique to the international criminal realm; in domestic systems too, goals as diverse as 'giving victims a voice' and reinstating confidence in public safety are invariably put forward by governments.[5]

What, then, are the accepted goals of international criminal proceedings? UN Security Council Resolutions 827 and 955, establishing the ICTY and the ICTR respectively, explicitly mentioned the aims of bringing perpetrators to justice; contributing to 'the process of national reconciliation and to the restoration and maintenance of peace', and deterring future perpetrations of international crimes as core aims in setting up such tribunals.[6] The ICTY's First Annual Report, in a Kelsenian manner,[7] noted the Tribunal's

[3] Eric Stover, *The Witnesses: War Crimes and the Promise of Justice in The Hague* (Philadelphia: University of Pennsylvania Press, 2007) 14; Mirjan R. Damaška, 'What is the Point of International Criminal Justice?' (2008) 83 *Chicago Kent LR* 329.

[4] Damaška (n 3). Compare Mark Klamberg, 'What are the Objectives of International Criminal Procedure? Reflections on the Fragmentation of a Legal Regime' (2010) 79 *Nordic JIL* 279 (arguing that it would be impossible to identify a 'fixed hierarchy' of goals).

[5] On the same problem in the context of the UK, see Andrew Ashworth, *Human Rights, Serious Crime and Criminal Procedure* (London: Sweet & Maxwell, 2002) 38–46. Duff et al. have defined the primary goal of the criminal trial as being one of judgment and publicly calling offenders into account: *The Trial on Trial, Volume III: Towards a Normative Theory of the Criminal Trial* (Oxford, Hart Publishing, 2007).

[6] UN Security Council Resolution 827 (1993) 25 May 1993, UN Doc. S/RES/827 (1993) preambular paras 5–7; UN Security Council Resolution 955 (1994) 8 November 1994, UN Doc. S/RES/955 (1994) preambular paras 6–8.

[7] Hans Kelsen, *Peace through Law* (New York: Garland Publishers, 1973); Silvia D'Ascoli, 'Reconciliation and Sentencing in the Practice of the Ad Hoc Tribunals', in William A. Schabas,

potential role in 'promoting reconciliation and restoring true peace'.[8] Similarly, Resolution 1315 on the situation in Sierra Leone, which led to the agreement between the United Nations and the government of Sierra Leone establishing the SCSL, referred to the objectives of 'bringing justice and ensuring lasting peace'.[9]

Fletcher and Ohlin have argued that it is more important to focus on the *criminal* rather than the *international* elements of international criminal proceedings, and they have advocated for a greater emphasis to be placed on general goals of criminal law in their judgments.[10] However, it is not completely accurate to say that the domestic goals of criminal law have been discarded or overlooked in the interest of promoting the purely international criminal law goals, such as ending impunity and creating a historical record.[11] Judgments have discussed deterrence and retribution, albeit often in the context of a conscious shift away from other goals central to domestic criminal sentencing, such as rehabilitation of offenders.[12]

Whether international criminal tribunals can actually play a role in deterring génocidaires and those who wish to commit war crimes or crimes against humanity is questionable, at best.[13] The most commonly-cited example of the inability of international criminal justice to deter offenders is the fact that the Srebrenica genocide happened after the ICTY had become fully operational. Most forcefully, Tallgren argued that international criminal law is an almost religious exercise in the manner in which it continues to perpetuate the myth of deterrence in spite of evidence that the existence of international criminal institutions does little or nothing to prevent such crimes from being committed, while in reality international criminal law would appear to be little more than an exercise in retributivism.[14]

Yvonne McDermott, and Niamh Hayes (eds), *The Ashgate Research Companion to International Criminal Law: Critical Perspectives* (Aldershot: Ashgate, 2013) 307, 312.

[8] First Annual Report of the International Criminal Tribunal for the former Yugoslavia, UN Doc. A/49/342-S/1994/1007 (29 August 1994) para 16.

[9] UN Security Council Resolution 1315 (2000) 14 August 2000, UN Doc. S/RES/1315 (2000) preambular para 9.

[10] George P. Fletcher and Jens David Ohlin, 'Reclaiming Fundamental Principles of Criminal Law in the Darfur Case' (2005) 3 *JICJ* 539.

[11] Compare Damaška (n 2) 613, referring to a 'mismatch' between the goals of international criminal tribunals and what they can actually do.

[12] *Prosecutor v. Delalić et al.*, Appeal Judgment, Case No. IT-96-21-A, 20 February 2001, para 806; *Prosecutor v. Nahimana et al.*, Appeal Judgment, Case No. ICTR-99-52-A, 28 November 2007, paras 1056–7.

[13] On the impossibility of the deterrence argument, see Martti Koskenniemi, 'Between Impunity and Show Trials' (2002) 6 *Max Planck Yearbook of United Nations Law* 1; Kate Cronin-Furman and Amanda Taub, 'Lions and Tigers and Deterrence, Oh My: Evaluating Expectations of International Criminal Justice', in Schabas, McDermott, and Hayes (eds) (n 7) 435.

[14] Immi Tallgren, 'The Sense and Sensibility of International Criminal Law' (2002) 13 *EJIL* 561.

The 1998 Report of the ICTY to the Security Council added the prevention of historical revisionism, such as preventing later genocide denial by legally confirming that the genocide did indeed take place, to the goals of the Tribunal.[15] Of course, this is only possible if the judgments on such findings—and the way that they are reached—are sufficiently thorough to be regarded as credible,[16] accurate,[17] and free from allegations of 'victors' justice'[18] or procedural impropriety. Furthermore, it has been argued that findings of individual wrongdoing can mitigate the dangers of collective guilt and can re-legitimize governmental authority.[19]

The goal of rebuilding the rule of law in postconflict societies stretches beyond the realms of setting a historical record and ensuring peace through justice. It also relates closely to the need to strengthen the affected countries' justice systems and their ability to prosecute perpetrators of international crimes in the future.[20] Resolution 955 establishing the ICTR added the objective of strengthening the judicial system of Rwanda, with a view to empowering the domestic justice system to 'deal with large numbers of suspects', as a goal.[21] Resolution 1315 on the situation in Sierra Leone noted the adverse impact that the conflict had played over the domestic justice system

[15] Fifth Annual Report of the International Tribunal for the Prosecution of Persons Responsible for Serious Violations of International Humanitarian Law Committed in the Territory of the former Yugoslavia, UN Docs A/53/219 and S/1998/737, 10 August 1998, para 202.

[16] On credibility, and particularly on the reliance of evidence in spite of inconsistencies, see Nancy Amoury Combs, 'Testimonial Deficiencies and Evidentiary Uncertainties in International Criminal Trials' (2009) 14 *UCLA J Int'l L & Foreign Aff* 235.

[17] John D. Jackson, 'Finding the Best Epistemic Fit for International Criminal Tribunals: Beyond the Adversarial-Inquisitorial Dichotomy' (2009) 7 *JICJ* 17, 19: 'amid the debate about the goals of international criminal justice, there is a consensus that when findings of guilt are made they must be predicated upon the international fair trial norms of the right to equality of arms and the right to adversarial procedure as these provide the foundation for a fair and accurate verdict'.

[18] David Luban, 'Fairness to Rightness: Jurisdiction, Legality, and the Legitimacy of International Criminal Law', in Samantha Besson and John Tasioulis (eds), *The Philosophy of International Law* (Oxford: OUP, 2010) 569, 579.

[19] UN Secretary General, *The Rule of Law and Transitional Justice in Conflict and Post-Conflict Societies, delivered to the Security Council*, UN Doc. S/2004/616, 23 August 2004, para 39; Martha Minow, *Between Vengeance and Forgiveness: Facing History After Genocide and Mass Violence* (Boston: Beacon Press, 1998) 25; Ruth Teitel, *Transitional Justice* (Oxford: OUP, 2000) 56.

[20] See further, Dermot Groome, 'Re-evaluating the Theoretical Basis and Methodology of International Criminal Trials' (2007) 25 *Penn State Int'l LR* 791, 795–7. Compare David Mendeloff, 'Truth-Seeking, Truth-Telling, and Postconflict Peacebuilding: Curb the Enthusiasm?' (2004) 6 *Int'l Studies Rev* 355, and Padraig McAuliffe, 'Hybrid Courts in Retrospect: Of Lost Legacies and Modern Futures', in Schabas, McDermott, and Hayes (eds) (n 7) 453.

[21] Resolution 955 (n 6) preambular paragraph 9: 'Stressing also the need for international cooperation to strengthen the courts and judicial system of Rwanda, having regard in particular to the necessity for those courts to deal with large numbers of suspects … '. Groome, ibid., 799–800, notes that the 'reconciliation and integration with local justice efforts' ought to be a goal of international criminal tribunals.

'and the pressing need for international cooperation to assist in strengthening the judicial system of Sierra Leone'.[22] Furthermore, the Resolution asserted, 'a credible system of justice ... would end impunity and would contribute to the process of national reconciliation and to the restoration and maintenance of peace'.[23] These references are an explicit acknowledgment of the tribunals' role in illustrating the best standards of justice and due process from the time of their establishment.

In tandem with the 'ending impunity' goal, the founding Resolutions explicitly envisioned the enactment of fair trial standards in their proceedings. Resolution 1315 stated that the international community would make every effort to bring those responsible for serious violations of the laws of armed conflict 'to justice in accordance with international standards of justice, fairness and due process of law'.[24] The Special Court was described as a 'strong and credible court',[25] thereby recognizing the need for legitimacy as well as effectiveness in such institutions.

The respect for fair trial norms was not explicitly listed as a goal of international criminal law upon the establishment of the ICTY, but rather, it was portrayed as an obvious fact that the new international tribunal would embrace the highest standards of fairness towards defendants. The Secretary General remarked that it was 'axiomatic' that the Tribunal would 'fully respect internationally recognised standards regarding the rights of the accused at all stages of its proceedings'.[26] These 'internationally recognised standards' were to be found, according to the Secretary General, in Article 14 of the ICCPR.[27] The adumbration 'in particular' before the reference to Article 14 left the Tribunal open to considering other sources of fair trial standards, such as the ECHR, which it has done in practice.[28]

[22] Resolution 1315 (n 9). See also, the prosecution's opening statement in *Prosecutor v. Taylor*, cited in Marlies Glasius and Tim Meijers, 'Constructions of Legitimacy: The Charles Taylor Trial' (2012) 6 *IJTJ* 229, 240.

[23] Resolution 1315 (n 9). On this point, see Jens David Ohlin, 'Meta-Theory of International Criminal Procedure: Vindicating the Rule of Law' (2009) 14 *UCLA J Int'l L & Foreign Aff* 77, arguing that international criminal procedure has a particular role to play, in that it returns process values to procedural vacuums.

[24] Resolution 1315 (n 9).

[25] Resolution 1315 (n 9). Christoph J.M. Safferling, *Towards an International Criminal Procedure* (Oxford: OUP, 2001) 46, stating that 'the main rationale for international criminal law' is 'the protection and promotion of human rights in the global society'.

[26] Report of the Secretary General Pursuant to Paragraph 2 of the Security Council Resolution 808 (1993) UN Doc. S/25704, 3 May 1993, para 106.

[27] ibid.

[28] e.g. *Prosecutor v. Tadić*, Appeal Judgment, Case No. IT-94-1-A, 15 July 1999, para 48; *Prosecutor v. Kordić and Čerkez*, Decision on the Application by Mario Čerkez for Extension of Time to Fill his Respondent's Brief, Case No. IT-95-14/2-A, 11 September 2001, para 5; *Prosecutor v. Kayishema and Ruzindana*, Judgment (Reasons), Case No. ICTR-95-1-A, 1 June 2001,

In 1994, the ICTY's first annual report stated that the term 'to do justice' could be taken as meaning 'to conduct a fair trial by a truly independent and impartial tribunal and to punish those found guilty'.[29] In a report following the establishment of the ICTR, the Secretary General remarked that 'the international character of the Rwanda Tribunal' was in itself 'a guarantee of the just and fair conduct of the legal process'.[30] In this respect, we can see that the international community took it as a given that an international tribunal should guarantee the highest human rights standards to defendants before them. Some years later, the Ad Hoc Committee of the General Assembly, in examining the International Law Commission's draft Statute of the ICC, said that the Court 'should be bound to apply the highest standards of justice, integrity and due process'.[31] Equally, Resolution 1664, which paved the way for the establishment of the STL, encouraged the establishment of a 'tribunal of an international character based on the highest international standards of criminal justice'.[32]

Thus, the idea that international criminal tribunals would both bring perpetrators to justice in accordance with international fair trial procedural standards and aid the rebuilding of domestic justice systems were goals of the contemporary international criminal tribunals upon their establishment. The need to set the fairest of procedural standards is clearly implicit in these two facets of postconflict rebuilding and bringing perpetrators to justice through fair proceedings. The arguments as to *why* such procedure ought to embrace a standard-setting function shall now be addressed.

para 67; *Prosecutor v. Stakić*, Judgment, Case No. IT-97-24-A, 22 March 2006, para 149; *Situation in the DRC: Prosecutor v. Lubanga*, Decision on the Prosecutor's 'Application for Leave to Reply to "Conclusions de la Défense en Réponse au Mémoire d'Appel du Procureur"', Case No. ICC-01/04-01/06, 12 September 2006, para 7 and Separate Opinion of Judge Pikis, paras 3–8. See further Nicholas Croquet, 'The International Criminal Court and the Treatment of Defence Rights: A Mirror of the European Court of Human Rights' Jurisprudence?' (2011) 11 *HRLR* 91; Wolfgang Schomburg, 'The Role of International Criminal Tribunals in Promoting Respect for Fair Trial Rights' (2009) 8 *Nw U J Int'l Hum Rts* 1; Patrick L. Robinson, 'The Right to a Fair Trial in International Law, with Specific Reference to the Work of the ICTY' (2009) 3 *Publicist* 1.

[29] First Annual Report of the International Criminal Tribunal for the former Yugoslavia (n 8) para 15.

[30] Report of the Secretary General Pursuant to Paragraph 5 of the Security Council Resolution 955 (1995) UN Doc. S/1995/134, 13 February 1995, para 42.

[31] Report of the Ad Hoc Committee on the Establishment of an International Criminal Court (1995) UNGA, Fiftieth Session, Supplement No. 22, UN Doc. A/50/22, para 129.

[32] UN Security Council Resolution 1664 (2006), 29 March 2006, UN Doc. S/RES/1664 (2006), para 1.

5.2 International Criminal Procedure and Standard Setting: The Case in Favour

5.2.1 References to standard setting in international criminal jurisprudence and by organs of the courts

Perhaps the most explicit justification for the hypothesis that international criminal tribunals should set the highest standards of fairness is the fact that they claim to do so already. As discussed in Section 5.1 above, the founding documents of the five courts not only stated that their goal was to bring perpetrators to justice, but to do so in a fair and impartial manner. The SCSL referred to the preambular paragraphs of Resolution 1315 in reiterating that the goal of the United Nations and Sierra Leone in establishing the court was to try and punish those most responsible in accordance with 'international standards of justice, fairness and due process of law'.[33] The letter sent by President Kabbah asking the United Nations to establish the Special Court noted that 'the framework is meant to produce a court that will meet international standards for the trial of criminal cases while at the same time having a mandate to administer a blend of international and domestic Sierra Leonean law on Sierra Leonean soil'. When the SCSL was faced with an issue regarding the concurrent jurisdiction of its mandate and that of the Truth and Reconciliation Commission for Sierra Leone, it reiterated that the Court 'provide[s] a fair trial according to international standards'.[34] Similarly, the ICTR has noted its role in providing a 'model of fairness' for other legal systems to follow,[35] while the STL's Statute explicitly mandates the judges to be guided by 'reference materials reflecting the highest standards of international criminal procedure, with a view to ensuring a fair and expeditious trial' when drafting their Rules of Procedure and Evidence.[36] In *Blaškić*, the ICTY noted that it was established 'to give effect to the highest standards of justice'.[37]

[33] *Prosecutor v. Kallon and Kamara*, Decision on Challenge to Jurisdiction: Lomé Accord Amnesty, Case No. SCSL-2004-15-AR72(E) 13 March 2004, para 11.

[34] *Prosecutor v. Norman*, Decision on appeal by the truth and reconciliation commission for Sierra Leone and chief Samuel Hinga Norman JP Against the decision of His Lordship, Mr Justice Bankole Thompson delivered on 30 October 2003 to deny the TRC's request to hold a public hearing with chief Samuel Hinga Norman JP, Case No. SCSL-2003-08-PT, 28 November 2003, para 44.

[35] *Prosecutor v. Ntagerura et al.*, Trial Judgment and Sentence, Case No. ICTR-99-46-T, 24 February 2004, Separate Opinion of Judge Pavel Dolenc, para 5.

[36] Article 28(2), STL Statute.

[37] *Prosecutor v. Blaškič*, Decision on the Objection of the Republic of Croatia to the Issuance of *Subpoenae Duces Tecum*, Case No. IT-95-14-T, 18 July 1997, para 61.

References to the fact that international criminal tribunals see themselves enshrining the highest standards of procedural fairness can be found not only in the tribunals' jurisprudence and founding instruments, but also in their external communications. The ICTY's website, with reference to the adjustments that had to be made to the proposed finished date for all trials in line with the completion strategy, explains the extra time needed as being necessary 'to ensure the highest standards of procedural fairness'.[38] Similarly, as Judge Meron assumed the office of President of the ICTY for the second time, he made a statement to the effect that the Tribunal embodied the 'international community's noblest aspirations for justice', adding that he would work to 'ensure that these proceedings are concluded in a timely fashion while upholding the highest standards of fairness'.[39] Judge Meron also noted that:

> [T]he Tribunal has made unprecedented contributions to the development of international criminal law and procedure. It has also served as an important model for other international courts and provided valuable assistance to national judiciaries trying war crimes cases.[40]

Through the statements of its President, we can see that the Tribunal's judges see themselves as both embracing the highest standards of fair procedures and setting an example for domestic jurisdictions in trying the most serious crimes. Similarly, Judge Kirk McDonald addressed an informal plenary of the Preparatory Committee on the Establishment of an ICC in 1997 and impressed on the Committee the need for the ICC's Statute to 'comport with the highest standards of fairness', thereby implying that the ICTY's practice also embodied those same standards.[41]

At the opening of the Arusha branch of the 'residual mechanism' for the international criminal tribunals,[42] Judge Meron emphasized the Tribunal's commitment to seeing that accused persons are 'treated in accordance with the highest standards of procedural and substantive fairness'.[43] In a similar vein, the late Judge Cassese wrote an expert report on the functioning of the SCSL in 2006, in light of its completion strategy and in order to strengthen its practice in the final years of its operation. On the terms of reference, he

[38] 'Completion Strategy', available online at http://www.icty.org/sid/10016 (last accessed 5 March 2015).

[39] 'Statement of the President of the Tribunal—Judge Theodor Meron', 17 November 2011.

[40] ibid.

[41] ICTY Press Release, 'Judge Kirk McDonald urges that the International Permanent Court "must be effective"', 14 August 1997.

[42] 'Remarks of President Theodor Meron, Opening of the Arusha Branch of the Mechanism for International Criminal Tribunals', 2 July 2012.

[43] ibid.

said that the UN Secretary General had appointed him 'with the objective of ensuring the most efficient use of the Court's resources and the completion of the Court's work in a timely manner while at the same time maintaining the highest standards of fairness, due process and respect for human rights'.[44]

Similar references to the judges' role in ensuring that international fair trial standards are fully respected can be found in the external statements of tribunal officials. In 2010, then-President of the ICTY, Judge Robinson, informed the Security Council that 'the Tribunal has continued to work as efficiently and expeditiously as possible in accordance with the highest standards of international due process'.[45] The ICTY Registrar, John Hocking, is on record as having stated that, 'The same institution that was created to prosecute alleged perpetrators and hold them accountable for their misdeeds, was also tasked to ensure that the right to fair trial was fully respected …'[46] The Prosecutor of the ICC has publicly stated that the accused before the Court will be guaranteed to receive a fair trial in accordance with the highest procedural standards on numerous occasions,[47] as have prosecution counsel in other international criminal tribunals.[48] Similarly, the tribunals' websites contain many references to the highest standards of fairness in their proceedings.[49]

[44] *Report on the Special Court for Sierra Leone submitted by the Independent Expert, Antonio Cassese*, 12 December 2006.

[45] ICTY Press Release, President Robinson's Address before the Security Council, 18 June 2010.

[46] 'Address of Mr John Hocking, Registrar, United Nations International Criminal Tribunal for the former Yugoslavia', *Meeting of Registrars of Final/Appellate, Regional and International Courts*, Ottawa, Canada, 14–16 April 2010.

[47] e.g. 'Statement by the Prosecutor of the International Criminal Court Mrs. Fatou Bensouda', Press Briefing, Nairobi, 22 October 2012.

[48] Opening statement of the Prosecution, *Prosecutor v. Lukić*, Transcript, 9 July 2008, 269 ('I give the Chamber, as well as Milan and Sredoje Lukić, my assurance, and the assurance of Mr Brammertz, that the Prosecution will conduct its case according to the highest standards of fairness and justice enabling this Chamber to reach a fair and just adjudication of the charges against these accused.')

[49] e.g. STL, 'Judges of the Special Tribunal for Lebanon', available online at http://www.stl-tsl.org/en/about-the-stl/biographies/judges-of-the-special-tribunal-for-lebanon (last accessed 8 October 2015): 'All judges will work to ensure that trials are conducted in accordance with the highest standards of international justice.'; ICTY Press Release, 'Tribunal Welcomes the Arrest of Radovan Karadzic', available online at http://www.icty.org/sid/9952 (last accessed 5 March 2015): 'Aware of the serious charges brought against him by the prosecution, the Tribunal is mindful that Karadzic enjoys the presumption of innocence and is committed to do all within its competences to ensure a fair and public trial in accordance with the highest standards of international law.'; ICC, 'About the Court: ICC at a Glance', available online at http://www.icc-cpi.int/en_menus/icc/about%20the%20court/icc%20at%20a%20glance/Pages/icc%20at%20a%20glance.aspx (last accessed 8 October 2015): 'In all of its activities, the ICC observes the highest standards of fairness and due process.'

5.2.2 Risk of wrongful conviction

It probably goes without saying that it would be extremely embarrassing for the international community if a court established by the community of nations and generously funded by a large number of states were found to be complicit in the wrongful conviction of an individual. As with domestic systems, one of the strongest arguments in favour of a robust protection of fair trial rights is that the greater the derogation from these rights, the greater the risk of convicting an innocent person. The need to avoid incorrect convictions increases in the international criminal law context, where the passing of judgments is linked with postconflict justice and rule of law reform.[50] If, as the founding documents of the ICTR and the SCSL suggested, these tribunals were intended to strengthen the domestic criminal justice systems of affected states,[51] a flawed procedural model which risks convicting the innocent cannot effectively meet that goal. Of course, no procedural model is infallible, and no matter how fair, there is always a risk that a wrongful conviction will be entered. Yet, models of the criminal process founded on due process are cautious of error and seek to avoid inaccuracy to a much greater extent than crime control systems.[52] There is a further theoretical argument that respect for the individual's rights needs to be central to the criminal process,[53] and this holds particularly true in relation to trials that bear a specific aim of spreading respect for the rule of law.

It may be argued that the evidence against renowned political and military leaders who find themselves on trial before international criminal tribunals is so overwhelming that the provision of all of the judicial guarantees is somewhat farcical and may just serve to protect the external image of the tribunals rather than being strictly necessary to ensure that innocent people are not convicted. But the fact remains that individuals have, in practice, been acquitted by the tribunals.[54] In one case before the ICTR, the defendant was acquitted on the basis of a successful alibi defence.[55] This proves that we

[50] See above, Section 5.2.1. [51] ibid.

[52] Herbert Packer, *The Limits of the Criminal Sanction* (Stanford: Stanford University Press, 1968) 164–5.

[53] Andrew Ashworth and Mike Redmayne, *The Criminal Process* (4th edn, Oxford: OUP, 2010) 20–61, 322.

[54] High-profile acquittals include: *Situation in the DRC, Prosecutor v. Chui*, Jugement rendu en application de l'article 74 du Statut, Case No. ICC-01/04-02/12, 18 December 2012; *Prosecutor v. Haradinaj et al.*, Retrial Judgment, Case No. IT-04-84-T, 29 November 2012; *Prosecutor v. Gotovina and Markač*, Appeals Judgment, Case No. IT-06-90-A, 16 November 2012, and *Prosecutor v. Bizimungu et al.*, Judgment and Sentence, Case No. ICTR-99-50-T, 30 September 2011.

[55] *Prosecutor v. Zigiranyirazo*, Appeals Judgment, Case No. ICTR-01-73-A, 16 November 2009.

cannot take it as a given that there is a strong case to be made against all those who are indicted by the tribunals. At the ICC, at the time of writing, seven of the fourteen individuals for whom warrants of arrest were issued have either been acquitted or had the charges against them withdrawn at an earlier stage in proceedings.[56] Moreover, the guilt of the accused must be proven 'beyond reasonable doubt'. Defendants must be given ample opportunity to raise any defence that might plant a reasonable doubt in the minds of the judges, and they can only be afforded this opportunity through having adequate time and facilities for the preparation of their defence,[57] the right to challenge the evidence against them,[58] and all of the other guarantees enshrined in Article 14 of the ICCPR and its equivalent in international criminal statutes. As Judge Dolenc stated in his separate opinion to the *Ntagerura* judgment, even if the evidence is overwhelming on some distinct counts in the indictment, this should not go to prove by extension the guilt of other counts which the accused has not been given adequate opportunity to challenge.[59]

In domestic law, miscarriages of justice are said to shake the citizens' confidence in the legal system as a whole. For example, the wrongful convictions of the 'Birmingham Six' and 'Guildford Four' in the UK stand as paradigmatic examples and led to the creation of the Runciman Commission to examine the foundations of the criminal justice system in England and Wales.[60] Arguably, the danger of people losing confidence in the international criminal justice system following a wrongful conviction carries even greater risks. As stated above, international tribunals seek to add to a credible historical record and prevent future revisionism by establishing at least part of the picture and deciding upon the individual responsibility of political

[56] *Situation in Kenya: Prosecutor v. Kenyatta*, Notice of withdrawal of the charges against Uhuru Muigai Kenyatta, Case No. ICC-01/09-02/11, 5 December 2014; *Situation in Kenya: Prosecutor v. Muthaura*, Decision on the Withdrawal of Charges against Mr Muthaura, Case No. ICC-01/09-02/11, 18 March 2013; *Situation in the DRC, Prosecutor v. Chui*, Jugement rendu en application de l'article 74 du Statut, ICC-01/04-02/12, 18 December 2012; *Situation in Darfur, Sudan: Prosecutor v. Abu Garda*, Decision on the Confirmation of Charges, Case No. ICC-02/05-02/09, 8 February 2010; *Situation in Kenya: Prosecutor v. Ruto, Kosgey and Sang*, Decision on the Confirmation of Charges Pursuant to Article 61(7)(a) and (b) of the Rome Statute, Case No. ICC-01/09-01/11, 23 January 2012 (declining to confirm the charges against Kosgey); *Situation in Kenya: Prosecutor v. Muthaura, Kenyatta and Hussein Ali*, Decision on the Confirmation of Charges Pursuant to Article 61(7)(a) and (b) of the Rome Statute, Case No. ICC-01/09-01/11, 23 January 2012 (declining to confirm the charges against Kosgey); *Situation in the DRC: Prosecutor v. Mbarushimana*, Decision on the Confirmation of Charges, Case No. ICC-01/04-01/10, 16 December 2011.

[57] See above, Section 3.11. [58] See above, Section 3.10.

[59] *Prosecutor v. Ntagerura et al.*, Trial Judgment and Sentence, Case No. ICTR-99-46-T, 24 February 2004, Separate Opinion of Judge Pavel Dolenc, para 3–6.

[60] See further, Kent Roach and Gary Trotter, 'Miscarriages of Justice in the War against Terror' (2004–2005) 109 *Penn St LR* 967, 968.

and military leaders.[61] If doubt were to be cast upon the soundness of such convictions as a result of an erroneous conviction, the international criminal justice project could be unhinged.

The *Barayagwiza* incident before the ICTR—where the accused was released 'with prejudice' after it was held that his rights had been violated by excessive pre-trial detention prior to his transfer to the tribunal—demonstrates that miscarriages of justice can have an adverse impact on state cooperation with international criminal institutions. Even though relations had been fraught between the Republic of Rwanda and the ICTR before the incident, and regardless of the fact that Rwanda's indignation was caused by the fact that a guilty man had been freed,[62] the same destabilizing effect that Rwanda's refusal to co-operate with the tribunal had could potentially result from a state's lack of faith in the institutions resulting from what is seen as a flawed set of rules.

By the same token, one of the reasons advanced by some commentators, in support of the United States of America's failure to ratify the Rome Statute, was the fact that trials before the ICC are not held before a jury.[63] Although most authors have argued that a jury trial is not an inescapable requirement of the right to a fair trial in international criminal trials,[64] this does demonstrate that procedural improprieties can be used as an excuse for states that are unwilling to co-operate due to political reasons. This negative view of the international criminal tribunals would be greatly enhanced if a wrongful conviction was entered by any of the tribunals, thus it is imperative that the fairest of procedures remain their watchword. In the *Katanga* admissibility decision before the ICC, the accused argued that he could not get a fair trial before the ICC as part of his admissibility challenge. In holding that fair trial considerations could not form part of an admissibility challenge, the Chamber held that the state parties had signed up to the ICC's legal regime

[61] Lower-ranking individuals were tried at the commencement of the ICTY and ICTR, but the point of international tribunals trying predominantly high-ranking individuals, usually infamous in their home countries, is true for at least the trials since the turn of the twenty-first century.

[62] The decision to release the accused was later overturned in *Prosecutor v. Barayagwiza*, Decision (Prosecutor's Request for Review or Reconsideration), Case No. ICTR-97-19-AR72, 31 March 2000, and Barayagwiza was later convicted in *Prosecutor v. Barayagwiza*, Judgment and Sentence, Case No. ICTR-99-52-T, 3 December 2003.

[63] Amy Powell, 'Three angry men: Juries in International Criminal Adjudication', (2004) 79 *NYU LR* 2341. Larry May, *Global Justice and Due Process* (New York: CUP, 2011) 35–7, stated that international criminal tribunals have a role in promoting fair trial rights, such as trial by jury, which is clearly a theoretical rather than a practical argument.

[64] See e.g. Cherie Booth, 'Prospects and Issues for the International Criminal Court: Lessons from Yugoslavia and Rwanda' in Philippe Sands (ed.), *From Nuremberg to The Hague: The Future of International Criminal Justice* (Cambridge: CUP, 2003) 157, 186–9.

'mindful of the consequences that [its seat in The Hague] would entail for the accused brought before the Court, and considered that they were not infringing their fundamental rights'.[65] This shows how closely interlinked state cooperation and the perception of fairness of ICC trials are.

5.2.3 Dangers of setting lower standards

If, as argued in Chapter 6, international criminal tribunals can encourage states to embrace higher standards of due process through the mechanisms of Rule 11*bis* referrals and complementarity, the converse is almost certainly the case. Those involved in policy-making at a domestic level might be forgiven for thinking that a period of ten years was a reasonable length for a trial on charges of genocide or other international crimes, based on the experience to date in some international criminal tribunals discussed in this work. This position was reflected in Libya's admissibility challenge to the Gaddafi case, where it stated that:

> Even this Court with its considerable resources has required several years to bring accused persons to justice in less complex cases. Libya is meeting the requirements of due process in accordance with international standards, and cannot be held to a requirement of achieving swift justice in circumstances that neither other States nor the ICC itself are required to meet.[66]

Indeed, some of the difficulties that have arisen in domestic prosecutions of international crimes mirror some of the key issues in international criminal procedure discussed in the present work. For example, Human Rights Watch published a report in 2012 on Uganda's International Crimes Division, where it reported the fact that an accused had not received the disclosure of prosecution witness statements until two years after his initial arrest.[67] A waiting period of two years between arrest and the first substantive disclosure would actually be better than international criminal procedure standards.[68] The danger here is that international criminal procedure's shortcomings can be used to justify a state's derogations from international due process norms. It would be reasonable for a state to argue that their procedures

[65] *Situation in the DRC: Prosecutor v. Katanga and Chui*, Reasons for the Oral Decision on the Motion Challenging the Admissibility of the Case (Article 19 of the Statute), Case No. ICC-01/04-01/07, 16 June 2009, paras 83–4.

[66] *Situation in Libya: Prosecutor v. Al-Islam Gaddafi and Al-Senussi*, Application on Behalf of the Government of Libya pursuant to Article 19 of the ICC Statute, Case No. ICC-01/11-01/11, 1 May 2012, para 94.

[67] Human Rights Watch, Justice for Serious Crimes before National Courts: Uganda's International Crimes Division (New York, 2012) 18.

[68] See above, Section 3.10.1.

comport with the standards set out by international criminal tribunals, and that the tribunals' practice should be seen as illustrative of international standards of due process. In practice, groups like Human Rights Watch have benchmarked their assessment of domestic trials for international crimes on the standards laid down by the ICC, based on the reasoning that defendants ought to receive equal treatment, whether they are tried in The Hague or in their home country.[69]

The dangers present in setting less than the highest standards of fairness were illustrated by a number of instances—in particular, in the United States at the turn of this century—where international criminal justice's shortcomings were used as a justification for states' own derogations from international standards of due process.[70] For example, Article 6(D) of the US Military Commission Order No. 1 allowed the admission of any evidence which the Presiding Officer deemed to bear probative value.[71] There is a clear parallel between this provision and Rules 89(C) of the Rules of Procedure and Evidence of the ICTY, ICTR, and SCSL and Rule 149 of the STL Rules, which provide that '[a] Chamber may admit any relevant evidence which it deems to have probative value.' However, these Rules come with a limitation clause—that the evidence may be excluded if its probative value is outweighed by the need to ensure a fair trial.[72] These provisions and related international practice, particularly as they pertained to the admissibility of hearsay evidence, evidence obtained through torture or other coercive means, and the testimony of anonymous witnesses, were hotly debated before the US House of Representatives in 2006.[73] The witnesses present were: Prof. Michael Scharf of Case Western University; Judge Patricia Wald, formerly a judge before the ICTY; Mr Gerald Gahima of the United States Institute for Peace, and Ms Jennifer Elsea, an Attorney with the Congressional Research Service. Judge Wald informed the House

[69] Human Rights Watch, 'Benchmarks for Justice for Serious Crimes in Northern Uganda: Human Rights Watch Memoranda on Justice Standards and the Juba Peace Talks', May 2007–February 2008, 13.

[70] See Human Rights Watch, 'Military Commissions Can't Compare to International Courts: Due Process Standards Much Lower for Proposed U.S. Trials', 4 December 2001; and Gerald Gahima, 'The Practice of International Criminal Tribunals and their Relevance to Military Commissions in Light of *Hamdan v. Rumsfeld*', Testimony before the House of Representatives Armed Services Committee, July 2006.

[71] Article 6(D), U.S. Department of Defense, Military Commissions Order No. 1 (21 March 2002).

[72] Rules 89(D).

[73] 'Standards of Military Commissions and Tribunals', Hearing before the Committee on Armed Services, House of Representatives, One Hundred Seventh Congress, Second Session, H.A.S.C. No. 109–17, 26 July 2006.

Committee on Armed Services that, in practice, judges 'move very carefully in terms of the weight that is given' to hearsay evidence, and she reiterated that the ICTY was guided by European Court of Human Rights jurisprudence which states that convictions cannot be substantially based on hearsay testimony.[74] Justification for this assertion can indeed be found in a number of judgments of the European Court of Human Rights, and in a number of decisions of the ICTY.[75]

While Section 949a(F) of the Military Commissions Act of 2006 states that hearsay evidence can be excluded if its probative value is outweighed '(i) by the danger of unfair prejudice, confusion of the issues, or misleading the commission; or (ii) by considerations of undue delay, waste of time, or needless presentation of cumulative evidence', this does not provide all of the same guarantees provided by the international criminal tribunals, because large swathes of evidence can be shielded from the accused for malleable 'national security' reasons, thereby limiting his/her ability to raise a challenge on the grounds of Section 949a(F)(i) or (ii).[76] Nonetheless, one member of the Senate Committee on Armed Services stated that:

> [I]f you compare our military commissions system, particularly the reformed version, to an international court trial at The Hague, we're much more, for lack of a better word, liberal in terms of providing due process and protections to the accused than you would get if you were going to go to The Hague.[77]

This assertion was apparently made on the basis that the only factor to be considered by the ICTY in assessing the admissibility of hearsay testimony was reliability.[78] Similarly, the Tribunal's extremely limited jurisprudence on the appropriateness of anonymous witnesses was relied upon by the

[74] ibid., 3–7.

[75] *Unterpertinger v. Austria* (1991) 13 EHRR 175, 24 November 1986, para 33; *Al-Khawaja and Tahery v. UK* (2012) 54 EHRR 23, 15 December 2011, para 147; *Prosecutor v. Prlić et al.*, Decision on Appeals against Decision Admitting Transcript of Jadranko Prlić's Questioning into Evidence, Case No. IT-04-74-AR73.6, 23 November 2007, para 53 and *Prosecutor v. Martić*, Decision on Appeal against the Trial Chamber's Decision on the Evidence of Witness Milan Babić, Case No. IT-95-11-AR73.2, 14 September 2006, para 20.

[76] Section 949(D) Military Commissions Act 2006.

[77] US Senate, Committee on Armed Services, Hearing to Receive Testimony on Legal Issues Regarding Military Commissions and the Trial of Detainees for Violations of the Law of War, 7 July 2009, 15 (Senator Graham).

[78] ibid., statement of Admiral MacDonald. See also, *Report of the Committee on Armed Services, House of Representatives on H.R. 6054*, 109th Congress, Second Session, 15 September 2006, 10 ('The committee notes that this standard for admission of evidence is similar to that used by international tribunals, such as the International Criminal Tribunal for the Former Yugoslavia (ICTY) and the International Criminal Tribunal for Rwanda (ICTR).').

President of the United States of America as justification for the military tribunals' shielding of witnesses from the accused and defence counsel, who said:

> For instance, the International Criminal Tribunal for the Former Yugoslavia has ruled that the accused's rights to a fair trial and to cross-examination are not violated when, out of concern for the safety of a witness, the court permits a witness to testify before the court while shielding the identity of the witness from the accused and defense counsel.[79]

This position was heavily criticized by Scharf, who pointed out the one-off nature of the *Tadić* decision on anonymous witnesses.[80] This reliance on the procedure of the ICTY (albeit wrongfully stated) as a justification for the dilution of the rights of the accused in the domestic context further illustrates the need for international tribunals to vigorously defend the rights of the accused in all circumstances. Thus, the need for the tribunals to provide fairness in their procedures stretches beyond the traditional impetus of protecting innocent people from wrongful conviction and into the realms of illustrating 'demonstrable principles of fairness'.[81]

5.2.4 The 'pull' of fair procedures: legitimacy and compliance

As mentioned earlier,[82] the *Tadić* jurisdiction decision interpreted compliance with full due process norms as being one interpretation of the requirement that tribunals be 'established by law'. The Chamber stated that:

> The important consideration in determining whether a tribunal has been 'established by law' is not whether it was pre-established or established for a specific purpose or situation; what is important is that it be set up by a competent organ in keeping with the relevant legal procedures, and should [*sic*] that it observes the requirements of procedural fairness.[83]

The human rights norms espoused by tribunals in their procedures have a resounding effect in terms of the external legitimacy of international criminal

[79] Message from the President of the United States transmitting a draft of proposed legislation entitled the 'Military Commissions Act of 2006', 109th Congress, 2nd Session, House Document 109–33, 7 September 2006, 6.

[80] 'Standards of Military Commissions and Tribunals', Hearing before the Committee on Armed Services (n 73) testimony of Prof. Michael Scharf.

[81] Anthony Duff et al., *The Trial on Trial, Volume III: Towards a Normative Theory of the Criminal Trial* (Oxford: Hart Publishing, 2007) 51.

[82] Section 2.1.

[83] *Prosecutor v. Tadić*, Decision on the Defence Motion for Interlocutory Appeal on Jurisdiction, Case No. IT-94-1-AR72, 2 October 1995, paras 45–7.

law.[84] Studies such as that carried out by Nancy Combs[85] that raise doubt as to the safety of international criminal convictions, carry a ripple effect which leads commentators to question the continued legitimacy of international criminal tribunals.[86] Furthermore, anything less than perfect standards can be pounced upon by the tribunals' detractors.[87]

The fairness of proceedings may also have an effect on the internal legitimacy of the courts, and the deference with which defendants treat their authority. Tyler has written several studies on the cooperation that arises when people believe the police or judiciary bears legitimate authority over them. Their legitimate authority, in turn, is derived from fair treatment of those within their authority, freedom from discrimination, bias and outside interference, and uniformity of application of the law.[88] Robertson has remarked that 'the most astonishing feature of the Nuremberg trial was how the adversary dynamics of the Anglo-American trial sucked in the defendants, who played an earnest and polite, at times desperate, part in making it work'.[89] In a similar vein, Luhmann's concept of 'legitimation through procedure', discussed in Chapter 2 above, states that parties will accept outcomes of a procedure if that procedure is flawless and the decision-makers adopt a neutral position.[90] In the words of Allan:

> The purpose of a criminal conviction is not merely to give the citizen a prudential incentive to obey the law, but to persuade him of the justice of the law's demands and therefore the wrongfulness of the conduct which it condemns.[91]

[84] Gabrielle McIntyre, 'Defining Human Rights in the Arena of International Humanitarian Law: Human Rights in the Jurisprudence of the ICTY', in William A. Schabas and Gideon Boas (eds), *International Criminal Law Developments in the Case Law of the ICTY* (Leiden: Brill/Nijhoff, 2003) 193.

[85] Nancy A. Combs, *Fact Finding without Facts: The Uncertain Evidentiary Foundations of International Criminal Convictions* (Cambridge: CUP, 2010).

[86] Beth S. Lyons, 'Enough is Enough: The Illegitimacy of International Criminal Convictions' (2011) 13 *J Genocide Res* 287; Augustine Brannigan, 'Is the Sun Setting on Cosmopolitan Justice?' (2011) 48 *Global Society* 420.

[87] Courtenay Griffiths, 'The International Criminal Court is hurting Africa' *The Telegraph*, London, 3 July 2012.

[88] Tom R. Tyler, *Why People Cooperate* (Princeton: Princeton University Press, 2010); Tom R. Tyler, *Why People Obey the Law* (Princeton: Princeton University Press, 2006); Tom R. Tyler (ed.), *Legitimacy and Criminal Justice: International Perspectives* (New York: Russell Sage Foundation, 2007).

[89] Geoffrey Robertson, *Crimes Against Humanity* (London: Penguin, 1999) 203.

[90] Heike Jung, 'Nothing but the Truth? Some Facts, Impressions and Confessions about Truth in Criminal Procedure' in Anthony Duff et al. (eds), *The Trial on Trial I: Truth and Due Process* (Oxford: Hart Publishing, 2004) 147, 150, referring to Luhmann's theory of legitimation through procedure ('*durch verfahren*').

[91] T.R.S. Allan, 'Procedural Fairness and the Duty of Respect' (1998) 18 *OJLS* 497, 506.

5.2.5 International criminal trials embody an idealized 'mixed' procedural model

Over the past number of years, scholarly works have examined the impact of human rights in general, and the European Convention of Human Rights in particular, on criminal procedure in domestic courts.[92] Some authors have suggested that the fact that large numbers of state parties have agreed upon provisions in human rights conventions on how the accused ought to be treated should in itself serve as evidence of an existing shared set of values, in spite of very different procedural traditions.[93] Within Europe, the creation of an Area of Freedom, Security and Justice which seeks to promote mutual recognition of judgments as well as a 'high level of confidence between Member States'[94] regarding each other's criminal justice systems illustrates some convergence between justice systems.

There is a strong case to be made that international criminal procedure, by representing a mixed procedural model which is (in theory, at least) acceptable to practitioners, judges, and perhaps most importantly, accused persons from across a broad spectrum of legal traditions, can best illustrate how to ensure the fairness of proceedings in the context of converging procedural traditions.[95]

[92] See, for example, Christopher Harding, Phil Fennell, Nico Jörg, and Bert Swart, *Criminal Justice in Europe: A Comparative Study* (Oxford: Clarendon Press, 1995); Diane Marie Amann, 'Harmonic Convergence? Constitutional Criminal Procedure in an International Context' (2000) 75 *Ind L J* 815; Marcel Lemonde, 'From the European Convention on Human Rights to the Treaty on European Union: Diversity in Reasoning' in Mireille Delmas-Marty (ed.), *What Kind of Criminal Policy for Europe?* (trans Mark A Summers, The Hague/London: Kluwer Law International, 1996) 33, 38; John D. Jackson, 'Transnational Faces of Justice: Two Attempts to Build Common Standards Beyond National Boundaries' in John D. Jackson, Máximo Langer, and Peter Tillers (eds), *Crime, Procedure and Evidence in a Comparative and International Context: Essays in Honour of Professor Mirjan R. Damaška* (Oxford: Hart Publishing, 2008) 221, 234; John D. Jackson, 'The Effect of Human Rights on Criminal Evidentiary Processes: Towards Convergence, Divergence or Realignment' (2005) 68 *MLR* 737; John Bell, *French Legal Cultures* (London: Butterworths, 2001) 102, and Peter Carmichael Keen, 'Tempered Adversariality: The Judicial Role and Trial Theory in the International Criminal Tribunals' (2004) 17 *LJIL* 767, 778.

[93] Sarah J. Summers, *Fair Trials: The European Procedural Tradition and the Practice of the European Convention on Human Rights* (Oxford: Hart Publishing, 2007) 17; Amann (n 92) 825.

[94] Council Framework Decision of 13 June 2002 on the European arrest warrant and the surrender procedures between Member States—Statements made by certain Member States on the adoption of the Framework Decision (2002/584/JHA) Official Journal L 190 (2002) P. 0001—0020, Recital 5.

[95] See e.g. Christoph J.M. Safferling, *Towards an International Criminal Procedure* (Oxford: OUP, 2001); Erik Møse and Joyce Aptel, 'Trial without Undue Delay before the International Criminal Tribunals' in Lal Chand Vohrah et al. (eds), *Man's Inhumanity to Man: Essays on International Law in Honour of Antonio Cassese* (The Hague: Kluwer Law International, 2003) 539, 550 have argued that '[i]n practice, the Chambers will usually find a solution acceptable to legal minds from both systems, thereby contributing to the construction of a new international

The standards of fairness developed by the international criminal tribunals can play an expository role for procedural standards to be applied in domestic courts, and thus it is imperative that these standards do represent optimal practice.

5.3 International Criminal Procedure and Standard Setting: The Case Against

5.3.1 Context of proceedings

It is unquestionably true that international criminal tribunals operate in a unique context. The path of an international criminal trial is often fraught with difficulty, not least because of the inconsistent nature of state cooperation. This has been evidenced by jurisprudence on the issuance of subpoenas,[96] the availability of evidence,[97] and the production of witnesses and defendants,[98] amongst others. But is this unique context sufficient to negate the role of international criminal tribunals in exemplifying the highest standards of procedural fairness?

Damaška, referring to the 'challenging international environment' in which international criminal tribunals operate, expressed doubts as to the

criminal jurisprudence.' Compare John D. Jackson and Sarah J. Summers, *The Internationalisation of Criminal Evidence* (Cambridge: CUP, 2012) 4.

[96] *Prosecutor v. Sesay, Kallon and Gbao*, Written reasoned decision on motion for issuance of a subpoena to H.E. Dr. Ahmad Tejan Kabbah, former President of the Republic of Sierra Leone, Case No. SCSL-04-15-T-1189, 30 June 2008; *Prosecutor v. Blaškić*, Decision on the Objection of the Republic of Croatia to the Issuance of *Subpoenae Duces Tecum*, Case No. IT-95-14-T, 18 July 1997, para 61.

[97] *Prosecutor v. Simić et al.*, Decision on the Prosecution Motion under Rule 73 for a Ruling Concerning the Testimony of a Witness, Case No. IT-95-9-PT, 27 July 1999; *Prosecutor v. Brđanin and Talić*, Decision on Interlocutory Appeal, Case No. IT-99-36-AR73.9, 11 December 2002; *Situation in the DRC: Prosecutor v. Lubanga Dyilo*, Decision on the Consequences of Non-Disclosure of Exculpatory Materials Covered by Article 54(3)(e) Agreements and the Application to Stay the Prosecution of the Accused, Together with Certain Other Issues Raised at the Status Conference on 10 June 2008', Case No. ICC-01/04-01/06, 13 June 2008.

[98] *Situation in Darfur, Sudan: Prosecutor v. Bashir*, Decision Pursuant to Article 87(7) of the Rome Statute on the Failure by the Republic of Malawi to Comply with the Cooperation Requests Issued by the Court with Respect to the Arrest and Surrender of Omar Hassan Ahmad Al Bashir, Case No. ICC-02/05-01/09, 12 December 2011; *Situation in Darfur, Sudan: Prosecutor v. Bashir*, Decision Pursuant to Article 87(7) of the Rome Statute on the Failure by the Republic of Chad to Comply with the Cooperation Requests Issued by the Court with Respect to the Arrest and Surrender of Omar Hassan Ahmad Al Bashir, Case No. ICC-02/05-01/09, 13 December 2011; *Prosecutor v. Naletilić and Martinović*, Decision on the Prosecutor's Request for Public Version of Trial Chamber's 'Decision on the Motion to admit Statement of Deceased Witnesses [...]' of 22 January 2002, Case No. IT-98-34-T, 27 February 2002.

full extent of their fair trial obligations.[99] He maintained that responsiveness to the unique context and challenges of international criminal law 'may require the abandonment, or relaxation, of some cherished domestic procedural arrangements',[100] and further argued that international criminal tribunals 'cannot successfully pursue their manifold objectives by strictly abiding by most demanding domestic rules of procedure'.[101]

There is a distinction to be drawn between universal fair trial obligations and procedural entitlements under domestic law, and indeed some 'domestic procedural arrangements' may be set aside in the international criminal trial, and it could still reach the highest standards of fairness. An example of this might be exclusionary rules of evidence, which Damaška conclusively proved in his earlier work, *Evidence Law Adrift*, to be based more in tradition than in concern for the rights of the accused.[102] However, where such arrangements include universal safeguards that are functions of the presumption of innocence, such as the right to a speedy trial (which is one of the elements that Damaška sees as being 'fair enough' in international criminal trials[103]), this presents cause for concern. Such exceptionalism when it comes to fair trial rights in criminal proceedings just because they are complex may lead the way for further erosions of rights, domestically and internationally.[104] As discussed above,[105] domestic trials can be just as complex as international cases, and this complexity should not serve to permit less than fair trial procedures. As Damaška said in an earlier work:

> It would ... be a disheartening irony if a justice system, designed to contribute to the protection of human rights, could properly function only by disregarding humanistic values rooted, *inter alia*, in the presumption of innocence.[106]

This brings us to the second prong of Damaška's argument—that by moving away from an overly burdensome regime of protections for the accused, international criminal tribunals free their energies to allow them to better focus

[99] Mirjan R. Damaška, 'Reflections on Fairness in International Criminal Justice' (2012) 10 *JICJ* 611.

[100] ibid., 612. See also, Colin Warbrick, 'International Criminal Courts and Fair Trial' (1998) 3 *J C & S L* 45, 46, 54.

[101] Damaška (n 99).

[102] Mirjan R. Damaška, *Evidence Law Adrift* (New Haven: Yale University Press, 1997).

[103] Damaška (n 99) 616.

[104] See similarly, William A. Schabas, 'Sentencing by International Tribunals: A Human Rights Approach' (1997) 7 *Duke J Comp & Int'l L* 461, 516: 'Wrong or even confusing signals from The Hague and Arusha may set human rights back decades, within the context of criminal justice.'

[105] Section 3.4.

[106] Mirjan R. Damaška, 'What is the Point of International Criminal Justice? (2008) 83 *Chicago Kent LR* 329, 355.

on their multiple goals. But, as discussed in Section 5.1 above, certain goals (such as deterrence and rebuilding respect for the rule of law) are difficult to achieve in any event, and difficult to measure, notwithstanding the fact that they are inextricably linked to the need for international tribunal to set the highest standards of fairness.

5.3.2 International criminal procedure as a *sui generis* system

International criminal law is a *sui generis* system of law bringing together pieces of procedure from a wide range of domestic legal regimes. Critics may argue that, as international tribunals are not party to any human rights instruments, they effectively work in a vacuum and a certain amount of leeway is granted to judges as to how to interpret the human rights standards repeated in their statutes, as they are not bound to follow the human rights jurisprudence based on those standards. Therefore, it could be argued that international criminal tribunals are free to pave their own way in terms of the procedures they adopt, modify, and put into practice on a daily basis.

However, in the light of the discussion above,[107] which highlighted international criminal law's acknowledged goal of strengthening the rule of law, their continued reference to their representation of the highest standards, and the dangers inherent in their adoption of anything less than the highest standards of fairness, it is clear that making reference to the *sui generis* nature of international criminal procedure does little to excuse any of its shortcomings.

5.3.3 Seriousness of the crimes charged

A third strand of the debate against the highest standards of fairness for the accused before international tribunals focuses on the gravity of the crimes with which they are accused. It could be argued that the role of international criminal tribunals is to end impunity for the most serious crimes known to man, and that therefore they can afford to be less concerned with standard-setting than human rights courts. For example, Boas argued that the 'nature of war crimes and their prosecution makes measures otherwise frowned upon in domestic criminal justice systems less egregious: retrospective extension of criminal provisions, extended jurisdiction, more relaxed evidentiary provisions may be considered appropriate and necessary'.[108]

[107] Section 5.1.

[108] Gideon Boas, 'War Crimes Prosecutions in Australia and Other Common Law Countries: Some Observations' (2010) 21 *CLF* 313, 327.

In response to this line of argument, it must be recalled that the primary goal of all criminal trials is to punish the guilty, regardless of the context of the trial and the crimes charged. To treat individual defendants with less than scrupulous fairness on the basis of the seriousness of the crimes they are charged with would be adverse to the presumption of innocence and would effectively be a form of punishment before judgment is passed.[109] Centuries of experience in criminal law in the domestic realm tells us that confidence in the outcome can only be derived from proper respect for procedures. Therefore, the value placed on the role of the fair trial in criminal law broadly cannot be sacrificed by the fact that international criminal trials are conducted in the context of an international environment that places weight on retribution for the most serious crimes.[110]

It might be argued that fair trial rights erect barriers to the effective prosecution of serious criminals,[111] and that insisting on the highest standards of fairness runs contrary to the legitimate right of victims to 'see justice done'. The interplay between the rights of the accused and other actors with an interest in the outcome of the trial was discussed in greater detail in Chapter 4 above, but suffice to say that an accused before an international criminal tribunal ought to receive a fair trial—not an easy one. It is well established that the procedures for fair trials serve as safeguards against abuse of power and wrongful convictions, regardless of the public interest in securing a conviction,[112] and also that the embodiment of such rights reflects the value that society places on liberty and the presumption of innocence.[113] By the same token, trials of alleged war criminals and génocidaires conducted with the fullest of respect for the fundamental human rights values which the international community holds dear reflects an international society which values the rights of each individual over the vengeful and retributivist reactions of the whole. The comments of Justice Murphy in *Yamashita* are as relevant today as they were in 1946:

> If we are ever to develop an orderly international community based upon a recognition of human dignity it is of the utmost importance that the necessary punishment of those guilty of atrocities be as free as possible from the ugly stigma of revenge and vindictiveness. Justice must be tempered by compassion rather than by vengeance ... We must insist, within the confines of our proper jurisdiction, that the highest

[109] Andrew Ashworth, *The Criminal Process: An Evaluative Study* (2nd edn, Oxford: OUP, 1998) 26.

[110] See also, George P. Fletcher and Jens David Ohlin, 'Reclaiming Fundamental Principles of Criminal Law in the Darfur Case' (2005) 3 *JICJ* 539, 540.

[111] Damaška (n 99) 614.

[112] *Klass v. Germany* (1979–1980) 2 EHRR 214.

[113] Ashworth (n 5) 38–51.

standards of justice be applied in this trial ... Otherwise stark retribution will be free to masquerade in a cloak of false legalism. And the hatred and cynicism engendered by that retribution will supplant the great ideals to which this nation is dedicated.[114]

Conclusion

This chapter aimed to contribute to the vast array of literature on fair trial rights in international criminal law by placing the international criminal tribunals' need to respect the right to a fair trial to the highest degree in the context of international criminal law's standard-setting role. It attempted to prove that international criminal tribunals do bear an obligation to set the highest standards of fairness through a number of distinct but related arguments.

First, it showed that the tribunals' standard-setting function is tied—implicitly or explicitly—to the goals of their establishment. Second, Section 5.2 developed some of the arguments in favour of the standard-setting function based on current practice and under-developed potential. A number of instances where organs of the courts themselves expressly referred to the fact that they do enshrine the highest standards of fairness were analysed. Along with the positive influence that international criminal tribunals can and do bear on fair trial standards domestically, as shall be discussed in greater detail in Chapter 6, the converse is also true. The impact that setting anything lower than the highest standards of fairness can have was examined in Sections 5.2.2, 5.2.3, and 5.2.4. These included the fact that low standards could pave the way for states to derogate from their fair trial obligations, and that less than full respect for the rights of the accused can run the risk of wrongful conviction. Last, the need for tribunals to set the highest standards of fairness was linked to their continuing legitimacy in the eyes of those affected by their proceedings.

Section 5.3 addressed a number of arguments that have been raised against the tribunals' standard-setting function. Although the international criminal tribunals operate in a complex environment that reflects a *sui generis* procedural regime, and in spite of the fact that they put individuals on trial for the most serious crimes, I argued that they still need to respect the highest standards of fairness, for reasons of their own legitimacy and role in spreading respect for the rule of law.

[114] Justice Murphy in *re Yamashita* (1946) 327 US 1, 28–30.

6

The Interplay between Domestic and International Jurisdictions on Fair Trial Matters

This chapter examines the extent to which international criminal tribunals can influence the protection of due process rights by states. As mentioned in the previous chapter, there is the danger that setting lower standards might bear a negative influence on such protection, insofar as the international criminal tribunals' practice might serve as a justification to those states that wish to derogate from the rights of the accused.[1] However, the primary focus of this chapter will be the extent to which international criminal tribunals can exert a positive influence over domestic practice in the realm of fair trial rights, through such practices as referral of cases and deferral to domestic states. The argument that the tribunals can and do play such a role is closely related to that raised in the previous chapter, that international criminal tribunals should set the highest standards of fairness in their procedures.

It is clear that international criminal law has borne a significant impact on substantive domestic criminal law. The ICC Statute, in its preamble, notes that 'it is the duty of every State to exercise its criminal jurisdiction over those responsible for international crimes'. Article 88 requires state parties to amend their national legislation, where necessary, in order to ensure that procedures for cooperation with the Court are in place. Many states availed themselves of this legislative opportunity to criminalize genocide, crimes against humanity, and war crimes, as defined by the Statute of the International Criminal Court, in their own national legislations.[2] While a

[1] See above, Section 5.2.3.

[2] A full database of such implementing legislation can be found online at: http://www.legal-tools.org/en/go-to-database/national-implementing-legislation-database/ (last accessed 14 June 2015). See further, Robert Cryer, 'International Criminal Law *vs* State Sovereignty: Another Round?' (2005) 16 *EJIL* 979; and Lisa J. Laplante, 'The Domestication of International Criminal Law: A Proposal for Expanding the International Criminal Court's Sphere of Influence' (2009–10) 43 *J. Marshall LR* 635.

number of states had jurisdiction over such crimes already,[3] such legislation is indicative of some uniformity in the approach towards international crimes, instigated by the entry into force of the Statute of the International Criminal Court. Judge Kirsch noted that 'these countries are now in a better position to investigate and prosecute [genocide, crimes against humanity, and war crimes] themselves' following the revision of domestic legislation to comply with the ICC Statute.[4]

The impact of international standards on substantive criminal law is not limited to the entry into force of the ICC Statute. Rule 11*bis* on the transfer of cases to domestic jurisdictions, discussed in greater detail below, has also had an effect on substantive criminal law. For example, the Netherlands had to amend its laws to include the criminalization of genocide committed since 1996, following an embarrassing incident in the *Bagaragaza* case. The case had been referred to the Netherlands in 2006, but the referral was revoked when it came to light that the state did not actually have jurisdiction over the crime of genocide, as charged.[5] The Dutch International Crimes Act criminalizes genocide,[6] but the District Court of The Hague held that Dutch courts did not have universal jurisdiction over genocide at the time of the Rwandan genocide in 1994.[7] In 2011, the Dutch Parliament passed a bill that would allow Dutch courts to have universal jurisdiction over any acts of genocide committed since 1966, when the Genocide Convention Implementation Act entered into force.[8]

The substance of international criminal law has resonated beyond the realms of domestic jurisdictions. International criminal judgments on the

[3] For example, the United Kingdom criminalized war crimes, genocide, and torture through the Geneva Conventions Act 1957, the Genocide Act 1967, and the Criminal Justice Act 1998.

[4] Philippe Kirsch, 'ICC Marks Five Years Since Entry into Force of Rome Statute' in Carsten Stahn and Goran Sluiter (eds), *The Emerging Practice of the International Criminal Court* (Leiden: Nijhoff, 2009) 11, 12.

[5] *Prosecutor v. Bagaragaza*, Decision on Prosecutor's Extremely Urgent Motion for Revocation of the Referral to the Kingdom of the Netherlands Pursuant to Rule 11*bis* (F) & (G), Case No. ICTR-2005-86-11*bis*, 17 August 2007.

[6] Act of 19 June 2003 Containing Rules Concerning Serious Violations of International Humanitarian Law (International Crimes Act), Netherlands.

[7] *Case against J.M.*, District Court of The Hague, Case Nos. 09/750009-06 + 09/750007-07, 24 July 2007, LJN BB0494. See further, Cedric Ryngaert, 'Universal Jurisdiction over Genocide and Wartime Torture in Dutch Courts: An Appraisal of the Afghan and Rwandan Cases (2007)' (2007) 2 *Hague Justice Journal* 13.

[8] See further, Thijs Bouwknegt, 'Holland to Close the Net on Old Genocide Suspects', *Radio Netherlands* (The Hague, 10 November 2011) online at: http://archief.wereldomroep.nl/english/article/holland-close-net-old-genocide-suspects (last accessed 12 October 2015) and Cedric Ryngaert, 'The Failed Referral of Michel Bagaragaza from the ICTR to the Netherlands', *Hague Justice Portal*, 14 October 2009, available online at http://www.haguejusticeportal.net/index.php?id=11116 (last accessed 17 June 2015).

definition of the crimes of rape and torture, amongst others, have been accepted by international human rights tribunals as being instructive.[9] These decisions show that international criminal tribunals are to be seen as leaders in setting human rights standards, and not mere followers of international human rights jurisprudence, and that there is a degree of symbiosis between the two branches of law. This symbiotic relationship is not limited to substantive criminal law provisions as they intersect with human rights violations. In Judge Sergio García-Ramírez's separate opinion in the judgment of the Inter-American Court of Human Rights in the case of *La Cantuta v. Peru*, reference was made to the principle of complementarity before the ICC—discussed further in Section 6.2 below—as evidencing that sham trials were not accepted by the international community.[10] It is clear that if the ICC and other tribunals were to accept less than fair trials in other jurisdictions (and it will be argued that the ICC did so in *Al Senussi*), this would send a negative message to domestic states that unfair trials are acceptable to the international community.

6.1 Rule 11*bis* before the ICTR and ICTY

The process of referral under Rules 11*bis* of the ICTY and ICTR Rules of Procedure and Evidence (RPE) allows the tribunals (in light of their 'completion strategies'[11]) to refer cases to national jurisdictions, provided the state in question has jurisdiction over the crime in question, that the case is of a level of gravity appropriate to be tried domestically, and the Referral Bench is satisfied that the accused would not be subject to the death penalty or to an unfair trial in the referral state. When referrals have been approved, international tribunals appoint monitors to ensure that these standards continue

[9] *M.C. v Bulgaria* (2005) 40 EHRR 20, 4 December 2003, paras 104–7 (referring to *Prosecutor v. Kunarac*, Judgment, Case No. IT-96-23-T, 22 February 2001); *Rantsev v. Cyprus* (2010) 51 EHRR 1, 7 January 2010, paras 142–3 (citing *Prosecutor v. Kunarac*, Judgment, Case No. IT-96-23-A, 12 June 2002); *Al-Adsani v. UK* (2002) 34 EHRR 11, 21 November 2001, paras 30–1 (citing *Kunarac* Trial Judgment; *Prosecutor v. Furundžija*, Judgment, Case No. IT-95-17/1-T, 10 December 1998, and *Prosecutor v. Delalić et al.*, Judgment, Case No. IT-96-21-T, 16 November 1998).

[10] *La Cantuta v. Peru* (2006) Series C, No. 162, Judgment of 29 November 2006.

[11] Assessment and Report of Judge Fausto Pocar, President of the International Criminal Tribunal for the Former Yugoslavia, Provided to the Security Council Pursuant to Paragraph 6 of Council Resolution 1534 (2004) Annex I to Letter dated 29 May 2006 from the President of the International Tribunal for the Prosecution of Persons Responsible for Serious Violations of International Humanitarian Law Committed in the Territory of the Former Yugoslavia since 1991, addressed to the President of the Security Council, UN Doc. S/2006/353, 31 May 2006; Letter dated 16 November 2007 from the President of the ICTR, Report on the Completion Strategy of the ICTR, UN Doc. S/2007/676, 20 November 2007.

to be met during the trial,[12] and the case may be sent back to the tribunal if any difficulties arise. Rule 11*bis* has certainly had an effect on the practice of applying the death penalty, in particular. Rwanda abolished the practice in 2007, in order to be eligible to try detainees transferred from the ICTR domestically.[13]

It would follow that the second guarantee—that the accused would not receive an unfair trial in the state of referral—ought to have had a similar impact on states which were keen to have cases referred to them. The principle enshrined in the Rule follows from the same starting point that rules out transfer to states that continue to impose the death penalty—that is, that defendants should receive the same level of treatment whether they are tried by a domestic or an international criminal court. The Referral Bench in *Limaj* stated that 'no distinction can be drawn between persons facing criminal procedures in their home country or on an international level'.[14] The application and assessment of fair trial rights against international benchmarks suggests a real role for the international criminal tribunals in setting the very highest standards of fairness, which would then have to be followed by domestic courts. This is evidenced by the comments of the Chief Prosecutor of the ICTR to the Security Council: 'Following the Appeals Chamber decisions rejecting referral cases to Rwanda for trial under rule 11 *bis* ... Rwanda is in the process of enacting ... additional legislation to meet the remaining concerns of the Appeals Chamber.'[15] In this respect, Rule 11*bis* has been described as a 'conduit for the [international tribunals] to influence domestic criminal procedural law'.[16]

Some might argue that to demand international standards of fairness from post-conflict states would be overly demanding, or perhaps even neo-colonial. A similar argument on the principle of complementarity was raised by the

[12] Rules 11*bis*, ICTR and ICTY RPE. In the ICTY, for example, referral has been aided by OSCE monitoring: David Tolbert and Aleksander Kontic, 'The International Criminal Tribunal for the Former Yugoslavia: Transitional Justice, the Transfer of Cases to National Courts and Lessons for the ICC' in Carsten Stahn and Goran Sluiter (eds), *The Emerging Practice of the International Criminal Court* (Leiden: Nijhoff, 2009) 135, 151.

[13] Organic Law N° 31/2007 of 25/07/2007 Relating to the Abolition of the Death Penalty, Rwanda, entered into force 25 July 2007.

[14] See also, *Prosecutor v. Limaj et al.*, Decision on Isak Musliu's Request for Provisional Release, Case No. IT-03-66-AR65.3, 31 October 2003, para 11.

[15] Statement by the Prosecutor of the ICTR, Justice Hassan B. Jallow to the United Nations Security Council, 4 June 2009, available online at http://41.220.139.198/tabid/155/Default.aspx?id=1029 (last accessed 12 October 2015).

[16] Sarah Nouwen and Dustin A. Lewis, 'Jurisdictional Arrangements and International Criminal Procedure', *University of Cambridge Faculty of Law Research Paper No. 50/2011*, 1 November 2011, available online at http://papers.ssrn.com/sol3/papers.cfm?abstract_id=1957578 (last accessed 17 June 2015) 18.

former Prosecutor of the ICTY, Louise Arbour, during the drafting of the Rome Statute.[17] However, as stated by Franck in response to criticisms that his vision of 'fairness' was too Western, there is no need to dash to protect every domestic practice 'as if it were the last ... white leopard'.[18] Moreover, states like Rwanda have, in practice, been able to embrace these fair trial standards in domestic procedural reforms, and referrals have subsequently taken place.[19] The individual assessment of each case, in light of the reforms enacted to meet international standards,[20] suggests that the tribunals' approach is both flexible, and that the standards expected of states are not beyond reach.

What factors, then, do the ICTR and ICTY see as imperative guarantees when deciding whether trials in a domestic state are fair enough to allow transfer to that state? The decisions on Rule 11*bis* referrals are not uniform in dealing with this question. In *Ademi and Norac*, the Referral Bench stated that 'the requirements of a fair trial' had been compared against the provisions in Croatian law, but did not explicitly state what those requirements were.[21] In the early decisions on transfer to Rwanda, where the safe transfer of defence witnesses and thereby the equality of arms was at issue, the ICTR referred to its own jurisprudence and that of the ECHR, which suggested that it required more than the minimum guarantees laid down in its own statutory provision on fair trial rights to be met, but did not expand on the full

[17] Sharon A. Williams and William A. Schabas, 'Article 17: Issues of Admissibility' in Otto Triffterer (ed.), *Commentary on the Rome Statute: Observers' Notes, Article by Article* (2nd edn, Munich: Beck, 2008) 605, 624.

[18] Thomas M. Franck, 'Epistemology at a Time of Perplexity' (2002) 13 *EJIL* 1025, 1030.

[19] e.g. *Prosecutor v. Uwinkindi*, Decision on Prosecutor's Request for Referral to the Republic of Rwanda, Case No. ICTR-2001-75-R11*bis*, 28 June 2011, upheld on appeal in *Prosecutor v. Uwinkindi*, Decision on Uwinkindi's Appeal against the Referral of His Case to Rwanda and Related Motions, Case No. ICTR-01-75-AR11*bis*, 16 December 2011; *Prosecutor v. Sikubwabo*, Decision on Prosecutor's Request for Referral of the Case to the Republic of Rwanda, Case No. ICTR-95-1D-R11*bis*, 26 March 2012; *Prosecutor v. Kayishema*, Decision on Prosecutor's Request for Referral to the Republic of Rwanda, Case No. ICTR-01-67-R11*bis*, 22 February 2012; *Prosecutor v. Ndimbati*, Decision on the Prosecutor's Request for Referral of the case of Aloys Ndimbati to the Republic of Rwanda, Case No. ICTR-95-1F-R11*bis*, 25 June 2012; *Prosecutor v. Munyarugarama*, Decision on Prosecutor's Request for Referral to the Republic of Rwanda; Case No. ICTR-02-79-R11*bis*, 28 June 2012. The European Court of Human Rights has also confirmed that fair trial rights are respected in Rwanda in the case of *Ahorugeze v. Sweden* (2012) 55 EHRR 2, 27 October 2011.

[20] e.g. *Prosecutor v. Ademi and Norac*, Decision for Referral to the Authorities of the Republic of Croatia Pursuant to Rule 11*bis*, Case No. IT-04-78-PT, 14 September 2005, para 56; *Prosecutor v. Uwinkindi*, Decision on Prosecutor's Request for Referral to the Republic of Rwanda (n 19) para 223.

[21] *Prosecutor v. Ademi and Norac*, Decision for Referral to the Authorities of the Republic of Croatia Pursuant to Rule 11*bis* (n 20) para 55. At para 56, the Bench stated that it 'accept[ed] the guarantees for a fair trial in Croatian law'.

extent of a state's fair trial obligations.[22] Interestingly, Human Rights Watch, in its amicus brief in *Kanyarukiga*, stated that 'on their face, Rwanda's laws comply with the fair trial provisions of Article 20 of the Statute',[23] suggesting that guarantees equivalent to those provided by Article 20 were the standard requirements of a fair trial. The latter interpretation appears to be reflected in the ICTR's decision on the transfer of Bagaragaza to the Netherlands, where the Dutch government had noted the influence of Article 14 of the ICCPR and Article 6 of the ECHR on its procedures, and the Tribunal concluded that the accused could be guaranteed a fair trial in the country, stating: 'The relevant provisions in the ECHR and the ICCPR are substantially similar to the rights enshrined in Article 20 of the ICTR Statute.'[24] Similarly, the Referral Bench's decision in *Sikubwabo* stated that 'Article 20 of the Statute provides guidance as to the rights that must be observed in order to ensure that the accused is given a fair trial.'[25]

One notable exception to these rather concise descriptions on the necessary components of the right to a fair trial is the Rule 11*bis* referral decision in *Stanković*, where the Referral Bench laid out a complete list of requirements for a fair criminal trial.[26] This was based on the provisions of Article 21 of the ICTY Statute, Article 14 of the ICCPR, and Article 6 of the ECHR. The Constitution, Criminal Procedure Code, and Law on the State Court of Bosnia and Herzegovina were assessed in the light of this full list of rights,[27] leading one commentator to argue that the Rule 11*bis* jurisprudence indicates that the tribunals are bound to ensure higher standards in the referral state than a domestic state would require for the purposes of extradition.[28]

In *Stanković*, the parties discussed at some length in their submissions whether the referral would impact on the accused's right to trial without undue delay. The Referral Bench was satisfied that, since the case could continue domestically from where the international tribunal left off, as the state Prosecutor planned to use the same indictment and the materials (such as

[22] *Prosecutor v. Kanyarukiga*, Decision on Request for Referral to Rwanda, Case No. ICTR-2002-78-R11*bis*, 6 June 2008, paras 74–81.

[23] ibid., para 31.

[24] *Prosecutor v. Bagaragaza*, Decision on Prosecutor's Request for Referral of the Indictment to the Netherlands—Rule 11*bis* of the Rules of Procedure and Evidence, Case No. ICTR-2005-86-11*bis*, 13 April 2007.

[25] *Prosecutor v. Sikubwabo*, Decision on the Prosecutor's Request for Referral of the Case to the Republic of Rwanda, Case No. ICTR-95-1D-R11*bis*, 26 March 2012, para 11.

[26] *Prosecutor v. Stanković*, Decision on Referral of Case under Rule 11*bis*, Case No. IT-96-23/2-PT, 17 May 2005, para 55.

[27] ibid., paras 56–65.

[28] Lorenzo Gradoni, '"You Will Receive a Fair Trial Elsewhere": The *Ad Hoc* International Criminal Tribunals Acting as Human Rights Jurisdictions' (2007) 54 *Netherlands Int'l LR* 1.

the pre-trial brief, witness and exhibit lists, and documentary evidence) provided by the Prosecutor of the international tribunal, this was not a cause for concern.[29] On the issue of availability of witnesses, the Referral Bench recalled that the international tribunal's regime of providing safe conduct to witnesses from abroad was often less effective than the domestic state's direct powers of enforcement over individuals residing within its borders, so this did not pose a difficulty.[30] The Referral Bench was satisfied that the state could guarantee a fair trial, given that it provided for all of the fair trial guarantees in its domestic law, had ratified the ECHR, and in light of the fact that the referral mechanism provided 'for a system to allow monitoring of the trial of a case which has been referred in order to ensure that the expectations of a fair trial are met'.[31]

By laying down the 'expectations of a fair trial' as pre-conditions for the referral of cases (referrals that can be revoked if the Tribunal is not satisfied that the trial proves to be sufficiently fair), the ICTR and ICTY willingly embrace a demonstrative function for the fair conduct of trials. The implication from Rule 11*bis* practice is that international criminal procedure is so fair that tribunals are in a position to adjudge the fairness of domestic courts by comparison to their standards, and to demand improvements where necessary. This standard-setting function is not unique to the ad hoc international criminal tribunals, where the international tribunal has primacy over domestic courts. It is also reflected in the ICC, through its practice of complementarity, despite the fact that that Court's jurisdiction is subsidiary to that of domestic courts, as shall now be discussed.

6.2 Complementarity before the ICC

The principle of complementarity as a bar to the exercise of jurisdiction over a case before the ICC means that the Court has to ensure the case has not been or is not in the process of being prosecuted domestically.[32] Where proceedings are ongoing, the Court will ask whether the state is 'unwilling or unable genuinely to carry out the investigation or prosecution'. In the event the domestic state is willing and able to prosecute the accused individual for the international crimes in the International Criminal Court's indictment against him, the Court is under a statutory obligation to declare the case against that individual inadmissible.[33]

[29] *Stanković* Referral Decision (n 26), paras 69–77. [30] ibid., para 85.
[31] ibid., para 68. [32] Article 17, ICC Statute.
[33] Article 17(1), ICC Statute; this obligation is reiterated in preambular paragraph 10 of the ICC Statute, which states that the Court's jurisdiction shall be complementary to that of states.

The first prong of an admissibility decision is to determine whether there has been action by a state to prosecute the person concerned.[34] If there has been no such action, and the case is of sufficient gravity to proceed,[35] then it will be admissible. In many admissibility decisions to date, the Court has deemed that neither prosecution nor 'concrete and progressive investigative steps' are ongoing or have been held,[36] or, where such investigations are underway, the accused has been charged with or investigated for different crimes or on the basis of different conduct.[37] If steps have been or are being taken by the state to investigate or prosecute the accused, the Court will have to consider whether the state is or was unwilling or unable genuinely to carry out the investigation or prosecution.[38]

There has been some debate on the so-called 'due process thesis' in academic discussions of the second prong of admissibility determinations—that is, whether a state can be deemed unwilling or unable to genuinely prosecute a case where it cannot guarantee full respect for the rights of the accused.[39]

[34] See Darryl Robinson, 'The "Inaction" Controversy: Neglected Words and New Opportunities' in Carsten Stahn and Mohamed El Zeidy (eds), *The International Criminal Court and Complementarity: From Theory to Practice* (Cambridge: CUP, 2011) 460, and Darryl Robinson, 'The Mysterious Mysteriousness of Complementarity' (2010) 21 *CLF* 67. This two-step assessment was used in *Situation in Libya: Prosecutor v. Gaddafi*, Decision, requesting further submissions on issues related to the admissibility of the case against Saif Al-Islam Gaddafi, Case No. ICC-01/11-01/11, 7 December 2012, paras 6–8.

[35] Article 17(1)(d), ICC Statute.

[36] e.g. *Situation in Uganda: Prosecutor v. Kony et al.*, Decision on the Admissibility of the Case under Article 19(1) of the Statute, Case No. ICC-02/04-01/05, 10 March 2009, para 52; *Situation in Côte d'Ivoire: Prosecutor v. Simone Gbagbo*, Decision on Côte d'Ivoire's Challenge to the Admissibility of the Case against Simone Gbagbo, Case No. ICC-02/11-01/12, 11 December 2014, para 35; *Situation in the CAR: Prosecutor v. Bemba*, Decision Pursuant to Article 61(7)(a) and (b) of the Rome Statute on the Charges of the Prosecutor Against Jean-Pierre Bemba Gombo, Case No. ICC-01/05-01/08, 15 June 2009, paras 24–5; *Situation in the DRC: Prosecutor v. Katanga and Ngudjolo*, Judgment on the Appeal of Mr Germain Katanga against the Oral Decision of Trial Chamber II of 12 June 2009 on the Admissibility of the Case, ICC-01/04-01/07, 25 September 2009, para 78; *Situation in Kenya: Prosecutor v. Ruto, Kosgey and Sang*, Decision on the Application by the Government of Kenya Challenging the Admissibility of the Case Pursuant to Article 19(2)(b) of the Statute, Case No. ICC-01/09-01/11, 30 May 2011, paras 68–70.

[37] *Situation in the DRC: Prosecutor v. Lubanga*, Decision Concerning Pre-Trial Chamber I's Decision of 10 February 2006 and the Incorporation of Documents into the Record of the Case against Mr Thomas Lubanga Dyilo, Case No. ICC-01/04-01/06, 10 February 2006, para 37; *Situation in Kenya: Prosecutor v. Muthaura, Kenyatta and Ali*, Judgment on the Appeal of the Republic of Kenya against the Decision of Pre-Trial Chamber II of 30 May 2011 entitled 'Decision on the Application by the Government of Kenya Challenging the Admissibility of the Case Pursuant to Article 19(2)(b) of the Statute', Case No. ICC-01/09-02/11, 30 August 2011, para 39.

[38] Articles 17(1)(a) and (b), ICC Statute. It will also have to consider whether there is a risk of double jeopardy under Article 20(3) with proceeding with the trial, pursuant to Article 17(1)(c); this is discussed in greater detail at Section 6.3 below.

[39] Frédéric Mégret and Marika Giles Samson, 'Holding the Line on Complementarity in Libya' (2013) 11 *JICJ* 571; Kevin Jon Heller, 'The Shadow Side of Complementarity: The Effect of Article 17 of the Rome Statute on National Due Process' (2006) 17 *CLF* 255.

Many scholars and practitioners have argued that it would be inappropriate for the ICC to consider whether the rights of the accused will be respected in domestic proceedings when determining admissibility, given that it is not a human rights court.[40] We might accept, as stated in the *Al-Senussi* admissibility decision, that, 'violations of the accused's procedural rights are not per se grounds for a finding of unwillingness or inability under article 17 of the Statute'.[41] However, such violations may stand as hallmarks of either unwillingness or inability to bring the accused to justice, and each of those elements will now be discussed in turn.

6.2.1 Unwillingness

According to Article 17(2) of the ICC Statute, unwillingness might be evidenced by a judicial system that fails to bring offenders to justice within a reasonable time, or by a lack of judicial impartiality or independence.[42] It has been argued that 'unwillingness' can only be proven if the domestic state's prosecution or investigation was inspired by an attempt to shield the accused from criminal accountability, which would appear to be the case from a literal reading of Article 17(2)(a), in particular, which demands that the Court must consider whether '[t]he proceedings were or are being undertaken or the national decision was made for the purpose of shielding the person concerned from criminal responsibility for crimes within the jurisdiction of the Court referred to in Article 5'.[43]

[40] The Prosecutor, visiting Libya in 2011, stated explicitly: 'We are not a human rights Court. We are not checking the fairness of the proceedings. We are checking the genuineness of the proceedings.' (Video available online at http://www.aljazeera.com/news/africa/2011/11/2011112395821170909.html (last accessed 19 June 2015)). See further, William Burke-White and Scott Kaplan, 'Shaping the Contours of Domestic Justice: The ICC and an Admissibility Challenge in the Uganda Situation' in Carsten Stahn and Goran Sluiter (eds), *The Emerging Practice of the International Criminal Court* (Leiden: Nijhoff, 2009) 79, 112; Compare Mark S. Ellis, 'The International Criminal Court and Its Implication for Domestic Law and National Capacity Building' (2002) 15 *Florida JIL* 215, 241; Office of the Prosecutor, *Paper on Some Policy Issues before the Office of the Prosecutor*, September 2003, available online at http://www.icc-cpi.int/nr/rdonlyres/1fa7c4c6-de5f-42b7-8b25-60aa962ed8b6/143594/030905_policy_paper.pdf (last accessed 20 June 2015), 5, stating that 'the principle underlying the concept of complementarity is that States remain responsible and accountable for investigating and prosecuting crimes committed under their jurisdiction and *that national systems are expected to maintain and enforce adherence to international standards*' (emphasis added).

[41] *Situation in Libya: Prosecutor v. Gaddafi and Al-Senussi*, Decision on the admissibility of the case against Abdullah Al-Senussi, Case No. ICC-01/11-01/11, 11 October 2013, para 235.

[42] Article 17(2), ICC Statute.

[43] Heller (n 39) 257 argued that there is no legal obligation on the ICC to assume jurisdiction where an unfair trial is going to be held, although a moral obligation to do so may exist. Jann Kleffner, *Complementarity in the Rome Statute and National Criminal Jurisdictions* (Oxford: OUP, 2008) stated that only Article 17(2)(b)—that is, undue delay inconsistent with an intent to bring

Articles 17(2)(b) and (c) of the Statute state that the Court shall also consider whether:

(b) There has been an unjustified delay in the proceedings which in the circumstances is inconsistent with an intent to bring the person concerned to justice;
(c) The proceedings were not or are not being conducted independently or impartially, and they were or are being conducted in a manner which, in the circumstances, is inconsistent with an intent to bring the person concerned to justice.

It is clear that these sub-paragraphs are worded slightly differently from Article 17(2)(a)'s formulation of 'shielding the person concerned from criminal responsibility for crimes within the jurisdiction of the Court'.[44] The question is whether the proceedings were held, or are being held, in a manner inconsistent with a desire to bring the accused person 'to justice'. It would appear, then, that the drafters intended the 'delay' and 'impartiality' prongs of the unwillingness test to mean something more than an unwillingness to convict the accused. The ICTY has interpreted the term 'justice' to mean respect for the rights of the accused as well as the rights of victims.[45] A number of authors have suggested that the notion of bringing an individual to justice goes beyond merely securing a conviction; justice would not be served when a conviction is handed down after a trial that fails to offer fundamental due process rights.[46] To read the term 'to bring the person to justice' as

the person to justice—can apply also to situations where the breach of due process is to the detriment of the accused.

[44] Enrique Carnero Rojo, 'The Role of Fair Trial Considerations in the Complementarity Regime of the International Criminal Court: From "No Peace without Justice" to "No Peace without Victor's Justice"?' (2005) 18 *LJIL* 829, 853.

[45] *Prosecutor v. Hadžihasanović et al.*, Decision granting provisional release to Enver Hadžihasanović, Case No. IT-01-47-PT, 19 December 2001, para 5.

[46] Federica Gioia, 'Comments on Chapter 3', in Jann Kleffner and Gerben Kor (eds), *Complementary Views on Complementarity* (Cambridge: CUP, 2006) 105, 112, argues that the term 'justice' requires the respect for due process rights. See also Carnero Rojo (n 44) 840, stating that Article 17(2) 'can also be construed as empowering the Court to take over domestic proceedings intentionally lacking due process of law'; Carsten Stahn, 'Libya, the International Criminal Court and Complementarity: A Test for "Shared Responsibility"' (2012) 10 *JICJ* 325, 345: 'The scope of scrutiny by the ICC over the fairness of domestic proceedings depends *inter alia* on the relationship between the chapeau and the notion of "intent to bring the person concerned to justice"'; Jo Stigen, 'The Relationship between the Principle of Complementarity and the Exercise of Universal Jurisdiction for Core International Crimes' in Morten Bergsmo (ed.), *Complementarity and the Exercise of Universal Jurisdiction for Core International Crimes* (Oslo: Torkel Opsahl Academic EPublisher, 2010) 133, 150, and in the same volume, Pål Lønseth, 'Between Territoriality and Universality: Reflections by a Core International Crimes Prosecutor' 161, 163: 'If the principle of complementarity is set to balance the principle of universality, maybe with the Rome Statute as a model, the "able and willing" criterion *needs to comprise a demand for fair trial* and principles that allow foreign jurisdictions to disregard mock trials, only set up to avoid interference from foreign jurisdictions' (emphasis added).

meaning 'to convict the accused' would run contrary to the presumption of innocence, and the Court is bound to interpret the law in a manner that is consistent with internationally recognized human rights,[47] which clearly include this presumption.

In light of the fact that the two prongs of the test in Article 17(b) and (c) fall under a *chapeau* which asks the Court to determine questions of whether there has been an unjustified delay or whether the proceedings were not conducted independently or impartially 'having regard to the principles of due process recognised by international law', it could be argued that an unfair trial at the expense of the accused might indeed render the trial admissible before the ICC. According to Robinson:

> During the drafting of Article 17, most delegates were concerned with sham or ineffective proceedings, and thought that the problem of overly-harsh national proceedings is one that could be taken up with a human rights body (which protects rights) not the ICC (which is about preventing impunity). Other delegates, including Mauro Politi of Italy (later a judge at the ICC) were of a different view, and secured an ambiguous but potentially significant reference to 'due process' in Article 17.[48]

Rule 51 of the ICC RPE explicitly states that, in its challenge to the admissibility of a case before the Court, a state can present information, inter alia, 'showing that its courts meet internationally recognised norms and standards for the independent and impartial prosecution of similar conduct'.[49] Judicial bias or a lack of independence that goes against the accused would clearly not meet those internationally recognized standards, thus supporting the view that a lack of independence and impartiality for the purposes of Article 17(2)(c) can act as a bar to admissibility where the bias was against the accused, as well as when it was in favour of him or her. Indeed, this would comport with the ordinary meaning of the term 'impartiality', which means 'not favouring one party or side more than another'.[50] Some have argued that the ordinary meaning of Article 17(2)(c), when read in its entirety, suggests that the lack of independence or impartiality must favour the accused,[51] given that it adds, '*and* they were or are being conducted in a manner which, in the

[47] Article 21(3), ICC Statute.

[48] Darryl Robinson, 'Three Theories of Complementarity: Charge, Sentence or Process? A Comment on Kevin Heller's Sentence-Based Theory of Complementarity' in William A. Schabas, Yvonne McDermott, and Niamh Hayes (eds), *The Ashgate Research Companion to International Criminal Law: Critical Perspectives* (Aldershot: Ashgate, 2013) 369, 378.

[49] Carsten Stahn, 'R2P, the ICC and the Libyan arrests' *Hague Justice Portal*, 24 November 2011, available online at http://www.haguejusticeportal.net/index.php?id=12998 (last accessed 17 June 2015).

[50] 'Impartial, adj.' *OED Online*, Oxford University Press, June 2015.

[51] Heller (n 39).

circumstances, is inconsistent with an intent to bring the person concerned to justice'.[52] Even if the term 'to bring the person concerned to justice' were interchangeable with 'to secure a conviction', this is not determinative, given that the Arabic version of the Statute uses the term 'or'.[53]

The 'due process' hypothesis appears to gain further credence from the admissibility decision in *Katanga*, where Trial Chamber II stated in the context of a self-referral from the Democratic Republic of the Congo:

> The Chamber is not in a position to ascertain the real motives of a State which expresses its unwillingness to prosecute a particular case... The reasons for such a decision may be because the State considers itself unable to hold a fair and expeditious trial or because it considers that circumstances are not conducive to conducting effective investigations or holding a fair trial.[54]

The Chamber stated that this interpretation was consistent with the drafters' intentions to 'bring an end to impunity while continuing to respect the primacy of national jurisdictions'.[55] However, it could be argued that this interpretation was consistent with the context of the case, where the state had voluntarily accepted the ICC's jurisdiction and thus did not challenge the admissibility of the case on the basis of complementarity. This contrasts with the cases in the *Libya* situation, where the state contested admissibility, while the defence argued in favour of trial before the ICC.

In its admissibility decision in the case against Abdullah Al-Senussi, Pre-Trial Chamber I stated that 'certain violations of the procedural rights of the accused may be relevant to the assessment of the independence and impartiality of the national proceedings that the Chamber is required to make, having regard to the principles of due process recognized under international law, under article 17(2)(c) of the Statute'.[56] However, this could only be the case where the lack of independence and impartiality was inconsistent with the intent to bring the accused to justice.[57] The Chamber did not expand further on its understanding of the term 'to bring the person to justice'. It merely noted in a footnote that the terms of Article 17(2)(c) were conjunctive, whereas Rule 9(ii) of the ICTY RPE was disjunctive, such that a lack of independence or impartiality alone could suffice for competence to

[52] Emphasis added.

[53] Wedad Elmaalul, *The Principle of Complementarity: A Critical Evaluation of its Legitimacy* (PhD thesis, Bangor University, July 2015) 136.

[54] *Situation in the DRC: Prosecutor v. Katanga and Chui*, Reasons for the Oral Decision on the Motion Challenging the Admissibility of the Case (Article 19 of the Statute), Case No. ICC-01/04-01/07, 16 June 2009, para 80.

[55] ibid., para 79.

[56] *Al-Senussi* admissibility decision (n 41) para 235.

[57] ibid.

be deferred to the ICTY, whereas for the ICC, it needed to be linked to a broader unwillingness to bring the accused to justice. In such circumstances, Article 17(2)(b) combined with Rule 51 may very well encourage states to ensure that proceedings are conducted in accordance with international standards on independence and impartiality, and with an intention to serve justice by reaching a final verdict in accordance with those standards.

The Appeals Chamber decision on the admissibility of the case was somewhat more explicit in rejecting the defence's position that a state could not be considered genuinely willing to conduct proceedings if it fails to respect the fair trial rights of the accused.[58] Based on the ordinary meaning, drafting history, and object and purpose of Article 17(2), and the overall aim of the Statute to end impunity, it concluded that Article 17(2) normally applied where the national proceedings were intended to allow the accused to 'evade justice'.[59] Nevertheless, it concluded that in some instances, 'the violations of the rights of the suspect are so egregious that it is clear that the international community would not accept that the accused was being brought to any genuine form of justice'.[60] Such proceedings should be deemed 'inconsistent with an intent to bring the person to justice' for the purposes of Article 17(2).[61] In other words, the Appeals Chamber did not completely close the door on the due process hypothesis—it will be for future Chambers ruling on admissibility to consider whether the violations of the rights of the accused are so egregious to render the case admissible before the ICC. The Appeals Chamber gave no particular examples of egregious violations that would meet this threshold, but presumably a clearly biased tribunal or one lacking in independence would meet the Article 17(2)(c) requirement, and an undue delay might fall foul of Article 17(2)(b). A failure to allow the accused adequate time and/or facilities to prepare his or her defence, trial *in absentia*, or a lack of access to a lawyer might also easily meet this threshold, depending on the circumstances. Thus, while the complementarity principle is not as explicit as Rule 11*bis*, it clearly has the potential to influence domestic jurisdictions to ensure that they respect the rights of the accused.

That being said, the Appeals Chamber's conclusions on Al-Senussi's lack of access to a lawyer are disappointing, and in clear contradiction to the findings on similar problems faced by his co-accused, Saif Gaddafi.[62] The

[58] *Situation in Libya: Prosecutor v. Gaddafi and Al-Senussi*, Judgment on the Appeal of Mr Abdullah Al-Senussi against the Decision of Pre-Trial Chamber I of 11 October 2013 entitled 'Decision on the Admissibility of the Case against Abdullah Al-Senussi', Case No. ICC-01/11-01/11, 24 July 2014, para 231.

[59] ibid., paras 229–31. [60] ibid., para 230. [61] ibid.

[62] *Situation in Libya: Prosecutor v. Gaddafi and Al-Senussi*, Decision on the Admissibility of the Case against Saif Al-Islam Gaddafi, Case No. ICC-01/11-01/11, 31 May 2013, para 214.

Pre-Trial Chamber found that Gaddafi's lack of access to a lawyer was an 'important difficulty' which could pose 'an impediment to the progress of proceedings' against the accused.[63] By contrast, the Appeals Chamber in *Al-Senussi* found that the lack of a lawyer for the accused was attributable to the security situation in the country, and found that this impediment did not illustrate a lack of willingness on the part of the state for the purposes of Article 17(2).[64] However, giving deference to the reasons given for acknowledged breaches of the rights of the accused is problematic for two reasons. First, it suggests that even egregious violations of the rights of the accused might be explained away by reference to extraneous factors, and that the protection of those rights can be diluted with reference to such ambiguous circumstances as 'the security situation in the country'. Second, the Chamber reached this conclusion on the basis of evidence provided by Libya, but the accused effectively could not challenge this evidence because Libya had denied him the right to communicate with counsel who represented his interests before the ICC. It would have been preferable for the Appeals Chamber to determine that a lack of access to a lawyer was inconsistent with a genuine intent to bring the accused to justice, and that the lack of access to a lawyer also suggested an inability to hold a trial in accordance with the due process standards established in domestic law and procedure. The finding in *Gaddafi* on the accused's lack of access to a lawyer was based on inability, as opposed to unwillingness, as we shall now discuss.

6.2.2 Inability

One of the hallmarks of inability is the domestic court's failure to try offenders in accordance with full due process standards where there has been a complete or partial breakdown in state structures, which renders the national justice system unable to arrest the accused, secure evidence or witnesses, or unable for some other reason to conduct a trial. The possibility that the accused might not be afforded a fair trial could clearly fall within the 'otherwise unable' proviso of Article 17(3). According to Benzing's reading of the *travaux préparatoires* on this provision, 'ineffectiveness' was designed to include situations where 'procedures did not guarantee full respect for the rights of the accused or could not be considered sufficiently impartial'.[65]

[63] ibid.

[64] *Al-Senussi*, Judgment on the Appeal of Mr Abdullah Al-Senussi against the Decision of Pre-Trial Chamber I of 11 October 2013 entitled 'Decision on the Admissibility of the Case against Abdullah Al-Senussi' (n 58) paras 191–2.

[65] Markus Benzing, 'The Complementarity Regime of the International Criminal Court: International Criminal Justice between State Sovereignty and the Fight against Impunity'

Similarly, given that the provision on securing witnesses is not limited to prosecution witnesses, it is possible that an inability to secure the testimony of defence witnesses may fall foul of Article 17(3) in the same way that Rwanda's difficulties in securing defence witnesses was a barrier in the early jurisprudence on transfer of cases to Rwanda from the ICTR.[66]

In *Gaddafi*, Pre-Trial Chamber I noted that the ability of a state to ensure the fair trial rights of the suspect was pertinent because if a state was not able to carry out a trial in accordance with the due process rights incorporated into its own law, it could not be said to be truly 'able' to conduct proceedings under that law.[67] It noted that Libya had not shown 'whether and how it will overcome the existing difficulties in securing a lawyer as a suspect',[68] and in a similar vein, the Pre-Trial Chamber in *Al-Senussi* noted that his lack of access to a lawyer could 'become a fatal obstacle to the progress of the case',[69] illustrating an inability to bring the case to trial. This shows that states must illustrate to the ICC how the rights of the accused will be respected if they are to mount a successful admissibility challenge. The ICC's standard-setting function and ability to encourage domestic jurisdictions to offer full respect for the rights of the accused cannot be overstated in this regard.

6.2.3 Conclusions on complementarity

This section illustrated that complementarity before the ICC can bear an influence on domestic prosecutions for international crimes and the rights of the accused therein. It showed that, in order to ensure that their admissibility challenges are successful, states should indicate that the accused's rights will be protected. Otherwise, it might be found that the violations of the rights of the accused are so egregious that the state cannot be found to be genuinely willing to bring the accused to justice, rendering the case admissible on the grounds of unwillingness, or that the trial of the accused cannot be granted

(2003) 7 *Max Planck Ybk UN L* 591, 597. See also, Office of the Prosecutor, International Criminal Court, *Informal Expert Paper: The Principle of Complementarity in Practice*, available online at http://www.icc-cpi.int/iccdocs/doc/doc654724.pdf (last accessed 17 June 2015) 8–9: 'Of course, although the ICC is not a "human rights court", human rights standards may still be of relevance and utility in assessing whether the proceedings are carried out genuinely.'

[66] See above (n 19).

[67] *Gaddafi*, Decision on the Admissibility of the Case against Saif Al-Islam Gaddafi (n 62), para 217.

[68] ibid., para 214.

[69] *Al-Senussi*, Judgment on the Appeal of Mr Abdullah Al-Senussi against the Decision of Pre-Trial Chamber I of 11 October 2013 entitled 'Decision on the Admissibility of the Case against Abdullah Al-Senussi' (n 58), para 307.

in accordance with domestic fair trial protections, and therefore the case is admissible due to inability.

Some might argue that such an interpretation goes against the ordinary meaning of Article 17, but it is clear from the above that the provisions of Article 17 are sufficiently ambiguous to allow a more expansive reading than was perhaps intended by the drafters. In a similar vein, it is reasonably clear from a reading of the Statute and the *travaux preparatoires* that the drafters did not intend for the Court to have subpoena powers but, as mentioned in Chapter 3, it was found to possess such powers in the *Ruto and Sang* case in 2014.[70] There is nothing to suggest that an equally creative interpretation of Article 17 might be taken in the future, and the decisions in *Gaddafi* and *Al-Senussi* certainly do not exclude this possibility.

It may also be argued that such an interpretation of the complementarity clause may allow the ICC to demand impossible standards from developing states, or those emerging from conflict situations,[71] and that even a less than fair trial in the domestic realm does more for transitional justice than an international trial respecting the highest due process standards.[72] But, as illustrated by the discussion on Rule 11*bis* above, these types of provisions can be as much an incentive to states that want to prosecute crimes falling within the jurisdiction of the court as an implement to defeat their ambitions. This conceptualization of complementarity as a carrot, rather than a stick, was dubbed 'positive complementarity' by Burke-White, who foresaw that the principle would encourage domestic states to prosecute international crimes.[73] He also envisioned the possibility that the Office of the Prosecutor, perhaps in partnership with non-governmental organizations, might monitor domestic prosecutions to ensure that they 'meet basic standards of due process and are genuine efforts to bring the accused to justice'.[74] In practice, the OTP has indeed monitored the case of Al-Senussi since the deferral of

[70] *Situation in Kenya: Prosecutor v. Ruto and Sang*, Decision on Prosecutor's Application for Witness Summonses and resulting Request for State Party Cooperation, Case No. ICC-01/09-01/11, 17 April 2014. See above, Section 3.10.2.

[71] William A. Schabas, *An Introduction to the International Criminal Court* (Cambridge: CUP, 2011) 196: 'Certainly, there is a danger that the provisions of Article 17 will become a tool for overly harsh assessments of the judicial machinery in developing countries'; Mauro Politi, 'The Establishment of an International Criminal Court at the Crossroads: Issues and Prospects After the First Session of the Preparatory Committee' (1999) 13 *Nouvelles Études Pénales* 115, 143; Williams and Schabas (n 17).

[72] David Luban, 'After the Honeymoon' (2013) 11 *JICJ* 505, 511–12.

[73] William W. Burke-White, 'Implementing a Policy of Positive Complementarity in the Rome System of Justice' (2008) 19 *CLF* 59. See also, Rod Rastan, 'Complementarity: Contest or Collaboration', in Morten Bergsmo (ed.), *Complementarity and the Exercise of Universal Jurisdiction for Core International Crimes* (Oslo: Torkel Opsahl Academic EPublisher, 2010) 83.

[74] Burke-White, ibid., 74.

jurisdiction to Libya, in partnership with Libyan authorities and independent trial monitors.[75] The Prosecutor noted in November 2014 that 'the on-going violence and alleged threats to judges, prosecutors and lawyers do not augur well for a fair trial that respects all the rights of an accused person', and that she would consider whether to apply for a review of the admissibility decision on that basis in due course.[76] This again illustrates the relationship between international and domestic courts on fair trial matters.

6.3 *Ne Bis in Idem*

The question of whether a case can be rendered admissible where proceedings have been unfair to the accused, as opposed to carried out in such a way as to shield him or her from full accountability, also arises in considerations of the *ne bis in idem* rule. Under Article 20(3) of the ICC Statute, a person cannot be tried by the Court if they have already been tried by a domestic court, unless those prior proceedings:

(a) Were for the purpose of shielding the person concerned from criminal responsibility for crimes within the jurisdiction of the Court; or
(b) Otherwise were not conducted independently or impartially in accordance with the norms of due process recognised by international law and were conducted in a manner which, in the circumstances, was inconsistent with an intent to bring the person concerned to justice.[77]

Some have argued that the ICC's clause can only apply where the accused benefitted from the domestic court's shortcomings.[78] On the contrary, if the term 'to bring the person concerned to justice' essentially means the same thing as shielding him/her from criminal responsibility, why would there be a need for two separate provisions? It would be most unusual if the drafters chose not only to include two consecutive legal provisions that were identical in meaning, but also that they would choose different wording for both provisions. Carnero-Rojo made a distinction between the concepts of bringing a person to justice and shielding an individual from criminal responsibility as they are present in both Articles 17 and 20.[79] He stated that the latter could be interpreted as meaning '"justice" as a result rather than as a process', while the former could incorporate general due process rights.[80] Thus, Article 20(3)(b) requires the Court to

[75] Statement to the United Nations Security Council on the Situation in Libya, pursuant to UNSCR 1970 (2011), Mrs Fatou Bensouda, Prosecutor of the International Criminal Court, 12 November 2014.

[76] ibid.

[77] Article 20(3), ICC Statute.

[78] Benzing (n 65) 598; Kleffner (n 43) 130.

[79] Carnero Rojo (n 44) 836–7.

[80] ibid.

determine whether the domestic trial was conducted in accordance with international due process norms, and whether the consequences of a failure to do so meant that justice was not done in the case.

In a similar vein, the statutes of the ICTY, ICTR, SCSL, and STL deem that *ne bis in idem* will not apply where the domestic proceedings were not independent or impartial, or where there was an intent to shield the person from justice, or the case was not diligently prosecuted.[81] Given that these terms are disjunctive (using 'or'), it is clear that a lack of independence, impartiality, or diligent prosecution of the case against the accused alone could justify the tribunal taking jurisdiction and trying him or her again in a fairer manner in an international forum. In other words, these flaws need not solely be linked to an intent to shield the person from justice to form an exception to the *ne bis in idem* rule.

Thus, the statutory provisions of all of the international criminal tribunals require an assessment of the genuineness of prior proceedings and the extent to which they were conducted impartially, independently, and diligently, in accordance with international due process standards. It would seem that the tribunals will not just be concerned with whether the unfairness or lack of compliance with international due process standards benefitted the accused; they will also examine those processes that failed to respect the rights of the accused.

Conclusion

This chapter argued that international criminal tribunals can encourage states to respect and protect the right to a fair trial. This is perhaps most explicit in the practice of the ICTY and ICTR under their Rule 11*bis*, where the tribunals will not defer jurisdiction to a state unless they can be satisfied that the accused can receive a fair trial. In this way, the international criminal tribunals encourage fairness in the trial practice of states, and this has been seen in practice from the improvements in due process protections domestically in order to be prepared for the transfer of cases.

It also advanced the 'due process hypothesis' for the principle of complementarity. While many commentators advance the theory that considerations of 'unwillingness' and 'inability' under Article 17 will only be concerned with impartiality and due process where the lack thereof favoured

[81] Article 10(2), ICTY Statute; Article 9(2), ICTR Statute; Article 9(2), SCSL Statute; Article 5(2), STL Statute.

the accused, a number of arguments were advanced to the contrary. First, the term 'to bring an individual to justice' must mean more than simply convicting him or her; justice could not be said to have been served in instances where the accused is convicted regardless of a failure to prove guilt beyond reasonable doubt. Second, the Rules of Procedure and Evidence allow a state to bring evidence that illustrates how its courts meet international standards for prosecution—those courts that are biased against the accused from the outset would not meet such standards. Third, the term 'impartiality' suggests that all sides must be treated equally—a bias against an accused would mean that the domestic court is as lacking in impartiality as a court that unduly favours the accused for the purposes of shielding him or her from the jurisdiction of the Court.

Lastly, the statutory provisions on *ne bis in idem* were examined to determine the extent to which they too could exert a positive influence over domestic jurisdictions on questions of fairness. It is clear from the disjunctive wording of Article 20(3) of the ICC Statute, which refers to 'shielding the person from criminal responsibility for crimes within the jurisdiction of the Court' and, in a later subsection, to an intent inconsistent with bringing the accused to justice. Again, the concept of bringing the accused to justice must mean more than shielding him or her from criminal responsibility. This chapter argued that where an accused had previously been subjected to an unfair trial in a state and been convicted of those crimes, the international criminal tribunals could use the unfairness of the domestic proceedings to justify taking jurisdiction and putting that individual on trial again, this time in a fairer international forum.

In light of the arguments on setting the highest standards of fairness in Chapter 5, all of the above discussion reiterates the norm-projecting role of the international criminal tribunal in illustrating best practice. The tribunals' ability to take jurisdiction over cases that have not been pursued diligently should convince domestic jurisdictions to emulate the high standards that they embrace. Relatedly, where less than the highest standards are incorporated by the international tribunal, there is a risk of 'rights dualism', whereby the international tribunal has illustrated lower standards for criminal trials than domestic trials, and an individual might expect to receive a fairer trial in a domestic forum.[82] This would lead to an overall weakening of the right to a fair trial, and international criminal tribunals should be mindful of that risk when adjudging upon the rights of the accused.

[82] Alexander Zahar, 'Pluralism and the Rights of the Accused in International Criminal Proceedings' in Elies van Sliedregt and Sergey Vasiliev (eds), *Pluralism in International Criminal Law* (Oxford: OUP, 2014) 225.

7
Conclusion

This work set out to examine the standards of due process embraced by the ICTY, ICTR, SCSL, STL, and ICC in the context of a broader discussion on the meaning of fairness in international criminal trials and the implications thereof. A key question that was raised throughout this book was to what extent international criminal tribunals could be said to bear a standard-setting function, setting an example of best practice for the conduct of domestic and international criminal trials by following the highest due-process standards. To this end, this book examined the interpretation of the concept of fairness in the context of international criminal trials, the components of the right to a fair trial in practice, the manner in which alleged breaches of the right to a fair trial have been treated, the tribunals' practice on the right to a fair trial of the Prosecutor and other parties, and the interplay between domestic and international jurisdictions on fairness issues.

In asking these questions, the present work built upon the extensive and burgeoning literature on fair trial rights in international criminal proceedings by undertaking an exposition of the wider implications of the realization of the right to a fair trial by international criminal tribunals. Many of the key works on fair trial rights in international criminal law have assessed the tribunals' procedural frameworks against human rights,[1] domestic procedural standards,[2] a mixture of both,[3] or their own statutory instruments by treating international criminal tribunals as *sui generis* legal regimes.[4] But these works have given the broader theoretical rationale as to *why* tribunals

[1] Salvatore Zappalà, *Human Rights in International Criminal Proceedings* (Oxford: OUP, 2003).

[2] Christoph J.M. Safferling, *Towards an International Criminal Procedure* (Oxford: OUP, 2001); Christian DeFrancia, 'Due Process in International Criminal Courts: Why Procedure Matters' (2001) 87 *Va LR* 1381; Gregory S. Gordon, 'Toward an International Criminal Procedure: Due Process Aspirations and Limitations' (2007) 45 *Columbia J Transnat'l L* 635.

[3] Goran Sluiter, Håkan Friman, Suzannah Linton, Salvatore Zappalà, and Sergey Vasiliev (eds), *International Criminal Procedure: Principles and Rules* (Oxford: OUP, 2013).

[4] Jens David Ohlin, 'Meta-Theory of International Criminal Procedure: Vindicating the Rule of Law' (2009) 14 *UCLA J Int'l L & Foreign Aff* 77; Frédéric Mégret, 'Beyond Fairness: Understanding the Determinants of International Criminal Procedure' (2009) 14 *UCLA J Int'l L & Foreign Aff* 37.

should espouse the highest standards of fairness only a perfunctory analysis. Indeed, some leading authors have expressed the view that international criminal tribunals do not need to set leading examples on every aspect of the right to a fair trial, but rather just need to be 'fair enough'.[5] This book has justified the need for international criminal tribunals to set the highest standards of fairness by presenting evidence of the extent to which the tribunals' standard-setting function is already happening on a consistent basis in practice.

A key theme throughout the work was that while the tribunals have for the most part been cognisant of international standards on the right to a fair trial, the actual application of these standards has been inconsistent. One might question whether consistency in procedure is a viable goal in the examination of five different tribunals, located in different parts of the world, and at different stages in their development. However, inconsistency in the application of fair trial standards was observed even between different chambers of the same tribunal. For example, we discussed the differing interpretations given to self-representation in the ICTY when faced with obstreperous, self-defending accused persons.[6] It is hoped that as the ICC becomes the primary (and perhaps only) international criminal tribunal in the near future, its practice will apply the highest standards of fairness in a consistent manner, in order to enhance the coherence and determinacy of the rules that have been developed on an ad hoc basis to date.

7.1 Findings and Recommendations

In Chapter 1, the distinction between international and hybrid tribunals, and what makes an international criminal tribunal 'international' was discussed. The five tribunals chosen in this work were international in nature not because of their judicial compositions, or the law that they apply, or the circumstances of their establishment, but because their founding instruments are part of either an international treaty or a Security Council Resolution.[7] This helps us to distinguish between the SCSL, an international criminal tribunal because its Statute was annexed to the international agreement between the United Nations and the Government of Sierra Leone, and the Extraordinary

[5] Mirjan R. Damaška, 'Reflections on Fairness in International Criminal Justice' (2012) 10 *JICJ* 611; Colin Warbrick, 'International Criminal Courts and Fair Trial' (1998) 3 *J C & S L* 45.

[6] See above, Section 3.8.

[7] See above, Section 1.1. William A. Schabas, *Unimaginable Atrocities: Justice, Politics and Rights at the War Crimes Tribunals* (Oxford: OUP, 2012) 19.

Chambers in the Courts of Cambodia (ECCC), a domestic tribunal trying individuals for international crimes, established by Cambodian domestic law.[8] The role of judges in making procedural law was also discussed. This role is explicit in those international criminal tribunals where the Rules of Procedure and Evidence are judge-made, but also implicit through judicial interpretation and practice, and resort to the 'inherent powers' doctrine.

Chapter 2 undertook a full exposition of the meaning of fairness in the context of international criminal trials. It suggested that the term 'fairness' was informed by a rich body of literature on theories of legitimacy, procedural justice, and rule of law, and that the principles derived therefrom could bear an influence over assessments of fairness in international criminal trials.[9] It also argued that the concept of 'fairness' in the sense of the fair trial could be seen as a standalone ideal, comprised of a number of minimum guarantees as enunciated in near-universal human rights and domestic constitutional provisions and reflected in the statutes of the international criminal tribunals.[10] The jurisprudence of the international criminal tribunals that suggested that not all of the trial needed to espouse perfect fairness so long as 'fairness as a whole' could be said to have been achieved[11] was criticized, as it was drawn from the practice of international human rights tribunals which carry out a very different function in undertaking *ex post facto* assessements of whether a trial was fair.[12] Moreover, this approach is dangerous in that it assumes that some components of the right to a fair trial can be temporarily suspended; the argument to the contrary presented throughout this book maintains that each of the components of the right to a fair trial plays a crucial role in levelling the playing field between prosecution and defence, allowing the accused to play a full role in proceedings, and facilitating the defendant to fully answer the charges against him or her. Therefore, Judge Van den Wyngaert's approach that emphasizes that all, and not just most, of the trial must be fair is a much better standard for international criminal trials to adopt.[13]

[8] Law on the Establishment of Extraordinary Chambers in the Courts of Cambodia for the Prosecution of Crimes Committed during the Period of Democratic Kampuchea, with inclusion of amendments as promulgated on 27 October 2004, NS/RKM/1004/006, available online at http://www.eccc.gov.kh/sites/default/files/legal-documents/KR_Law_as_amended_27_Oct_2004_Eng.pdf (last accessed 30 June 2015).

[9] See above, Section 2.1.

[10] See above, Section 2.2.

[11] *Prosecutor v. Milošević*, Separate Opinion of Judge Shahabuddeen, Decision on Admissibility of Evidence-in-Chief in the form of Written Statements, Case No. IT-02-54-AR 73.4, 30 September 2003, para 16.

[12] See above, Section 2.3.

[13] *Prosecutor v. Katanga*, Judgment, Case No. ICC-01/04-01/07, 7 March 2014, Minority Opinion of Judge Van den Wyngaert, para 311.

Chapter 3 then considered the constituent parts of the right to a fair trial, and their interpretation by the international criminal tribunals. We saw, for example with reference to the practical application of the presumption of innocence, that tribunal practice can inform us not just of the importance of the accused's right to be presumed innocent, but also how that right might be practically implemented.[14] In the case of the presumption of innocence, such practical implementation is reflected in the treatment of the accused at pre-trial, including the granting of provisional release, and the measures taken to ensure that the burden of proof remains with the prosecution.[15] Broadly positive practice on the rights to silence,[16] to an impartial tribunal,[17] to presence at trial (with the exception of the STL, where trials *in absentia* are permitted),[18] to defence counsel of one's choosing,[19] to an appeal,[20] and to the free assistance of an interpreter (especially before the ICC)[21] were noted. Some areas where there is room for improvement in a number of the tribunals were also highlighted. These included the rights to trial without undue delay,[22] to present and examine witnesses and evidence,[23] and to remedies for a breach of the rights of the accused.[24] An unwillingness to find breaches of fair trial rights in a number of instances was noted, either through a finding that the accused had not fully proven the case of a breach, such as the strict requirements for showing that the accused had suffered 'prejudice', when they had been in detention in a different country to their family home for several years without provisional release,[25] or through an excessively strict interpretation of a right, for example, through finding that 'equality of arms' did not require full equality, but rather a freedom from substantial disadvantage.[26] It was suggested that a broader range of available remedies might result in a more open approach to potential breaches.[27] Overall, the discussion in this chapter was nuanced, and the extent to which the tribunals had embraced the highest standards of fairness was found to really depend on the tribunal concerned, and occasionally a tribunal-wide practice could not be identified owing to discrepencies in interpretation between different chambers of the same tribunal.

Chapter 4 examined the actors to whom the right to a fair trial has been found to be owed, with a particular focus on the prosecutor's alleged right to a fair trial. It was recognized that some might view the case law on prosecutorial

[14] See above, Section 3.1.
[15] See above, Section 3.1.
[16] See above, Section 3.2.
[17] See above, Section 3.3.
[18] See above, Section 3.7.
[19] See above, Section 3.8.
[20] See above, Section 3.12.
[21] See above, Section 3.6.
[22] See above, Section 3.4.
[23] See above, Section 3.10.
[24] See above, Section 3.16.
[25] See above, Section 3.4.
[26] See above, Section 3.10.2.
[27] See above, Section 3.4.

fair trial rights and on extended procedural rights for victims (outside of those limited rights provided for in the ICC Statute and RPE) as proving that the tribunals have acted in cognisance of their standard-setting role, and have sought to create a new norm in human rights by extending fair trial rights to the prosecution and other actors.[28] On the contrary, it was argued that the extension of fair trial rights in this manner can and does impact negatively on the rights of the accused, as evidenced by the *Haradinaj* retrial fiasco.[29] This chapter recommended that the tribunals should move away from this interpretation and reinstate the accused as being the only holder of due process rights at trial. A distinction was drawn between 'ordinary' human rights, such as the right to life and those attaching to one's status, including victims' right to present their views and concerns.[30] In that regard, there was no difficulty in recognizing that the rights of the accused do sometimes need to be balanced against the witnesses' right not to be placed in danger of death or harm, where witnesses' rights might be unjustifiably imperilled by the trial. Normally, however, witness protection measures that fall short of full anonymity will be able to ensure that the rights of the accused and of witnesses are duly protected.

Chapter 5 argued that international criminal tribunals have a role in setting the highest standards of fairness, with reference to a number of factors. First, quite simply, the tribunals have consistently reminded observers, through their case law and external communications, that they offer defendants the highest standards of fairness.[31] Second, an examination of the purported goals of international criminal law, as reflected in the tribunals' founding documents, revealed the spread of the rule of law and the strengthening of domestic criminal justice systems to be a key aim.[32] These goals are clearly linked to the need to set the highest standards of fairness; if anything less were to be developed as acceptable procedural standards, some domestic states with malevolent intentions could rely on those lower standards as justification for their unfair practices.[33] This danger is not illusory; a number of examples were discussed where the ICTY's early practices on the use of anonymous witnesses and the acceptance of hearsay evidence before the Tribunal were used as justification for domestic due-process breaches.[34] In addition, of course, the higher the standards of fair trial embraced by the tribunal, the lower the risk is of wrongful conviction.[35] For the purpose of

[28] See above, Section 4.1.

[29] *Prosecutor v. Haradinaj et al.*, Judgment, Case No. IT-04-84-A, 19 July 2010. See Section 4.2 above for a full discussion.

[30] See above, Section 4.3.

[31] See above, Section 2.2.3.

[32] See above, Section 5.1.

[33] See above, Section 5.2.3.

[34] See above, Section 5.2.3.

[35] See above, Section 5.2.2.

testing the hypothesis, a number of arguments that may be made against it were explored.[36] Some of these arguments were garnered from the existing literature on the subject, and included protestations based on the tribunals' resources, the complexity of the cases, and the seriousness of the crimes they prosecute. In response to these counter-arguments, a number of factors were pointed to, including: the huge budgets allocated to the tribunals in proportion to the number of cases they prosecute; the fact that complex cases, such as those involving white collar crime, are prosecuted in domestic contexts, and states are still required to implement the full panoply of fair trial rights in these cases;[37] and the point that human rights are applicable to all persons, regardless of the seriousness of the crime with which they are charged.[38] To deny the accused fair trial rights based on the seriousness of the crimes with which they are charged would contravene the presumption of innocence and the principle that there should be no punishment unless and until a finding of guilt has been reached.[39]

On a related note, Chapter 6 discussed the rules relating to complementarity before the ICC, Rule 11*bis* transfers before the ICTY and ICTR, and *ne bis in idem* before all of the tribunals. The practice on deferral of jurisdiction to domestic states in accordance with Rule 11*bis* has borne a clear influence over the fair conduct of international criminal trials in domestic states.[40] While complementarity before the ICC is somewhat different, and many argue that due process considerations have no place in assessments of whether a state is unwilling or unable to put an accused on trial,[41] it was argued that Article 17 is drafted in sufficiently ambiguous terms, including references to 'justice' and 'the principles of due process recognized by international law', to allow such an interpretation.[42] Furthermore, following the *Gaddafi* admissibility decision, it would seem that a state that cannot guarantee a fair trial might be deemed 'unable' to bring that individual to justice.[43] A state that cannot guarantee the rights of the accused might also be found 'unwilling' to bring the accused to justice if 'the violations of the rights of the suspect are so egregious that it is clear that the international community

[36] See above, Section 5.3.

[37] *Saunders v. UK,* Application No. 43/1994/490/572, Judgment, 17 December 1996.

[38] See above, Section 5.3. [39] See above, Section 5.3.3.

[40] See above, Section 6.1.

[41] e.g. Frédéric Mégret and Marika Giles Samson, 'Holding the Line on Complementarity in Libya' (2013) 11 *JICJ* 571; Kevin Jon Heller, 'The Shadow Side of Complementarity: The Effect of Article 17 of the Rome Statute on National Due Process' (2006) 17 *CLF* 255.

[42] See above, Section 6.2.

[43] *Situation in Libya: Prosecutor v. Gaddafi and Al-Senussi,* Decision on the Admissibility of the Case against Saif Al-Islam Gaddafi, Case No. ICC-01/11-01/11, 31 May 2013, para 214.

would not accept that the accused was being brought to any genuine form of justice'.[44] It was posited that the fact that these rules, and the rules on *ne bis in idem*,[45] permit the international tribunal to assess whether the domestic system enshrines or enshrined international fair trial procedures highlights their role in enunciating the fairest trial practice.[46]

7.2 Fairness in International Criminal Trials: Continuing Challenges

(a) Internal fragmentation

The issue of inconsistencies in procedural standards throughout international criminal tribunals, and even between individual Chambers within the same tribunal, is a result not just of rule-making from the bench in the ad hoc tribunals.[47] It also arises from the fact that a procedural culture is not engrained; the status of international criminal procedure as a 'clash of legal cultures' is well documented.[48] Judges, counsel and legal support staff come from a variety of legal cultures and do not tend to stay in post for as long as those in domestic legal appointments do.[49]

International criminal procedure, being a result of 'the gradual decanting of national criminal concepts and rules into the international receptacle',[50] offers practitioners the opportunity to suggest the adoption of procedures poached from their own legal tradition.[51] Transposed into the breeding ground of

[44] *Situation in Libya: Prosecutor v. Gaddafi and Al-Senussi*, Judgment on the Appeal of Mr Abdullah Al-Senussi against the Decision of Pre-Trial Chamber I of 11 October 2013 entitled 'Decision on the Admissibility of the Case against Abdullah Al-Senussi', Case No. ICC-01/11-01/11, 24 July 2014, para 230.

[45] See above, Section 6.3. [46] See above, Chapter 6, 166–168.

[47] See above, Section 1.3.2. For a discussion of judicial rule-making in greater detail, see Megan A. Fairlie, 'Rule-Making from the Bench: A Place for Minimalism at the ICTY' (2004) 39 *Texas Int'l L J* 257.

[48] e.g. Christine Schuon, *International Criminal Procedure: A Clash of Legal Cultures* (The Hague: T.M.C. Asser Press, 2010) and Kai Ambos, 'International Criminal Procedure: "Adversarial", "Inquisitorial" or Mixed?' (2003) 3 *ICLR* 1. According to Immi Tallgren, 'The Sense and Sensibility of International Criminal Law' (2002) 13 *EJIL* 561, 566–7, 'the international criminal justice system is assumed to function following mechanisms of an idealized national system that cannot be localized anywhere'.

[49] Elena A. Baylis, 'Tribunal Hopping with the Post-Conflict Justice Junkies' (2008) 10 *Oregon Rev Int'l L* 361; Rosemary Byrne, 'The New Public International Lawyer and the Hidden Art of International Criminal Trial Practice' (2010) 25 *Connecticut JIL* 243.

[50] *Prosecutor v. Erdemović*, Judgment, Separate and Dissenting Opinion of Judge Cassese, Case No. IT-96-22-A, 7 October 1997, para 4.

[51] Judge Levi Carneiro, in his Dissenting Opinion in the ICJ's *Anglo-Iranian Oil Co. (United Kingdom v. Iran)* case, (Judgment, 1952 ICJ Reports 20 (22 July 1952) at 161 para 14) referred to

international criminal procedure, this practice may offer reasonable solutions for short-term problems, but may not be grounded in an overarching theoretical framework suitable to international criminal procedure: it thereby offers little in its development of a coherent system of law.[52] These procedural solutions may not be implemented by the other tribunals, leading to further fragmentation. The coherence of procedural standards is therefore far from obvious and undermines international criminal procedure's standard-setting function. It is submitted that international criminal judges should be more reflective in adopting procedures in the future. They should be guided by questions such as whether the procedure in question is desirable in the long term, or whether it may need to be later amended; whether the procedure comports fully with statutory provisions and other rules and regulations, and whether this practice sets a desirable standard that they would be happy to have applied to all crimes, and not just those of the particularly serious nature that they are prosecuting.

(b) Context of international criminal proceedings

Aside from the fact that international criminal procedure's status as a *sui generis* or hybrid creature allows judges to be selective in merging domestic procedural elements, other unique elements of the international criminal legal process allow judges to step away from their standard-setting role. As pointed out by Damaška, international criminal trials operate in a challenging legal and political environment.[53] Investigations are often complex cross-border affairs, carried out long after the atrocities under investigation occurred and without judicial oversight. The trial process is beset with difficulty in obtaining witness attendance, communicating thousands of pages of documents between the parties and limiting complex legal arguments to reasonable time-frames. Occasionally, trial chambers have the added burden of ensuring that obstreperous defendants do not use the process for their own political gains.[54] Moreover, tribunals face external pressures and often unrealistic expectations from an international community with a desire to achieve

the fact that '[i]t is inevitable that every one of us in this Court should retain some trace of his legal education and his former legal activities in his country of origin.' The same could clearly be said for practitioners in the international criminal law arena, where lawyers and judges train and qualify in a domestic jurisdiction before moving to the international criminal system.

[52] It may also be the case that dominant judges drive the development of procedural rules towards their home model or another preferred model, but further research would be needed to assess whether this has been the case in the practice of the international criminal tribunals. The STL RPE are clearly heavily influenced by the ICTY RPE, so it would seem not to be the case before the STL, at least.

[53] Mirjan R. Damaška, 'Reflections on Fairness in International Criminal Justice' (2012) 10 *JICJ* 611.

[54] Patricia M. Wald, *Tyrants on Trial* (New York: Open Society Institute, 2009) 16.

retribution for the grave atrocities of the past and to establish a full historical record of those events to grant peace and to give closure to the victims. There is additional expectation and pressure from those who fund the Court, particularly in the case of those who financially support the ad hoc tribunals and the Special Court for Sierra Leone, to act with expediency in line with their completion strategies.[55] That being said, the completion strategies do not seem to have hurried some judges in issuing judgments, as discussed in detail in Chapter 3.[56]

This truly exceptional context, however, does not provide a justification for the tribunals' espousing of anything less than the highest standards of fairness. Chapter 5 above outlined many reasons why the tribunals should be seen to bear a standard-setting function with regard to the rights of the accused. It is submitted, then, that international criminal tribunals should move away from some of the more questionable practices highlighted in Chapters 3 and 4 of the present work, and fully embrace their standard-setting function. This can be achieved by, inter alia, recognizing that fair trial rights attach to the accused alone and that these rights can only be balanced against the rights, as opposed to interests, of other actors at trial; taking a more proactive approach to the right to a speedy trial and the right to prepare one's defence, especially as regards the disclosure of evidence at the pre-trial stage; and embracing a definition of equality of arms that aims for parity between the parties, as opposed to freedom from substantial disadvantage on the part of the defence.

(c) Priorities

It could be argued that international criminal judges have not fully embraced their standard-setting role because they have not been aware of this role until the present work was completed. This is unlikely, given the references to the tribunals' highest standards discussed in Section 5.2.1 above. In the alternative, it could be said that the manifold goals of international criminal justice (discussed in Section 5.1 above) render it simply impossible (or even undesirable) for tribunals to attempt to carry out all of the goals that they were designed to achieve, and that it is unreasonable to impose yet another goal upon them.

However, the standard-setting goal is far more achievable than some of the pre-established goals of international criminal justice, such as bringing peace

[55] *Prosecutor v. Nyiramasuhuko et al.*, Decision in the Matter of Proceedings under Rule 15*bis* (D), Case No. ICTR-98-42-A15*bis*, 24 September 2003, Dissenting Opinion of Judge David Hunt, para 17.

[56] See above, Section 3.4.

to the affected regions, which are often cited in judgments without dispute.[57] It is hoped that one of the broader policy implications of the present study will be an enhanced cognisance of the standard-setting function and a move towards operationalizing it in the tribunals' future practice, particularly in the practice of the ICC. As regards the rights and interests of parties at trial, in balancing the rights of the accused against, for example, the international community's right to a speedy trial, or the rights of victims to have their voices heard, the tribunals appear to have made a conscious effort to avoid the inevitable criticism that they act in disregard of the suffering incurred by the innocent victims of the conflicts within their jurisdictions.

Conclusion

This book has offered a definitive exposition of the wider importance of fair trial rights in international criminal law, and has argued that international criminal trials can influence the fairness of proceedings before domestic courts. In justifying the position that international criminal tribunals should lay down the highest standards of fairness in their procedure, a number of distinct arguments were developed, including: that the need to set the highest standards of fairness is implicit in many of the declared goals of international criminal tribunals; that judges already declare that tribunal practice represents the fairest procedures for the rights of the accused; and that the legitimacy of the international criminal justice project is closely interwoven with the need to set the highest standards of fairness. It is hoped that the standard-setting function will be taken into account by international criminal law practitioners, judges, scholars, and policy-makers in the future.

As international criminal law has developed, its procedures have been refined to address the rights of the accused in a more satisfactory manner. Some important examples of this include more expansive rules on the right to provisional release, and the jurisprudence on witness protection measures. By pointing to a number of distinct areas where the highest standards of fairness have not been realized, including the extension of rights to actors other than the accused, the application of the right to a speedy trial and the practice on remedies for breaches of the rights of the accused, the author hopes to have illustrated some areas that provide room for improvement, as contemporary international criminal justice continues into its third decade.

[57] See above, Section 2.1.

Bibliography

BOOKS

Arai-Takahashi, Y., *The Margin of Appreciation Doctrine and the Principle of Proportionality in the Jurisprudence of the ECHR* (Antwerp: Intersentia, 2002)

Ashworth, A., *The Criminal Process: An Evaluative Study* (2nd edn, Oxford: OUP, 1998)

Ashworth, A., *Human Rights, Serious Crime and Criminal Procedure* (London: Sweet & Maxwell, 2002)

Ashworth, A. and Redmayne, M., *The Criminal Process* (4th edn, Oxford: OUP, 2010)

Bayles, M.D., *Procedural Justice* (Dordrecht: Kluwer, 1990)

Bell, J., *French Legal Cultures* (London: Butterworths, 2001)

Bergsmo, M. (ed.), *Human Rights for the Downtrodden: Essays in Honour of Asbjørn Eide* (Leiden: Martinus Nijhoff, 2003)

Bergsmo, M. (ed.), *Complementarity and the Exercise of Universal Jurisdiction for Core International Crimes* (Oslo: Torkel Opsahl Academic EPublisher, 2010)

Besson, S. and Tasioulis, J. (eds), *The Philosophy of International Law* (Oxford: OUP, 2010)

Bingham, T., *The Rule of Law* (London: Allen Lane, 2010)

Black, H.C., *Black's Law Dictionary* (5th edn, St Paul, MN, USA: West Publishing Co., 1979)

Boas, G., *The Milošević Trial: Lessons for the Conduct of Complex International Criminal Proceedings* (Cambridge: CUP, 2007)

Boister, N. and Cryer, R., *The Tokyo International Military Tribunal—A Reappraisal* (Oxford: OUP, 2008)

Bowring, J. (ed.), *The Complete Works of Jeremy Bentham: Vol. 2* (Edinburgh: William Tait, 1838–1843)

Bradley, C.M. (ed.), *Criminal Procedure: A Worldwide Study* (Durham, N.C.: Carolina Academic Press, 1999)

Broomhall, B., *International Justice and the International Criminal Court: Between Sovereignty and the Rule of Law* (Oxford: OUP, 2004)

Carter, L. and Pocar, F. (eds), *International Criminal Procedure: The Interface of Civil Law and Common Law Legal Systems* (Cheltenham: Edward Elgar, 2013)

Cassese, A., *International Criminal Law* (Oxford: OUP, 2003)

Cassese, A. (ed.), *The Oxford Companion to International Criminal Justice* (Oxford: OUP, 2009)

Cassese, A., Gaeta, P., and Jones, J.R.W.D. (eds), *The Rome Statute of the International Criminal Court: A Commentary* (Oxford: OUP, 2002)

Chand Vohrah, L., Pocar, S., Featherstone, Y., Fourmy, O., Graham, C., Hocking, J., and Robson, N. (eds), *Man's Inhumanity to Man: Essays on International Law in Honour of Antonio Cassese* (The Hague: Kluwer Law International, 2003)

Clark, P., *The Gacaca Courts, Post-Genocide Justice and Reconciliation in Rwanda* (Cambridge: CUP, 2010)

Combs, N.A., *Fact Finding without Facts: The Uncertain Evidentiary Foundations of International Criminal Convictions* (Cambridge: CUP, 2010)

Cryer, R., Friman, H., Robinson, D., and Wilmhurst, E., *An Introduction to International Criminal Law and Procedure* (3rd edn, Cambridge: CUP, 2014)

Damaška, M.R., *The Faces of Justice and State Authority: A Comparative Approach to the Legal Process* (New Haven: Yale University Press, 1986)

Damaška, M.R., *Evidence Law Adrift* (New Haven: Yale University Press, 1997)

Darcy, S. and Powderly, J. (eds), *Judicial Creativity at the International Criminal Tribunals* (Oxford: OUP, 2010)

Darcy, S., *Judges, Law, and War: The Judicial Development of International Humanitarian Law* (Cambridge: CUP, 2014)

David, R. and Brierley, J.E.C., *Major Legal Systems in the World Today: An Introduction to the Comparative Study of Law* (3rd edn, London: Stevens & Sons, 1985)

De Brouwer, A.M., *Supranational Criminal Prosecution of Sexual Violence* (Antwerp: Intersentia, 2005)

Delmas-Marty, M. (ed.), *What Kind of Criminal Policy for Europe?* (trans M.A. Summers, The Hague/London: Kluwer Law International, 1996)

Delmas-Marty, M. (ed.), *The Criminal Process and Human Rights: Towards a European Consciousness* (Dordrecht: Martinus Nijhoff, 1997)

Delmas-Marty, M., *Towards a Truly Common Law: Europe as a Laboratory for Legal Pluralism* (trans N. Norberg, Cambridge: CUP, 2002)

Dicey, A.V., *An Introduction to the Study of the Law of the Constitution* (1885; 9th edn, Macmillan, 1945)

Dijk, P. van and Hoof, G.J.H. van, *Theory and Practice of the European Convention on Human Rights* (3rd edn, The Hague: Kluwer Law International, 1998)

Drumbl, M., *Atrocity, Punishment and International Law* (Cambridge: CUP, 2007)

Duff, A. (ed.), *Philosophy and the Criminal Law* (Cambridge: CUP, 1998)

Duff, A., Farmer, L., Marshall, S., and Tadros, V. (eds), *The Trial on Trial, Volume I: Truth and Due Process* (Oxford: Hart Publishing, 2004)

Duff, A., Farmer, L., Marshall, S., and Tadros, V. (eds), *The Trial on Trial, Volume II: Judgment and Calling to Account* (Oxford: Hart Publishing, 2006)

Duff, A., Farmer, L., Marshall, S., and Tadros, V., *The Trial on Trial, Volume III: Towards a Normative Theory of the Criminal Trial* (Oxford: Hart Publishing, 2007)

Dworkin, R., *Taking Rights Seriously* (Cambridge, MA: Harvard University Press, 1977)

Dworkin, R., *A Matter of Principle* (Cambridge, MA: Harvard University Press, 1985)

Dworkin, R., *Law's Empire* (London: Fontana, 1986)

El Zeidy, M., *The Principle of Complementarity in International Criminal Law* (Leiden: Nijhoff, 2008)
Emmerson, B. and Ashworth, A., *Human Rights and Criminal Justice* (London: Sweet & Maxwell, 2001)
Fennell, P., Harding, C., Jörg, N., and Swart, B., *Criminal Justice in Europe: A Comparative Study* (Oxford: Clarendon Press, 1995)
Findlay, M. and Henham, R., *Beyond Punishment: Achieving International Criminal Justice* (London: Palgrave Macmillan, 2010)
Fletcher, G.P., *Basic Concepts of Legal Thought* (Oxford: OUP, 1996)
Franck, H.G., *The Barbaric Punishment: Abolishing the Death Penalty* (revised and edited by W.A. Schabas, The Hague: Martinus Nijhoff, 2003)
Franck, T.M., *The Power of Legitimacy Among Nations* (Oxford: OUP, 1990)
Franck, T.M., *Fairness in International Law and Institutions* (New York: OUP, 1995)
Freeman, S., *Rawls* (Abingdon: Routledge, 2007)
Fuller, L.L., *The Law in Quest of Itself* (Chicago: Northwestern University Press, 1940)
Fuller, L.L., *The Morality of Law* (New Haven and London: Yale University Press, 1969)
Galligan, D.J., *Due Process and Fair Procedures: A Study of Administrative Procedures* (Oxford: Clarendon Press, 1996)
Goss, R., *Criminal Fair Trial Rights* (Oxford: Hart, 2014)
Groenhuijsen, M.S. and Letschert, R.M. (eds), *Compilation of International Victims' Rights Instruments* (Nijmegen: Wolf Legal Publishers, 2012)
Harding, C., Fennel, P., Jörg, N., and Swart, B., *Criminal Justice in Europe: A Comparative Study* (Oxford: Clarendon Press, 1995)
Hart, H.L.A., *The Concept of Law* (2nd edn, Oxford: Clarendon, 1994)
Henham, R., *Punishment and Process in International Criminal Trials* (Aldershot: Ashgate, 2005)
Henham, R. and Behrens, P. (eds), *The International Law of Genocide* (Aldershot: Ashgate, 2007)
Jackson, J.D., Langer, M., and Tillers, P. (eds), *Crime, Procedure and Evidence in a Comparative and International Context: Essays in Honour of Professor Mirjan Damaška* (Oxford: Hart Publishing, 2008)
Jackson, J.D. and Summers, S.J., *The Internationalisation of Criminal Evidence: Beyond the Common Law and Civil Law Traditions* (Cambridge: CUP, 2012)
Keane, D. and McDermott, Y. (eds), *The Challenge of Human Rights: Past, Present and Future* (Cheltenham: Edward Elgar, 2012)
Kelsen, H., *Peace through Law* (New York: Garland Publishers, 1973)
Khan, K., Buisman, C., and Gosnell, C. (eds), *Principles of Evidence in International Criminal Justice* (Oxford: OUP, 2010)
Klamberg, M., *Evidence in International Criminal Trials: Confronting Legal Gaps and the Reconstruction of Disputed Events* (Leiden: Nijhoff, 2013)
Kleffner, J., *Complementarity in the Rome Statute and National Criminal Jurisdictions* (Oxford: OUP, 2008)

Kleffner, J. and Kor, G. (eds), *Complementary Views on Complementarity* (Cambridge: CUP, 2006)
Klip, A. and Sluiter, G. (eds), *Annotated Leading Cases of International Criminal Tribunals, Vol. XXV: The International Criminal Tribunal for Rwanda, 2006–2007* (Antwerp: Intersentia, 2010)
Klip, A. and Sluiter, G. (eds), *Annotated Leading Cases of International Criminal Tribunals: Vol. XXXV: The International Criminal Tribunal for the Former Yugoslavia 2007–2008* (Antwerp: Intersentia, 2012)
Koskenniemi, M., *The Politics of International Law* (Oxford: Hart, 2011)
Lind, A. and Tyler, T.R., *The Social Psychology of Procedural Justice* (New York: Plenum, 1988)
Luhmnann, N., *Legitimation durch Verhafen* (Darmstadt: Luchterhand, 1969)
May, L., *Global Justice and Due Process* (New York/Cambridge: CUP, 2011)
May, L. and Hoskins, Z. (eds), *International Criminal Law and Philosophy* (Cambridge: CUP, 2010)
May, R. and Wierda, M., *International Criminal Evidence* (Ardsley, NY: Transnational Publishers, 2002)
Mettraux, G. (ed.), *Perspectives on the Nuremberg Trial* (Oxford: OUP, 2008)
Minow, M., *Between Vengeance and Forgiveness: Facing History after Genocide and Mass Violence* (Boston: Beacon Press, 1998)
Örücü, E. and Nelken, D. (eds), *Comparative Law: A Handbook* (Oxford: Hart Publishing, 2007)
Packer, H., *The Limits of the Criminal Sanction* (Stanford: Stanford University Press, 1968)
Pakes, F.J, *Comparative Criminal Justice* (Cullompton; Portland, OR: Willan, 2004)
Raímondo, F.O., *General Principles of Law in the Decisions of International Criminal Courts and Tribunals* (Leiden: Nijhoff, 2008)
Rawls, J., *A Theory of Justice* (Harvard: Harvard University Press, 1971)
Rawls, J., *A Theory of Justice* (revised edn, Cambridge, MA: Harvard University Press, 1999)
Rawls, J., *Justice as Fairness: A Restatement* (Cambridge, MA: Belknap Press, 2001)
Raz, J., *The Authority of Law: Essays on Law and Morality* (Oxford: Clarendon Press, 1979)
Roberts, P. and Zuckerman, A., *Criminal Evidence* (2nd edn, Oxford: OUP, 2010)
Roberts, P. and Hunter, J. (eds), *Criminal Evidence and Human Rights: Reimagining Common Law Procedural Traditions* (Oxford: Hart Publishing, 2012)
Robertson, G., *Crimes Against Humanity* (London: Penguin, 1999)
Röhl, K.F. and Machura, S. (eds), *Procedural Justice* (Dartmouth: Ashgate, 1997)
Romano, C.P., Nollkaemper. A., and Kleffner, J.K. (eds), *Internationalized Criminal Courts: Sierra Leone, East Timor, Kosovo and Cambodia* (Oxford: OUP, 2004)
Sadat, L.N. and Scharf, M. (eds), *The Theory and Practice of International Criminal Law: Essays in Honour of M. Cherif Bassiouni* (Leiden: Nijhoff, 2008)
Safferling, C.J.M., *Towards an International Criminal Procedure* (Oxford: OUP, 2001)
Safferling, C.J.M., *International Criminal Procedure* (Oxford: OUP, 2012)

Sands, P. (ed.), *From Nuremberg to The Hague: The Future of International Criminal Justice* (Cambridge: CUP, 2003)

Schabas, W.A., *Genocide in International Law: The Crime of Crimes* (Cambridge: CUP, 2000)

Schabas, W.A., *The UN International Criminal Tribunals: The Former Yugoslavia, Rwanda and Sierra Leone* (Cambridge: CUP, 2006)

Schabas, W.A., *The International Criminal Court: A Commentary on the Rome Statute* (Oxford: OUP, 2010)

Schabas, W.A. and Boas, G. (eds), *International Criminal Law Developments in the Case Law of the ICTY* (Leiden: Brill/Nijhoff, 2003)

Schabas, W.A., *An Introduction to the International Criminal Court* (Cambridge: CUP, 2011)

Schabas, W.A., *Unimaginable Atrocities* (Oxford: OUP, 2012)

Schabas, W.A., McDermott, Y., and Hayes, N. (eds), *The Ashgate Research Companion to International Criminal Law: Critical Perspectives* (Aldershot: Ashgate, 2013)

Schuon, C., *International Criminal Procedure: A Clash of Legal Cultures* (The Hague: T.M.C. Asser Press, 2010)

Sen, A., *The Idea of Justice* (London/New York: Allen Lane, 2009)

Shahabudden, M., *International Criminal Justice at the Yugoslav Tribunal: A Judge's Recollection* (Oxford: OUP, 2012)

Shany, Y., *Assessing the Effectiveness of International Courts* (Oxford: OUP, 2014)

Sluiter, G., Friman, H., Linton, S., Zappalà, S., and Vasiliev, S. (eds), *International Criminal Procedure: Principles and Rules* (Oxford: OUP, 2013)

Sluiter, G. and Vasiliev, S. (eds), *International Criminal Procedure: Towards a Coherent Body of Law* (New York: Cameron May Publishing, 2009)

Stahn, C. and El Zeidy, M. (eds), *The International Criminal Court and Complementarity: From Theory to Practice* (Cambridge: CUP, 2011)

Stavros, S., *The Guarantees for Accused Persons under Article 6 of the European Convention on Human Rights: An Analysis of the Application of the Convention and a Comparison with other Instruments* (Dordrecht: Martinus Nijhoff, 1993)

Stover, E., *The Witnesses: War Crimes and the Promise of Justice in The Hague* (Philadelphia: University of Pennsylvania Press, 2007)

Stover, E. and Weinstein, H.M. (eds), *My Neighbour, My Enemy: Justice and Community in the Aftermath of Mass Atrocity* (Cambridge: CUP, 2004)

Struett, M.J., *The Politics of Constructing the International Criminal Court: NGOs, Discourse, and Agency* (London: Palgrave Macmillan, 2008)

Summers, S.J., *Fair Trials: The European Criminal Procedural Tradition and the European Court of Human Rights* (Oxford: Hart Publishing, 2007)

Swart, B., Zahar, A., and Sluiter, G. (eds), *The Legacy of the International Criminal Tribunal for the Former Yugoslavia* (Oxford: OUP, 2011)

Tamanaha, B.Z., *On the Rule of Law* (Cambridge: CUP, 2004)

Teitel, R., *Transitional Justice* (Oxford: OUP, 2000)

Tochilovsky, V., *Jurisprudence of the International Criminal Courts and the European Court of Human Rights: Procedure and Evidence* (Leiden: Nijhoff, 2008)

Trechsel, S., *Human Rights in Criminal Proceedings* (Oxford: OUP, 2006)
Triffterer, O. (ed.), *Commentary on the Rome Statute: Observers' Notes, Article by Article* (2nd edn, Munich: Beck, 2008)
Tyler, T.R., *Why People Obey the Law* (Princeton: Princeton University Press, 2006)
Tyler, T.R. (ed.), *Legitimacy and Criminal Justice: International Perspectives* (New York: Russell Sage Foundation, 2007)
Tyler, T.R., *Why People Cooperate* (Princeton: Princeton University Press, 2010)
Van Sliedregt, E. and Vasiliev, S. (eds), *Pluralism in International Criminal Law* (Oxford: OUP, 2014)
Vogler, R., *A World View of Criminal Justice* (Aldershot: Ashgate, 2005)
Waldron, J. (ed.), *Theories of Rights* (Oxford: OUP, 1984)
Weber, M., *Economy and Society: An Outline of Interpretative Sociology* Vol. 1, (Guenther Roth and Claus Wittich (eds), originally published in 1922, Berkeley: University of California Press, 1978)
Weissbrodt, D., *The Right to a Fair Trial under the Universal Declaration of Human Rights and the International Covenant on Civil and Political Rights* (The Hague: Martinus Nijhoff, 2001)
Weissbrodt, D. and Wolfrum, R. (eds), *The Right to a Fair Trial* (Berlin: Springer, 1997)
Wilson, R.A., *Writing History in International Criminal Trials* (Cambridge: CUP, 2011)
Zahar, A. and Sluiter, G. *International Criminal Law: A Critical Introduction* (Oxford: OUP, 2007)
Zappalà, S., *Human Rights in International Criminal Proceedings* (Oxford: OUP, 2003)

ARTICLES AND CHAPTERS IN EDITED VOLUMES

Acquaviva, G. and Heikkilä, M., 'Protective and Special Measures for Witnesses' in Sluiter, G., Friman, H., Linton, S., Zappalà, S., and Vasiliev, S. (eds), *International Criminal Procedure: Principles and Rules* (Oxford: OUP, 2013) 818–58
Affolder, N.A., '*Tadić*, the Anonymous Witness and the Sources of International Procedural Law' (1997–98) 19 *Michigan JIL* 445–95
Alexander, L., 'Are Procedural Rights Derivative Substantive Rights?' (1998) 17 *Law & Phil* 19–42
Allan, T.R.S., 'Procedural Fairness and the Duty of Respect' (1998) 18 *OJLS* 497–515
Amann, D.M., 'Harmonic Convergence? Constitutional Criminal Procedure in an International Context' (2000) 75 *Ind L J* 815–45
Amann, D.M., ' "The Only Thing Left is Justice": Cherif Bassiouni, Saddam Hussein, and the Quest for Impartiality in International Criminal Law' in Sadat, L. and Scharf, M. (eds), *The Theory and Practice of International Criminal Law: Essays in Honour of M. Cherif Bassiouni* (Leiden: Nijhoff, 2008) 365–95
Ambos, K., 'International Criminal Procedure: "Adversarial", "Inquisitorial" or Mixed?' (2003) 3 *ICLR* 1–37
Aptel, C., 'Some Innovations in the Statute of the Special Tribunal for Lebanon' (2007) 5 *JICJ* 1107–1124

Ashworth, A., 'Responsibilities, Rights and Restorative Justice' (2002) 42 *Brit J Criminol* 578–95

Bassiouni, M.C., 'International Crimes: *Jus Cogens* and *Obligatio Erga Omnes*' (1996) 59 *LCP* 63–74

Baumgartner, E., 'Aspects of Victim Participation in the Proceedings of the International Criminal Court' (2008) 90(870) *Int'l Rev Red Cross* 409–440

Baylis, E.A., 'Tribunal Hopping with the Post-Conflict Justice Junkies' (2008) 10 *Oregon Rev Int'l L* 361–90

Baylis, E.A., 'Rebuilding National Courts through Transnational Networks' (2009) 50 *Boston Coll LR* 1–85

Baylis, E.A., 'Outsourcing Investigations' (2009) 14 *UCLA J Int'l L & Foreign Aff* 121–48

Benzing, M., 'The Complementarity Regime of the International Criminal Court: International Criminal Justice between State Sovereignty and the Fight against Impunity' (2003) 7 *Max Planck Ybk UN L* 591–632

Besson, S., 'Institutionalising Global "Demoi"-cracy', in Meyer, L.H. (ed.), *Legitimacy, Justice and Public International Law* (Cambridge: CUP, 2009) 58–91

Bibas, S. and Burke-White, W., 'International Idealism meets Domestic Criminal Procedure Realism' (2009–2010) 59 *Duke LJ* 637–704

Boas, G., 'Creating Laws of Evidence for International Criminal Law: The ICTY and the Principle of Flexibility' (2001) 12 *CLF* 41–90

Boas, G., 'War Crimes Prosecutions in Australia and Other Common Law Countries: Some Observations' (2010) 21 *CLF* 313–30

Bohlander, M., 'The International Criminal Judiciary: Problems of Judicial Selection, Independence and Ethics' in Bohlander, M. (ed.), *International Criminal Justice: A Critical Analysis of Institutions and Procedures* (New York: Cameron May, 2007) 325–90

Bohlander, M., 'Radbruch Redux: The Need for Revisiting the Conversation between Common and Civil Law at Root Level at the Example of International Criminal Justice' (2011) 24 *LJIL* 393–410

Booth, C., 'Prospects and Issues for the International Criminal Court: Lessons from Yugoslavia and Rwanda' in Sands, P. (ed.), *From Nuremberg to The Hague: The Future of International Criminal Justice* (Cambridge: CUP, 2003) 157–92

Bourgon, S., 'Procedural Problems Hindering Expeditious and Fair Justice' (2004) 2 *JICJ* 526–32

Brady, H., Costi, M., Friman, H., Guariglia, F., and Stuckenberg, C.-F., 'Charges', in Sluiter, G., Friman, H., Linton, S., Zappalà, S., and Vasiliev, S. (eds), *International Criminal Procedure: Principles and Rules* (Oxford: OUP, 2013) 381–488

Brannigan, A., 'Is the Sun Setting on Cosmopolitan Justice?' (2011) 48 *Global Society* 420–5

Broomhall, B. and Kress, C., 'Implementing Cooperation Duties under the Rome Statute' in Kress, C., Broomhall, B., Lattanzi, F., and Santori, V., *The Rome Statute and Domestic Legal Orders: Volume II* (Baden-Baden: Nomos, 2005) 515–43

Broomhall, B., 'Article 22: *Nullum Crimen Sine Lege*' in Triffterer, O., (ed.), *Commentary on the Rome Statute of the International Criminal Court—Observers' Notes, Article by Article* (2nd edn, Munich: Beck, 2008) 713–30

Burke-White, W.W., 'Implementing a Policy of Positive Complementarity in the Rome System of Justice' (2008) 19 *CLF* 59–85

Burke-White, W.W. and Kaplan, S., 'Shaping the Contours of Domestic Justice: The ICC and an Admissibility Challenge in the Uganda Situation' in Stahn, C. and Sluiter, G. (eds), *The Emerging Practice of the International Criminal Court* (Leiden: Nijhoff, 2009) 79–114

Burke-White, W.W. and Slaughter, A.-M., 'The Future of International Law Is Domestic (or, the European Way of Law)' (2006) 47 *Harvard Int'l L J* 327–52

Byrne, R., 'The New Public International Lawyer and the Hidden Art of International Criminal Trial Practice' (2010) 25 *Connecticut JIL* 243–303

Caianiello, M., 'Law of Evidence at the International Criminal Court: Blending Accusatorial and Inquisitorial Models' (2011) 36 *N C J Int'l L & Com Reg* 287–318

Carmichael Keen, P., 'Tempered Adversariality: The Judicial Role and Trial Theory in the International Criminal Tribunals' (2004) 17 *LJIL* 767–814

Carnero Rojo, E., 'The Role of Fair Trial Considerations in the Complementarity Regime of the International Criminal Court: From "No Peace without Justice" to "No Peace without Victor's Justice"?' (2005) 18 *LJIL* 829–69

Cassese, A., 'Opinion: The ICTY and Human Rights' (1997) 2 *European Human Rights L Rev* 320–52

Cassese, A., 'Foreword by Judge Antonio Cassese, former President of the International Criminal Tribunal for the former Yugoslavia' (1997) *International Review of the Red Cross* No. 321, 602

Cassese, A., 'The Statute of the International Criminal Court: Some Preliminary Reflections' (1999) 10 *EJIL* 144–71

Cassese, A., 'The Influence of the European Court of Human Rights on International Criminal Tribunals: Some Methodological Remarks' in Bergsmo, M. (ed.), *Human Rights for the Downtrodden: Essays in Honour of Asbjørn Eide* (Leiden: Martinus Nijhoff, 2003) 19–52

Cassese, A., 'The International Criminal Court Five Years On: *Andante* or *Moderato?*' in Stahn, C. and Sluiter, G. (eds), *The Emerging Practice of the International Criminal Court* (Leiden: Martinus Nijhoff, 2009) 21–30

Cerruti, E., 'Self-Representation in the International Arena: Removing a False Right of Spectacle' (2009) 40 *Georgetown JIL* 919–84

Charney, J.I., 'Is International Law Threatened by Multiple International Tribunals?' (1998) 271 *Recuil des Cours* 101–382

Chinkin, C., 'Due Process and Witness Anonymity' (1997) 91 *AJIL* 75–9

Christie, N., 'Conflicts as Property' (1977) 17 *Brit J Criminol* 1–15

Chung, C.H., 'Victims' Participation at the International Criminal Court: Are Concessions of the Court Clouding the Promise?' (2007–2008) 6 *Nw U J Int'l Hum Rts* 459–545

Clapham, A., 'The Rights and Responsibilities of Armed Non-State Actors: The Legal Landscape and Issues Surrounding Engagement' (1 February 2010) available online at http://papers.ssrn.com/sol3/papers.cfm?abstract_id=1569636

Cogan, J.K., 'International Criminal Courts and Fair Trials: Difficulties and Prospects' (2002) 27 *Yale JIL* 111–40

Combs, N.A., 'Testimonial Deficiencies and Evidentiary Uncertainties in International Criminal Trials' (2009) 14 *UCLA J Int'l L & Foreign Aff* 235–74

Cronin-Furman, K. and Taub, A., 'Lions and Tigers and Deterrence, Oh My: Evaluating Expectations of International Criminal Justice' in Schabas, W.A., McDermott, Y., and Hayes, N. (eds), *The Ashgate Research Companion to International Criminal Law: Critical Perspectives* (Aldershot: Ashgate, 2013) 435–52

Croquet, N.A.J., 'The International Criminal Court and the Treatment of Defence Rights: A Mirror of the European Court of Human Rights' Jurisprudence?' (2011) 11 *HRLR* 91–131

Cryer, R., 'International Criminal Law *vs* State Sovereignty: Another Round?' (2005) 16 *EJIL* 979–1000

Cullen, H., 'The Role of History in Franck's *Fairness*' (2002) 13 *EJIL* 927–40

Damaška, M., 'Evidentiary Barriers to Conviction and Two Models of Criminal Procedure: A Comparative Study' (1972–1973) 121 *U Penn LR* 506–89

Damaška, M.R., 'Structures of Authority and Comparative Criminal Procedure' (1974–1975) 84 *Yale L J* 480–544

Damaška, M.R., 'Epistemology and Legal Regulation of Proof' (2003) 2 *LPR* 117–30

Damaška, M., 'Assignment of Counsel and Perceptions of Fairness' (2005) 3 *JICJ* 3–8

Damaška, M.R., 'What is the Point of International Criminal Justice?' (2008) 83 *Chicago Kent LR* 329–65

Damaška, M.R., 'Problematic Features of International Criminal Procedure' in Cassese, A. et al. (eds), *The Oxford Companion to International Criminal Justice* (Oxford: OUP, 2009) 175–86

Damaška, M.R., 'The International Criminal Court: Between Aspiration and Achievement' (2009) 14 *UCLA J Int'l L & Foreign Aff* 19–37

Damaška, M.R., 'Reflections on Fairness in International Criminal Justice' (2012) 10 *JICJ* 611–20

Danner, A.M., 'Enhancing the Legitimacy and Accountability of Prosecutorial Discretion at the International Criminal Court' (2003) 97 *AJIL* 510–52

Danner, A.M. and Martinez, J.S., 'Guilty Associations: Joint Criminal Enterprise, Command Responsibility, and the Development of International Criminal Law' (2005) 93 *California LR* 75–169

D'Ascoli, S., 'Reconciliation and Sentencing in the Practice of the International Criminal Tribunals' in Schabas, W.A., McDermott, Y., and Hayes, N. (eds), *The Ashgate Research Companion to International Criminal Law: Critical Perspectives* (Aldershot: Ashgate, 2013) 307–31

Davidson, C., 'May It Please the Crowd? The Role of Public Confidence, Public Order and Public Opinion in Bail for International Criminal Defendants' (2012) 43 *Columbia Hum Rts LR* 349–414

DeFrancia, C., 'Due Process in International Criminal Courts: Why Procedure Matters', (2001) 87 *Va LR* 1381–1440

De Hemptinne, J., 'The Creation of Investigating Chambers at the ICC' (2007) 5 *JICJ* 402–18

Delmas-Marty, M., 'The Contribution of Comparative Law to a Pluralist Conception of International Criminal Law' (2003) 1 *JICJ* 13–25

De Meester, K., Pitcher, K., Rastan, R., and Sluiter, G., 'Investigation, Coercive Measures, Arrest and Surrender' in Sluiter, G., Friman, H., Linton, S., Zappalà, S., and Vasiliev, S. (eds), *International Criminal Procedure: Principles and Rules* (Oxford: OUP, 2013) 171–380

Donat-Cattin, D., 'Article 68' in Triffterer, O. (ed.), *Commentary on the Rome Statute of the International Criminal Court: Observers' Notes, Article by Article* (3rd edn, Baden-Baden: Beck, 2015) 1677–1707

Donlon, F., 'The Role of the Judges in the Definition and Implementation of the Completion Strategies of the International Criminal Tribunals' in Darcy, S. and Powderly, J. (eds), *Judicial Creativity at the International Criminal Tribunals* (Oxford: OUP, 2010) 353–83

Doran, K., 'Provisional Release in International Human Rights Law and International Criminal Law' (2011) 11 *ICLR* 707–43

Duff, A., 'Authority and Responsibility in International Criminal Law' in Besson, S. and Tasioulis, J. (eds), *The Philosophy of International Law* (Oxford: OUP, 2010) 589–604

Dworkin, R., 'Rights as Trumps' in Waldron, J. (ed.), *Theories of Rights* (Oxford: OUP, 1984) 153–67

Ellis, M.S., 'Achieving Justice before the International War Crimes Tribunal: Challenges for the Defense Counsel' (1996–1997) 7 *Duke J Comp & Int'l L* 519–38

Ellis, M.S., 'The International Criminal Court and Its Implication for Domestic Law and National Capacity Building' (2002) 15 *Florida JIL* 215–242

Ellis, M.S., 'The Saddam Trial: Challenges to Meeting International Standards of Fairness with Regard to the Defense' (2006–2008) 39 *Case Western Res JIL* 171–94

Fairlie, M.A., 'Due Process Erosion: The Diminution of Live Testimony at the ICTY' (2003) 34 *California Western Int'l L J* 47–83

Fairlie, M.A., 'Rule-Making from the Bench: A Place for Minimalism at the ICTY' (2004) 39 *Texas Int'l L J* 257–85

Fairlie, M.A., 'The Marriage of Common and Continental Law at the ICTY and Its Progeny, Due Process Deficit', (2004) 4 *ICLR* 243–319

Fairlie, M.A., 'The Precedent of Pretrial Release at the ICTY: A Road Better Left Less Traveled' (2010) 33 *Fordham Int'l L J* 1101–77

Fallon, R.H., and Melzer, D.J., 'Habeas Corpus Jurisdiction, Substantive Rights, and the War on Terror' (2006–2007) 120 *Harv LR* 2029–112

Fenwick, H., 'Procedural "Rights" of Victims of Crime: Public or Private Ordering of the Criminal Justice Process?' (1997) 60 *MLR* 317–33

Ferencz, B.B., 'Nuremberg Trial Procedure and the Rights of the Accused' (1948–1949) 39 *J Crim L & Criminol* 144–51

Findlay, M., 'Synthesis in Trial Procedures? The Experience of International Criminal Tribunals' (2001) 50 *ICLQ* 26–53

Fletcher, G.P., 'Parochial versus Universal Criminal Law' (2005) 3 *JICJ* 20–34

Fletcher, G.P., and Ohlin, J.D., 'Reclaiming Fundamental Principles of Criminal Law in the Darfur Case' (2005) 3 *JICJ* 539–61

Franck, T.M., 'Epistemology at a Time of Perplexity' (2002) 13 *EJIL* 1025–30

Fry, E., 'Between Show Trials and Sham Prosecutions: The Rome Statute's Potential Effect on Domestic Due Process Protections' (2012) 23 *CLF* 35–62

Fuller, L.L., 'Positivism and Fidelity to Law: A Reply to Professor Hart' (1957) 71 *Harv LR* 630–72

Gaeta, P., 'To be (Present) or not to be (Present): Trials *In Absentia* before the Special Tribunal for Lebanon' (2007) 5 *JICJ* 1165–74

Galbraith, J., 'The Pace of International Criminal Justice' (2009) 31 *Michigan JIL* 79–156

Garapon, A., 'Three Challenges for International Criminal Justice' (2004) 2 *JICJ* 716–26

Gibson, K., and Lussiaa-Berdou, C., 'Disclosure of Evidence' in Khan, K. et al. (eds), *Principles of Evidence in International Criminal Justice* (Oxford: OUP, 2010) 306–74

Gioia, F., 'Comments on Chapter 3' in Kleffner, J. and Kor, G. (eds), *Complementary views on Complementarity* (Cambridge: CUP, 2006) 105–14.

Glasius, M., and Meijers, T., 'Constructions of Legitimacy: The Charles Taylor Trial' (2012) 6 *IJTJ* 229–52

Goldstein, A.S., 'Reflections on Two Models: Inquisitorial Themes in American Criminal Procedure' (1974) 26 *Stanford LR* 1009–25

Gordon, G.S., 'Toward an International Criminal Procedure: Due Process Aspirations and Limitations' (2007) 45 *Columbia J Transnat'l L* 635–710

Gosnell, C., 'Damned If You Don't: Liability for Omissions in International Criminal Law' in Schabas, W.A., McDermott, Y., and Hayes, N. (eds), *The Ashgate Research Companion to International Criminal Law: Critical Perspectives* (Aldershot: Ashgate, 2013) 101–32.

Gradoni, L., '"You Will Receive a Fair Trial Elsewhere": The *Ad Hoc* International Criminal Tribunals Acting as Human Rights Jurisdictions' (2007) 54 *Netherlands Int'l LR* 1–49

Groome, D., 'Re-evaluating the Theoretical Basis and Methodology of International Criminal Trials' (2007) 25 *Penn State Int'l LR* 791–802

Harmon, M.B., 'The Pre-Trial Process at the ICTY as a Means of Ensuring Expeditious Trials: A Potential Unrealised' (2007) 5 *JICJ* 377–93

Hart, H.L.A., 'Positivism and the Separation of Law and Morals' (1958) 71 *Harv LR* 593–629

Hart, H.L.A., 'Book Review: *The Morality of Law* by Lon L. Fuller' (1964–1965) 78 *Harv LR* 1281–1310

Heller, K.J., 'The Shadow Side of Complementarity: The Effect of Article 17 of the Rome Statute on National Due Process' (2006) 17 *CLF* 255–80

Heller, K.J., 'What Happens to the Acquitted?' (2008) 21 *LJIL* 663–80

Herlin-Karnell, E., 'The Lisbon Treaty and the Area of Criminal Law and Justice' (2008) 3 *European Policy Analysis* 1–10

Higgins, G., 'The Development of the Right to Self-Representation before the International Criminal Tribunals' in Darcy, S. and Powderly, J. (eds), *Judicial Creativity at the International Criminal Tribunals* (Oxford: OUP, 2010) 252–85

Hildebrandt, M., 'Trial and 'Fair Trial': From Peer to Subject to Citizen' in Duff, A., Farmer, L., Marshall S., and Tadros, V. (eds), *The Trial on Trial, Volume II: Judgment and Calling to Account* (Oxford: Hart Publishing, 2006) 15–37

Hirsch, A. von and Schorscher, V.C., 'A System of International Criminal Justice for Human Rights Violations: What is the General Justification for its Existence?' in Zedner, L. and Roberts, J.V. (eds), *Principles and Values in Criminal Law and Criminal Justice: Essays in Honour of Andrew Ashworth* (Oxford: OUP, 2012) 209–22

Hoyano, L., 'What is Balanced on the Scales of Justice? In Search of the Essence of the Right to a Fair Trial' [2014] *Crim LR* 4–29

Jackson, J.D., 'The Effect of Human Rights on Criminal Evidentiary Processes: Towards Convergence, Divergence or Realignment' (2005) 68 *MLR* 737–64

Jackson, J.D., 'Transnational Faces of Justice: Two Attempts to Build Common Standards Beyond National Boundaries' in Jackson, J.D., Langer, M., and Tillers, P. (eds), *Crime, Procedure and Evidence in a Comparative and International Context: Essays in Honour of Professor Mirjan Damaška* (Oxford: Hart Publishing, 2008) 221–50

Jackson, J.D., 'Finding the Best Epistemic Fit for International Criminal Tribunals: Beyond the Adversarial-Inquisitorial Dichotomy' (2009) 7 *JICJ* 17–39

Jackson, J., 'Re-Conceptualizing the Right of Silence as an Effective Fair Trial Standard' (2009) 58 *ICLQ* 835–61

Jacobs, D., The Importance of Being Earnest: The Timeliness of the Challenge to Admissibility in *Katanga*' (2010) 23 *LJIL* 331–42

Jacobs, D., 'A Shifting Scale of Power: Who is in charge of the charges at the International Criminal Court?' in Schabas, W.A., McDermott, Y., and Hayes, N. (eds), *The Ashgate Research Companion to International Criminal Law: Critical Perspectives* (Aldershot: Ashgate, 2013) 205–22

Jalloh, C.C., 'The Contribution of the Special Court for Sierra Leone to the Development of International Law' (2007) 15 *Afr J Int'l & Comp L* 165–207

Jalloh, C.C., 'Self-representation and the Use of Assigned, Standby and Amicus Counsel', in Carter, L. and Pocar, F. (eds), *International Criminal Procedure: The Interface of Civil Law and Common Law Legal Systems* (Cheltenham: Edward Elgar, 2013) 125–65

Jalloh, C.C. and DiBella, A., 'Equality of Arms in International Criminal Law: Continuing Challenges' in Schabas, W.A., McDermott, Y., and Hayes, N. (eds), *The Ashgate Research Companion to International Criminal Law: Critical Perspectives* (Aldershot: Ashgate, 2013) 251–88

Janis, M.W., 'The Nature of *Jus Cogens*' in May, L. and Brown, J. (eds), *Philosophy of Law: Classical and Contemporary Readings* (Malden: Wiley-Blackwell, 2010) 184–86

Jones., J.R.W.D. and Zgonec-Rozej, M., 'Rights of Suspects and Accused', in Alamuddin, A., Jurdi, N.N., and Tolbert, D. (eds), *The Special Tribunal for Lebanon: Law and Practice* (Oxford: OUP, 2014) 177–207

Jones, R.K., 'Untangling the Right to Self-Representation in the International Criminal Tribunal for the Former Yugoslavia' (2009) 43 *Georgia LR* 1285–1319

Jorda, C., 'The Major Hurdles and Accomplishments of the ICTY: What the ICC Can Learn from Them' (2004) 2 *JICJ* 572–84

Jordash, W., Parker, T., 'Trial *in Absentia* before the Special Tribunal for Lebanon: Incompatibility with International Human Rights Law' (2010) 8 *JICJ* 487–509

Jordash, W., 'Joint Criminal Enterprise Liability: Result Orientated Justice' in Schabas, W.A., McDermott, Y., and Hayes, N. (eds), *The Ashgate Research Companion to International Criminal Law: Critical Perspectives* (Aldershot: Ashgate, 2013) 133–64

Jorgensen, N.H.B., 'The Right of the Accused to Self-Representation Before International Criminal Tribunals' (2004) 98 *AJIL* 711–44

Jorgensen, N.H.B., 'The Right of the Accused to Self-Representation Before International Criminal Tribunals: Further Developments' (2005) 99 *AJIL* 495–502

Jorgensen, N.H.B., 'The Problem of Self-Representation at International Criminal Tribunals' (2006) 4 *JICJ* 64–77

Jung, H., 'Nothing but the Truth? Some Facts, Impressions and Confessions about Truth in Criminal Procedure' in Duff, A., Farmer, L., Marshall, S., and Tadros, V. (eds), *The Trial on Trial I: Truth and Due Process* (Oxford: Hart Publishing, 2004) 147–56

Katz Cogan, J., 'International Criminal Courts and Fair Trials: Difficulties and Prospects' (2002) 27 *Yale JIL* 111–40

Kay, S., 'The Move from Oral Evidence to Written Evidence: "The Law is always Too Short and Too Tight for Growing Humankind"' (2004) 2 *JICJ* 495–502

Keefe, A., Landis, W.B. Jr, and Shaad, R.B., 'Sense and Nonsense about Judicial Notice' (1950) 2 *Stanford Law Review* 664–90

Kekes, J., 'Morality and Impartiality' (1981) 18 *American Philosophical Quarterly* 295–303

Khan, K.A.A. and Buisman, C., 'Sitting on Evidence? Systematic Failings in the ICC Disclosure Regime—Time for Reform' in Stahn, C. (ed.), *The Law and Practice of the International Criminal Court* (Oxford: OUP, 2015) 1029–62

Kirsch, P., 'ICC Marks Five Years Since Entry into Force of Rome Statute', in Stahn, C. and Sluiter, G. (eds), *The Emerging Practice of the International Criminal Court* (Leiden: Nijhoff, 2009) 11–12

Klamberg, M., 'What are the Objectives of International Criminal Procedure? Reflections on the Fragmentation of a Legal Regime' (2010) 79 *Nordic JIL* 279–302

Koskenniemi, M., 'Between Impunity and Show Trials' (2002) 6 *Max Planck Yearbook of United Nations Law* 1–35

Kranzbuhler, O., 'Nuremberg Eighteen Years Afterwards' (1964–1965) 14 *DePaul Law Review* 333–47

Kress, C., 'The Procedural Law of the International Criminal Court in Outline: Anatomy of a Unique Compromise' (2003) 1 *JICJ* 603–17

Kress, C. and Holtzendorff, L. von, 'The Kampala Compromise on the Crime of Aggression' (2010) 8 *JICJ* 1179–1217

Kwon, O., 'Procedural Challengers Faced by International Criminal Tribunals and the Value of Codification' in Sluiter, G., Friman, H., Linton, S., Zappalà, S., and Vasiliev, S. (eds), *International Criminal Procedure: Principles and Rules* (Oxford: OUP, 2013) 1415–1418

Langbein, J.H. and Weinreb, L.L., 'Continental Criminal Procedure: "Myth" and Reality' (1978) 87 *Yale L J* 1549–69

Langer, M., 'The Rise of Managerial Judging in International Criminal Law' (2005) 53 *AJIL* 835–909

Langer, M., and Doherty, J.W., 'Managerial Judging Goes International, but Its Promise Remains Unfulfilled: An Empirical Assessment of the ICTY Reforms' (2011) 36 *Yale JIL* 241–305

Langford, I., 'Fair Trial: The History of an Idea' (2009) 8 *Journal of Human Rights* 37–52

Laplante, L.J., 'The Domestication of International Criminal Law: A Proposal for Expanding the International Criminal Court's Sphere of Influence' (2009–2010) 43 *J. Marshall LR* 635–80

Legrand, P., 'European Legal Systems are Not Converging' (1996) 45 *ICLQ* 52–81

Leigh, M., 'The Yugoslav Tribunal: Use of Unnamed Witnesses against Accused' (1996) 90 *AJIL* 235–38

Leigh, M., 'Witness Anonymity is Inconsistent with Due Process' (1997) 91 *AJIL* 80–3

Lemonde, M., 'From the European Convention on Human Rights to the Treaty on European Union: Diversity in Reasoning' in Delmas-Marty, M. (ed.), *What Kind of Criminal Policy for Europe?* (trans Mark A Summers, The Hague/London: Kluwer Law International, 1996) 33–9

Lønseth, P., 'Between Territoriality and Universality: Reflections by a Core International Crimes Prosecutor' in Bergsmo, M. (ed.), *Complementarity and the Exercise of Universal Jurisdiction for Core International Crimes* (Torkel Opsahl Academic EPublisher: Oslo, 2010) 161–64

Luban, D., 'The Legacies of Nuremberg' in Mettraux, G. (ed.), *Perspectives on the Nuremberg Trial* (Oxford: OUP, 2008) 638–72

Luban, D., 'Fairness to Rightness: Jurisdiction, Legality, and the Legitimacy of International Criminal Law' in Besson, S. and Tasioulis, J. (eds), *The Philosophy of International Law* (Oxford: OUP, 2010) 569–88

Luban, D., 'After the Honeymoon' (2013) 11 *JICJ* 505–15

Lyons, B.S., 'Enough is Enough: The Illegitimacy of International Criminal Convictions' (2011) 13 *J Genocide Res* 287–312

McAuliffe, P., 'Hybrid Courts in Retrospect: Of Lost Legacies and Modern Futures' in Schabas, W.A., McDermott, Y., and Hayes, N. (eds), *The Ashgate Research Companion to International Criminal Law: Critical Perspectives* (Aldershot: Ashgate, 2013) 453–74

McDermott, Y., 'Some are More Equal than Others: Victim Participation in the International Criminal Court' (2008) 5 *Eyes on the ICC* 23–48

McDermott, Y., 'Victims and International Law: Remedies in the Courtroom?' (2009) 4 *Hague Justice Journal* 199–213

McDermott, Y., 'Double Speak and Double Standards: Does the Jurisprudence on Retrial following Acquittal under International Criminal Law Spell the End of the Double Jeopardy Rule?' in Keane, D. and McDermott, Y. (eds), *The Challenge of Human Rights: Past, Present and Future* (Cheltenham: Edward Elgar, 2012) 176–93

McDermott, Y., 'Case commentary: *Prosecutor v. Krajišnik*, Decision on Momčilo Krajišnik's Motion to Reschedule Status Conference and Permit Alan Dershowitz Appear' in Klip, A. and Sluiter, G. (eds), *Annotated Leading Cases of International Criminal Tribunals: Vol. XXXV* (Antwerp: Intersentia, 2012) 181–84

McDermott, Y., 'Rights in Reverse: A Critical Analysis of Fair Trial Rights under International Criminal Law' in Schabas, W.A., McDermott, Y., and Hayes, N. (eds), *The Ashgate Research Companion to International Criminal Law: Critical Perspectives* (Aldershot: Ashgate, 2013) 165–80.

McDermott, Y., 'General Duty to Ensure the Right to a Fair and Expeditious Trial' in Sluiter, G., Friman, H., Linton, S., Zappalà, S., and Vasiliev, S. (eds), *International Criminal Procedure: Principles and Rules* (Oxford: OUP, 2013) 770–817

McDermott, Y., 'General Duty to Ensure the Integrity of the Proceedings' in Sluiter, G., Friman, H., Linton, S., Zappalà, S., and Vasiliev, S. (eds), *International Criminal Procedure: Principles and Rules* (Oxford: OUP, 2013) 743–69

McDermott, Y., 'The Admissibility and Weight of Written Witness Testimony in International Criminal Law: A Socio-Legal Analysis' (2013) 26 *LJIL* 971–89

McDermott, Y., 'The Legacy of the International Criminal Tribunal for Rwanda in Promoting Respect for International Due Process Standards' [2013] *African Yearbook of International Humanitarian Law* 45–65

McDermott, Y. and Elmaalul, W., 'Legitimacy and the Administration of International Justice' in Schabas, W.A., and Murphy, S. (eds), *Research Handbook on International Courts and Tribunals* (Cheltenham: Edward Elgar, 2016) (forthcoming)

McDonald, W.F., 'Towards a Bicentennial Revolution in Criminal Justice: The Return of the Victim' (1976) 13 *Am Crim LR* 649–74

McHarg, A., 'Reconciling Human Rights and the Public Interest: Conceptual Problems and Doctrinal Uncertainty in the Jurisprudence of the European Court of Human Rights' (1999) 62 *MLR* 671–96

McIntyre, G., 'Defining Human Rights in the Arena of International Humanitarian Law: Human Rights in the Jurisprudence of the ICTY' in Schabas, W.A., and Boas, G. (eds), *International Criminal Law Developments in the Case Law of the ICTY* (Leiden: Brill/Nijhoff, 2003) 193–238

McIntyre, G., 'Equality of Arms—Defining Human Rights in the Jurisprudence of the International Criminal Tribunal for the Former Yugoslavia' (2003) 16 *LJIL* 269–320

MacSweeney, D., 'International Standards of Fairness, Criminal Procedure and the International Criminal Court' (1997) 68 *RIDP* 233–89

Mahoney, P., 'Right to a Fair Trial in Criminal Matters under Article 6 E.C.H.R.' (2004) 4 *Judicial Studies Institute Journal* 107–29

May, R., and Wierda, M., 'Trends in International Criminal Evidence: Nuremberg, Tokyo, The Hague, and Arusha', (1999) 37 *Columbia J Transnat'l L* 725–66

Mégret, F., 'Beyond Fairness: Understanding the Determinants of International Criminal Procedure' (2009) 14 *UCLA J Int'l L & Foreign Aff* 37–76

Mégret, F. and Samson, G.S., 'Holding the Line on Complementarity in Libya' (2013) 11 *JICJ* 571–89

Mendeloff, D., 'Truth-Seeking, Truth-Telling, and Postconflict Peacebuilding: Curb the Enthusiasm?' (2004) 6 *Int'l Studies Rev* 355–80

Mettraux, G., 'Crimes against Humanity in the Jurisprudence of the International Criminal Tribunals for the Former Yugoslavia and for Rwanda' (2002) 43 *Harv Int'l L J* 237–316

Mettraux, G., 'Comparing the Comparable: 2006 Military Commissions v. the ICTY' (2007) 5 *JICJ* 59–66

Møse, E., and Aptel, J., 'Trial without Undue Delay before the International Criminal Tribunals' in Chand Vohrah, L. et al. (eds), *Man's Inhumanity to Man: Essays on International Law in Honour of Antonio Cassese* (The Hague: Kluwer Law International, 2003) 539–65

Mundis, D.A., 'From "Common Law" to "Civil Law": The Evolution of the ICTY Rules of Procedure and Evidence' (2001) 14 *LJIL* 367–82

Mundis, D.A., 'The Judicial Effects of the "Completion Strategies" on the Ad Hoc International Criminal Tribunals' (2005) 99 *AJIL* 142–57

Murphy, C., 'Lon Fuller and the Moral Value of the Rule of Law' (2005) 24 *Law & Phil* 239–62

Murphy, P., 'Excluding Justice or Facilitating Justice? International Criminal Law would benefit from Rules of Evidence' (2008) 12 *Int'l J of Evidence and Proof* 1–31

Murphy, P., 'No Free Lunch, No Free Proof: The Indiscriminate Admission of Evidence is a Serious Flaw in International Criminal Trials' (2010) 8 *JICJ* 539–73

Nelson, W., 'The Very Idea of Pure Procedural Justice' (1980) 90 *Ethics* 502–11

Nice, G., Vallieres-Roland, P., 'Procedural Innovations in War Crimes Trials', in Abtahi, H. and Boas, G. (eds), *The Dynamics of International Criminal Justice: Essays in Honour of Sir Richard May* (Leiden: Nihoff, 2006) 141–68

Nijboer, J.F., 'Common Law Tradition in Evidence Scholarship Observed from a Continental Perspective' (1993) 41 *Am J Comp L* 299–338

Ntanda Nsereko, D.D., 'Rules of Procedure and Evidence of the International Tribunal for the Former Yugoslavia' (1994) 5 *CLF* 507–55

Ohlin, J.D., 'Three Conceptual Problems with the Doctrine of Joint Criminal Enterprise' (2007) 5 *JICJ* 69–90

Ohlin, J.D., 'Meta-Theory of International Criminal Procedure: Vindicating the Rule of Law' (2009) 14 *UCLA J Int'l L & Foreign Aff* 77–120

Orie, A., 'Accusatorial v Inquisitorial Approach in International Criminal Proceedings Prior to the Establishment of the ICC and in the Proceedings before the ICC' in Cassese, A., Gaeta, P., and Jones, J.R.W.D. (eds), *The Rome Statute of the International Criminal Court: A Commentary, Vol. II* (Oxford: OUP, 2002) 1439–95

Osiel, M., 'In Defence of Liberal Show Trials—Nuremberg and Beyond' in Mettraux, G. (ed.), *Perspectives on the Nuremberg Trial* (Oxford: OUP, 2008) 704–25

O'Sullivan, E. and Montgomery, D., 'The Erosion of the Right to Confrontation under the Cloak of Fairness at the ICTY' (2010) 8 *JICJ* 511–38

Packer, H., 'Two Models of the Criminal Process' (1964) 113 *U Penn LR* 1–68

Pakes, F.J., 'Styles of Trial Procedure at the International Criminal Tribunal for the Former Yugoslavia' in Koppen, P.J. van and Penrod, S.D. (eds), *Adversarial versus Inquisitorial Justice: Psychological Perspectives on Criminal Justice Systems* (New York: Kluwer Academic/Plenum Publishers, 2003), 309–20

Piragoff, D.K., 'Protection of National Security Information' in Lee, R.S. (ed.), *The International Criminal Court: The Making of the Rome Statute* (The Hague: Kluwer Law International, 1999) 270–93

Pizzi, W., 'Overcoming Logistical and Structural Barriers to Fair Trials at International Tribunals' (2006) 4 *Int'l Commentary on Evidence* Issue 1, Article 4

Politi, M., 'The Establishment of an International Criminal Court at the Crossroads: Issues and Prospects After the First Session of the Preparatory Committee' (1999) 13 *Nouvelles Études Pénales* 115–57

Powell, A., 'Three Angry Men: Juries in International Criminal Adjudication' (2004) 79 *NYU LR* 2341–80

Raab, D., 'Evaluating the ICTY and its Completion Strategy: Efforts to Achieve Accountability for War Crimes and their Tribunals' (2005) 3 *JICJ* 82–102

Rapp, S.J., 'Achieving Accountability for the Greatest Crimes—The Legacy of the International Tribunals' (2006–2007) 55 *Drake LR* 259–310

Rastan, R., 'Testing Co-Operation: The International Criminal Court and National Authorities' (2008) 21(2) *LJIL* 431–56

Rastan, R., 'Complementarity: Contest or Collaboration' in Bergsmo, M. (ed.), *Complementarity and the Exercise of Universal Jurisdiction for Core International Crimes* (Oslo: Torkel Opsahl Academic EPublisher, 2010) 83–132

Rearick, D.J., 'Innocent until Alleged Guilty: Provisional Release at the ICTR' (2003) 44 *Harv Int'l L J* 577–96

Redmayne, M., 'Hearsay and Human Rights: *Al-Khawaja* in the Grand Chamber' (2012) 75 *MLR* 865–78

Riachy, R., 'Trial *in Absentia* in the Lebanese Judicial System and at the Special Tribunal for Lebanon: Challenge or Evolution?' (2010) 8 *JICJ* 1295–1305

Rigney, S., '"The Words Don't Fit You": Recharacterisation of the Charges, Trial Fairness, and Katanga' (2014) 15(2) *Melbourne JIL* 515–33

Roach, K., 'Wrongful Convictions: Adversarial and Inquisitorial Themes' (2010) 35 *N C J Int'l L & Com Reg* 387–446

Roach, K. and Trotter, G., 'Miscarriages of Justice in the War against Terror' (2004–2005) 109 *Penn St LR* 967–1042

Roberts, P., 'On Method: The Ascent of Comparative Criminal Justice' (2002) 22 *OJLS* 539–61

Roberts, P., 'Comparative Law for International Criminal Justice' in Nelken, D. and Örücü, E. (eds), *Comparative Law: A Handbook* (Oxford: Hart Publishing, 2007) 339–70

Roberts, P., 'Comparative Criminal Justice Goes Global' (2008) 28 *OJLS* 369–91

Roberts, P., 'Does Article 6 of the European Convention on Human Rights Require Reasoned Verdicts in Criminal Trials?' (2011) 11 *HRLR* 213–35

Roberts, P., 'The Priority of Procedure and the Neglect of Evidence and Proof: Facing Facts in International Criminal Law' (2015) 13 *JICJ* 479–506

Roberts, P., and Hunter, J., 'Introduction' in Roberts, P. and Hunter, J. (eds), *Criminal Evidence and Human Rights* (Oxford: Hart Publishing, 2012) 1–23

Roberts, R.C.E., 'The Lubanga Trial Chamber's Assessment of Evidence in Light of the Accused's Right to the Presumption of Innocence' (2012) 10 *JICJ* 923–43

Robinson, D., 'The Identity Crisis of International Criminal Law' (2008) 21 *LJIL* 925–63

Robinson, D., 'The Mysterious Mysteriousness of Complementarity' (2010) 21 *CLF* 67–102

Robinson, D., 'The "Inaction" Controversy: Neglected Words and New Opportunities' in Stahn, C. and El Zeidy, M. (eds), *The International Criminal Court and Complementarity: From Theory to Practice* (Cambridge: CUP, 2011) 460–502

Robinson, D., 'Three Theories of Complementarity: Charge, Sentence or Process? A Comment on Kevin Heller's Sentence-Based Theory of Complementarity' in Schabas, W.A., McDermott, Y., and Hayes, N. (eds), *The Ashgate Research Companion to International Criminal Law: Critical Perspectives* (Aldershot: Ashgate, 2013) 369–86

Robinson, P.L., 'Ensuring Fair and Expeditious Trials at the International Criminal Tribunal for the Former Yugoslavia' (2000) 11 *EJIL* 569–89

Robinson, P.L., 'Rough Edges in the Alignment of Legal Systems in the Proceedings at the ICTY' (2005) 3 *JICJ* 1037–58.

Robinson, P.L., 'The Right to a Fair Trial in International Law, with Specific Reference to the Work of the ICTY' (2009) 3 *Publicist* 1–11

Rohan, C.M., 'Rules Governing the Presentation of Testimonial Evidence' in Khan, K., Buisman, C., and Gosnell, C. (eds), *Principles of Evidence in International Criminal Justice* (Oxford: OUP, 2010) 499–550

Rohan, C.M., 'Protecting the Rights of The Accused in International Criminal Proceedings: Lip Service Or Affirmative Action?' in Schabas, W.A., McDermott, Y., and Hayes, N. (eds), *The Ashgate Research Companion to International Criminal Law: Critical Perspectives* (Aldershot: Ashgate, 2013) 289–306

Röhl, K.F., 'Procedural Justice: Introduction and Overview' in Röhl, K.F., and Machura, S. (eds), *Procedural Justice* (Dartmouth: Ashgate, 1997) 1–36

Ryngaert, C., 'Universal Jurisdiction over Genocide and Wartime Torture in Dutch Courts: An Appraisal of the Afghan and Rwandan cases (2007)' (2007) 2 *Hague Justice Journal* 13–36

Schabas, W.A., 'Sentencing by International Tribunals: A Human Rights Approach' (1997) 7 *Duke J Comp & Int'L L* 461–517

Schabas, W.A., 'State Policy as an Element of International Crimes' (2008) 98 *J Crim L & Criminol* 953–82

Schabas, W.A., 'Article 67' in Otto Triffterer (ed.), *Commentary on the Rome Statute: Observers' Notes, Article-by-Article* (2nd edn, Munich: Beck, 2008) 1247–74

Schabas, W.A., 'Synergy or Fragmentation? International Criminal Law and the European Convention on Human Rights' (2011) 9 *JICJ* 609–32

Scharf, M.P., 'Self-Representation Versus Assignment of Defence Counsel before International Criminal Tribunals' (2006) 4 *JICJ* 31–46

Schlesinger, R.B., 'Comparative Criminal Procedure: A Plea for Utilizing Foreign Experience', (1977) 26 *Buff LR* 361–86

Schmid, E., 'A Few Comments on a Comment: The UN Human Rights Committee's General Comment No. 32 on Article 14 of the ICCPR and the Question of Civilians Tried by Military Courts' (2010) 14 *Intl J Hum Rts* 1058–71

Schmidt, V.H., 'Procedural Aspects of Distributive Justice' in Röhl, K.F., and Machura, S. (eds), *Procedural Justice* (Dartmouth: Ashgate, 1997) 161–80

Schomburg, W., 'The Role of International Criminal Tribunals in Promoting Respect for Fair Trial Rights' (2009) 8 *Nw U J Int'l Hum Rts* 1–29

Schuon, C., 'The Appeals Decision in the ICC's Jean-Pierre Bemba Gombo Case on the Trial Chamber's "Decision on the Admission into Evidence of Materials Contained in the Prosecution's List of Evidence"' (2012) 25 *LJIL* 511–20

Schwartz, H., 'Trials in Absentia' (1996) 4(1) *Human Rights Brief* 12–14

Scobbie, I., 'Tom Franck's Fairness' (2002) 13 *EJIL* 909–25

Shahabuddeen, M., 'Judicial Creativity and Joint Criminal Enterprise' in Darcy, S. and Powderly, J. (eds), *Judicial Creativity at the International Criminal Tribunals* (Oxford: OUP, 2010) 184–203

Shannon, K.G., 'Passing the Poisoned Chalice: Judicial Notice of Genocide by the ICTR' (2006) 19 *Revue Québécoise de Droit International* 95–122

Shany, Y., 'Assessing the Effectiveness of International Courts: A Goal-Based Approach' (2012) 106 *AJIL* 225–70

Sivakumaran, S., 'Courts of Armed Opposition: Fair Trials or Summary Justice?' (2009) 7 *JICJ* 489–513

Skilbeck, R., 'Frankenstein's Monster: Creating a New International Procedure' (2010) 8 *JICJ* 451–62

Sluiter, G., 'International Criminal Proceedings and the Protection of Human Rights' (2003) 37 *New England L R* 935–48

Sluiter, G., 'Fairness and the Interests of Justice: Illusive Concepts in the Milošević Case' (2005) 3 *JICJ* 9–19

Sluiter, G., 'The ICTR and the Protection of Witnesses' (2005) 3 *JICJ* 962–76

Sluiter, G., '"I Beg You, Please Come Testify"—The Problematic Absence of Subpoena Powers at the ICC' (2009) 12 *New Criminal Law Review* 590–608

Smith, L., 'Victims' Participation at the International Criminal Court: Benefit or Burden?' in Schabas, W.A., McDermott, Y., and Hayes, N. (eds), *The Ashgate Research Companion to International Criminal Law: Critical Perspectives* (Aldershot: Ashgate, 2013) 181–204

Spencer, J.R., 'Orality and the Evidence of Absent Witnesses' [1994] *Crim LR* 628–44

Spencer, J.R., 'The Case for a Code of Criminal Procedure' [2000] *Crim LR* 519–33

Stahn, C., 'Libya, the International Criminal Court and Complementarity: A Test for "Shared Responsibility"' (2012) 10 *JICJ* 325–49

Stavros, S., 'The Right to a Fair Trial in Emergency Situations' (1992) 41 *ICLQ* 343–65

Stewart, J.G., 'The End of "Modes of Liability" for International Crimes' (2012) 25 *LJIL* 165–219

Stigen, J., 'The Relationship between the Principle of Complementarity and the Exercise of Universal Jurisdiction for Core International Crimes' in Bergsmo, M. (ed.), *Complementarity and the Exercise of Universal Jurisdiction for Core International Crimes* (Oslo: Torkel Opsahl Academic Epublisher, 2010) 133–60

Summers, R.S., 'Evaluating and Improving Legal Process—A Plea for "Process Values"' (1974) 60 *Cornell LR* 1–52

Swaak-Goldman, O.Q., 'The ICTY and the Right to a Fair Trial: A Critique of the Critics' (2004) 10 *LJIL* 215–21

Swart, B., 'Damaška and the Faces of International Criminal Justice' (2008) 6 *JICJ* 87–114

Tallgren, I., 'The Sense and Sensibility of International Criminal Law' (2002) 13 *EJIL* 561–95

Tasioulas, J., 'International Law and the Limits of Fairness' (2002) 13 *EJIL* 993–1023

Temminck Tuinstra, J., 'Assisting an Accused to Represent Himself: Appointment of *Amici Curiae* as the Most Appropriate Option' (2006) 4 *JICJ* 47–63

Temminck Tuinstra, J., 'Defending the Defenders: The Role of Defence Counsel in International Criminal Trials' (2010) 8 *JICJ* 463–86

Temminck Tuinstra, J., 'The ICTY's Continuing Struggle with the Right to Self-Representation' in Swart, B., Zahar, A., and Sluiter, G. (eds), *The Legacy of the International Criminal Tribunal for the Former Yugoslavia* (Oxford: OUP, 2011) 345–76

Thayer, J.B., 'Judicial Notice and the Law of Evidence' (1890) 3 *Harvard Law Review* 285–312

Tochilovsky, V., 'Trial in International Criminal Jurisdictions: Battle or Scrutiny?' (1998) 6 *Eur J Crime Crim L & Crim Just* 55–9

Tochilovsky, V., 'Proceedings in the International Criminal Court: Some Lessons to Learn from ICTY Experience' (2002) 10 *Eur J Crime Crim L & Crim Just* 268–75

Tolbert, D. and Kontic, A., 'The International Criminal Tribunal for the Former Yugoslavia: Transitional Justice, the Transfer of Cases to National Courts and Lessons for the ICC' in Stahn, C. and Sluiter, G. (eds), *The Emerging Practice of the International Criminal Court* (Leiden: Nijhoff, 2009) 135–62

Trechsel, S., 'Why Must Trials Be Fair?' (1997) 31 *Isr LR* 94–119

Turner, J.I., 'Nationalizing International Criminal Law' (2005) 41 *Stanford JIL* 1–51

Turner, J.I., 'Defense Perspectives on Law and Politics in International Criminal Trials' (2008) 48 *Va JIL* 529–94

Tyler, T.R., 'The Role of Perceived Injustice in Defendants' Evaluations of their Courtroom Experience' (1984) 18 *Law and Society Review* 51–74

Tyler, T.R., 'Procedural Justice, Legitimacy, and the Effective Rule of Law' (2003) 30 *Crime & Justice* 283–357

Van Schaack, B., 'Legality and International Criminal Law' [2009] *ASIL Proceedings* 101–104

Vidmar, N., 'Procedural Justice and Alternative Dispute Resolution' in Röhl, K, F., and Machura, S., (eds), *Procedural Justice* (Dartmouth: Ashgate 1997) 121–36

Voeten, E., 'Public Opinion and the Legitimacy of International Courts' (2013) 14 *Theoretical Inquiries in Law* 411–36

Wald, P.M., 'To "Establish Incredible Events by Credible Evidence": The Use of Affidavit Testimony in Yugoslavia War Crimes Tribunal Proceedings' (2001) 42 *Harv Int'l L J* 535–53

Wald, P.M., 'The International Criminal Tribunal for the former Yugoslavia Comes of Age: Some Observations on Day-to-Day Dilemmas of an International Court' (2001) 5 *Wash U J L & Pol'y* 87–118

Wallach, E., 'The Procedural and Evidentiary Rules of Post World War II War Crimes Trials: Did They Provide an Outline for International Legal Procedure?' (1999) 37 *Columbia J Transnat'l L* 851–83

Warbrick, C., 'International Criminal Courts and Fair Trial' (1998) 3 *J C & S L* 45–64

Webb, P., 'Individual Criminal Responsibility', in Alamuddin, A., Nabil Jurdi, N., and Tolbert, D. (eds), *The Special Tribunal for Lebanon: Law and Practice* (Oxford: OUP, 2014) 88–110

Weisbord, N. and Smith, M.A., 'The Reason Behind the Rules: From Description to Normativity in International Criminal Procedure' (2010–2011) 36 *N C J Int'l L & Com Reg* 255–76

Weissbrodt, D. and Zinsmaste, K.K., 'Protecting the Fair Trial Rights of the Accused in International Criminal Law: Comparison of the International Criminal Court and the Military Commissions in Guantánamo' in Brown, B.S. (ed.), *Research Handbook on International Criminal Law* (Cheltenham: Edward Elgar, 2011) 261–83

Whiting, A., 'Disclosure Challenges at the International Criminal Court' in Stahn, C. (ed.), *The Law and Practice of the International Criminal Court* (Oxford: OUP, 2015) 1007–28

Williams, J., 'Slobodan Milošević and the Guarantee of Self-Representation' (2006–2007) 32 *Brooklyn JIL* 553–602

Williams, S.A. and Schabas, W.A., 'Article 17: Issues of Admissibility' in Triffterer, O. (ed.), *Commentary on the Rome Statute: Observers' Notes, Article by Article* (2nd edn, Oxford: Hart Publishing, 2008) 605–26

Wolfrum, R., 'Legitimacy in International Law from a Legal Perspective: Some Introductory Remarks' in Wolfrum, R. and Röben, V. (eds), *Legitimacy in International Law* (Berlin: Springer. 2008) 1–24

Wright, Q., 'Due Process and International Law' (1946) 40 *AJIL* 398–406

Wright, Q., 'The Law of the Nuremberg Trial' (1947) 41 *AJIL* 38–72

Young, A.N., 'Two Scales of Justice: A Reply' (1993) 35 *Crim L Q* 355–75

Zacklin, R., 'The Failings of *Ad Hoc* International Tribunals' (2004) 2 *JICJ* 541–45

Zahar, A., 'Legal Aid, Self-Representation, and the Crisis at the Hague Tribunal' (2008) 19 *CLF* 241–63

Zahar, A., 'The Problem of False Testimony at the International Criminal Tribunal for Rwanda' in Klip, A. and Sluiter, G. (eds), *Annotated Leading Cases of International Criminal Tribunals, Vol. XXV: International Criminal Tribunal for Rwanda, 2006–2007* (Antwerp: Intersentia, 2010) 509–22

Zahar, A., 'Pluralism and the Rights of the Accused in International Criminal Proceedings' in Elies van Sliedregt and Sergey Vasiliev, *Pluralism in International Criminal Law* (Oxford: OUP, 2014) 225–50

Zakerhossein, M.H. and De Brouwer, A., 'Diverse Approaches to Total and Partial *In Absentia* Trials by International Criminal Tribunals' (2015) 26 *CLF* 181–224

Zappalà, S., 'The Rights of Victims v. the Rights of the Accused' (2010) 8 *JICJ* 137–64

Zemach, A., 'Fairness and Moral Judgments in International Criminal Law: The Settlement Provision in the Rome Statute' (2003) 41 *Columbia J Transnat'l L* 123–49

REPORTS AND STATEMENTS OF THE INTERNATIONAL CRIMINAL TRIBUNALS (CHRONOLOGICAL ORDER)

Exceptions to the Exhaustion of Domestic Remedies (Arts. 46.1, 46.2a and 46.2.b, American Convention on Human Rights) Inter-American Court of Human Rights Advisory Opinion OC-11/90, 10 August 1990

Report of the Secretary-General Pursuant to Paragraph 2 of the Security Council Resolution 808 (1993) UN Doc. S/25704, 3 May 1993

First Annual Report of the International Criminal Tribunal for the Former Yugoslavia, UN Doc. A/49/342–S/1994/1007, 29 August 1994

ICTY Press Release, 'Judge Kirk McDonald urges that the International Permanent Court "must be effective"', 14 August 1997, available online at http://www.icty.org/sid/7478/en

Fifth Annual Report of the International Tribunal for the Prosecution of Persons Responsible for Serious Violations of International Humanitarian Law Committed in the Territory of the Former Yugoslavia, UN Docs A/53/219 and S/1998/737, 10 August 1998

Report of the Expert Group to Conduct a Review of the Effective Operation and Functioning of the International Criminal Tribunal for the Former Yugoslavia and the International Criminal Tribunal for Rwanda, UN Doc. A/54/634, 22 November 1999

Office of the Prosecutor, *Paper on Some Policy Issues before the Office of the Prosecutor* (September 2003) available online at http://www.icc-cpi.int/nr/rdonlyres/1fa7c4c6-de5f-42b7-8b25-60aa962ed8b6/143594/030905_policy_paper.pdf

Office of the Prosecutor, International Criminal Court, *Informal Expert Paper: The Principle of Complementarity in Practice*, ICC-OTP-2003, available online at http://www.icc-cpi.int/iccdocs/doc/doc654724.pdf

ICTY Press Release, 'Prlić, Stojić, Praljak, Petković, Corić and Pušić Initial Appearance', 6 April 2004, available online at http://www.icty.org/sid/8439

Assessment and Report of Judge Fausto Pocar, President of the International Criminal Tribunal for the Former Yugoslavia, Provided to the Security Council Pursuant to Paragraph 6 of Council Resolution 1534 (2004), Annex I to Letter dated 29 May 2006 from the President of the International Tribunal for the Prosecution of Persons Responsible for Serious Violations of International Humanitarian Law Committed in the Territory of the Former Yugoslavia since 1991, addressed to the President of the Security Council, UN Doc. S/2006/353, 31 May 2006

Report on the Special Court for Sierra Leone submitted by the Independent Expert, Antonio Cassese, 12 December 2006, available online at http://www.sc-sl.org/LinkClick.aspx?fileticket=VTDHyrHasLc=&

ICTY Digest, 15 January 2007, available online at http://www.icty.org/x/file/About/Reports%20and%20Publications/ICTYDigest/icty_digest_5_en.pdf

Letter dated 16 November 2007 from the President of the ICTR, Report on the Completion Strategy of the ICTR, UN Doc. S/2007/676, 20 November 2007

ICTY Press Release, 'Tribunal Welcomes the Arrest of Radovan Karadzic', 21 July 2008, available online at http://www.icty.org/sid/9952

ICTY/UNICRI, *ICTY Manual on Developed Practices* (Turin, 2009) available online at http://www.icty.org/x/file/About/Reports%20and%20Publications/ICTY_Manual_on_Developed_Practices.pdf

Ninth Annual Report of the International Criminal Tribunal for the former Yugoslavia, UN Doc. A/57/379-S/2002/985, 4 September 2002

Statement by the Prosecutor of the ICTR, Justice Hassan B. Jallow to the United Nations Security Council, 4 June 2009, available online at http://41.220.139.198/tabid/155/Default.aspx?id=1029

STL, 'RPE – Explanatory Memorandum by the Tribunal's President', 10 November 2009, available online at http://www.stl-tsl.org/en/documents/rules-of-procedure-and-evidence/rules-of-procedure-and-evidence-explanatory-memorandum-by-the-tribunal-s-president-10-november-2009

'Address of Mr John Hocking, Registrar, United Nations International Criminal Tribunal for the former Yugoslavia', *Meeting of Registrars of Final/Appellate, Regional and International Courts*, Ottawa, Canada, 14–16 April 2010, available online at http://www.icty.org/x/file/Press/Statements%20and%20Speeches/Registrar/100414_reg_hocking_ottawa.pdf

ICTY Press Release, President Robinson's Address before the Security Council, 18 June 2010, available online at http://www.icty.org/sid/10422/en

Report of the International Tribunal for the Former Yugoslavia, UN Docs A/65/205 and S/2010/413, 30 July 2010

Eighth Annual Report of the President of the Special Court for Sierra Leone, May 2011, available online at http://www.sc-sl.org/LinkClick.aspx?fileticket=kK8RBeHGowQ%3D&tabid=53

'Statement of the President of the Tribunal—Judge Theodor Meron', 17 November 2011, available online at http://www.icty.org/sid/10856

'Remarks of President Theodor Meron, Opening of the Arusha Branch of the Mechanism for International Criminal Tribunals', 2 July 2012, available online at http://www.icty.org/x/file/Press/Statements%20and%20Speeches/President/120702_pdt_meron_arusha_mict_en.pdf

'Statement by the Prosecutor of the International Criminal Court Mrs. Fatou Bensouda', Press Briefing, Nairobi, 22 October 2012, available online at http://www.icc-cpi.int/en_menus/icc/structure%20of%20the%20court/office%20of%20the%20prosecutor/reports%20and%20statements/statement/Pages/otpstatement221012.aspx

REPORTS OF NON-GOVERNMENTAL ORGANIZATIONS

Amnesty International, *Fair Trial Manual* (2nd edn, London, 2014)

Human Rights Watch, *Military Commissions Can't Compare to International Courts: Due Process Standards Much Lower for Proposed U.S. Trials* (4 December 2001)

Human Rights Watch, *Benchmarks for Justice for Serious Crimes in Northern Uganda: Human Rights Watch Memoranda on Justice Standards and the Juba Peace Talks* (May 2007–February 2008)

Human Rights Watch, *Justice for Serious Crimes before National Courts: Uganda's International Crimes Division* (New York, 2012)

International Law Commission, Report on the work of its forty-fifth sessions (3 May–23 July 1993) UN Doc. A/48/10

International Bar Association, ICC Programme Legal Opinion, *Rule 68 Amendment Proposal* (November 2013) available online at http://www.ibanet.org/Human_Rights_Institute/ICC_Outreach_Monitoring/IBA_ICC_Position_Papers.aspx

War Crimes Research Office, *Victims Participation at the Case Stage of Proceedings* (February 2009) available online at http://www.wcl.american.edu/warcrimes/icc/documents/WCROReportonVictimParticipationattheCaseStageofProceedingsFebruary2009.pdf

NEWSPAPER ARTICLES AND WEB SOURCES

Al Jazeera, 'Kenyatta failure deals blow to ICC' (11 December 2014) available online at http://america.aljazeera.com/opinions/2014/12/uhuru-kenyatta-crimesagainsthumanityinternationalcriminalcourt.html

BBC News, 'ICC Promises to Investigate Libya Staff if Released' (London, 23 June 2012) available online at http://www.bbc.co.uk/news/world-africa-18561515

Bouwknegt, T., 'Dutch to close the net on old genocide suspects', *Radio Netherlands*, The Hague (10 November 2011) available online at http://www.rnw.nl/international-justice/article/dutch-close-net-old-genocide-suspects

Easterday, J., 'A Closer Look at Regulation 55 at the ICC' *International Justice Monitor* (28 May 2013) available online at http://www.ijmonitor.org/2013/05/a-closer-look-at-regulation-55-at-the-icc/

'First Kenya, now Sudan: The International Criminal Court takes another bad knock', *The Economist* (20 December 2014) available online at http://www.economist.com/news/middle-east-and-africa/21636780-international-criminal-court-takes-another-bad-knock-first-kenya-now-sudan

Gahima, G., 'The Practice of International Criminal Tribunals and their Relevance to Military Commissions in Light of *Hamdan v. Rumsfeld*', Testimony before the House of Representatives Armed Services Committee (July 2006) available online at http://www.usip.org/publications/practice-international-criminal-tribunals-and-their-relevance-military-commissions-light-h

Gibson, K., 'The Arrest of ICTR Defense Counsel Peter Erlinder in Rwanda' (2010) 14 *ASIL Insights*, available online at http://www.asil.org/files/insight100811pdf.pdf

Griffiths, C., 'The International Criminal Court is hurting Africa' *The Telegraph*, London (3 July 2012) available online at http://www.telegraph.co.uk/news/worldnews/africaandindianocean/kenya/9373188/The-International-Criminal-Court-is-hurting-Africa.html

House of Representatives, 'Standards of Military Commissions and Tribunals', Hearing before the Committee on Armed Services, One Hundred Seventh Congress, Second Session, H.A.S.C. No. 109-117 (26 July 2006) available online at http://www.gpo.gov/fdsys/pkg/CHRG-109hhrg32982/html/CHRG-109hhrg32982.htm

House of Representatives, 'Report of the Committee on Armed Services, House of Representatives on H.R. 6054', 109th Congress, Second Session (15 September 2006) available online at http://www.loc.gov/rr/frd/Military_Law/pdf/H-Rep-109-664-1.pdf

International Criminal Court, 'About the Court: ICC at a Glance', available online at http://www.icc-cpi.int/en_menus/icc/about%20the%20court/icc%20at%20a%20glance/Pages/icc%20at%20a%20glance.aspx

International Criminal Tribunal for the Former Yugoslavia, 'Completion Strategy', available online at http://www.icty.org/sid/10016

Jallow, H.B., 'Fair Trial in International Criminal Justice', *United Nations Audiovisual Library of International Law*, published online (February 2015)

McDermott, Y., 'Some Thoughts on the Ntaganda and Gbagbo Confirmation of the Charges Decisions at the ICC', *PhD Studies in Human Rights* (14 June 2014) available online at http://humanrightsdoctorate.blogspot.ie/2014/06/some-thoughts-on-ntaganda-and0gbagbo.html

May, L., 'International Criminal Law and the Inner Morality of Law' paper presented at a conference on the Hart/Fuller debates at the Law School of Australian National University (18 December 2008), available online at https://law.anu.edu.au/sites/all/files/may_on_international_criminal_law.pdf

Nouwen, S. and Lewis, D.A., 'Jurisdictional Arrangements and International Criminal Procedure', *University of Cambridge Faculty of Law Research Paper No. 50/2011*, 1 November 2011, available online at http://papers.ssrn.com/sol3/papers.cfm?abstract_id=1957578

Physicians for Human Rights, 'Libya Should Surrender Saif al-Islam Qaddafi to the ICC', Press Release (April 2012) available online at http://physiciansforhumanrights.org/library/statements/libya-should-surrender-saif-al-islam-qaddafi-to-the-icc.html

President of the United States of America, 'Message from the President of the United States transmitting a draft of proposed legislation entitled the "Military Commissions Act of 2006"', 109th Congress, 2nd Session, House Document 109–33 (7 September 2006) available online at http://www.loc.gov/rr/frd/Military_Law/pdf/Hdoc_109-133.pdf

Ryngaert, C., 'The Failed Referral of Michel Bagaragaza from the ICTR to the Netherlands' *Hague Justice Portal* (14 October 2009) available online at http://www.haguejusticeportal.net/index.php?id=11116

Schmelzle, C., 'Evaluating Governance: Effectiveness and Legitimacy in Areas of Limited Statehood', SFB-Governance Working Paper Series 26 (November 2011), available online at http://www.sfb-governance.de/en/publikationen/working_papers/wp26/SFB-Governance-Working-Paper-26.pdf

Stahn, C., 'R2P, the ICC and the Libyan arrests' *Hague Justice Portal* (24 November 2011) available online at http://www.haguejusticeportal.net/index.php?id=12998

US Senate, Committee on Armed Services, Hearing to Receive Testimony on Legal Issues Regarding Military Commissions and the Trial of Detainees for Violations of the Law of War (7 July 2009) available online at http://www.loc.gov/rr/frd/Military_Law/pdf/Senate-Armed-Services-July-7-2009.pdf

Vasiliev, S., 'Fairness and its Metric in International Criminal Procedure' in *International Criminal Trials: A Normative Theory* (Oxford: OUP, 2016) (forthcoming), available online at http://ssrn.com/abstract=2253177

Wyngaert, C. Van den, 'Victims before International Criminal Courts, Some Views and Concerns of an ICC Trial Judge', Lecture delivered to Case Western Reserve University (21 November 2011) available online at http://law.case.edu/journals/JIL/Documents/(22)%20Van%20den%20Wyngaert_Darby.pdf

Index

The manufacturer's authorised representative in the EU for product safety is Oxford University Press España S.A. of el Parque Empresarial San Fernando de Henares, Avenida de Castilla, 2 – 28830 Madrid (www.oup.es/en or product.safety@oup.com). OUP España S.A. also acts as importer into Spain of products made by the manufacturer.

www.ingramcontent.com/pod-product-compliance
Lightning Source LLC
LaVergne TN
LVHW011755200926
848484LV00003B/710